The United States of Anonymous

THE UNITED STATES OF ANONYMOUS

How the First Amendment Shaped Online Speech

JEFF KOSSEFF

CORNELL UNIVERSITY PRESS
ITHACA AND LONDON

First published 2022 by Cornell University Press

Printed in the United States of America

Library of Congress Cataloging-in-Publication Data

Names: Kosseff, Jeff, 1978– author.
Title: The United States of anonymous : how the First Amendment shaped online speech / Jeff Kosseff.
Description: Ithaca [New York] : Cornell University Press, 2022. | Includes bibliographical references and index.
Identifiers: LCCN 2021020494 (print) | LCCN 2021020495 (ebook) | ISBN 9781501762383 (hardcover) | ISBN 9781501762406 (ebook) | ISBN 9781501762390 (pdf)
Subjects: LCSH: United States. Constitution. 1st Amendment. | Freedom of speech—United States. | Anonymous persons—Legal status, laws, etc.—United States. | Privacy, Right of—United States. | Internet—Law and legislation—United States. | United States. Constitution. 1st Amendment.
Classification: LCC KF4772 .K67 2022 (print) | LCC KF4772 (ebook) | DDC 342.7308/53—dc23
LC record available at https://lccn.loc.gov/2021020494
LC ebook record available at https://lccn.loc.gov/2021020495

This book is dedicated to the memory of Kurt Wimmer. An extraordinarily generous mentor. A true friend. And an unrelenting believer in free speech and privacy.

CONTENTS

ACKNOWLEDGMENTS AND DISCLAIMERS

Thanks to the many people who helped me track down information, served as sounding boards, or reviewed drafts of this book, including Annemarie Bridy, Anupam Chander, Danielle Citron, Gabriella Coleman, Sophia Cope, Joan Donovan, Matthew Dziennik, Timothy Edgar, Tori Smith Ekstrand, Ellis Fenske, Bill Frimel, A. Michael Froomkin, Brian Frye, Mara Gassmann, Cathy Gellis, Carrie Goldberg, Eric Goldman, Jennifer Granick, Megan Gray, Jeff Jarvis, Kate Klonick, Brad Kutner, Lyrissa Lidsky, Mike Masnick, Travis Mayberry, Riana Pfefferkorn, David Post, Alan Rozenshtein, Pamela Samuelson, Paul Schwartz, Paul Syverson, and Michael Vogel. Special thanks to Paul Alan Levy of Public Citizen, whose archive of the early filings from the online subpoena cases were particularly valuable to my research. Thanks also to the incredibly talented and patient librarians in the Library of Congress Manuscript Division and Law Library. As always, I'm thankful for the support of my family, including Crystal Zeh, Julia Kosseff, Chris and Betty Kosseff, and Eileen Peck.

I am deeply grateful to Laura Moraff and Liz Seif for exceptional research assistance and cite checking, and to Karen Laun and Jack Rummel for excellent editing. Thanks to Emily Andrew and her wonderful colleagues at Cornell University Press for helping to shape this book.

Thanks to the many midshipmen and faculty at the United States Naval Academy (Hooyah!) with whom I often discuss and debate the complex and stimulating issues related to online speech.

This book was made possible in part by a grant from Carnegie Corporation of New York during my time as an Andrew Carnegie Fellow. The statements made and views expressed are solely the responsibility of the author and do not represent the Carnegie Corporation of New York, Defense Department, Department of Navy, or Naval Academy.

Although this book focuses on legal issues, this book is not intended to be a substitute for legal advice from a licensed lawyer.

Some of the cases and incidents described in this book involve explicit language. To illustrate the full extent of the harms that people have experienced, this book includes that explicit language.

The United States of Anonymous

INTRODUCTION

The review, titled "A Scandal!" fit right in on Glassdoor.com. Since 2008, the site has hosted more than fifty million reviews from current, former, and prospective employees of companies worldwide.[1] Many reviews are not flattering, highlighting incompetent management, low salaries, and intolerable working conditions.

Among the claims in the June 21, 2015, review of video game developer Machine Zone was that the Silicon Valley company's management "spreads unreal information to both outside [venture capitalists] and employees" and the company has a "terrible work-life balance, except for the platform team, which do not know what to work on." The reviewer claimed that Machine Zone "has invested heavily in the platform team (there are 70–80 engineers)," but "after one year, nothing has been done by that team." The reviewer alleged that Machine Zone's chief executive said at a meeting that he did not "expect products and revenue from the platform team" and that the platform is intended "only for attracting investments from [venture capitalists.]" The review concluded with some "advice" for the company: "Stop telling the investors and employees the unreal information. A company cannot survive forever by cheating!"[2]

The next day, Machine Zone complained to Glassdoor that the review revealed "confidential information regarding Machine Zone's valuation and fundraising, as well as internal, confidential statements made by Machine Zone's CEO and management regarding Machine Zone's confidential and strategic business plans." The entire review was removed from Glassdoor a day later.[3]

Still, Machine Zone believed that the poster had violated a nondisclosure agreement required of its employees. About a week after the post, Machine Zone sued the anonymous poster for breach of contract. The complaint alleged that the poster "provided details concerning undisclosed technology Machine Zone has and is developing, the stage of development of that technology and the scope of Machine Zone's investment therein" and that the post quoted Machine Zone's chief executive's "confidential internal statements concerning that technology," but the complaint did not specify precisely what confidential information the poster had disclosed.[4] Machine Zone named the poster "John Doe," and issued a subpoena to Glassdoor for information that would allow Machine Zone to identify the author.[5]

Glassdoor opposed the subpoena, but a California state trial court judge ordered the company to provide the identifying information.[6] Glassdoor appealed. What made Glassdoor believe that it could defeat a rather standard discovery request?

The First Amendment.

For more than a half century, the Supreme Court has held that the First Amendment provides a right to speak anonymously. Courts have applied this right to the Internet and found a robust—though not absolute—ability for people to control the identifying information they reveal online. "Lawsuits such as the one filed by Machine Zone and Machine Zone's subpoena to Glassdoor are examples of how this constitutional right can be undermined by resourced companies that want to strip individuals of their anonymity as a means of improperly silencing them," Glassdoor's lawyers wrote in a brief to the California Court of Appeal.[7]

The appellate judges unanimously agreed that Glassdoor did not have to help Machine Zone unmask the poster, reasoning that Machine Zone failed to demonstrate that the review contained confidential information that violated the nondisclosure agreement.[8] The rigorous scrutiny that the court applied to the subpoena rested on a line of US Supreme Court cases beginning in the 1950s, which themselves are grounded in the American tradition of anonymous speech dating to the Federalist Papers and colonial pamphleteers. These First Amendment protections have allowed countless John and Jane Does to communicate controversial, intimate, embarrassing, harmful, or even revolutionary ideas online without facing the personal repercussions of being linked to that speech.

Anonymity is deeply rooted in the constitutional values and social norms of the United States. Anonymity has allowed minorities to communicate unpopular political viewpoints, whistleblowers to expose their employers' illegal schemes, and citizen journalists to document corruption and fraud. Anonymity is also employed for nefarious uses, such as defamation, persistent harassment, and online crimes. The longstanding US tradition of anonymous speech has enabled Americans to often separate their identities from the words and thoughts that they communicate. In this book, I examine how the First Amendment protections, combined with technology that prevents identities from being associated with online activities, have created a culture of anonymity empowerment.

Anonymity is "the condition of avoiding identification."[9] What does it mean to empower anonymity? Does anonymity empowerment simply mean allowing people to hide their names when they post thoughts online? What about allowing them to wear masks in public? Are they anonymous if they are required to display license plates, which, with some work, might be used to identify them?

My conception of anonymity empowerment is broad. Anonymity empowerment allows people to control what, if any, details about their identity to reveal. It includes, but goes beyond, merely separating a person's name from that person's speech or action; anonymity empowerment includes the protection of details that could increase the likelihood of the speaker being identified. Even when we try to separate our identities from our expression, we may leave clues that could lead to our identification. Consider the author of an unsigned political pamphlet who distributes the literature to mailboxes at night. If that author is caught on a surveillance camera while distributing the pamphlets, she may be identified based on her facial features. Still, legal protections can help prevent the local government from forcing her to sign her real name to the pamphlet, because that compelled signature would further increase the chances of her being identified immediately.

The culture of anonymity empowerment includes both true anonymity, when no identifiers are linked to expression or activity, and pseudonymity, when speech or activity is associated with a pen name that does not directly identify the author, but stays with that person over time. (Chapter 6 explores the taxonomy for the different types of online pseudonymity and anonymity.) The culture of anonymity empowerment has been an essential component of American democracy, protecting the ability of citizens to communicate and receive information without fear of persecution or harm.

Part I of this book explores the origins of the legal right to anonymity. The First Amendment right to anonymous speech dates to eighteenth-century England and the American colonies. The nation's Founders made their case for independence and our indirect democracy in part by circulating anonymous pamphlets and writing inflammatory newspaper columns under pseudonyms. With that history in mind, the US Supreme Court has recognized a qualified right to anonymous speech, striking down laws that require the NAACP to disclose its membership lists and prohibitions on the circulation of anonymous political materials. Lower courts have applied this right by striking down prohibitions on Ku Klux Klan members wearing masks and by protecting whistleblowers' anonymity in litigation.

Part II examines how courts have applied these First Amendment anonymity values to the Internet. Courts have tried to remain faithful to this First Amendment tradition as they protected anonymity on the Internet. Beginning in the 1990s, companies tried to use the court system to unmask people who criticized their business practices on online bulletin boards (and, if the posters turned out to be employees, they often would be fired). Judges gradually developed a process, rooted in the First Amendment, by which they only would order online service providers to reveal identifying information if the plaintiffs had a particularly strong case and satisfied other requirements. The right to anonymity exists in some other countries, but is especially strong in the United States. These legal rights, however, are not the only protections for anonymity. For instance, Tor, based on a technology developed by the Naval Research Laboratory in the 1990s, allows people to protect their online anonymity. Technology such as Tor, coupled with the First Amendment anonymity safeguards, have fostered substantial protections for those who wish to separate their online words from their identities.

Part III considers how these robust online anonymity protections shape everyday life in the United States. The culture of anonymity empowerment in the United States has enabled citizen journalists, like a privacy blogger with the pseudonym of Dissent Doe, to challenge the powerful in ways they never would have been able to do under their real names. Anonymity has also been a tool in some substantial harms, such as people who ruin the lives of innocent people, hiding enough of their identifying information to at least temporarily avoid prosecution. Anonymity is a blunt instrument that protects not only those who express minority views, but also those who harm and attack others.

Part IV contemplates how to continue to empower anonymity. The First Amendment addresses only government intrusions on free speech; its anonymity protections, like the other First Amendment safeguards, generally do not restrict the actions of private companies. Some platforms require their users to operate under their real names. And technological advancements have not only led to anonymity protections, but also to increased surveillance by the government and the private sector, often making it harder for people to remain truly anonymous. Technologies like facial recognition and geolocation allow companies to have unprecedented access to information that often can easily identify someone. Thus, I argue that to continue the US tradition of anonymity, lawmakers should supplement the First Amendment rights and anonymity technology with robust privacy laws that restrict the ability of private parties and the government to collect, use, and share identifying information.

This book examines many sides of the anonymity debate, including the substantial benefits and costs of a culture that guards anonymity. I ultimately conclude that we must preserve and improve upon the culture of anonymity empowerment, even though the equities are more complex than ever. It is difficult to imagine the American conception of free speech surviving without some anonymity protections. Anonymity allows people to express their views and influence the future. I do not argue for absolute protections for anonymity; even if such a goal were achievable, in extraordinary cases we should pierce the veil of anonymity. Such circumstances are rare, but remedies should be available to combat particularly egregious anonymous online behavior.

Given the wide range of online harms, it might be tempting to call for an end to online anonymity in the United States, such as by imposing real-name requirements that other countries have adopted.[10] Some in the United States have proposed requirements that people register their real names when speaking online.[11] I agree with free speech expert Jillian York, who has called such proposals the "White Man's Gambit." LGBT teenagers, domestic abuse survivors, and other vulnerable groups often are the ones that rely most on anonymity and pseudonymity, York wrote. "And anyone with unpopular or dissenting political opinions may choose not to risk their livelihood by identifying with a pseudonym," she correctly concluded.[12]

As with other free speech and privacy rights, courts and lawmakers should provide balanced protections that capture the benefits of anonymity, while reducing the likelihood of the most dangerous anonymous behavior. This is possible, but it requires a critical examination of the way that courts currently apply First Amendment anonymity protections, as well as new laws to protect the privacy of particularly sensitive information. First, we must understand the historical roots of the longstanding American tradition of anonymity.

Part I

DEVELOPING THE RIGHT TO ANONYMITY

The US Constitution does not expressly guarantee a right to anonymity. Yet many Framers who wrote and negotiated the document had long relied on pseudonyms to persuade the masses and criticize the powerful. Anonymity and pseudonymity undergird American democracy. From colonial pamphleteers to the authors of the Federalist Papers to the Jim Crow–era NAACP, Americans have had good reason to separate their identities from their words and actions.

Even with no mention of anonymity in the Constitution, US courts have recognized a right to anonymous speech, grounded in the First Amendment. This right to anonymous speech is strong, but it has limits. The First Amendment anonymity right—like all of its free speech guarantees—only restricts "state action." This means that the First Amendment restricts the ability of a court, legislature, or government agency from unmasking anonymous speakers. But it does not limit a private company from piercing someone's anonymity, providing that it does not rely on government resources such as a court subpoena.[1]

The First Amendment right to anonymity also is far from absolute. Although courts have recognized that anonymous speech is fundamental to American democracy, they have concluded that in some cases the need to know a speaker's identity outweighs the chilling effect that compelled disclosure would have on speech.

This part of the book traces the development of the First Amendment right to anonymous speech. It begins by highlighting the anonymous speech that was fundamental to the establishment of America's constitutional democracy. It then examines the battles over civil rights and political speech, beginning in the 1950s, that led the US Supreme Court to conclude that the First Amendment provides a strong, but limited, right to anonymity. And it assesses how lower courts have applied that right to anonymity in assessing antimask laws intended to curb the activities of the Ku Klux Klan.

1

AMERICA, THE ANONYMOUS

"Sir," the letter began. "The submission of a free people to the executive authority of government is no more than a compliance with laws which they themselves have enacted. While the national honour is firmly maintained abroad, and while justice is impartially administered at home, the obedience of the subject will be voluntary, cheerful, and, I might almost say, unlimited."[1]

By contemporary standards, such a letter would be unobjectionable, and likely unnoticed. A paean to self-governance. But this letter was published on January 21, 1769, in London's *Public Advertiser* newspaper. At the time, King George III was facing resistance in the colonies, and such a letter reminded the British people of their civil liberties and right to self-determination. The author signed the letter only as "Junius."

Junius's letters are among the most prominent examples of pseudonymous and anonymous speech that proliferated in England and the American colonies throughout the eighteenth century. This history is essential to understanding why US courts recognize a robust First Amendment right to anonymous speech.

Despite his controversial tone, Junius may have escaped the limelight had nobody noticed. But Sir William Draper drew attention to Junius in a response in the *Public Advertiser*, calling him one of the "felonious robbers of private character [who] stab in the dark, without having the courage to sign their real names to their malevolent and wicked productions."[2]

Between 1769 and 1772, *Public Advertiser* publisher Henry Sampson Woodfall would print more than sixty letters from and to Junius (or "Philo Junius"), in either the newspaper or a book. Woodfall published these letters with care to not reveal the identity of Junius. In a private letter to Woodfall dated July 15, 1769, Junius wrote that he suspected that Woodfall may need to communicate with him. "If that be the case, I beg that you will be particular; and also that you will tell me candidly whether you know or suspect who I am. Direct a letter to Mr. William Middleton to be left at the bar of the New Exchange Coffee-house on Monday, as early as you think proper."[3]

John Mason Good, the editor of an 1812 compilation of Junius's letters, wrote of the various locations where Junius asked Woodfall and other correspondents to leave letters to him, and the likelihood that Junius used his own intermediaries to safeguard his identity. "That a variety of schemes were invented and actually in motion to detect him there can be no doubt," Good wrote, "but the extreme vigilance he at all times evinced, and the honourable forbearance of Mr Woodfall, enabled him to baffle every effort, and to persevere in his concealment to the last."[4]

In a September 18, 1771, letter to radical politician John Wilkes, Junius wrote of the value of anonymity to his ability to deliver his message. "Besides every personal consideration, if I were known, I could no longer be an useful servant to the public," he wrote. "At present there is something oracular in the delivery of my opinions. I speak from a recess which no human curiosity can penetrate, and darkness, we are told, is one source of the sublime. The mystery of Junius increases his importance."[5]

But Junius clearly was also concerned that he might face retaliation for his strident views. In a private letter to Woodfall, Junius asked Woodfall to deliver a message to another man, but to send it in Woodfall's own handwriting to avoid Junius's handwriting being "too commonly seen." "I must be more cautious than ever," Junius wrote. "I am sure I should not survive a discovery three days; or, if I did, they would attaint me by bill."[6] Junius asked Woodfall to change the drop-off point for their communications.[7]

Indeed, Junius anonymously attacked some of the most powerful men in England. Among the most frequent targets was the prime minister, the Third Duke of Grafton. "The injuries you have done this country are such as demand not only redress, but vengeance," Junius wrote in a public letter to the prime minister, published by the newspaper on July 8, 1769.[8] Junius also attacked the prime minister's personal life. "Did not the duke of Grafton frequently lead his mistress into public, and even place her at the head of his table, as if he had pulled down an ancient temple of Venus, and could bury all decency and shame under the ruins?" Junius wrote in a June 12, 1769, letter.[9] The Duke of Grafton resigned as prime minister about six months later, and scholars attributed his downfall at least partly to Junius's relentless criticism. Junius's criticism of the Duke of Grafton exposed his "incompetency and profligacy," Fred H. Peterson wrote.[10]

Junius also took up defense of the inhabitants of the American colonies, including their opposition to the duties imposed on tea. "It is not pretended that the continuation of the tea duty is to produce any direct benefit whatsoever to the mother country," Junius wrote. "What is it then, but an odious, unprofitable exertion of a speculative right, and fixing a badge of slavery upon the Americans, without service to their masters? But it has pleased God to give us a ministry and a parliament, who are neither to be persuaded by argument, nor instructed by experience."[11]

Junius's letters, seeking to improve the political system in England, had immediate impact. "All England marvelled and talked about these letters with mingled fear and surprise; those in the public service were in abject terror of being flayed or of seeing their actions dissected and held up to ridicule and scorn," Peterson wrote.[12]

Junius's most controversial letter, however, was not directed to the Duke of Grafton. Addressed to the king and published in the *Public Advertiser* on December 19, 1769, it began:

Sir,
    It is the misfortune of your life, and originally the cause of every reproach and distress which has attended your government, that you should never have been acquainted with the language of truth, until you heard it in

the complaints of your people. It is not, however, too late to correct the error of your education. We are still inclined to make an indulgent allowance for the pernicious lessons you received in your youth, and to form the most sanguine hopes from the natural benevolence of your disposition.[13]

Woodfall printed 1,750 additional copies of the newspaper containing the letter to the king, and Horace Walpole deemed the letter "the most daring insult ever offered to a prince but in times of open rebellion."[14] Within days of the publication, a prosecutor began investigating whether the publication was criminally libel. Junius wrote to reassure Woodfall, advising him to "stand firm (I mean with all the humble appearances of contrition). If you trim or falter, you will lose friends without gaining others."[15]

Six months later, Woodfall stood trial for seditious libel. According to an account of the trial in the *Universal Magazine*, the prosecutor told the jury that "the letter in question was totally and universally abhorred."[16] Woodfall's lawyer argued that Woodfall "published it with the truly laudable motive of informing his fellow-subjects" and that "the public acts of Government often demanded public scrutiny," the magazine reported.[17]

The judge, Lord Mansfield, instructed the jury that they needed to consider two points: first, "the printing and publishing the paper in question," and second, "the sense and meaning of it."[18] Lord Mansfield limited their inquiry to those two facts, and instructed the jury that it was unnecessary to make legal judgments about libel. In criminal libel prosecutions, Lord Mansfield instructed the jury, it was "immaterial whether the publication be false or true; that it is no defence to say it is true, because it is a breach of the peace, and therefore criminal."[19] After more than nine hours of deliberation, the jury delivered its verdict, "guilty of printing and publishing Only."[20]

The limited verdict caused Lord Mansfield to order a new trial. But there was a problem: the jury foreman from the first trial had apparently destroyed the original copy of the newspaper, making it difficult for the prosecutor to prove publication. When the prosecutor raised this concern with Lord Mansfield, the judge replied, "That is not my fault, Mr. Attorney" and ended the trial.[21]

Although Woodfall escaped punishment for Junius's letter, he endured great fear and legal expense just because he published an anonymous letter that criticized the king. The actual author (or authors)—who operated under the pseudonymous construct of Junius—managed to survive the trial without being prosecuted or unmasked, thanks to his careful efforts to conceal his identity. Still, after Woodfall's trial, Junius could not help but publish a long letter in which he eviscerated Lord Mansfield's character. "Our language has no term of reproach, the mind has no idea of detestation, which has not already been happily applied to you, and exhausted," Junius wrote.[22]

His steps to safeguard his identity worked. More than two centuries after Junius shook the power structure in England, there still is no entirely uncontested consensus as to who he was. Historians have persisted in seeking any clues, with many certain that they identified Junius. Edward J. White counted twenty-three different men being named at one time or another as the authors of Junius's letters, including Thomas Paine, Treasury department clerk Charles Lloyd, George Sackville, John Wilkes, Edmund Burke, and Pitt of Chatham.[23]

The person most frequently speculated to be Junius is Sir Philip Francis. In 1871, a handwriting expert asserted that Junius's letters were written by Francis, a Parliament member. Yet later that year, Herman Merivale, editor of Francis's memoirs, wrote that any handwriting similarities do not necessarily mean that Francis was Junius. "It is still open to contend, for those who love a difficult cause, that the author may have been some great personage, who employed the penmanship of Francis," Merivale wrote.[24]

Merivale's hypothetical would require Junius to have taken great operational precautions to secure his anonymity. That is not impossible, particularly given Junius's repeated statements to Woodfall and Wilkes to safeguard his anonymity. Even if Francis were Junius, the more confident attempts at attribution did not come until about a hundred years after Woodfall published Junius's letters. Either way, Junius's anonymity safeguards worked.

And these protections were essential to Junius's ability to question England's most powerful men, at a time when free speech protections were far less robust in the country than they are today. As Lord David Edmond Neuberger, president of the Supreme Court of the United Kingdom, observed in a 2014 speech, Junius "was able to make criticisms of the powerful for which others of his time faced prosecution," and "offered a voice of firm if sometimes scurrilous criticism, prompting both political and legal change."[25]

Based on Junius's own letters and the impact that they had, we can deduce many potential motivations for his seeking anonymity. These motivations apply not only in eighteenth-century England, but also in the modern disputes over online anonymity in the United States.

First is the Legal Motivation for anonymity. Exposure of his identity could lead to substantial criminal or civil liability for Junius. He had good reason to avoid the same criminal prosecution that Woodfall faced merely for publishing his letters.

Second is the Safety Motivation. Junius may have faced personal retaliation, such as being physically attacked, for criticizing some of the most powerful people in England. His opponents may have destroyed his property, or harmed his family. Junius's private letters suggested that he doubted whether he could survive unmasking. As Victoria Smith Ekstrand wrote in a thorough analysis of the various reasons for anonymity, there are cases in which "the message is often deemed critical to circulate, but so controversial that having the author's name attached would put the author in some kind of danger, either a physical threat or a serious threat to one's reputation."[26]

Third is the Economic Motivation. Depending on his occupation, Junius may have lost his job if his name had been publicly associated with his writing. If Junius operated his own business, he may have faced a decline in revenues due to the controversy.

Fourth is the Privacy Motivation. Junius may have wanted to avoid public attention. Robert Natelson wrote that an eighteenth-century author "might wish to participate in public life in some minimal way (e.g., by writing a letter or helping to publish a pamphlet) without exposing himself and his family to full 'public figure' status."[27] Anonymity and privacy are separate concepts,[28] but protecting privacy can help to protect anonymity, and vice versa. The privacy scholar Helen Nissenbaum wrote in 1999 that "the value of anonymity lies not in the capacity to be unnamed, but in the possibility of acting or participating while remaining out of reach, remaining unreachable. Being unreachable means that no-one will come knocking on your door demanding explanations, apologies, answerability, punishment or payment."[29] Junius may have wanted to separate his private life from his very public statements and the surrounding controversy. Junius appeared to consider his identity to be deeply private information, and safeguarding that information may have been essential to his protection of his right to be let alone.

Fifth is the Speech Motivation. His identity may have distracted readers from the content of his message, which was strong enough to upset the powerful and cause political change. For instance, his opponents may have accused Junius of making his arguments due to personal economic interests or grudges. By maintaining his pseudonymity, Junius forced his readers to focus on the substance of his arguments. Likewise, as Junius himself suggested, the mystery of Junius's identity may have drawn more attention to his writing. Had the writings been linked to the name of a politician or writer, they might not have had the same allure. As Ekstrand observed, the "rhetorical power of anonymous speech is significant."[30]

Sixth is the Power Motivation.[31] By remaining anonymous, Junius had tremendous influence that he likely could not have had if he were forced to associate his identity with his words. Without anonymity, Junius may not have felt free to speak out against the king and others, so he simply would not have spoken at all. Because he was able to speak, Junius used his words to shape public opinion among the most powerful—and dangerous—men in England. For Junius and so many other dissidents, anonymity affords power that they otherwise never would have.

Junius may be one of the most notorious pseudonymous writers of eighteenth-century England—or, for that matter, of all time—but pseudonymous and anonymous writing was common then, and it was a thorn in the side of the monarchy. Joseph Addison, an English playwright and member of Parliament, wrote in 1712 of a proposal "to oblige every Person that writes a Book, or a Paper, to swear himself the Author of it, and enter down in a publick Register his Name and Place of Abode."[32]

Writing in his daily publication, *The Spectator*, Addison predicted that such an identification requirement would, indeed, eliminate "printed Scandal," but it would have far more negative consequences. "But it is to be feared, that such an Expedient would not only destroy Scandal, but Learning," Addison wrote. "It would operate promiscuously, and root up the Corn and Tares together." Few "Works of Genius," Addison observed, are initially associated with their authors' real names. "The Writer generally makes a Tryal of them in the World before he owns them; and,

I believe, very few, who are capable of Writing, would set Pen to Paper, if they knew, before-hand, that they must not publish their Productions but on such Conditions."[33]

Anonymity often shaped the views in England of the unrest in the American colonies. Political pamphlets were a common method of circulating these writings.[34] In a review of more than two thousand British pamphlets published about America between 1763 and 1783, Thomas R. Adams found that about 75 percent were anonymously authored. Adams attributed the widespread anonymity in part to "fear of prosecution" and "fear of displeasing influential men."[35] But Adams also posited that booksellers generally preferred to stick to a tradition of selling pamphlets based on the ideas that they contained, rather than their authors' identities.[36]

The colonial press in America shared England's passionate—and often anonymous—speech. Consider the *New York Weekly Journal*, which years after the *Spectator*'s 1712 closure would continue to publish Addison's old *Spectator* essays, as well as many anonymous screeds.[37] John Peter Zenger began publishing the *Weekly Journal* in 1733 on behalf of followers of New York Supreme Court chief justice Lewis Morris (known as "Morrisites"); the *Journal* was overseen by Morrisite lawyer James Alexander. Morris was engaged in a public and bitter feud with William Cosby, who had become New York's governor a year earlier.[38] Along with Addison's essays, the newspaper included many anonymous criticisms of Governor Cosby. Although the authors were anonymous, Zenger faced liability because he was publicly identified as the newspaper's publisher.[39] Zenger also declined to tell authorities who wrote the critical pieces.[40]

Cosby argued that Alexander was "the head of a scheme to give all imaginable uneasiness to the government by infusing into and making the worst impressions on the minds of the people," and that Morris's "open and implacable malice against me has appeared weekly in false and scandalous libels printed in Zenger's *Journal*."[41] Among the anonymous writings in the newspaper was one that stated that "the People of this City and Province think as matters now stand that their liberties and properties are precarious, and that slavery is like to be intailed on them and their Posterity, if some past things be not amended, and this they collect from many past Proceedings."[42] This statement, along with other essays in the *Weekly*

Journal, formed the basis for the attorney general to charge Zenger with publishing "false, malicious, seditious and scandalous libels."[43]

The articles in Zenger's newspaper may have been true, but truth was immaterial to a criminal libel trial at the time.[44] As in Woodfall's trial in England, the jury's primary duty was to determine whether Zenger published the articles. Yet after hearing arguments from both sides, the jury returned a verdict of not guilty. "Then, as after the flash in a thunderstorm, the tensions broke in a crash of applause and cheers that spread to the street outside and left the judges no choice but to withdraw in silent impotence," Walker Lewis wrote in a 1960 summary of the trial. "Zenger was free and so, through him, was the American press."[45]

Zenger's trial was a landmark verdict for the press in the colonial times, when free speech rights were far less robust than they currently are. The primary issue was whether the government could punish a critic via seditious libel laws. The trial did not center on the fact that the authors were anonymous or pseudonymous; the government was trying to hold Zenger accountable as the publisher of the newspaper. Yet the Zenger case highlighted the importance of anonymous speech in American political discourse, decades before the Declaration of Independence. The anonymous words were so threatening to Governor Cosby that the government ordered both the burning of the papers and the prosecution of its publisher. As US Supreme Court justice Clarence Thomas would write more than two centuries later, Zenger's case "signified at an early moment the extent to which anonymity and the freedom of the press were intertwined in the early American mind."[46]

The case also illustrates the sliding scale of anonymity that has existed for centuries. Even if a communication does not bear the author's true name, it may include some clues that suggest a likelihood of the author's identity. The *Weekly Journal*'s writers, for instance, were known to be among the Morrisites. A reasonable observer may have concluded that the author was part of that group. But the government could not specifically identify—and prosecute—the author or authors. Anonymity protected the *Weekly Journal* authors from economic or personal reprisals, as Jeffrey L. Pasley has observed.[47]

The anonymous and pseudonymous commentary was pervasive in the colonies, particularly as resistance to England grew. Thomas R. Adams has conducted a separate bibliographical review of political pamphlets published in America between the passage of the controversial Stamp Act of 1765 and the 1776 signing of the Declaration of Independence. Forty percent of the pamphlets were published anonymously, he found.[48]

In a different analysis of colonial political pamphlets from 1763 through 1765—when the Stamp Act controversy was at its peak—John Howe found that 55 percent did not carry the authors' names.[49] Howe attributed the widespread pseudonymity in part to the Legal and Safety Motivations I mention above, that "to reveal one's identity in the intensely personal world of eighteenth-century politics was to risk quick retribution by governmental authorities or personal enemies."[50] But Howe also attributed the phenomenon to both the Speech Motivation and the Privacy Motivation. He described "a culture deeply grounded in the limited commercialization of American printing, epistemological assumptions concerning the production of political knowledge, republican admonitions to subordinate personal fame to the larger public good, and concern by genteel writers to shield themselves from an expanding, increasingly 'promiscuous' reading public."[51]

Parliament in 1767 enacted the Townshend Acts, which taxed the colonies via import duties. One provision sought to penalize New York for failing to pay for the quartering of British soldiers. Like their predecessor, the Stamp Act, the Townshend Acts faced great resistance in the colonies.[52] Some opposition came in a series of twelve weekly letters in the *Pennsylvania Chronicle and Universal Advertiser,* under the heading of "Letters from a Farmer in Pennsylvania to the Inhabitants of the British Colonies."

The Farmer's first letter, published in the November 30–December 3, 1767, edition of the newspaper, focused on the penalties that the Parliament tried to impose on New York for its failure to quarter soldiers. "It is parliamentary assertion of the supreme authority of the British legislature over these colonies in the part of taxation; and is intended to COMPEL New York unto a submission to that authority," the Farmer wrote in his first letter. "It seems therefore to me as much a violation of the liberty of the people of that province, and consequently of all these colonies, as if the parliament had sent a number of regiments to be quartered upon them till they should comply."[53]

The Farmer also protested the import duties, which he likened to the Stamp Act. "The single question is, whether the parliament can legally preparing the minds of plain men for independence and in shifting their loyalty from the British Crown to the American republic."[70]

Why did Paine publish *Common Sense* anonymously? He gave some hint in the preface to the third edition of *Common Sense*. "Who the Author of this Production is, is wholly unnecessary to the Public, as the Object for Attention is the *Doctrine itself*, not the *Man*," he wrote. "Yet it may not be unnecessary to say, That he is unconnected with any party, and under no sort of Influence, public or private, but the influence of reason and principle."[71] This statement suggests that the Speech Motivation drove Paine's anonymity; he wanted the readers to focus on his arguments rather than his identity. Yet it is hard to ignore the personal risks that he faced by arguing for independence from Great Britain in a widely read pamphlet; thus, the Legal and Safety Motivations likely contributed to his decision to use a pseudonym.

Anonymous political speech did not stop when the colonies gained independence. When the government under the Articles of Confederation proved to be weak and ineffective, a Constitutional Convention in 1787 drafted a new framework for a stronger federal government. In a thorough examination of political writings during the constitutional debate, Victoria Smith Ekstrand and Cassandra Imfeld Jeyaram concluded that anonymity played a crucial role in delivering the often heated arguments by allowing the debate to focus on the proposals rather than the speakers' characters.[72] The anonymous nature of the communications, they argued, also contributed to the efficacy of their arguments.[73]

In New York newspapers, Anti-Federalist pseudonymous writers including Brutus and Federal Farmer argued against ratification of the new Constitution.[74] After some Federalist newspaper publishers in Massachusetts required Anti-Federalists to disclose their identities to the publishers in order to publish opinion pieces, Anti-Federalist writer Federal Farmer wrote: "What can be the views of those gentlemen in Boston, who countenanced the Printers in shutting up the press against a fair and free investigation of this important system in the usual way?"[75]

But Federalists also relied on pseudonymity. To rebut the Anti-Federalist criticism and urge ratification, Alexander Hamilton, James Madison, and John Jay published a series of eighty-five articles, known as *The Federalist*, in New York newspapers. The Federalist Papers address specific aspects of the Constitution, including taxation, separation of powers, the military, and elections. The essays also highlight the deficiencies of the government under the Articles of Confederation.

The authors' real names do not appear in the Federalist Papers. They used the pseudonym of Publius, from 500 BCE Roman ruler Publius Valerius.[76] "My motives must remain in the depository of my own breast," Hamilton wrote in Federalist No. 1. "My arguments will be open to all, and may be judged of by all. They shall at least be offered in a spirit which will not disgrace the cause of truth."[77]

Although the three men disclosed their authorship to a few close associates, at the time of publication most people did not know who Publius was.[78] Madison even wrote about his involvement with the Federalist Papers in cipher.[79] According to one commentary on the development of the Constitution, only a few newspapers at the time speculated that Hamilton was behind the Federalist Papers.[80] More often, people identified in private letters some or all of the authors.[81] On March 10, 1788, Henry Knox wrote to George Washington that "the publication signed Publius is attributed to the joint efforts of Mr Jay, Mr Maddison and Colo Hamilton. It is highly probable that the general conjecture on this case is well founded."[82]

Why did Hamilton, Madison, and Jay avoid using their real names? The authors were unlikely to have faced legal liability or personal endangerment due to the Federalist Papers. The Speech Motivation likely played a role in their choice to write under a pseudonym. "Perhaps Hamilton and Madison felt that praising a Constitution that they had helped to write would appear immodest," Gregory E. Maggs speculated. "Maybe they wanted to make arguments that they later could distance themselves from. They might have wanted to avoid accusations that they were violating the confidentiality of the Constitutional Convention. Or they could have decided that their group should use just one name to cover the work of all three authors."[83]

Eran Shalev also hypothesizes that the pseudonymity was for literary effect. Publius represented "the Roman's act of banishing a king and founding a great republic."[84] The pseudonym added traditional effect to the authors' arguments, Shalev wrote.[85]

Whatever the motivation, the pseudonymous nature of the Federalist Papers and the commentary opposing it was the norm at the time. As Robert G. Natelson summarized, during the founding of the United impose duties to be paid *by the people of these colonies only* FOR THE SOLE PURPOSE OF RAISING A REVENUE, *on commodities which she obliges us to take from her alone,* or, in other words, whether the parliament can legally take money out of our pockets, without our consent," the Farmer wrote. "If they can, our boasted liberty is but *Vox et praeterea nihil.* A sound, and nothing else."[54]

The letters were signed only "A Farmer," though the first letter began with a vague description of the author's purported identity. "I AM a FARMER, settled, after a variety of fortunes, near the banks, of the river *Delaware,* in the province of *Pennsylvania,*" the Farmer wrote. "I received a liberal education, and have been engaged in the busy scenes of life: but am now convinced, that a man may be as happy without bustle as with it. My farm is small, my servants are few, and good; I have a little money at interest; I wish for no more: my employment in my own affairs is easy; and with a contented grateful mind, I am completing the number of days allotted to me by Divine Goodness."[55]

Newspapers throughout America reprinted the twelve letters, and they also were distributed a few months later as a pamphlet.[56] In a review of the reactions to the Letters, Carl F. Kaestle estimated that the combined circulation of the Letters was at least fifteen thousand, and no previous American political work had had such reach or impact.[57] Kaestle noted the importance of the "Farmer" pseudonym. Although such political writings often bore pseudonyms, they often were simply initials or locations. "The idea of a farmer, on the other hand, appealed to an almost universal American conviction about the good life of the soil," Kaestle wrote. "What better atmosphere for clear-headed political theorizing than the uncorrupted, unhurried farm estate?"[58] The Farmer pseudonym, Kaestle wrote, "proved to be not just a mask, but a full character."[59]

For months, the Farmer's identity was unknown, and the subject of great intrigue. "The endless speculation provoked by the mystery of the 'Farmer's' identity further whetted popular interest," Arthur M. Schlesinger wrote.[60] Lord Hillsborough, the British minister who oversaw the colonies, speculated that Ben Franklin was the author of the "well written" and "extremely wild" letters.[61] Although Franklin did not fully agree with the letters' reasoning, he ensured that the letters were reprinted in England, and John Wilkes, Junius's correspondent, stated that the Farmer "perfectly understood" liberty.[62]

The Farmer's true identity was not publicly revealed until the following spring.[63] He was a Pennsylvania lawyer named John Dickinson who had opposed the Stamp Act. Dickinson later would hold various positions in Pennsylvania and Delaware state politics, and would later serve as a delegate to the Constitutional Convention. But the twelve Farmer's letters would remain his most enduring legacy. "The 'Pennsylvania Farmer' was more famous than John Dickinson, and Dickinson himself was referred to simply as 'the Farmer' in letters and even diaries for years after," Kaestle wrote.[64]

Dickinson's work was a clear example of the Speech Motivation for anonymity. The Farmer persona added to that literary value. Letters from lawyer John Dickinson would not have been as compelling and resonant throughout the colonies. As Philip Davidson wrote in 1941, his letters were "called the most brilliant literary event of the entire Revolution."[65]

Less than a decade after the pseudonymous distribution of the Farmer's letters, a pamphlet entitled *Common Sense* was published in Philadelphia. The four-part pamphlet was a clear and direct call for colonial independence from England. Although the colonies may have "flourished" under Great Britain, the author wrote, it is "fallacious" to suggest that America's prosperity depends on that relationship. "We may as well assert that because a child has thrived upon milk, that it is never to have meat, or that the first twenty years of our lives is to become a precedent for the next twenty," the author wrote. "But even this is admitting more than is true; for I answer roundly, that America would have flourished as much, and probably much more, had no European power taken any notice of her."[66]

Common Sense would be reprinted in twenty-five editions that year, with up to 120,000 copies of the pamphlet printed.[67] Some versions of the pamphlet were signed "Written by an Englishman," but the author's true name was not included. As with Dickinson's letters, some speculated that Benjamin Franklin was the author. Others suggested that Samuel Adams or John Adams was behind *Common Sense*.[68] But the author was Thomas Paine, who indeed was an Englishman, having immigrated to Philadelphia little more than a year before the publication of *Common Sense*.

Common Sense made the case for independence. In April 1776, George Washington wrote that "common sense is working a powerful change [in Virginia] in the Minds of many Men."[69] As Alfred Aldridge would write in his 1959 biography of Paine, the pamphlet's "great contribution" was "in

States, anonymity was considered to be among the protections of freedom of the press. "As a matter of practice, authors of newspaper letters and essays and of pamphlets, at least on political subjects, nearly always wrote anonymously or pseudonymously," he wrote. "This was certainly true of writing on the Constitution, as on other political issues."[86]

At various times during the nation's founding, all six motivations for anonymity justified protecting the author's name from disclosure, though the Speech Motivation appeared to be common; writers such as Thomas Paine urged the readers to focus on their arguments rather than their identities. Yet the other motivations for speech also underpinned this culture of anonymity. Authors had very good reason to fear for their safety, or to seek to avoid prosecution. Publicly linking their identities to their writing could cause significant personal economic harm, and compromise the privacy of the writers and their families. And anonymity afforded power that these dissidents otherwise would not have had.

For all of these reasons, the culture of anonymity empowerment is engrained in US history, and as the next three chapters will show, has shaped the Supreme Court's strong—but not absolute—protection of identities from compelled disclosure. Just as the Speech Motivation was so central to protecting anonymity in the eighteenth century, the Supreme Court's protection for anonymity is rooted in the First Amendment right to free speech.

2

EMPOWERING ANONYMOUS
ASSOCIATION

The Supreme Court's long journey to recognizing a qualified First Amendment right to anonymity began not with a crusading newspaper editor or an obstinate political pamphleteer. Rather, it emerged from the turmoil of the civil rights battles of the 1950s. Civil rights groups made gradual progress in school desegregation and fighting Jim Crow laws. With their victories, the groups—and their members—faced tremendous backlash. These groups had an existential need to protect the anonymity of their members, lest they face threats to their personal safety.

The backlash was exacerbated after May 17, 1954, when the Supreme Court issued its opinion in *Brown v. Board of Education*. In the opinion, the Supreme Court struck down the "separate but equal" policy of segregating schools by race, reasoning that "separate educational facilities are inherently unequal" under the Fourteenth Amendment's equal protection clause.[1] Although many elected officials—particularly in the South—remained ardent opponents of desegregation and other civil liberties—the

Supreme Court had taken a more progressive stance, particularly after Earl Warren became chief justice of the United States in 1953. For the next decade, many state and local officials would seek avenues to circumvent the rulings of the Warren Court.

Leading the court battles for civil rights was the National Association for the Advancement of Colored People. With a Legal Defense and Educational Fund led by future Supreme Court justice Thurgood Marshall, the NAACP fought against discriminatory laws and policies throughout the United States.[2] The NAACP's work in Alabama was particularly challenging, as it confronted decades of post–Civil War institutionalized segregation and discriminatory laws.[3]

The NAACP had operated affiliate chapters in Montgomery and Selma since 1918, and in 1951 opened its Southeast Regional Office in Birmingham in rented office space, employing three staffers there, but relying mostly on volunteers.[4] The organization represented African Americans in court cases to establish their rights to equal treatment in public facilities, voting, and desegregated schools. The NAACP also advocated for due process rights in criminal cases.[5]

While operating in Alabama, the NAACP did not register as a foreign corporation with the Alabama secretary of state. Although Alabama law required the registration, the NAACP did not believe that the registration requirement applied to its activities.[6] In 1956, Alabama attorney general John Patterson disagreed with the group's assessment of the registration law. Patterson was a staunch segregationist who would become governor in 1959.[7] He made no efforts to hide his goal of shutting down the NAACP in Alabama.

And he pursued the goal. Patterson filed a complaint against the NAACP, and sought an injunction to effectively close down the group's operations. Not only was its adversary a segregationist, but so was the state court judge presiding over the case. In 1957, Judge Walter B. Jones would write a column for the *Montgomery Advertiser* newspaper, entitled "I Speak for the White Race." In the column, Jones asserted that the top artists, writers, philosophers, and inventors were white. "So when you call the roll of the world's noble and useful spirits, the men and women of the white race stand up in honor and glory with a just pride in the race's achievements," Jones wrote. "We have all kindly feelings for the world's other races, but we will maintain at any and all sacrifices the purity of our blood strain and race. We shall never submit to the demands of integrationists. The white race shall forever remain white."[8]

The NAACP said that it received no notice of the state's concerns with its failure to register, so it had no opportunity to correct the bureaucratic mistake.[9] Still, Jones granted the request and temporarily prohibited the NAACP from soliciting memberships and raising money in Alabama.[10] "We cannot stand idly by and raise no hand to stay these forces of confusion who are trying to capitalize upon racial factors for private gain or advancement," Patterson declared on the day that Jones issued the injunction.[11]

But Jones did not merely freeze the organization's operations in Alabama; as part of pretrial discovery, Jones granted the state's request to force the NAACP to disclose the names and addresses of all NAACP members in Alabama.[12]

The NAACP had good reason to protect the anonymity of its members. All six of the overarching motivations for anonymity justified opposition of this discovery request. Perhaps the most compelling was the Safety Motivation. The NAACP had good reason to fear that its members, once unmasked, could face the threat of severe physical harm in the South. Likewise, the Economic Motivation may have driven the group's quest for anonymity, as its members could face retaliation from their employers. And anonymity gave the NAACP power to speak against oppressive forces.

Robert L. Carter, the lawyer who represented the NAACP in Jones's courtroom (and whom Richard Nixon would later appoint to be a federal judge in Manhattan), recalled in his memoir that he was convinced that this order violated the First Amendment and wanted to defy it. But Thurgood Marshall, then the head of the NAACP Legal Defense and Education Fund, "was adamant at first that we had to obey the court's order because our legal program relied on courts issuing orders in our favor."[13] Yet after consulting with the board, the NAACP ultimately refused to comply.[14]

On July 25, Jones fined the group $10,000 for violating the pretrial discovery order, with the fine to increase to $100,000 if the group did not comply within five days.[15] "The present willful and deliberate, and considered, defiance of the court's order is not to be lightly taken," Jones wrote. "It is not such an act which admits of any but severe punishment. The court cannot permit its orders to be flouted. It cannot permit a party, however wealthy and influential, to take the law in his own hands, set himself up above the law, and contumaciously decline to obey the orders of a duly constituted court made under the law of the land and in the exercise of an admitted and ancient jurisdiction."[16]

The NAACP twice appealed the contempt order to the Supreme Court of Alabama, which denied both requests to hear the appeal.[17] The court ruled that procedural requirements prevented it from reviewing the merits of the NAACP's arguments at that stage. Still, the state high court revealed its frustration with the NAACP's refusal to comply with the lower court's order. The Alabama high court's unanimous opinion blasted the NAACP's "brazen defiance of the order of the court."[18]

With no other options for appeal in Alabama, the NAACP asked the US Supreme Court to review the case. In its petition to the Supreme Court, the NAACP wrote of the hostility that integrationists faced in Alabama, citing, for instance, the burning of a cross in the yard of a federal judge who had voted to desegregate Montgomery's transportation system.[19] Disclosing its membership list, the NAACP wrote, "would inevitably lead to serious economic pressure, loss of employment, mental harassment, threatened or actual violence."[20] Such reprisals, the NAACP wrote, would violate the First Amendment because they "would inhibit members from speaking, writing, petitioning, or assembling to end racial discrimination as individuals."[21]

Patterson and the other attorneys representing Alabama argued that Jones's order did not infringe the First Amendment rights of NAACP members, and that it was a routine discovery order. "It makes the best of sense that a party who refuses to divulge information necessary to the conduct of a case should be prevented continuing with it," the state's lawyers wrote in their opposition brief.[22] Alabama's procedural argument was not enough for Warren's Supreme Court to look the other way, and it granted the NAACP's motion to review the case.

A coalition of organizations, including the American Civil Liberties Union, American Jewish Committee, Japanese American Citizens League, and Workers Defense League, filed an amicus brief in support of the NAACP. Pointing to the anonymous publication of the Federalist Papers and other foundational documents, the groups argued that the Constitution protects a "right of anonymity that may not be infringed in the absence of an overriding communal interest which the state is constitutionally competent to protect. The right of anonymity is an incident of a civilized society and a necessary adjunct to freedom of association and to full and free expression in a democratic state."[23]

The groups also pointed to contemporary practices to shield anonymity in letters to newspapers, public polling, and employer's suggestion systems. "Underlying all these practices, anonymous polls, letters to the editor and the like, is the well-founded belief that anonymity in the expression of views contributes to the free play of ideas and hence to the ultimate search for truth, the same search for truth that the founding fathers sought to foster by the guarantees of the First Amendment."[24]

The challenge for these groups, and the NAACP, was to convince the Supreme Court to explicitly recognize a right to anonymity. Although they pointed to historical anonymity practices and compelling reasons for shielding the compelled disclosure of speakers' identities, the Supreme Court had never clearly recognized a right to anonymity.

The Supreme Court's precedent suggested that the groups would face an uphill climb. In a 1928 opinion, *Bryant v. Zimmerman*, the Supreme Court upheld the constitutionality of a New York statute, as applied to the Ku Klux Klan, that required organizations to disclose the names of their officers and members.[25] "It is difficult to see why Alabama may not obtain, by judicial order, evidence relevant to issues in a proceeding to enforce its corporation laws, similar to that which New York may constitutionally extract from corporations by virtue of a statute," Alabama's attorneys argued to the Supreme Court.[26]

The Supreme Court held oral arguments on January 15, 1958. Carter emphasized the discovery order's significant infringement on free speech and argued that Alabama demonstrated no legitimate need for the member list. "There is no necessity, no need that has been shown as to why . . . the Attorney General desires to know who our members are," Carter told the justices.[27] Carter received mostly procedural questions from the justices, and the argument appeared to flow smoothly.

Edmon L. Rinehart, a lawyer representing Alabama, spent much of his oral argument trying to convince the justices that the way the NAACP appealed was invalid. His argument about the merits of the state's action encountered skepticism. Justice Hugo Black asked Rinehart whether any Alabama law states that a corporation cannot register because it is delinquent in filing its registration forms, and Rinehart said there was not.

Rinehart also acknowledged to Black that the state had never taken such action against any organization other than the NAACP.[28]

Justice William Brennan asked Rinehart why the membership list was relevant to the state's case, and Rinehart responded that he didn't "believe a corporation has any right of privacy and that any case of this Court . . . has ever held any such thing."[29] That drew some skepticism, even from conservative Justice Felix Frankfurter.

"What you're saying is that Alabama tomorrow can subpoena a lot of individuals in this litigation, suppose this proceeds because you're allowed to proceed at the ouster proceeding?" Frankfurter said. "What you're saying is that as a matter of substantive constitutional law, if Alabama [subpoenaed] Smith Jones Robinson and asked . . . him or her on the stand, 'Are you now or were you a member of N.A.A.C.P.?' They could not say, 'Your Honor, in every respect, I decline to answer because I'm protected by the Constitution.' That's what you say, is it?"[30]

"I think that we would have to show that our questions were relevant to the issues in the case," Rinehart replied.

"I'm assuming there, yes," Frankfurter said.

"I don't believe that he could," Rinehart said. "In fact, I deny that he could."[31]

After oral argument, the justices deliberated in private conference whether to reverse the Alabama Supreme Court. Papers in the justices' personal files suggest that they initially were inclined to reverse the lower court in a short, unsigned opinion known as per curiam (Latin for "by the court").[32] Since *Brown*, the Court had disposed of many segregation-related cases with these shorter opinions, and it planned to do so with the Alabama dispute. Justice John Marshall Harlan II was assigned the task of writing the unsigned opinion.

But on April 22, 1958, Harlan sent a memorandum to his colleagues, urging them to agree to a "fully reasoned opinion" in the case, rather than a per curiam opinion. "In my view, the considerations here are quite different from those which have led us to *per cur* all of the cases in this field which have come to us since the original segregation cases were decided," he wrote. "Having found it impossible to write a satisfactory opinion within the normal compass of a *per curiam*, as originally proposed, I have ventured to prepare a full-scale opinion."[33]

Harlan circulated a full opinion, reversing the Alabama Supreme Court and finding for the NAACP. The justices concluded not only that the Alabama Supreme Court should have reviewed the constitutionality of the discovery order, but also that the discovery order violated the members' First Amendment rights.

Harlan wrote that it is "beyond debate" that the freedom of association is protected by the First Amendment's free speech and assembly rights, which apply to states owing to the Due Process Clause of the Fourteenth Amendment.[34] The production order, Harlan wrote, entails "the likelihood of a substantial restraint" on the NAACP members' freedom of association.[35] The NAACP has proven that when its members' identities have been revealed in the past, they have faced "economic reprisal, loss of employment, threat of physical coercion, and other manifestations of public hostility," he wrote.[36] Thus, the compelled disclosure would harm the ability of NAACP members "to pursue their collective effort to foster beliefs which they admittedly have the right to advocate, in that it may induce members to withdraw from the Association and dissuade others from joining it because of fear of exposure of their beliefs shown through their associations and of the consequences of this exposure."[37]

Harlan rejected Alabama's contention that its interest in the compelled production of the membership list outweighs the harms to free association. Harlan noted that the litigation centered on two issues: whether the NAACP must register with Alabama, and whether the NAACP may be banned from operating in the state. Harlan wrote that the court is "unable to perceive that the disclosure of the names of [NAACP's] rank-and-file members has a substantial bearing on either of them."[38]

Harlan also disagreed with Alabama's argument that its statute was justified under the 1928 decision that upheld New York's required disclosure of the Ku Klux Klan's members and officers. "The decision was based on the particular character of the Klan's activities, involving acts of unlawful intimidation and violence, which the Court assumed was before the state legislature when it enacted the statute, and of which the Court itself took judicial notice," he wrote.[39]

At first, the lone dissenter from Harlan's ruling was Justice Tom Clark, who wrote a two-paragraph dissent in which he argued that rather than ruling on the First Amendment issue, the US Supreme Court should send the case back to the Alabama Supreme Court for it to evaluate the constitutionality of the discovery order. But on the day that the opinion was published, he withdrew the dissent, meaning that Harlan's opinion was backed by all nine justices.[40]

The unanimous opinion, coming just four years after *Brown v. Board of Education*, was a huge victory for the NAACP and the civil rights movement. But it was more than that. The opinion also marked the Supreme Court's recognition that the First Amendment protects not only the right to association, but also the right to exercise it anonymously. As Anita L. Allen has aptly observed, *NAACP v. Alabama* protects a wide range of political and religious groups from being forced to disclose their membership rosters.[41]

The Supreme Court demonstrated the value of anonymity not only to traditional free speech interests, but to the basic functions of civil rights. Without the ability for its members and supporters to be shielded from government persecution, it is hard to conceive of how the NAACP could have operated safely in the 1950s.

Nearly a year after the NAACP's victory against the state of Alabama, Robert Carter would ask the Supreme Court to review another attempt to unmask the identity of NAACP members and leaders, this time involving NAACP officials in Arkansas. The outcome would further lay the groundwork for the robust anonymity rights that US courts would recognize.

Arkansas state law allowed municipalities to levy occupational license taxes on businesses operating within their borders, but charitable organizations were exempt from these taxes. On October 14, 1957, the City of Little Rock passed Ordinance 10638, an amendment to its occupational license tax ordinance, requiring any "organization operating or functioning within the City of Little Rock" to file with the city clerk a number of pieces of information, including a list of officers and employees and a financial statement including a list of all contributors, which includes any dues-paying members. The ordinance required that any information filed under the ordinance "shall be deemed public and subject to the inspection of any interested party at all reasonable business hours."[42] The City of North Little Rock passed an identical ordinance.[43]

The NAACP branches in both cities provided the city clerks with all required information except the lists of contributors.[44] "We cannot give you any information with respect to the names and addresses of our members and contributors or any information which may lead to the ascertainment of such information," the Little Rock chapter wrote in its filing with the city clerk. "We base this refusal on the anti-NAACP climate in this State. It is our good faith and belief that the public disclosure of the names of our members and contributors might lead to their harassment, economic reprisals, and even bodily harm."[45]

Daisy Bates, the Arkansas president of the NAACP and custodian of records for the Little Rock branch, and Birdie Williams, president of the North Little Rock branch, were fined in municipal court and appealed to the Circuit Court of Pulaski County.[46] On February 11, 1958, Bates appeared for a trial in the Pulaski County Circuit Court. At the beginning of the trial, Judge William J. Kirby made clear his skepticism of the NAACP's position that disclosure of members and donors implicates the First Amendment. "I cannot see how the ordinance is going to affect the right of freedom of speech or assembly either one," Kirby said. "The City certainly has a right to tax this organization. It looks like the NAACP is a little too apprehensive about what will happen."[47]

Bates testified that the Little Rock ordinance caused 100 or 150 people to refrain from renewing their NAACP memberships.[48] "For the most part, professional people are afraid if their names are published they will be subjected to harassment the same as I," Bates said.[49] Kirby refused to allow testimony from Bates and other local NAACP officials who sought to establish the harms of the local ordinance on NAACP membership and fundraising. He stuck with his preliminary conclusion that the ordinance was valid and issued a twenty-five dollar fine to Bates.[50]

Later that month, Kirby presided over an appeal of the conviction of Birdie Williams. At her hearing, Williams testified about the harassment that she experienced due to her association with the NAACP. "I received a letter threatening my life and they threaten my life over the telephone," she said.[51] As with Bates, Williams could not convince Kirby that the ordinance was unconstitutional. He affirmed the conviction and issued a twenty-five dollar fine.[52]

Bates and Williams appealed the convictions to the Arkansas Supreme Court, which issued its opinion on December 22, 1958, roughly six months *after* the US Supreme Court ruled for the NAACP in its dispute with Alabama. Still, the Arkansas Supreme Court distinguished the Arkansas ordinances from the Alabama case and affirmed Kirby's fines.

"The ultimate aim in *NAACP v. State of Alabama* was to stop the activities of NAACP; but in the case at bar, the disclosure of NAACP's list of members and contributors is a mere incident to see if legal taxation is being evaded," wrote Justice Ed F. McFaddin. "The ordinance here under attack does not single out NAACP and require information of it only: rather, the ordinance requires information of all organizations seeking exemption from privilege tax. Other organizations have complied: why should this one have immunity as though it were a favored child?"[53]

The Arkansas court's justification for the ordinances—particularly considering the Alabama ruling—was flimsy at best. Was the public availability of the names of all of the NAACP members truly necessary to effectively administer the tax system? Bates and Williams said no, and asked the US Supreme Court to review the decision. In the petition seeking Supreme Court review, Carter wrote that the local NAACP branches aren't even subject to the privilege or occupation license taxes.[54] "The reasons which led the Court to hold that compelled disclosure of the names and addresses of NAACP members in Alabama was an unconstitutional restraint on individual freedom, apply with equal vigor here," Carter wrote.[55]

The US Supreme Court agreed to review the case and held oral arguments on November 18, 1959. Carter urged the justices to examine the true purpose of the tax ordinances. "The most effective way to curb the activities of the association in areas in the South is by the publication, public disclosure of the names of the members and contributors because this, as the record in this case discloses, is a frightening thing for people," Carter said. "And what will happen is the people become afraid to participate in the organizational activities."[56]

Joseph C. Kemp, the lawyer for Little Rock, told the justices that the ordinance "was designed to determine in an investigatory manner whether or not organizations allegedly charitable and benevolent and nonprofit were in fact nonprofit or were in fact profit making organizations." The justices appeared skeptical of this argument, peppering Kemp with questions about the need for the information disclosures in the cities' administration of their tax system.[57]

Not surprisingly, soon after the argument the justices voted to overturn the Arkansas Supreme Court and rule for the NAACP. Although the Court was unanimous in the judgment, the justices disagreed as to the reasoning that the Court would apply to reach the result. And that ultimately would be crucial to the case's relevance in the world of anonymity.

Potter Stewart was assigned the opinion. In his initial draft, Stewart wrote that the compelled disclosure of members' identities "would work a significant interference with the freedom of association of their members."[58] But that did not immediately make the ordinances unconstitutional, he wrote. "It merely poses the problem—the recurring problem to which this Court must address itself whenever state action is challenged as an unconstitutional intrusion into the protected domain of individual liberty," Stewart wrote. "As our decisions show, the task the Court must then undertake is to weigh the gravity of the threatened impairment to freedom against the substantiality of the state interest relevantly to be served."[59] Applying this balancing test, Stewart concluded that the state interests did not outweigh the harms to individual liberty.

The NAACP won under this legal analysis, but it left the door open for judges in other cases to conclude that the government interests strongly outweighed any First Amendment interests. This opaque balancing test did not sit well with Justice William Brennan, one of the Court's stalwart liberals. On January 5, 1960, he wrote a letter to Justice Hugo Black, perhaps the most adamant First Amendment defender to ever sit on the Supreme Court. "Does Potter's opinion in the above give you the trouble I have with it?" Brennan wrote. "It seems to me he has unnecessarily emphasized the 'balancing approach.'"[60] Two days later, Brennan wrote to Stewart with suggestions to delete the "balancing" portion of the opinion. "Basically my suggestion is that discussion is not necessary to the decision and its omission might be a way of reconciling the differences among us in that regard," Brennan wrote.[61]

Stewart heard these concerns. On January 19, he circulated to his colleagues a revised opinion, accompanied by a note: "In this revision I have taken out the discussion of 'balancing' and have deleted some of the citations on page 8," Stewart wrote. "In organization the opinion is now almost a Chinese copy of *NAACP v. Alabama*. Those of our brethren who have previously concurred in the opinion are agreeable to these changes if they will serve to achieve unanimity."[62] The changes satisfied Brennan, who wrote to Stewart on February 1 that he was joining the opinion "with great pleasure and satisfaction."[63]

In the final version of the opinion, Stewart relied heavily on the evidence of harassment of NAACP members. "This repressive effect, while in part the result of private attitudes and pressures, was brought to bear only after the exercise of governmental power had threatened to force disclosure of the members' names," he wrote. "Thus, the threat of substantial government encroachment upon important and traditional aspects of individual freedom is neither speculative nor remote." Such significant harm, Stewart wrote, can survive a constitutional challenge only if the government shows a "subordinating interest which is compelling."[64]

Although the government's need to administer taxes is a "fundamental" interest, Stewart wrote, it did not justify this abridgement of free association because there was not a "reasonable relationship" between the rationale for the law and the restrictions that it imposes.[65] The cities failed to demonstrate that the NAACP's activities would be subject to the license tax. "If the organizations were to claim the exemption which the ordinance grants to charitable endeavors, information as to the specific sources and expenditures of their funds might well be a subject of relevant inquiry," he wrote. "But there is nothing to show that any exemption has ever been sought, claimed, or granted—and positive evidence in the record to the contrary."[66]

Stewart removed the explicit balancing test from the final version of the opinion, but even the revised version was far from an absolute prohibition on unmasking the members of a political association. Under Stewart's analytical framework, a law could pass muster if its unmasking requirement had a "reasonable relationship" to a compelling interest.

For Justice Black and Justice William Douglas, who also believed in strong application of First Amendment protections, Stewart's test did not go far enough. They wrote a two-paragraph concurring opinion, agreeing with the result but arguing for stronger protections. They argued that "First Amendment rights are beyond abridgment either by legislation that directly restrains their exercise or by suppression or impairment through harassment, humiliation, or exposure by government."[67]

Despite the pushback from Black and Douglas, Stewart's opinion represented progress for those who wanted to prevent the compelled disclosure of identities. Combined with the recent opinion involving Alabama, *Bates v. Little Rock* meant that the government, at the very least, must make a strong demonstration of the need to identify members of groups involved in significant public controversy.

In the decades since the ruling in *NAACP v. Alabama*, there has been considerable debate over the impetus behind this landmark decision. In a 2012 article, Dale E. Ho aptly characterized the two general views of the Court's reasoning: "anti-chilling" and "anti-suppression." Under the "anti-chilling" rationale, Ho wrote, the case "stands for a neutral proposition that, because compelled disclosure of a speaker's identity may deter that person (or entity) from speaking, such requirements should generally be viewed with suspicion, regardless of to whom they are applied."[68] Under the "anti-suppression" perspective, the opinion "can also be understood from a different perspective that acknowledges its historical context and the fact that the target of disclosure in that case was a protected minority group."[69] Ho argued that the latter view of *NAACP v. Alabama* is more effective and historically appropriate, as it helps to provide a voice to minorities who otherwise may not have been heard.[70]

It is impossible to ignore the historical context of both NAACP cases. The organizations and people seeking anonymity were fighting segregation and discrimination against some of the most powerful elements of society. As would become clear as the modern Internet took shape decades later, anonymous and pseudonymous speech is vital for vulnerable groups that are more likely to face retaliation for their views. The ability to associate one's real name with one's speech is too often an unappreciated privilege of the majority. Anonymity and pseudonymity have been a key tool for the speech of those who do not normally have a voice in the mainstream debate.

Yet the rulings that rely on these NAACP opinions were not limited to an antisuppression context. Later cases would adopt a broad antichilling rationale to rely on the cases in protecting anonymity in a wide range of contexts.

The Court's rulings in the NAACP cases addressed only one aspect of anonymity: association with an organization whose members might face harassment and retaliation. What about protecting the identities of people who write controversial articles or leaflets, as they did during the earliest days of America? Does the First Amendment protect anonymous speech, just as it protects anonymous association? The justices would gradually develop the rules of the road for anonymity over the next four decades, in a series of cases involving political pamphleteering and canvassing. And these rules would shape anonymity both online and offline.

3

EMPOWERING ANONYMOUS SPEECH

Manuel Talley founded the Los Angeles chapter of the Congress of Racial Equality and dedicated his life to fighting discrimination. Talley was action director of National Consumer Mobilization, which organized boycotts of discriminatory businesses throughout the 1950s and 1960s.[1] He also twice ran for Congress and worked on registering Black voters before dying at age sixty-eight in 1986.[2]

Talley promoted peaceful means of protesting racial discrimination. In 1950, Talley and two friends were denied service in an Albuquerque café that refused to allow Black customers. After Talley questioned the denial of service, three employees argued with Talley, and one hit him on the head with a ketchup bottle.[3] Talley asked a local judge to dismiss criminal charges against the three men because "what is needed is a program for racial understanding."[4]

One of his longest lasting impacts, however, was not on civil rights law but the First Amendment rules governing anonymity. A dispute over an unsigned boycott flyer that he distributed in Los Angeles reached the Supreme Court, and the 1960 opinion established a First Amendment right to anonymous speech.

The dispute began on March 22, 1958, when Talley distributed two handbills outside of the A&D Market in Los Angeles.[5] The first read:

We are boycotting the A and D Market at 5501 Holmes Avenue.

Why?
    Because he carries in his store goods that come from manufacturers who will not offer equal employment opportunity to Negroes, Mexicans, and Orientals.

What are the unfair goods?
    Our entire unfair list is at the center of this sheet. Articles with *'s by them are sold in grocery stores.

Why not trade at A&D Market but not buy the blacklisted goods?
    If you buy a pound of meat, you help keep this business open so he can sell unfair bread or milk.
    This boycott will probably last for six months. Do not trade at A&D Market until this boycott is over.[6]

The handbill then included a list of brands subject to the boycott, a sign-up sheet for new members in the National Consumers Mobilization group, and the following contact information: "National Consumers Mobilization, Box 6533, Los Angeles 55, Calif. For further information, call Pleasant 9–1576."[7]

The second handbill similarly urged a boycott of A&D Market, alleging that "Nick Mirolla, operator of the A&D Market, says he will close his market and move before he will cooperate in this fair employment program, which will open more jobs for Negroes, Mexicans and Orientals." The handbill included the same post office box and phone number for National Consumers Mobilization.[8]

A Los Angeles Police Department sergeant observed Talley distributing the handbills,[9] and Talley was arrested and charged with violating Los Angeles Municipal Ordinance No. 77,000, sec. 28.06, which stated:

No person shall distribute any handbill in any place under any circumstances, which does not have printed on the cover, or the face thereof, the name and address of the following:

(a) The person who printed, wrote, compiled or manufactured the same.

(b) The person who caused the same to be distributed; provided, however, that in the case of a fictitious person or club, in addition to such fictitious name, the true names and addresses of the owners, managers or agents of the person sponsoring said handbill shall also appear thereon.[10]

Talley was tried before Judge John G. Barnes in Los Angeles Municipal Court on May 27, 1958.[11] At trial, Talley's lawyer, Herbert W. Simmons, argued that prosecutors held Talley to a double standard. Simmons introduced a handbill that A&D Market distributed on the street to promote its products. Before Talley was arrested, the market's handbills only carried the name of A&D Market, and not the person who "wrote, compiled, or manufactured" the handbills.[12] After Talley was arrested, the market's handbill began noting that it was printed by the Hollywood Lithograph Company.[13]

Simmons was trying to argue that by arresting Talley but allowing the market to distribute its anonymous handbills, the police unequally enforced the law.[14] But he struggled to demonstrate that A&D Market was a fictitious name, and not the company's formal name of incorporation, calling market employees to testify who simply did not know how the market was incorporated.[15] Judge Barnes appeared to lose patience, finally ruling that even if A&D Market were a fictitious name, the unequal enforcement defense "falls short of proof."[16]

Simmons then began to argue that the ordinance was unconstitutional, but he acknowledged that a California state appellate court had rejected that argument just four years earlier in *People v. Arnold*, a case that Simmons had lost.[17]

"Who am I to argue with them?" Barnes asked. "Those wise ones up there know much more about these things than I do."

"I know you would be bound by that, your Honor," Simmons conceded.

Barnes found Talley guilty of a misdemeanor and issued a $10 fine.[18] Talley appealed to the same California appellate court that had upheld the Los Angeles handbill ordinance four years earlier.

At first glance, it might appear futile to ask a state appeals court to reverse its own stance on the handbill ordinance. But developments in Washington, DC, could have forced the California court to reconsider how the First Amendment applies. Talley's trial took place a month before the US Supreme Court would issue its opinion in *NAACP v. Alabama*, its most forceful articulation ever of a right to anonymous expression. By the time that the California appeals court would hear the case, it would have guidance from the higher court, calling into question not only Barnes's ruling, but its earlier decision in *People v. Arnold*.

The California appellate court issued its opinion in Talley's case nearly five months after the *NAACP v. Alabama* ruling. Despite the new national First Amendment precedent, the California court refused to back away from its conclusion that the Los Angeles ordinance was constitutional. "The requirement that the desired information be placed upon a handbill, does not serve in any way to restrict what may be said, except the purely speculative personal possibility that someone might hesitate to identify himself with his own statements therein contained," the majority wrote.[19]

The majority acknowledged the Supreme Court's new opinion protecting the NAACP, but noted that the Court had not overruled the 1928 case, *Bryant v. Zimmerman*, which allowed the compelled disclosure of the membership list of the Ku Klux Klan. "It seems accepted that the names of the officials or employees of the organization could be validly required," the California court wrote. "One can find no differences between organizations, except that one was considered malignant, and the other benign, and the situation out of which the latter case evolved perhaps led to the fear that disclosure was only sought as a prelude to the deprivation of other constitutional rights; not a speculative but an imminent deprivation."[20]

Judge Swain concurred, noting the conflict in precedent between the NAACP and Ku Klux Klan opinions. "The distinction which Mr. Justice Harlan draws between the two seems to be that the members of N.A.A.C.P. are good guys and the members of Ku Klux Klan are wicked men," he wrote.[21]

Presiding Judge Bishop dissented, noting that the bill's purpose was to hold the author or distributor of a handbill accountable for its content. "In order to accomplish this purpose in the relatively few instances where there has been an abuse of the right freely to communicate ideas by hand-bills (and plainly defendant's handbill was not obscene, libelous, nor did it otherwise abuse the right), the municipal code would impose restraint upon all occasions where it is desired to use them. I remain convinced that this may not be done," he wrote.[22]

The southern California chapter of the American Civil Liberties Union took on Talley's case, and convinced the US Supreme Court to hear the appeal. In Talley's Supreme Court brief, the ACLU traced the history of anonymity back to the Renaissance and Reformation, when writers faced "severe penalties," through the anonymous works of the eighteenth century to modern periodicals, such as *Foreign Affairs*, which routinely used pseudonyms.[23] The right to anonymous speech, the lawyers wrote, is particularly important for social reformers. "People usually resent change, and greet it only with hostile reluctance," they wrote. "For this reason, ideas which tamper with deep-rooted prejudices may expect to encounter serious—and even violent—opposition. The simplest way to discourage such opinions, therefore, is to expose their proponents to a resentful community."[24]

In defense of the ordinance, the government relied partly on *Lewis Publishing Co. v. Morgan*,[25] a 1913 case in which the US Supreme Court affirmed a federal law that required publications sent via the mail to file with the postmaster general and postmaster "a sworn statement setting forth the names and post office addresses of the editor and managing editor, publisher, business managers, and owners," among other information.[26] "Under the *Lewis* decision it appears that those who share responsibility in newspaper endeavors have no constitutional right to go unnoticed," Los Angeles's city attorneys wrote. "The reader is entitled to know of their identity."[27]

The 1913 case proved to be a challenge for Talley's attorneys at oral argument on January 13, 1960. Justice Felix Frankfurter asked Hugh R. Manes, a lawyer for Talley, whether *Lewis* "qualifies this absolute statement of yours about the right to anonymity."

"I say, Your Honor, that we do not contend that the right to anonymity is an unlimited right by any means," Manes responded. "We say that there are times and circumstances when . . . the State has the right to limit anonymity. We say only that it cannot be an unlimited right to suppress anonymity or the right to anonymity so completely and so broadly as is done here." *Lewis*, Manes said, involved "a commercial profit-making venture which is very much unlike our particular leaflet here."[28]

That did not appear to satisfy Frankfurter. "If Tom Paine had published his *Common Sense* as a periodical and sought to send it through the mail," Frankfurter reasoned, "he would under the *Lewis* case, as I understand it, have to disclose who owns his paper." Manes pointed out that disclosing the identity of the owner and publisher of the publication is not necessarily the same thing as disclosing the writer. Frankfurter responded that those are the "people who really run the show and own it."[29]

"That's correct, Your Honor," Manes said, "but the fact remains that the writers of the articles within the newspaper are not compelled to be disclosed."[30]

Justice Charles E. Whittaker appeared unpersuaded. He noted that the ordinance merely requires the handbill to include the identity of the creator or distributor.

Manes acknowledged that was the only requirement. "But its impact . . . has a farther reach, Your Honor, because what we are trying to suggest to the Court is that there are times and circumstances when speech can only be freely uttered anonymously or if . . . the author or the speaker remains anonymous, so that he does not leave a trail to the door for those who are hostile to his ideas," Manes said.[31]

Despite the justices' apparent skepticism of Manes's argument, his client prevailed. In a 6–3 ruling, the Supreme Court struck down the Los Angeles ordinance as unconstitutional. In the majority opinion, First Amendment stalwart Justice Hugo Black noted that in a 1938 case, *Lovell v. Griffin,* the Court had struck down a Georgia ordinance that required a license to distribute literature.[32] Black reasoned that the requirement for identification in the Los Angeles ordinance "would tend to restrict freedom to distribute information, and thereby freedom of expression."[33] Black outlined the longstanding importance of the ability to publish anonymously.

His opinion contained the Supreme Court's first extended discussion of the historical justification for protecting anonymous speech. "Before the Revolutionary War colonial patriots frequently had to conceal their authorship or distribution of literature that easily could have brought down on them prosecutions by English-controlled courts," Black wrote. "Along about that time, the Letters of Junius were written and the identity of their author is unknown to this day. Even the Federalist Papers, written in favor of the adoption of our Constitution, were published under fictitious names. It is plain that anonymity has sometimes been assumed for the most constructive purposes."[34] Likewise, Black reasoned, the two recent NAACP rulings were grounded in the reasoning that "identification and fear of reprisal might deter perfectly peaceful discussions of public matters of importance." The Los Angeles ordinance, he concluded, "is subject to the same infirmity."[35]

In a letter to Black while the opinion was being circulated among the justices, Justice Harlan noted that although he agreed with the outcome of the case, he believed that California should lose because it failed to demonstrate a compelling interest. "I realize that I can hardly expect you to meet my difficulties on this score because of your distaste for the 'balancing' process in this type of case," Harlan wrote on February 10, 1960.[36] Harlan wrote a concurrence, emphasizing that there are some circumstances in which intrusions on anonymity can pass constitutional muster, though this was not one of them. The city justified the ordinance, he wrote, by claiming that "the circulation of all anonymous handbills must be suppressed in order to identify the distributors of those that may be of an obnoxious character."[37] Such rationale falls short of the "compelling" interest required for restrictions on anonymity, he wrote. "In the absence of a more substantial showing as to Los Angeles' actual experience with the distribution of obnoxious handbills, such a generality is for me too remote to furnish a constitutionally acceptable justification for the deterrent effect on free speech which this all-embracing ordinance is likely to have."[38]

Black's opinion was a monumental development for the right to anonymity. The NAACP protected the ability of people to anonymously join organizations. But Talley's victory meant that the First Amendment protects not only the right to associate anonymously, but also the right to speak anonymously. An article the next year in the *Ohio State Law Journal* observed that "the aim of the *Talley* majority is clearly in the direction of the protection of anonymous speech, or, the protection of anonymity from arbitrary infringement."[39]

The opinion immediately received some criticism. In a column distributed by the *New York Herald Tribune* the week that the opinion issued, David Lawrence noted the conflict with the *Lewis* opinion. "Even the best lawyers in the country must be baffled now in attempting to say just what the 'law of the land' is today with reference to the distribution of anonymous handbills," he wrote.[40]

Black's bold statements about anonymity also received criticism from some justices. Soon after Black circulated a draft of his opinion in February 1960, Frankfurter sent a memo to his colleagues in which he announced his plans to write a dissent unless another justice planned to do so. "I certainly cannot agree to an opinion which does not differentiate the invalidation of this legislation against anonymity from the great body of enactments requiring disclosure in a field that so deeply touches the protection of free discussion of public matters as against 'the fear of reprisal' etc. in the exercise of the voting franchise in political elections," Frankfurter wrote.[41]

Justice Clark wrote a dissent, not surprisingly joined by Frankfurter and Whittaker. Clark observed that Los Angeles may well have had a valid reason for the identification requirement, such as combatting false advertising.[42] And Talley failed to show that he would face harm by identifying himself on the handbills, he reasoned. "I stand second to none in supporting Talley's right of free speech—but not his freedom of anonymity," Clark wrote. "The Constitution says nothing about freedom of anonymous speech."[43] Clark pointed to state election laws that require campaign materials to identify the author. "The fact that some of these statutes are aimed at elections, lobbying, and the mails makes their restraint no more palatable, nor the abuses they prevent less deleterious to the public interest, than the present ordinance," he wrote.[44] Clark was correct that it had been generally accepted that anonymity rights did not necessarily extend to the distribution of election-related writing. Did Manuel Talley's victory in the Supreme Court mean that these state election laws also were unconstitutional?

The Supreme Court's answer to that question—and its most forceful articulation of the right to anonymous speech—emerged from a 1988 meeting at Blendon Middle School in Westerville, Ohio, nearly three decades after the *Talley* ruling. The Court's clear and enduring statement can be traced to Margaret McIntyre and her adamant opposition to a local school tax levy. McIntyre was so vocal about her stances on local issues such as the school tax that she was an unlikely torchbearer for the right to anonymous speech. She made her beliefs known in Westerville, the Columbus, Ohio, suburb where she lived with her family.

"If she believed in something, she'd stay and fight with it until the end," her husband, Joseph McIntyre, told a newspaper.[45]

On April 27, 1988, the Westerville school district's assistant superintendent, J. Michael Hayfield, saw Margaret McIntyre distributing a flyer at the school. The flyer, which she created on her home computer, read:

> VOTE NO
> ISSUE 19 SCHOOL TAX LEVY
> Last election Westerville Schools, asked us to vote yes for new buildings and expansions programs. We gave them what they asked. We knew there was crowded conditions and new growth in the district.
> Now we find out there is a 4 million dollar deficit—WHY?
> We are told the 3 middle schools must be split because of over-crowding, and yet we are told 3 schools are being closed—WHY?
> A magnet school is not a full operating school, but a specials school.
> Residents were asked to work on a 20 member commission to help formulate the new boundaries. For 4 weeks they worked long and hard and came up with a very workable plan. Their plan was totally disregarded—WHY?
> WASTE of tax payers dollars must be stopped. Our children's education and welfare must come first. WASTE CAN NO LONGER BE TOLERATED.
> PLEASE VOTE NO
> ISSUE 19
> THANK YOU,
> CONCERNED PARENTS
> AND
> TAXPAYERS
> NOT PAID FOR BY PUBLIC FUNDS[46]

Hayfield told McIntyre that the flyer violated an Ohio election law, which required any publication designed "to promote the adoption or defeat of any issue" to include the "name and residence or business address of the chairman, treasurer, or secretary of the organization" that issues the publication.[47] This warning did not daunt McIntyre; the next day she distributed another unsigned flyer at a public meeting.[48]

The school levy failed twice, before being approved at the November 1988 election.[49] Hayfield filed a complaint against McIntyre with the Ohio Elections Commission, alleging, among other things, that she failed to include the required disclaimer on the flyers.[50] McIntyre told the commission that "a few copies" of the flyers had "incomplete information" and were erroneously distributed. "At no time was there any intent to hide my identity or to issue any false statements," she wrote to the commission.[51] McIntyre told the commission that another version of the flyer, including her name and address, was also distributed at the meeting.[52]

At a commission hearing on Hayfield's complaint, McIntyre not only argued that the omission of her name from some flyers was accidental, but that she had a constitutional right to distribute the unsigned literature.

"Now I feel that being denied passing this literature out would definitely be an infringement of my First Amendment rights, because I was working as an individual, not as a committee, not as a group," she said at the March 19, 1990, hearing. "Therefore, I didn't need to file anything."[53]

"Except you didn't identify yourself as an individual," replied Michael Igoe, the commission's chairman. "You identified yourself as a group."[54]

The commission unanimously found her in violation of the statute and imposed a $100 fine.[55] McIntyre appealed to the Common Pleas Court of Franklin County, which reversed the commission's decision.[56] Judge Tommy L. Thompson concluded that although there is a need to "protect the voting process from scandalous, libelous, or malicious attempts to degrade its integrity," people also have the right to express their opinions about issues.[57] Applying the identification requirement to McIntyre, he reasoned, violates the First Amendment. "The record does not reflect any attempt by Ms. McIntyre to mislead the public nor act in a surreptitious manner."[58]

The election commission appealed the decision, and the Court of Appeals of Ohio reversed, reinstating the fine. The court acknowledged that the Supreme Court had struck down the Los Angeles ordinance in Manuel Talley's case, but reasoned that there is a more compelling reason for the Ohio requirement: "The state has a greater interest in prohibiting anonymous political communication to protect against fraudulent and corrupt practices than it has in prohibiting anonymous communications generally."[59]

McIntyre appealed to the Ohio Supreme Court, which also affirmed the commission's fine. The identification requirement is constitutional, the majority wrote, because it "neither impacts the content of their message nor significantly burdens their ability to have it disseminated." The majority interpreted Supreme Court precedent to conclude that state laws that impose nondiscriminatory burdens on free speech are subject to a fairly deferential standard of review, and are typically justified by "the State's important regulatory interests."[60]

Justice J. Craig Wright dissented, stressing the historical importance of anonymity in foundational documents such as the Federalist Papers. "I think that James Madison, the author of the Bill of Rights, would be very surprised by the decision of the majority that a citizen does not have the right to issue anonymous statements expressing her views on ballot issues," Wright wrote.[61] Because the law restricted the speech of an individual citizen, rather than a political candidate or political committee, he wrote, the majority should have applied the more rigorous constitutional standard.[62]

Representing McIntyre was David Goldberger, an Ohio State University law professor who had long worked as an ACLU attorney and was known for a 1977 US Supreme Court case in which he successfully challenged a court order that prohibited neo-Nazis from demonstrating in Skokie, Ill. Goldberger asked the US Supreme Court to review the decision in McIntyre's case and on February 22, 1994, the Supreme Court granted the request. "She was really ecstatic," her husband, Joseph, recalled later that year. "She said, 'It isn't very often a little person gets their case to the Supreme Court.'"[63] McIntyre died of ovarian cancer less than three months later, and the Court allowed Joseph to pursue her claim.[64]

The case's fate, however, was far from clear. Goldberger was not arguing to Chief Justice Earl Warren's court, where Manuel Talley had won more than three decades earlier. This was the more conservative court of Chief Justice William Rehnquist, and Goldberger seemed to face an uphill battle in convincing the Rehnquist Court to interpret the right to anonymity even more broadly than the Warren Court did.

At oral argument on October 12, 1994, some justices appeared a bit skeptical of Goldberger's argument that McIntyre had a First Amendment right to anonymously distribute campaign literature. Shortly after Goldberger began his argument, Justice Sandra Day O'Connor noted that at the federal level, campaign expenditures of more than $250 must be disclosed to the Federal Election Commission, along with the name of the person who spent the money. Does that violate the First Amendment?[65]

"I believe, Your Honor, that a disclosure requirement on any leaflet, when the leaflet . . . constitutes core political speech or is pure speech, would violate the First Amendment," Goldberger replied.

"Well, that wasn't my question," O'Connor responded. The federal law, she said, does not require identity disclosure on the campaign material, but to the federal agency. Is that a First Amendment violation?

"We do not believe that the expenditure disclosure requirements are by any means," Goldberger responded, "when appropriately framed, unlawful or unconstitutional, but we—"

"What about a requirement on a television ad that the identity of the people running the ad be shown?" O'Connor interjected.

"I believe that's a different kind of a case, Your Honor, because television is a conduit for a great variety of communication, and there's a potential for confusion when a viewer is watching television as to who's saying what and under what circumstances," Goldberger said. "In addition, television as a form of broadcasting is governed by the federal Communications Act, and I believe is subject to a separate and distinct set of rules."

Justices seized on Goldberger's emphasis on "potential for confusion" with television advertising. "Well, isn't there an equal potential for confusion when I walk up to the polling place and I'm handed 6 or 8 or 10 or 12 leaflets saying, vote for this, that, or the other person or issue on the way up to vote?" Justice David Souter asked.

"Your Honor, I believe that the voters are capable of deciding for themselves," Goldberger replied. "They operate in a political climate—"

"You just did not see my puzzlement last September when I was on my way into the primary," Souter joked.

Justice Ruth Bader Ginsburg wanted to know how the Ohio law could be unconstitutional if the Supreme Court has already upheld laws that require corporations to disclose campaign expenditures.

"Are you drawing a line between individuals like McIntyre and corporations?" Ginsburg asked.

"I believe that the Court should draw a line between individuals like McIntyre and corporations," Goldberger replied.

"What about rich individuals versus poor corporations?" Ginsburg said, to laughter.

Ginsburg and Souter noted that this case was different from the NAACP's dispute with Alabama because McIntyre intended to include her name on the literature.

Goldberger acknowledged that McIntyre had first defended the anonymous brochure as an inadvertent error, but noted that the school officials waited to file the complaint until a year later, after the tax levy had finally passed.

"She and every other resident of the village or City of Westerville are now on notice that when they take on school officials in these tax levy referenda, they do so knowing that the school officials are going to fight back, and very hard," Goldberger said.

Andrew Sutter, the Ohio assistant attorney general who was defending the identification requirement, also faced tough questioning from the justices. O'Connor asked him whether Ohio would have been able to mandate the identification of the authors of the Federalist Papers.

"No, Your Honor," Sutter said. "We think this is a much more limited statute that addresses only campaign literature or broadcast media."

"Well, if they were circulated in support of a referendum on whether the Constitution should be adopted or ratified," O'Connor said, "you would say it would have been perfectly okay to require disclosure."

"Your Honor, the circumstances then were somewhat different," Sutter said. "We think that the protections of the First Amendment make a difference, but if today the Federalist Papers were being circulated, we would argue that the State had a compelling interest in requiring the speakers to place their name on the literature. There would be no difference, and that is our point here."

Sutter received some support from conservative Justice Antonin Scalia, who observed that it's safe to assume that Ohioans like the disclosure law.

"Your Honor, there haven't been any initiatives or referenda on the ballot to repeal it," Sutter said.

"And presumably would rather know who is putting out these pamphlets than not know," Scalia reasoned.

Sutter replied, "I think that's correct, and that reflects—"

"Most people in Ohio," Ginsburg asked, "don't know a thing about the existence of this law?" The courtroom again erupted in laughter.

"Your Honor, I wouldn't want to speculate either way, but I would say that the vast majority of legislators in the Congress think that this is important legislation," Sutter responded.

Both Sutter and Goldberger faced tough questions, so it was hard to predict the outcome based on the justices' comments at oral argument. About six months later, the Supreme Court released an opinion in which it held the Ohio law unconstitutional. Justice Stevens, joined by five of his colleagues, wrote the majority opinion.

"Under our Constitution, anonymous pamphleteering is not a pernicious, fraudulent practice, but an honorable tradition of advocacy and of dissent," Stevens wrote. "Anonymity is a shield from the tyranny of the majority. It thus exemplifies the purpose behind the Bill of Rights, and of the First Amendment in particular: to protect unpopular individuals from retaliation—and their ideas from suppression—at the hand of an intolerant society."[66]

Stevens began the legal analysis portion of the opinion with an overview of the historical importance of anonymity and pseudonymity in political writing such as the Federalist Papers, and in literature by authors such as Voltaire, Mark Twain, and George Eliot.

"Great works of literature have frequently been produced by authors writing under assumed names," Stevens wrote. "Despite readers' curiosity and the public's interest in identifying the creator of a work of art, an author generally is free to decide whether or not to disclose his or her true identity. The decision in favor of anonymity may be motivated by fear of economic or official retaliation, by concern about social ostracism, or merely by a desire to preserve as much of one's privacy as possible."

Although *Talley* involved a boycott of a supermarket, Stevens concluded that "the Court's reasoning embraced a respected tradition of anonymity in the advocacy of political causes."[67] The Los Angeles ordinance in *Talley*, Stevens acknowledged, more broadly prohibited all anonymous pamphleteering, while Ohio's law only applied to writing intended to influence an election.[68] Nonetheless, he reasoned, the law burdens "core political speech," and is therefore subject to "exacting scrutiny," meaning that it can be upheld "only if it is narrowly tailored to serve an overriding state interest."[69]

Stevens concluded that the Ohio law could not survive this high level of scrutiny. The state sought to justify the law by identifying two government interests: providing voters with necessary information and combatting fraud and libel. Providing relevant information to voters, Stevens wrote, cannot justify the identification requirement.[70] Nor can prevention of fraud or libel justify the Ohio law, he wrote, as the ban on unsigned election materials "encompasses documents that are not even arguably false or misleading."[71]

Although his condemnation of Ohio's law was clear, Stevens did not foreclose the possibility of more targeted restrictions on anonymous speech. "We recognize that a State's enforcement interest might justify a more limited identification requirement, but Ohio has shown scant cause for inhibiting the leafletting at issue here," he wrote.[72] While this standard is rigorous, it provides more leeway for unmasking than Justice Black's opinion in *Talley*, which Justice Harlan believed was too absolutist.

Crucial to the *McIntyre* decision was its reliance on the "marketplace of ideas" theory of free speech, which Justice Holmes famously articulated in 1919: "The best test of truth is the power of the thought to get itself accepted in the competition of the market."[73] Stevens extended the marketplace theory to anonymous speech, writing that "the identity of the speaker is no different from other components of the document's content that the author is free to include or exclude."[74] Stevens quoted an earlier Supreme Court case in which the Court observed that the "inherent worth of the speech in terms of its capacity for informing the public does not depend upon the identity of its source, whether corporation, association, union, or individual."[75] Stevens placed a fairly heavy burden on audience members to evaluate the veracity of anonymous speech. As Lyrissa Barnett Lidsky and Thomas F. Cotter wrote, "The Court merely expresses faith in the audience's ability to discount anonymous speech, reducing (but not eliminating) any potential harm that might flow from it."[76]

Justice Ginsburg joined Stevens's opinion, but wrote a brief concurrence to reiterate that the right to anonymity is not absolute. "The Court's decision finds unnecessary, over intrusive, and inconsistent with American ideals the State's imposition of a fine on an individual leafleteer who, within her local community, spoke her mind, but sometimes not her name," she wrote. "We do not thereby hold that the State may not in other, larger circumstances require the speaker to disclose its interest by disclosing his identity."[77]

Justice Stevens was firmly entrenched in the liberal wing of the Supreme Court, and conservatives Scalia and Rehnquist were the two justices to dissent, with Scalia writing that the opinion is an "imposition of free-speech imperatives that are demonstrably not those of the American people today."[78]

To Scalia, the question was not whether anonymous election communications took place when the First and Fourteenth Amendments were adopted, but whether such communications were viewed as constitutional liberties. "Evidence that anonymous electioneering was regarded as a constitutional right is sparse, and as far as I am aware evidence that it was *generally* regarded as such is nonexistent," Scalia wrote.[79]

Scalia pointed to the difficulty of discerning a workable and predictable framework for anonymity from the majority's opinion. "Must a public university that makes its facilities available for a speech by Louis Farrakhan or David Duke refuse to disclose the on-campus or off-campus group that has sponsored or paid for the speech?" Scalia wrote. "Must a municipal 'public-access' cable channel permit anonymous (and masked) performers? The silliness that follows upon a generalized right to anonymous speech has no end."[80]

Scalia also voiced a more general hostility toward anonymous political speech, questioning whether "mudslinging" and dirty tricks would increase in an anonymous world. "How much easier—and sanction free!—it would be to circulate anonymous material (for example, a *really* tasteless, though not actionably false, attack upon one's own candidate) with the hope and expectation that it will be attributed to, and held against, the other side," Scalia wrote.[81]

Yet Justice Clarence Thomas, also a conservative, not only concurred in Stevens's judgment, but wrote a separate opinion in which he called for an even bolder recognition of the right to anonymous speech. Rather than simply relying on the longstanding history of anonymous speech in the United States, Thomas argued that when the Bill of Rights was drafted, the First Amendment's provision for freedom of the press was understood to include a right to anonymity, pointing to the drafting of the Federalist Papers, the Zenger trial, and other events and publications in the years around the Constitution's adoption. "The large quantity of newspapers and pamphlets the Framers produced during the various crises of their generation show the remarkable extent to which the Framers relied upon anonymity," Thomas wrote.[82]

Thomas wrote separately because he is an originalist, who believes that the Constitution should be interpreted based on the meaning of the words as they were understood when the Founders wrote the Constitution. Although Thomas agreed with the result of the case, he disagreed with Stevens's focus on the tradition of anonymous speech and his balancing of the benefits and harms of anonymity.

"Whether 'great works of literature'—by Voltaire or George Eliot have been published anonymously should be irrelevant to our analysis, because it sheds no light on what the phrases 'free speech' or 'free press' meant to the people who drafted and ratified the First Amendment," Thomas wrote. "Similarly, whether certain types of expression have 'value' today has little significance; what *is* important is whether the Framers in 1791 believed anonymous speech sufficiently valuable to deserve the protection of the Bill of Rights."[83]

To Thomas, the key question was whether the Framers expected the First Amendment's protections for freedom of speech and the press to protect anonymous political communications. And he believed that they did. "After reviewing the weight of the historical evidence, it seems that the Framers understood the First Amendment to protect an author's right to express his thoughts on political candidates or issues in an anonymous fashion," Thomas wrote.[84]

McIntyre was perhaps the most significant legal development ever for the right to anonymity in the United States. *Talley* was issued by a far more liberal Supreme Court, and the Court had not significantly expanded on the opinion for more than three decades. Yet liberals such as Stevens, moderates such as O'Connor, and conservative Thomas agreed that the Ohio law violated McIntyre's First Amendment rights. And the breadth of the protections for anonymity in *McIntyre* was even greater than that articulated in *Talley*. As Jonathan Turley wrote: "Whether *McIntyre* created a de facto right to anonymity would remain a question for academic debate. However, it was clear that the Court viewed anonymity as a critical component of speech under the First Amendment."[85]

The Court in *McIntyre* also applied First Amendment values to both anonymity *and* pseudonymity, a trend that would continue as courts grappled with subpoenas for the identities of pseudonymous online posters. As David Post wrote in 1996, the Court repeatedly referred to pseudonymous works such as the Federalist Papers. "The *McIntyre* Court implicitly recognized this principle that restrictions on anonymity necessarily restrict pseudonymity as well," Post wrote.[86]

Although *McIntyre* expanded the anonymity right set forth in *Talley* and the NAACP cases, its rationale was somewhat different. Margot Kaminski observed that *Talley* focused on the fear of reprisal that looms over those who express unpopular views.[87] In contrast, she wrote, *McIntyre* focused more on the literary value of the anonymous speech.[88]

At first glance, Margaret McIntyre's case might seem to be less urgent than Manuel Talley's. Talley was organizing boycotts during the civil rights era, and he had very pragmatic reasons to hide his group's name from the fliers. McIntyre, on the other hand, only mistakenly circulated her anonymous campaign literature. The Supreme Court's ruling in her favor made clear that courts should not make value judgments and only protect particular forms of anonymous speech with particular outcomes.

The majority opinions in *Talley* and *McIntyre* set forth a doctrinal balancing test for determining whether government restrictions on anonymous speech violate the First Amendment. In the years since both opinions, there has been considerable normative debate in scholarly literature on whether these anonymity protections promote free speech both online and offline.

As described later in this book, while anonymous online communications create substantial benefits for society, in some cases they also enable trolls, harassers, and criminals to cloak their identities. A handful of malicious actors can cause great harm, and the normative question that we must address is how to protect the valuable anonymous speech, such as advocacy of abolition and suffrage, while minimizing the harm.

Frederick Schauer articulated the value of a balanced assessment of both the costs and benefits of anonymity. On one hand, he wrote, anonymity protects those who wish to express unpopular views but are unwilling to be the next Joan of Arc. "Not everyone is willing to be burned at the stake for their principles and their beliefs, and for the rest of us—with at best a normal and not exceptional amount of courage—the fear of various unpleasant consequences is often sufficient to get us to keep our mouths shut and our beliefs to ourselves," he wrote. "And thus it seems clear that a First Amendment in which *Talley* and *McIntyre*, in particular, were decided differently would be a First Amendment less sensitive to the realities of speaker incentives, and more willing to tolerate an environment in which only—or at the very least disproportionately—the bold were full participants in public discourse."[89]

Yet Schauer also notes the value of knowing the identity of a speaker. Were the Federalist Papers necessarily more persuasive *without* the names of their authors, as the Speech Motivation might suggest? Schauer points to the value of identifying particularly trustworthy sources of information. "Once we recognize that most of the contributions to public debate that we especially value (as well as those we most abhor) rely on assertions that the reader or listener or viewer is expected to take on faith, we can understand that treating identity as largely a matter of idle or voyeuristic curiosity misconceives the nature of public discussion," Schauer wrote. "If someone says to me that President Obama was born in Kenya or Indonesia and is therefore an ineligible imposter to the presidency, I want to know who said so, not (only) as a matter of curiosity, and not only because I want to learn about who is taking which positions in public debate so that I can learn something about *them*, but because knowing who said something enables me to evaluate the substance of the statement. That is what the claim of authority- and trust-dependent knowledge is all about, and it infuses our epistemic existence."[90]

The doctrinal framework set forth in *McIntyre* implicitly reflects these competing social and expressive values. Rather than setting a bright-line rule prohibiting anonymity restrictions, the Supreme Court has adopted a flexible balancing test to weigh the competing benefits and harms of anonymity.

With flexibility comes unpredictability. A bright-line rule could provide more certainty both for speakers and for governments. But such absolutism would also deprive courts of the ability to make case-specific judgments that look at unique burdens on speech and harms both to expression and other interests such as privacy.

After the *McIntyre* opinion, it was apparent that the Supreme Court valued anonymity and wanted courts to take reasonable steps to protect it. But the Court had not fully articulated when it believed anonymity rights apply, and the extent to which courts must impose safeguards for anonymity. Those outer limits would emerge somewhat over the next decade.

THE SCOPE OF ANONYMITY
EMPOWERMENT

Anonymity is "the condition of avoiding identification."[1] But anonymity empowerment is not always binary. As with the political pamphlets written during colonial times, anonymous speakers may disclose some details that could lead to their identification, but hide other details. Anonymity empowerment may make it more difficult for a sleuth to identify an anonymous speaker, but unmasking still may be possible with enough work.

If we agree that the First Amendment protects anonymity, what types of information should it protect? Jeffrey Skopek rightly argues that "namelessness" is "neither a sufficient nor a necessary condition for anonymity," as there are some cases in which someone can be identified by characteristics other than name, and other cases in which the speaker's name might not be specific enough to identify the person; Skopek uses the example of a book that lists "John Smith" as the author. "If there are thousands of people named 'John Smith,' the book will be effectively anonymous absent further information," Skopek writes.[2]

Other than names, what types of information could be combined with other information to, at the very least, increase the chances of identifying someone? Imagine that rather than listing my name on the cover of this book, the publisher wrote that it was authored by a cybersecurity law professor at the US Naval Academy who has previously written a book about Section 230 for this same publisher? Because I am the only person who fits this profile, it hardly would stand to reason that my publisher's approach rendered me entirely anonymous.

As you can see, my publisher did, in fact, print my name on the cover of this book. As far as I am aware, I am the only "Jeff Kosseff" in the United States, if not the world.[3] My authorship of this book, therefore, is not anonymous. But if, as in Skopek's example, my name were "John Smith" or another common name, would I be anonymous unless my publisher included other details, such as my picture, employer, or other biographical information? On the other hand, would disclosure of only one of those pieces of information be seen as compromising my anonymity?

In support of a nonbinary approach to anonymity empowerment, David G. Post uses an example of graffiti on a subway platform, which "informs us that the author was literate and was physically present on that particular platform at some point during the period since the platform was last painted, all of which significantly reduces our uncertainty about the author's identity by ruling out the vast majority of individuals in the world of possible authors."[4] Bryan H. Choi compares anonymity to "a curtain that we draw between our confidants and distrusted outsiders. We remain effectively anonymous to those outsiders as long as the curtain remains intact, though anyone within its curtilage has the ability to welcome others inside."[5]

While it is hard, and in many cases impossible, to be entirely anonymous forever, it is possible for legal, administrative, and technological barriers to make it more difficult to identify a speaker. The culture of anonymity empowerment provides speakers with the ability to withhold at least some of their identifying information from some people for some length of time. While the speakers eventually may be identified, the culture of anonymity empowerment allows them to at least temporarily dissociate their identifying details from their messages.

This nonbinary view of anonymity empowerment comports with America's earliest days of anonymous speech. Anonymity and pseudonymity are often temporary. The names of the authors of *Common Sense* and *Letters from a Farmer in Pennsylvania* were a mystery at the time that they were published, but eventually both Thomas Paine and John Dickinson were publicly identified. And speakers may be anonymous to most—but not all—of their audience members. Alexander Hamilton, James Madison, and John Jay were not identified as the authors of the Federalist Papers, but some of their powerful allies were aware that they were Publius. This aligns with Skopek's broader definition of anonymity: "a condition in which something associated with a person (such as an action, idea, object, etc.) is known only through traits that are not, without further information or investigation, unique and connected in a way that provides a relevant form of access to that person in a given context."[6]

The earliest Supreme Court anonymity cases did not clearly define the full scope of anonymity empowerment that the First Amendment provides. The attempts to force the NAACP to disclose its membership lists could lead to the identification of members who otherwise never would have been associated with the group. The Los Angeles and Ohio laws prohibited authors from removing any hints of their identities from their pamphlets; because those laws were invalidated, an author of a political pamphlet could theoretically remain entirely anonymous.

But anonymity can be more complicated. Consider people who canvass door-to-door or in public places, either to spread messages or collect signatures for petitions. These canvassers are not entirely anonymous, in that their faces are visible, and the person to whom they are speaking might be able to recognize them. Yet in many cases, their facial characteristics may not immediately inform the person of their identity.

Should the First Amendment protect these canvassers from being forced to reveal all of their identifying information? Or have they already surrendered the right to remain anonymous by revealing some of their identifying details? In two decisions around the turn of the century, the Supreme Court would protect the identities of canvassers.

The culture of anonymity empowerment provides not only for absolute anonymity, but also for people to control precisely how much of their identifying information they choose to reveal.

In 1910, the Colorado Direct Legislation League convinced the young state's legislature and governor to amend its Constitution to allow citizens to collect ballot signatures to place legislative referendums on the ballot.[7] Since then, Coloradans have used the process to pass laws on the environment, nuclear fracking, tax limits, legalizing marijuana, working conditions, worker's compensation, and many other issues.[8]

Colorado's Constitution allows the legislature to pass laws that regulate the petitioning process if they are "designed to prevent fraud, mistake, or other abuses."[9] In 1993, the state legislature passed new restrictions on petitioning that attracted fierce opposition. First, the legislature required unpaid petition circulators to "display an identification badge that includes the words 'VOLUNTEER CIRCULATOR' in bold-faced type which is clearly legible and the circulator's name," and paid circulators to wear a similar badge with the words "PAID CIRCULATOR."[10] Second, when a petition is filed with the secretary of state, petition organizers must file a report listing "the name, address, and county of voter registration of all circulators who were paid to circulate any section of the petition, the amount paid per signature, and .the total amount paid to each circulator."[11] They also must file with the state monthly reports listing the proponents' names, the names and addresses of paid circulators, and the amount of money that was paid to each circulator.[12]

Groups and people who circulated petitions filed a federal lawsuit challenging this new law as well as other restrictions on petitioning.[13] At a bench trial before Colorado federal judge Richard Paul Matsch, the challengers and other witnesses testified about the burdens that the new law would impose on their efforts to promote initiatives.

The Economic Motivation for anonymity appeared to drive at least part of their concerns. For instance, Paul Grant, who had tried to pass transportation deregulation initiatives, testified that supporters did not necessarily want to publicly identify with those efforts, fearing reprisal. "The people most involved in the industry were the people most leery of being publicly identified as being associated with us," he testified. "They didn't want their names, for the most part, listed on our letterhead. They didn't want to contribute money because their names would be reported to the State and they didn't want to circulate petitions too openly because they were afraid it might have repercussions against them in future dealings with their competitors and with the Public Utilities Commission which regulates them."[14] Likewise, Jon Baraga, who organized a hemp ballot initiative petition, said that he had been harassed while petitioning and that people were less likely to circulate his petitions because of the new badge law.[15]

The state tried to justify the badge requirement by introducing evidence of misrepresentations by some petition circulators and arguing that identification is necessary for the public to file reports with authorities. Judge Matsch ruled that the requirement was unconstitutional and that misrepresentation does not meet the high constitutional standard for justifying this encroachment on anonymity. "Misstating the expected consequences of changes in the law is not uncommon in the political process," he wrote. "Inaccuracies in political discourse do not necessarily rise to the level of calculated falsehood or criminal fraud."[16] Matsch also struck down Colorado's requirement for organizers to file reports listing the identities of petition circulators. "This requirement prevents anonymity of the circulators and thus exposes them to intimidation, harassment and retribution in the same manner as the badge requirement," he wrote.[17]

The state appealed to the US Court of Appeals for the Tenth Circuit, which affirmed the district court's invalidation of the badge and monthly report requirements. The state argued that because petition circulators needed to attach signed affidavits to the petitions, the circulators have a "diminished interest in anonymity."[18] Judge Mary Beck Briscoe, writing for the panel, rejected this argument, concluding that an affidavit does not impose the same burden on anonymity as a badge.

"Information contained on an identification badge is much more accessible than information attached to a filed petition and, unlike the affidavit requirement, the badge requirement forces circulators to reveal their identities at the same time they deliver their political message," Briscoe wrote. "The badge requirement operates when the reaction to their message may be the most intense, emotional, and unreasoned. Thus, as opposed to the affidavit requirement, the badge requirement deprives circulators of their anonymity at the precise moment their interest in anonymity is greatest."[19]

Briscoe also agreed with Matsch's invalidation of the requirements that petition organizers file reports that contain the petition circulators' identities both when the petition is filed and on a monthly basis. Briscoe ruled that the public has an interest in petition organizers filing final reports that shed light on the proponents of the measure, but the reports need not identify those who circulated the petitions. "Requiring proponents to provide a detailed roster of all who were paid to circulate compromises the expressive rights of paid circulators, but sheds little light on the relative merit of the ballot issue," she wrote.[20]

The state of Colorado asked the US Supreme Court to reverse the Tenth Circuit. Petitions, the state argued, are more like ballots than political literature, and should be subject to regulation. "The circulators are fiduciaries for the petition signers," the state wrote in its petition to the Supreme Court. "Disclosing the circulator's name and status as a paid or volunteer circulator on a badge is not intrusive; it is necessary. A signer should have easy access to the name of the person who will be submitting the signer's signature for review."[21]

The Supreme Court agreed to review the case, and at oral argument in October 1998, Colorado attorney general Gale Norton faced skepticism about the need for petition circulators to wear name badges.

"Why does the State insist that the circulator have to have the circulator's name on a badge, as opposed to just saying, volunteer, or paid circulator?" Justice Sandra Day O'Connor asked.

"That is to address the problem that we have of trying to maintain the integrity of the process as it is going along," said Norton, who later would serve as the interior secretary under President George W. Bush. "If the Secretary of State's office receives a phone call that says, 'I saw a petition circulator paying people to sign petitions,' which is clearly a violation of state law, we get a call that says, 'It was a man with brown hair standing at the corner of Sixth and Broadway,' at that point in time, we don't have any petitions. We can't look at the signature on that."[22]

Justice Antonin Scalia asked whether there have been any recent prosecutions for such violations, and Norton acknowledged there had not been. Scalia speculated that the Colorado legislators' true reason for imposing such restrictions is that they dislike ballot initiatives, which are "usually collected in order to do something that the legislature doesn't want it to, or to undo something that the legislature has done."

Three months after oral argument, the Supreme Court upheld the Tenth Circuit rulings, concluding that both the badge and disclosure requirements violate the First Amendment. Writing for the majority, Justice Ruth Bader Ginsburg likened the badge requirement to Ohio's restrictions on handbills. "Both involve a one-on-one communication," Ginsburg wrote. "But the restraint on speech in this case is more severe than was the restraint in *McIntyre*. Petition circulation is the less fleeting encounter, for the circulator must endeavor to persuade electors to sign the petition."[23] On the other hand, she reasoned, the requirement to file an affidavit along with the petition is permissible under *McIntyre* because the requirement "must be met only after circulators have completed their conversations with electors."[24]

Like the Tenth Circuit, Ginsburg also concluded that the mandatory disclosure of petition circulators' names and addresses in monthly and final reports was a First Amendment violation. The ruling did not prohibit the state from requiring the reports to contain information about the groups that are paying for the ballot initiatives. Ginsburg wrote that the "added benefit" of requiring disclosure of the circulators' names and payment amounts "is hardly apparent and has not been demonstrated."[25] Elizabeth Garrett later noted that the Court's opinion did not strike down the "most important disclosure provisions," which reveal the ballot initiatives' supporters.[26]

As he did in *McIntyre*, Justice Thomas wrote a separate concurring opinion in which he argued that the Court should have clarified that it was applying a high level of scrutiny to the Colorado laws. For instance, he observed that the state attempted to justify its badge law as an effort to combat fraud. "Even assuming that this is a compelling interest, plainly, this requirement is not narrowly tailored," Thomas wrote. "It burdens all circulators, whether they are responsible for committing fraud or not. In any event, the State has failed to satisfy its burden of demonstrating that fraud is a real, rather than a conjectural, problem."[27]

Chief Justice William Rehnquist dissented, writing that although the badge provision is unconstitutional, the disclosure report provision is constitutional. He noted that the affidavits that must be attached to each petition already contain the name and address of the circulator. "The only additional piece of information for which the disclosure requirement asks is thus the amount paid to each circulator," he wrote.[28]

O'Connor, joined by Justice Stephen Breyer, partly dissented, agreeing that the badge rule was unconstitutional but disagreeing about the disclosure reports. "The disclosure required here advances Colorado's interest in law enforcement by enabling the State to detect and to identify on a timely basis abusive or fraudulent circulators," she wrote.[29] She disagreed with the invalidation of the disclosure report provision. "Colorado's disclosure provision is a step removed from the one-on-one, communicative aspects of petition circulation, and it burdens this communication in only an incidental manner," she wrote.[30]

Even with the various concurrences and dissents, Colorado's loss in the Supreme Court was a bold statement that the Court recognized a right to anonymous speech not only for writing, but also in person. But the Colorado law restricted only political speech, which is more likely to receive sweeping First Amendment protection. It would take a few years for the Supreme Court to clarify whether this anonymity right extends to other forms of speech.

The Village of Stratton, Ohio, population of about three hundred, sits across the Ohio River from West Virginia. The W. H. Sammis coal power plant is the Village's largest private employer.[31] Less than ten miles north of Stratton is Wellsville, the home of a Jehovah's Witness congregation that in the late 1990s had about fifty-nine members.[32] True to the religion's beliefs, the members of the congregation canvassed businesses and homes in Stratton and other nearby towns to discuss the Bible.[33]

The congregation claims that it had many conflicts with Stratton's mayor and police officers and was told that the congregation members would face arrest if they did not "get out of town."[34] The members claimed that in the early nineties, a police officer told them that "I could care less about your rights," and that in 1998, the village's mayor allegedly told four female members of the congregation that they would have been jailed if they were male.[35]

Soon after the confrontation with the mayor, Stratton enacted an ordinance that regulated "canvassers, solicitors, peddlers, hawkers, iterant merchants or transient vendors of merchandise or services."[36] Unless they first obtained the property owner's permission or a permit from the village, they could not enter private property "for the purpose of advertising, promoting, selling and/or explaining any product, service, organization, or cause," among other reasons. Obtaining a permit required each canvasser to register with the mayor's office and provide their name, home address, the addresses that the canvasser intended to visit, and other information related to their canvassing.[37] While canvassing, each person must "carry upon his person his permit" and present it upon request by the police or anyone who is solicited.[38] The ordinance imposed other canvassing restrictions, such as limiting the activities to daytime hours.[39]

The ordinance caught the attention of Watchtower Bible and Tract Society of New York, the central administrative organization for Jehovah's Witnesses congregations. On June 3, 1999, the group, along with the local congregation, filed an eight-count lawsuit against Stratton and its mayor, John M. Abdalla, arguing that the ordinance violated free speech and religion rights provided in the US and Ohio constitutions.[40] Watchtower asked federal judge Edmund Sargus Jr. to grant an injunction blocking enforcement of the ordinance. At a hearing before Sargus, the village's solicitor testified that the ordinance was intended to combat "flimflam" con artists.[41]

In an August 18, 1999, order, Sargus upheld the registration portion of the ordinance, though his analysis primarily focused on the requirement that canvassers list the addresses that they plan to visit. He struck down parts of the ordinance, including the portion that limited canvassing to no later than 5:00 p.m.[42] Yet the opinion did not thoroughly analyze whether the requirement to disclose names or addresses violated a First Amendment anonymity right. (He issued his opinion less than a year after the Supreme Court ruled on the Colorado petitioning law.)

Watchtower appealed to the US Court of Appeals for the Sixth Circuit, which affirmed Sargus's ruling. Unlike Sargus, the Sixth Circuit thoroughly addressed—and rejected—Watchtower's argument that the village's ordinance violates the right to anonymity that the Supreme Court recognized in *McIntyre*. Writing for the majority, Judge Cornelia Groefsema Kennedy distinguished Stratton's canvassing ordinance from the Ohio election law invalidated in *McIntyre* because canvassers, unlike pamphlet authors, cannot remain entirely anonymous. "As we see it, individuals going door-to-door to engage in political speech are not anonymous by virtue of the fact that they reveal a portion of their identities—their physical identities—to the residents they canvass," Kennedy wrote. "In other words, the ordinance does not require canvassers going door-to-door to reveal their identities; instead, the very act of going door-to-door requires the canvassers to reveal a portion of their identities."[43]

The Supreme Court recognized an anonymity right in the First Amendment, Kennedy reasoned, to protect against retaliation and suppression of ideas. "Once the political canvassers are before the resident, the ability to protect them from those dangers is substantially diminished," she wrote. "Accordingly, there is little reason to read the Court's holding as protecting political canvassers from being required to reveal a portion of their identities when their very activity will reveal other portions of their identity and subject them to scrutiny."[44]

A shortcoming of Kennedy's analysis was its failure to meaningfully address the Supreme Court's ruling against Colorado just a few years earlier. How was Stratton's ordinance substantially different from Colorado's referendum circulator law? Both involved the compelled disclosure of the names of people whose facial features were apparent to the public.

Watchtower convinced the US Supreme Court to review Kennedy's opinion, including her dismissal of its anonymity arguments. Watchtower emphasized the difficulty of squaring the Sixth Circuit's ruling with the Supreme Court's invalidation of Colorado's law. "Revealing one's name to the Mayor removes anonymity as effectively as a badge requirement," Watchtower wrote in its brief to the Supreme Court.[45]

Watchtower emphasized the Safety and Economic Motivations for anonymity. "What if a person wants to discuss the need for a new mayor, or his dissatisfaction with the current Mayor's treatment of minority religious groups?" Watchtower's lawyers wrote. "Especially within the small community of Stratton, when he applies for a permit and reveals his name, would he not be exposed to the fear of economic or official retaliation?"[46]

In response, Stratton noted that the Supreme Court had struck down Colorado's badge requirement, and that Ginsburg had suggested that its separate requirement for completing an affidavit was constitutional. Stratton's ordinance, the village argued, is more like the affidavit requirement than the badge requirement, and therefore passes constitutional muster. "It in no way inhibits anonymous political discourse in any public forum," the village wrote in its brief. "It does not require the recipient of a Solicitation Permit to wear a badge or outwardly identify themselves in any manner. It does not require a person engaging in door-to-door political discourse to disclose his identity until the resident requests identification."[47]

The Supreme Court rejected this distinction. In its June 17, 2002, opinion, the Court ruled that Stratton's ordinance violated the First Amendment right to anonymous speech. Justice John Paul Stevens rebuffed Stratton's attempts to distinguish its ordinance from the Colorado requirement that the Court had struck down. "The fact that circulators revealed their physical identities did not foreclose our consideration of the circulators' interest in maintaining their anonymity," Stevens wrote.

"In the Village, strangers to the resident certainly maintain their anonymity, and the ordinance may preclude such persons from canvassing for unpopular causes."[48] As Margot Kaminski observed, Stevens acknowledged "that anonymity may be contextual rather than absolute," and the opinion "treats anonymity as a communicative tool employed by speakers within the context of a relationship."[49]

Stevens recognized that precluding anonymity may be necessary in some cases, such as fighting commercial fraud. "The Village ordinance, however, sweeps more broadly, covering unpopular causes unrelated to commercial transactions or to any special interest in protecting the electoral process," Stevens wrote.[50]

The ordinance, Stevens reasoned, also prevents patriotic citizens from speaking because "they would prefer silence to speech licensed by a petty official."[51] And the ordinance prevents citizens from engaging in "spontaneous speech" because they must first obtain the permit, he wrote. "A person who made a decision on a holiday or a weekend to take an active part in a political campaign could not begin to pass out handbills until after he or she obtained the required permit," Stevens wrote. "Even a spontaneous decision to go across the street and urge a neighbor to vote against the mayor could not lawfully be implemented without first obtaining the mayor's permission."[52]

Stevens pointed to World War II–era Supreme Court cases, which recognized the First Amendment rights of Jehovah's Witnesses to canvass homes. "The rhetoric used in the World War II–era opinions that repeatedly saved petitioners' coreligionists from petty prosecutions reflected the Court's evaluation of the First Amendment freedoms that are implicated in this case," he wrote. "The value judgment that then motivated a united democratic people fighting to defend those very freedoms from totalitarian attack is unchanged. It motivates our decision today."[53]

Chief Justice Rehnquist dissented, pointing to a recent New Hampshire double murder by teenagers who pretended to be conducting surveys of homes. Stratton, he wrote, sought to reduce the risks of such harms. "The residents did not prohibit door-to-door communication; they simply required that canvassers obtain a permit before going door-to-door," Rehnquist wrote. "And the village does not have the discretion to reject an applicant who completes the application."[54]

Despite Rehnquist's concerns about physical safety, the majority of the Supreme Court held that the Stratton ordinance's intrusion on the anonymous speech rights of canvassers was greater. Indeed, Stevens wrote that criminals could visit people at their homes under other guises that do not require permits. "They might, for example, ask for directions or permission to use the telephone, or pose as surveyers or census takers," he wrote. "Or they might register under a false name with impunity because the ordinance contains no provision for verifying an applicant's identity or organizational credentials."[55]

The twin losses of Colorado and the Village of Stratton represent a high-water mark for anonymity in the Supreme Court. In both cases, the Supreme Court protected the right of people to decline to reveal their name, even though their physical characteristics were not hidden. And the Court decided that anonymity outweighed important interests such as ballot integrity and crime prevention.

The two canvasser cases, combined with *Talley* and *McIntyre*, suggest that there are few limits to the Supreme Court's recognition of the First Amendment right to anonymity. Although *Talley* and *McIntyre* firmly established a qualified right to anonymous speech, particularly in the political sphere, the Supreme Court also made abundantly clear that this right was not absolute. The Court recognized that there are circumstances, particularly related to campaign finance, in which the public interest in disclosure of a person or corporation's identity outweighs the value in maintaining anonymity.

As James A. Gardner has written, anonymity is expected in some realms of politics, such as voting, yet in other areas, such as campaign finance, there may be a public interest in disclosure.[56] The Court articulated a public interest in campaign finance-related identity disclosure in a 1976 case, *Buckley v. Valeo*, a challenge to many portions of the Federal Election Campaign Act of 1971.[57] Relevant to anonymity was a challenge to the law's disclosure provisions, which required political committees to register with the Federal Election Commission.[58] The law also required political committees and candidates to file public reports listing the name, address, and occupation of anyone who contributed more than a hundred dollars in a year, among other disclosure requirements.[59]

The Supreme Court recognized that under the precedent of *NAACP v. Alabama*, "compelled disclosure has the potential for substantially infringing the exercise of First Amendment rights," but that "there are governmental interests sufficiently important to outweigh the possibility of infringement, particularly when the free functioning of our national institutions is involved."[60]

The disclosure requirements in the federal campaign law, the court ruled, did indeed justify the infringement on anonymity for three reasons: (1) they provide voters with information about how candidates receive and spend money; (2) they "deter actual corruption and avoid the appearance of corruption by exposing large contributions and expenditures to the light of publicity;" and (3) they are necessary to police campaign contribution violations.[61]

Some of the campaign finance law's challengers urged the court to exempt independent candidates and minor parties from the disclosure requirements, arguing that there is a less immediate public interest in the information, and their supporters face more potential repercussions. The Court rejected this argument, concluding that the litigants failed to present the same "record of harassment" that the NAACP displayed in Alabama.[62]

Buckley v. Valeo is a reminder that although the Supreme Court recognizes a strong right to anonymity, it is willing to find that some public interests are so great that they justify the abrogation of that right. The Supreme Court reinforced this principle in 2003, when it upheld the disclosure requirements of the Bipartisan Campaign Reform Act of 2002 in *McConnell v. Federal Election Commission*.[63] Among the requirements at issue in *McConnell* was a provision that required anyone who spends more than ten thousand dollars in a year on "electioneering communications" to file a report with the Federal Election Commission. As in *Buckley*, the Supreme Court upheld the disclosure requirements because they serve the interests of "providing the electorate with information, deterring actual corruption and avoiding any appearance thereof, and gathering the data necessary to enforce more substantive electioneering restrictions."[64]

Justice Thomas dissented from his colleagues' affirmation of the disclosure provision, expanding on his views that the First Amendment provides robust anonymity protections. Thomas noted that only a few years earlier in *McIntyre*, the Court recognized the strong interest in anonymous speech. "The Court now backs away from this principle, allowing the established right to anonymous speech to be stripped away based on the flimsiest of justifications," he wrote.[65] Lyrissa Barnett Lidsky and Thomas F. Cotter noted the "deep theoretical inconsistency" between the *McIntyre* and *McConnell* opinions. "The *McConnell* opinion rests on paternalistic notions about the abilities of voters; as opponents of campaign finance reform have argued, even the assumption that money influences outcomes paternalistically implies that voters cannot sift through various information to make decisions," they wrote. "*McIntyre*, on the other hand, assumes voters are savvy consumers of political information, able to discern the partisan motivations behind campaign literature and make informed decisions even without knowing the identity of the author."[66]

The Supreme Court's most recent affirmation of the ability to require disclosure of campaign finance matters occurred in its 2010 opinion, *Citizens United v. Federal Election Commission*, considering a challenge to campaign finance laws brought by Citizens United, the producer of a documentary critical of Hillary Clinton.[67] The brunt of the public attention to the opinion was because of its recognition of the ability of corporations to spend in support of candidates.

Citizens United had also challenged a federal law that required televised electioneering communications to include a statement that "_____ is responsible for the content of this advertising" if the advertising was not paid for by the candidate. Campaign finance law also required annual disclosure statements that provide information about expenditures and certain contributors' identities.[68]

The Supreme Court rejected the challenge to these provisions, concluding that Citizens United failed to provide evidence of the prospect of its members experiencing retaliation. "To the contrary, Citizens United has been disclosing its donors for years and has identified no instance of harassment or retaliation," Justice Anthony Kennedy wrote for the majority.[69] Kennedy also rejected Citizens United's claim that there is not an informational interest in the advertising disclosure. "Even if the ads only pertain to a commercial transaction, the public has an interest in knowing who is speaking about a candidate shortly before an election," he wrote.[70]

Although Citizens United warned that compelled disclosure of donors could cause donors to face retaliation, Kennedy wrote that such concerns would render a disclosure law unconstitutional only if "there were a reasonable probability that the group's members would face threats, harassment, or reprisals if their names were disclosed," and Citizens United had not presented evidence of such potential harms.[71] As in the earlier anonymity cases, Kennedy's ruling was a balancing test rather than an absolute prohibition on any incursions upon anonymous speech.

To Kennedy, the disclosure requirements were necessary to help people understand the source of the political speech that the rest of the opinion promoted. "The First Amendment protects political speech; and disclosure permits citizens and shareholders to react to the speech of corporate entities in a proper way," Kennedy wrote. "This transparency enables the electorate to make informed decisions and give proper weight to different speakers and messages."[72]

Justice Thomas once again dissented, arguing that the disclosure requirement violates the right to speak anonymously. Thomas pointed to the harassment experienced by some supporters of Proposition 8, California's 2008 ballot proposition that defined marriage as being between a man and woman.[73] California law required the public disclosure of anyone who contributed more than a hundred dollars to a campaign related to the proposition, so its opponents posted the home and work addresses of supporters online. This publicity led to death threats, property damage, boycotts, and other harms, Thomas wrote.[74] He argued that "disclaimer and disclosure requirements enable private citizens and elected officials to implement political strategies *specifically calculated* to curtail campaign-related activity and prevent the lawful, peaceful exercise of First Amendment rights."[75]

The Court further rejected Thomas's calls for strong anonymity protections later in 2010 when it issued its opinion in *Doe v. Reed*.[76] That case involved a challenge to an attempt to use the Washington state public records law to reveal the names of people who signed a referendum petition related to same-sex couple benefits.[77]

The Supreme Court affirmed the constitutionality of the public records law, applying the "exacting scrutiny" balancing test. Chief Justice John Roberts, writing for the majority, concluded that the law was justified by Washington state's interest in "preserving the integrity of the electoral process by combating fraud, detecting invalid signatures, and fostering government transparency and accountability."[78] The plaintiffs generally alleged harm resulting from the disclosure, but Roberts wrote that they "provided us scant evidence or argument beyond the burdens they assert disclosure would impose" on the signatories of petitions.[79]

Justice Antonin Scalia wrote an opinion concurring in the judgment, in which he agreed with the result upholding the disclosure but argued that the Court need not engage in a balancing test for anonymous speech. "Our Nation's longstanding traditions of legislating and voting in public refute the claim that the First Amendment accords a right to anonymity in the performance of an act with governmental effect," Scalia wrote.[80] Scalia, who dissented in *McIntyre v. Ohio*, added that he continued to believe that the right to anonymous political speech created by the opinion was flawed. "Requiring people to stand up in public for their political acts fosters civic courage, without which democracy is doomed," Scalia wrote.[81]

Thomas wrote a dissent, in which he once again advocated for a strong right to anonymous speech and argued for an even tougher level of constitutional scrutiny for restrictions on anonymity. The state's interest in "transparency and accountability" cannot justify the disclosure, Thomas wrote, as the state and its supporters pointed to only eight cases of fraud related to ballot initiatives. "If anything, these meager figures reinforce the conclusion that the risks of fraud or corruption in the initiative and referendum process are remote and thereby undermine Washington's claim that those two interests should be considered compelling for purposes of strict scrutiny," he wrote.[82] Nor does the interest in providing voters with relevant information justify the burden on anonymous speech, Thomas wrote.[83]

Although Thomas and Scalia often were aligned in their conservative jurisprudence, on the issue of anonymous speech, they represented two opposing views. Justice Thomas has long advocated for the strongest possible protections for anonymous speech, while Justice Scalia had concluded that anonymity is not among the rights that the First Amendment protects. The exacting scrutiny framework, on which most of the Court has settled, provides courts with some flexibility to allow or prohibit restrictions on anonymous speech. With this flexibility also comes uncertainty, as seen in the campaign finance cases.

Although the Supreme Court has found a right to anonymity for canvassing, pamphleteering, and to some extent, campaign finance, in other areas it is less likely to provide robust protection. In my former career as a newspaper reporter, I worked on investigative projects that required me to gather information from anonymous sources. They had good reason to insist on remaining anonymous, as their unmasking could lead to their firings, lawsuits, harassment, and other retaliation. I guaranteed sources that I would not reveal their identities, even if I were subpoenaed by the government or private litigants. Without that promise, these sources would not have spoken with me or provided me with the documents necessary for my reporting about corporate malfeasance and corruption.

But what if I were to receive a subpoena to testify about the identities of my confidential sources? If I were to refuse to comply with the subpoena (as I promised my sources), a judge could hold me in contempt of court and throw me in jail. Fortunately, I never received a subpoena, but I was fully prepared to serve time in jail so that I could protect the anonymity of my sources.

Should a journalist be forced to choose between going to jail and compromising the confidentiality of sources? After all, the First Amendment explicitly protects both freedom of speech and of the press. If the First Amendment prevents pamphleteers from being forced to reveal their identities, shouldn't it also guard against journalists going to jail for refusing to identify their confidential sources?

The Supreme Court has been less enthusiastic about protecting the anonymity of journalists' sources. In the 1972 *Branzburg v. Hayes* opinion, decided on a narrow 5–4 vote, the Supreme Court declined to rule that the First Amendment prevents grand juries from requiring journalists to testify about the identities of their anonymous news sources.[84] Writing for the majority, Justice Byron White concluded that there is "no basis for holding that the public interest in law enforcement and in ensuring effective grand jury proceedings is insufficient to override the consequential, but uncertain, burden on news gathering that is said to result from insisting that reporters, like other citizens, respond to relevant questions put to them in the course of a valid grand jury investigation or criminal trial."[85]

Yet the Supreme Court in *Branzburg* did not entirely rule out the possibility of First Amendment safeguards in all cases. Justice White wrote that "grand jury investigations, if instituted or conducted other than in good faith, would pose wholly different issues for resolution under the First Amendment," and that "official harassment of the press undertaken not for purposes of law enforcement but to disrupt a reporter's relationship with his news sources would have no justification."[86] In a short concurring opinion, Justice Lewis Powell, one of the five justices in the majority, wrote that a journalist may be able to rely on the First Amendment to quash a subpoena if the journalist "is called upon to give information bearing only a remote and tenuous relationship to the subject of the investigation, or if he has some other reason to believe that the testimony implicates confidential source relationships without a legitimate need of law enforcement."[87]

Since its *Branzburg* opinion, the Supreme Court has not again revisited the reporter's privilege, but lower courts have applied the ruling to find a limited privilege for anonymous sources. The courts are generally more likely to recognize this privilege in civil cases rather than criminal cases or grand jury investigations.[88] Yet the strength and scope of a federal reporter's privilege varies by the circuit in which a court is located.

To address the uncertainty, for years members of Congress have attempted to pass a federal "shield law" that protects journalists from being compelled to reveal their sources in certain circumstances. Although these federal proposals received significant support from members of both parties, Congress has not yet passed a shield law. Most state legislatures, however, have passed their own shield law statutes.[89] This means that in many states' courts, reporters will have stronger protections than they would have in federal courts, even those in the same city.

The states' passage of shield laws provides an important lesson for anonymity protection in general. The First Amendment protections for reporters' source anonymity were limited at best, so many state legislatures decided to pass shield laws that go beyond the First Amendment.

The First Amendment's protections for anonymity often are strong in some areas, but in other instances do not provide the safeguards that we desire. Rather than relying exclusively on the First Amendment to protect anonymity, we also should evaluate whether privacy laws and other statutes could supplement the First Amendment guarantees. Shield laws are good examples of statutes that fill the gaps in anonymity protection when First Amendment caselaw has fallen short. In chapter 16, I argue that Congress should more broadly address gaps in the First Amendment's anonymity protections by passing a comprehensive statute that protects the privacy of identifying information.

But in some cases, statutes abrogate the right to anonymity in the name of combatting substantial harms, such as racist organizations that hide behind masks. In those cases, the courts must determine whether the statutes' interests outweigh the benefits of anonymous expression. These competing values were tested in many courts over the years as they assessed laws that prohibited people from wearing masks.

5

ANTIMASK

In the 1990s, Jeff Berry of Butler, Indiana, founded the American Knights of the Ku Klux Klan. Berry's group was particularly active in Goshen, a northern Indiana city of about thirty thousand residents whose high school had drawn media attention for disciplining a student for wearing a T-shirt with a racial slur.[1]

Like many organizations that had long been affiliated with the Ku Klux Klan, the American Knights supported racial segregation. But unlike some other Klan groups, the American Knights proclaimed itself a religion, with seven "sacred symbols," including a robe and a hood with a mask. During the group's activities, such as church services and cross burnings, members would wear hoods that covered their faces.[2] The members also would obscure their faces with the masks while distributing leaflets and engaging in other public activities, in part because they feared the harassment stemming from their association with the religion.[3]

Berry's Ku Klux Klan would benefit from the anonymous free speech precedent that the NAACP and Manuel Talley had established decades ago in the Supreme Court, even though the principles underlying his group were fundamentally at odds with those of the civil rights groups. Berry's battle for his group members' anonymity reveals the difficult trade-offs that often are at issue in anonymity disputes.

The racism at the heart of other Klan groups permeated the American Knights. A Goshen, Indiana, member of the American Knights, using the pseudonym Janet Williams, left no doubt why she joined the group. "I would like to see the races kept separate—but equal," she told a newspaper reporter in 1998. "In Goshen, our problem is more with the Mexicans than with the blacks. A couple of times in the past, I had children beaten up by gangs of them."[4]

Berry, too, had long used racist rhetoric to get national attention, appearing on news programs and talk shows such as *The Jerry Springer Show*. "We use the hate speech," he said in 1999. "Sometimes you have to, to get a point across."[5] The group held rallies, where members would inflame protesters by hurling racist and anti-Semitic epithets, using Bible passages to bolster their message.[6] The rallies carried a hefty price tag for local governments. Goshen spent nearly a quarter of its police overtime budget keeping the peace at five events related to the Klan group. Klan members also appeared in their masks at a Goshen city council meeting, and asked to be included in a July parade.[7]

"We're tired of spending overtime dollars on keeping the peace when they come to town," Goshen mayor Allan Kauffman told the Associated Press at the time. "There comes a point at which spending money to keep the peace at these kinds of rallies divert your attention from other things, and we're tired of that and we're looking at anything to discourage this kind of activity."[8]

Goshen city officials also heard complaints from residents about the fear they experienced due to the presence of hooded Klan members in their community. Kauffman would later state that "fear and intimidation is reduced when we know who our adversaries are and we can have discussion with them."[9] To address this growing problem in the community, Kauffman and his colleagues on the city council considered an "antimask" ordinance, modeled after state laws that about one-third of the states had passed to address growing Klan movements starting in the 1920s. Goshen's proposal was unique because it was at the municipal level rather than statewide.[10]

At its meeting on June 16, 1998, the Goshen Common Counsel considered Ordinance 3829, which stated that it is illegal "for any person 18 year [*sic*] of age or older to wear a mask, hood or other device in any public place for the purpose of disguising or concealing his or her identity." The ordinance contained exceptions for "religious, safety, or medical reasons," and imposed a fine of up to $2,500 on violators.[11]

In an interview with me, Kauffman recalled that Klan members attended the council meeting in hoods and masks, sitting in the back row. Kauffman told the group that they could not speak at the meeting unless they removed their masks and identified themselves. One member did so, but he at first gave a fake name. The police chief recognized him from the community, Kauffman said, causing Kauffman to ask him again to give his real name.[12]

The council initially approved the ordinance in a 4–2 vote, but Goshen resident John Stith, speaking at the meeting, asked the two dissenters to change their vote. "Although I commend the council for the four-to-two vote, if you two gentlemen were black, the vote would be unanimous," Stith said. The two holdouts reversed their votes, and the passage was unanimous.[13]

Despite the successful passage, it was unclear even to the ordinance's supporters whether it would withstand the inevitable court challenge. "We can't guarantee that we're on firm constitutional ground," Kauffman said that evening. "All we can do is try."[14]

After the ordinance's passage, the Goshen police department informed the American Knights that it would enforce the ordinance against the group's members if they wore masks in public.[15] The next month, the American Knights sued Goshen in federal court, alleging that the ordinance was unconstitutional. The Indiana Civil Liberties Union represented the American Knights, and as part of the litigation deposed Kauffman.

The Indiana Civil Liberties Union pressed Kauffman about the scope of the ordinance. Did the ordinance, for instance, prohibit adults from wearing masks on Halloween? Kauffman pointed to the ordinance's focus on whether the *purpose* of the mask was to conceal or disguise. "If the reason was to observe the holiday, if the reason was entertainment, or if the reason really was that you don't want somebody to know who you are on Halloween night, it may be argued as to why I wear a mask on Halloween," he said in a deposition.[16]

Kauffman acknowledged in the deposition that the ordinance provides the police officer and judge with leeway in interpretation of intent, stating that "the ultimate decision, I guess, gets made in the court about what the purpose of wearing a mask was. The officer may need to use some discretion about what he thinks the purpose is."[17]

The case went before Judge Robert L. Miller Jr., a Reagan appointee to the US District Court for the Northern District of Indiana, in the courthouse in South Bend. The Indiana Civil Liberties Union relied on both the Safety Motivation and the Speech Motivation for anonymity: they argued that the masks were necessary both to ensure the safety of the Klan members and to allow them to fully express themselves. "Without the protection afforded by anonymity, many members will not be willing to appear at all," the group wrote in its summary judgment brief. "Without wearing the full uniform, observers will not be able to see and receive the full message that the American Knights wishes to impart and members will not be able to share fully in their membership experience. As a matter of fact, therefore, the wearing of the mask is expressive conduct and allows expressive conduct to take place."[18]

While the Klan members do, indeed, have a valid Safety Motivation for seeking anonymity, their argument minimizes the safety concerns for others that arise from the Klan members' anonymity. Even if these Klan members did not intend to commit violence, Ku Klux Klan groups for more than a century were associated with violence such as lynching and cross burning.[19] The security that the Klan members felt from their masks and hoods understandably would cause feelings of insecurity among the targets of their protests.

After the parties conducted their discovery and presented evidence to Miller in summary judgment briefs, Miller ruled for the American Knights, concluding that the ordinance violated the First Amendment.[20] Goshen had argued that the antimask ordinance was constitutional because only some of the Klan's members wore masks, while others did not. This did not persuade Judge Miller. "One person's choice to reveal his or her identity does not delimit another person's First Amendment rights," he wrote.[21]

Miller concluded that there is "no doubt" that Goshen's antimask ordinance harms the Klan members' free speech rights.[22] He likened the Goshen ordinance to the leafletting restrictions challenged by Manuel

Talley and Margaret McIntyre in the Supreme Court, though he acknowledged that Goshen's ordinance is different, as it requires the disclosure of faces instead of names. "But those are distinctions without
differences: the evidence reveals rallies and demonstrations within the
members' own community, where facial recognition might be expected
to disclose name, address and other commonly known information,"
Miller wrote.[23]

Like the leafletting restrictions, Goshen's ordinance failed the "exacting scrutiny" test established by the Supreme Court, Miller wrote, because
it was not "narrowly tailored to serve an overriding or compelling state
interest."[24] Miller focused on the burdens that the ordinance imposed on
the Klan members' speech, noting that his analysis must not consider the
"worthiness" of the Klan's ideas; "if anything, the unpopularity of their
ideas enhances the argument for protecting anonymity," he wrote.[25]

The Goshen ordinance, Miller reasoned, imposed a substantial burden
on the Klan members' ability to express themselves. "By requiring unmasked faces, it specifically links the members to their unpopular ideas,
unlike a more general disclosure requirement," Miller wrote. "Although
the disclosure exists only as long as the person appears in public, as opposed to the more permanent publication of a list or printing of a name on
a leaflet, it occurs at the very moment the American Knights deliver their
message, when the reaction to that message is most intense."[26]

Miller acknowledged that some disclosure requirements—such as
those for campaign finance filings—survive the exacting scrutiny test. But
such requirements are constitutional only if the government convinces the
court of the need for them, and Goshen failed to do so, he wrote. Although Goshen presented evidence of public safety hazards at previous
Klan appearances, Miller reasoned that the city did not sufficiently link
the use of masks with this unrest.[27] Even if the mask ordinance actually
had a link to reducing chaos at rallies, Miller wrote, it was not "narrowly tailored" for that goal. "The ordinance prohibits anonymity and/
or has the effect of directly chilling speech, which amount to serious and
far-reaching limitations on free speech and association," Miller wrote.
"The ordinance simply burdens more speech than is necessary to serve
Goshen's purpose of preventing violence."[28]Miller also rejected Goshen's
alternative explanation for its ordinance: helping law enforcement identify and apprehend people who commit crimes. "Masks obviously hinder

identification, but the summary judgment record does not support any connection between the antimask ordinance and Goshen's purported need to see faces to identify and apprehend criminals," Miller wrote. "Goshen's materials do not suggest that AKKKK members engaged in criminal activity while masked."[29]

The irony in the outcome was not lost on Miller. "More than a century ago, the Ku Klux Klan wore masks to terrorize persons they wanted to drive from their communities," he wrote. "Today, the Klan's descendant organization uses its masks to conceal the identities of those who hold ideas the community wishes to drive off. Still, a generation after the Ku Klux Klan's final heyday in Indiana, brave and unmasked men, women and children faced violence and thuggery in hostile southern streets, where Klansmen once rode, to establish the principle that the Constitution applies to all of us."[30]

Goshen decided not to appeal. The city had already incurred about fifty thousand dollars in legal fees defending the ordinance in trial court. "The attorneys recommended we not take it to another level because we'd probably lose there too," Kauffman said.[31]

After the court struck down the antimask ordinance, Kauffman said that the KKK did not stage any more rallies or protests in the community. Despite the significant legal fees and the ultimate defeat in court, he said, he does not regret his attempts to deter the Klan's rallies. He said that his championship of the ordinance never took a political toll on him; he served as mayor for nearly nineteen years before stepping down in 2015. "We did the right thing," he said in 2020.[32]

Although Berry's KKK group started in the Midwest, he gained followers nationwide during the 1990s. One particularly fast-growing chapter was in New York and New Jersey, led by Grand Dragon Jim Sheeley, a middle-aged computer services company employee. As Sheeley told the New York Times in 1999, he joined the KKK out of frustration that "other groups are encouraged to have pride, but not whites."[33]

In September 1999, Sheeley applied to the New York City Police Department for permission to hold a demonstration on October 23 at the city's Criminal Court Building.[34] At a meeting with the NYPD on October 13, Sheeley said that the demonstration would consist of between fifty and eighty hooded and masked participants.[35]

The NYPD informed Sheeley that wearing masks violated New York State Penal Law Section 240.35(4), which provided that a person is guilty of the crime of loitering if that person "being masked or in any manner disguised by unusual or unnatural attire or facial alteration, loiters, remains or congregates in a public place with other persons so masked or disguised, or knowingly permits or aids persons so masked or disguised to congregate in a public place; except that such conduct is not unlawful when it occurs in connection with a masquerade party or like entertainment." The New York law is even broader than the Goshen ordinance, which was limited to the wearing of masks "for the purpose of disguising or concealing his or her identity" in a "public place." New York first passed an antimask law in 1845, in response to tenant farmers in the Hudson Valley who had worn disguises while carrying out armed insurrections.[36]

At the meeting, Sheeley told the NYPD that the mask ban was unconstitutional, and that his members would wear masks at the rally.[37] His assertion that the members would violate the state law caused the NYPD to deny the permit for the event.[38]

The national American Knights organization quickly drew media attention to the permit denial. In an interview with the *New York Post*, Berry attacked the police department's actions as unconstitutional and predicted that the mask ban would be struck down, as Goshen's was. "Are they going to tell the pope to take off his hood when he comes to New York?" Berry told the newspaper. "Are they going to tell a Jewish person to shave off his beard and take off his hat? Are they going to make SWAT team members take their masks off?"[39]

Four days before the scheduled rally, the American Knights sued the city in the US District Court for the Southern District of New York, and asked the court to grant a preliminary injunction, ordering the city to allow the rally to occur with masked participants.

The Reverend Al Sharpton's National Action Network, a civil rights group that often conducted nonviolent protests in New York, filed an amicus brief in the case. But the brief did not oppose the position of the KKK, a group that espoused views that are antithetical to those of Sharpton. Rather, the National Action Network urged the court to recognize the KKK members' right to express themselves anonymously. "One purpose of the First Amendment is to protect speech and ideas that many citizens, if not most, find disturbing and disagreeable," the group wrote. "It is for the general marketplace of ideas, not statutes, to determine which ideas will be accepted and which will be discarded. While the organization seeking this permit does not espouse views which decent people may wish to hear, it is nevertheless essential to the political rights of the millions of members of quality civil rights organizations like the National Action Network, Inc., which must be protected."[40]

New York City defended the mask ban as necessary to promote public safety at crowded public events. In an affidavit filed to oppose the KKK's motion, Thomas Graham, commanding officer of the NYPD's Disorder Control Unit, described the chaos and crime that had occurred at large sporting events, concerts, demonstrations, and other gatherings. "Facial recognition is an essential element for witness and law enforcement identifications," Graham wrote. "Facial anonymity in a group can create a total shield to apprehension and may embolden a group or individual to engage in criminal activity. Where a group is organized with a cohesive mission and the ability to identify them is impaired, the potential for unsafe conditions or criminal conduct increases."[41]

On October 21—two days before the KKK had planned to hold its rally—New York federal judges Harold Baer and Alvin Hellerstein held a hearing on the KKK's preliminary injunction motion, as well as the Partisan Defense Committee's plans to hold a counterprotest. "The courts have long recognized a right to engage in anonymous political expression, and this First Amendment right of anonymity is especially strong where, as here, such anonymity is requested by a despised dissident organization," Norman Siegel, a New York Civil Liberties Union lawyer representing the KKK, told the judges.[42]

Berry was the first witness to testify for the KKK. He explained the need for his members to wear masks in public, which he attributed to the Safety Motivation. "The reason they need to hide their identity is because so many of the members has had people destroy their property, damage their cars, bust their windows out," he said. "I personally myself because they know who I am, I've had my house bombed about 14 times. This is all in the police record. People can check it out. I've had my house burnt down with a Molotov cocktail. My daughter has been shot at. I have been shot at. I have been beaten."[43]

Under questioning from another New York Civil Liberties Union attorney, Beth Haroules, Berry recounted his family receiving "threatening
phone calls," and Judge Baer asked him when and where he received the
calls.

"The most recent one is, I got a phone call three days ago, no disre-
spect, Judge, because of the New York accent," Berry said. "He said he
was from New York and it sounded to me, if we show up there we will
be dead."

"Do you have a New York accent?" Judge Hellerstein asked.

"No, sir," Berry replied.

"Where do you come from?" Judge Baer asked.

"I was born in Indiana, sir," Berry said.

"Do you have an Indiana accent?" Judge Hellerstein asked.

"I believe so," the KKK leader responded.

"Miss Haroules, do you have a New York accent?" Judge Hellerstein
asked Berry's lawyer.

"No, your Honor," she replied.

"How about you, Mr. Siegel?" Judge Hellerstein asked.

"I sure do," Siegel said.

"I'm not from New York originally," Haroules added.[44]

After that sideshow, Berry reverted to the need to protect his group's
free speech rights given the substantial threats.

"They single out, we're going to get you, the Ku Klux Klan, you're a
hate group, you kill people, you hang people," Berry said. "I have never
hung anybody. I have never killed anybody, and I have never beaten up
anybody because of their religious beliefs or the color of their skin."

"What prompted you to grace us with this prospect of this rally?" Baer
asked.

"We have members in this area around here and we want to come to
New York," Berry said. "This is basically where a lot of people express
their views. We wanted a white unity or white pride rally."[45]

Under cross-examination from an attorney for New York City, Berry
explained that the masks not only protect the safety of KKK members but
they are fundamental to the group's religious beliefs.

"We hide our face from Jesus or Messiah, whatever anybody wants
to call him, because we are sinners," Berry said. "We are in the dark just

like the Catholic goes into a dark confession booth to confess their sins. When we have our cross lighting they ask for forgiveness for sins with their masks down. They ask for it. We light the cross so the light of Jesus will [shine] down and make this a better world to live in. And the people hide their face."[46]

Both judges pushed back on Berry's characterization of his group, pointing to the Ku Klux Klan's violent history. "What I wonder is whether you have the same kinds of tenets to your organization as the Klan of 40, 50 years ago, or whether you have a very different outlook on what the Klan is about and what your organization in particular is about?" Judge Baer asked.

"I have a different outlook, you know," Berry said. "We're nonviolent Christian white civil rights group. I'm not going out there just because I disagree with what somebody does. I'm not going out and murder somebody because of that. This is the nineties. Like Rodney King said, 'why can't we all get along?' We are out there to let people know we are not this hate group. Whether they agree, sometimes we have different language that they would like to hear, but that's our constitutional right. We have a right to express our views."[47]

From their statements during the testimony of Berry and others, it did not appear that the judges were sympathetic to the Klan's arguments. But after hearing the testimony and briefly recessing to confer, the judges ruled for the Klan and issued the preliminary injunction, requiring the city to allow the group to hold its event while wearing masks.

"But the mask itself, although reflective of certain standards of hatred and fear, also may well reflect a fear of the speaker and a fear of the listener to such an extent as to discourage free speech and the exercise of First Amendment rights, and that seems to us to be inconsistent with the cases," Judge Hellerstein said.[48]

New York City immediately appealed, and the next day, the US Court of Appeals for the Second Circuit stayed the preliminary injunction, effectively upholding the city's prohibition on the use of masks at the rally. The court did not issue a written opinion; rather, reading from the bench at the end of the appellate argument, Judge Jose A. Cabranes briefly stated that he and two other judges concluded "that this case is distinguishable from those cases in which the Supreme Court has protected the anonymity of organizations and individuals seeking to exercise First

Amendment rights of association and speech."[49] He did not elaborate on the panel's reasoning.

New York City mayor Rudy Giuliani lauded the appellate court's decision. "The Court of Appeals has upheld the wisdom of the Police Department saying this is an organization that wore masks in order to kill people," he said to the press. "The Police Department has a public safety reason that's very, very sound in saying that you should not be able to do that in hiding, anonymously."[50]

Ruth Bader Ginsburg, the Supreme Court justice who heard emergency appeals from the Second Circuit, denied the KKK's request to overturn the appeals court. The next day, seventeen people held the rally in New York in KKK regalia but without masks. Even after the October 23 rally, the KKK continued to litigate the case before Judge Baer, seeking a permanent ruling that would preserve its right to wear masks at future events in New York.[51]

After hearing more arguments, on November 19, 2002, Judge Baer granted the KKK's request for a permanent injunction, reasoning that the New York antimask law violated the group members' First Amendment anonymity right. In his written opinion, Baer made clear that the KKK was not a terribly sympathetic litigant. "No one disputes the fact that plaintiff is a notorious racist organization, at least not this Court," Baer wrote. "The focus here, however, is on the constitutional protections, spelled out in the Federalist papers by our founding fathers, and on whether the conduct here and of concerns to the police should be protected."[52]

Just as the NAACP and other groups relied on anonymity to avoid reprisals for their speech, Baer wrote, so too did the KKK. "Like the NAACP members, the citizen distributing leaflets and the donors to political campaigns, the American Knights have produced unrefuted evidence that it has a legitimate fear of reprisal if its members reveal their identities at public American Knights' events," Baer wrote. "Members who have taken part in demonstrations without their masks, including those at the October 23 rally, describe the reprisals as pervasive and as having serious consequences in their lives including loss of employment, physical injury and threats to their children's safety."[53] Baer reasoned that the New York statute failed to meet the "exacting scrutiny" test established by the Supreme Court in its anonymity cases.

New York City continued to justify the antimask law as necessary to maintain order and public safety, yet Baer reasoned that this justification fails to satisfy the requirement of the exacting scrutiny test that the law must be "narrowly tailored." The antimask law applies to all groups equally, even if they might engage in illegal conduct. "No evidence was submitted supporting the argument that the police department had any reason to believe that the members of the American Knights would engage in unlawful behavior on October 23, and, in fact, they did not," he wrote. "Yet the statute applies regardless of the propensity of the group for illegal behavior. This blunderbuss approach, which encompasses so many lawful demonstrators, cannot be considered 'narrowly tailored.'"[54]

Baer also questioned whether the government had a "compelling state interest," another requirement of the exacting scrutiny test. Baer pointed to the statute's exception, allowing participants in a "masquerade party or like entertainment" to wear masks. "Surely, if masked events posed such a significant problem for the police department, the exception would not have found its way into the statute," he wrote. "In fact, the determination of whether any particular event presents a risk of disruption must be made on an individualized, case-by-case basis in which the police consider the various factors."[55] Besides finding the statute to violate the right to anonymous speech, Baer also concluded that it violated the right to symbolic speech, that its distinction between entertainment and other types of gatherings is content based and unconstitutional on its face, and that its selective enforcement constitutes illegal viewpoint discrimination.[56]

Judge Baer's conclusion about symbolic speech is particularly important. Because Judge Miller's opinion in *Goshen* focused on the potential retaliation that unmasked Klan members faced, he did not address the Klan's argument that the ordinance violated their ability to express themselves through masks. As Scott Skinner-Thompson argued in a 2017 article, "Attempts to preserve a degree of privacy or anonymity in public are often a form of performative and expressive opposition to an ever expanding surveillance society and, as such, may be protected as symbolic conduct."[57] By wearing masks, Klan members are not only preventing others from knowing their identities, but they are communicating that fact via their conduct.

New York City appealed the permanent injunction to the Second Circuit. The three judges randomly assigned to the panel were Dennis Jacobs, an appointee of George H. W. Bush; Jose Cabranes, a former Yale University general counsel appointed by Bill Clinton; and Sonia

Sotomayor, a Clinton appointee to the Second Circuit who would later rise to the Supreme Court.

The judges unanimously reversed Baer, disagreeing with all of his reasons for striking down the New York antimask law. The judges rejected Baer's extension of the First Amendment right to anonymity to the antimask statute. They recognized that the Supreme Court had recognized anonymity rights for groups such as the NAACP and people such as Margaret McIntyre, but noted that "the Supreme Court has never held that freedom of association or the right to engage in anonymous speech entails a right to conceal one's appearance in a public demonstration."[58]

Writing for the panel, Cabranes challenged Baer's conclusion that prohibiting the use of masks necessarily results in a First Amendment violation. "While the First Amendment protects the rights of citizens to express their viewpoints, however unpopular, it does not guarantee ideal conditions for doing so, since the individual's right to speech must always be balanced against the state's interest in safety, and its right to regulate conduct that it legitimately considers potentially dangerous," Cabranes wrote. "Because every civil and criminal remedy imposes some conceivable burden on First Amendment protected activities, a conduct-regulating statute of general application that imposes an incidental burden on the exercise of free speech rights does not implicate the First Amendment."[59]

Because Cabranes concluded that the antimask statute did not involve a constitutional right to anonymity, he found it unnecessary to analyze whether the ban satisfies the exacting scrutiny test.[60] His opinion also failed to address the rationale of other judges—such as Judge Miller in Indiana—who struck down antimask ordinances on First Amendment grounds.

The primary shortcoming in Cabranes's opinion is that it implicitly assumed that *McIntyre*, *Talley*, and the other Supreme Court anonymity cases were limited to disclosure of membership lists and author names. Although the Supreme Court never addressed the constitutionality of an antimask statute, nothing in the holdings limits the First Amendment anonymity concerns to the compelled disclosure of names rather than faces.

Although disclosure of names might be a more efficient way of identifying people than disclosure of their physical features, facial characteristics can easily reveal a person's identity. The same concerns about compelled disclosure of names are present when group members are forced to reveal their faces. As Judge Miller wrote in his opinion striking down Goshen's ordinance, banning KKK members from wearing masks will link them to "unpopular ideas" and subject them to potential retaliation.

Judge Cabranes also disagreed with Baer's conclusion that wearing masks constitutes protected symbolic speech. While the entirety of the Klan outfit—a robe, mask, and hood—may be expressive, Cabranes emphasized that the New York statute only prohibited wearing masks. "The mask that the members of the American Knights seek to wear in public demonstrations does not convey a message independently of the robe and hood. That is, since the robe and hood alone clearly serve to identify the American Knights with the Klan, we conclude that the mask does not communicate any message that the robe and the hood do not. The expressive force of the mask is, therefore, redundant."[61]

The robe and hood, Cabranes wrote, already sufficiently link the American Knights members with the Klan. "A witness to a rally where demonstrators were wearing the robes and hoods of the traditional Klan would not somehow be more likely to understand that association if the demonstrators were also wearing masks."[62]

Like his conclusion about the scope of the right to anonymous speech, Cabranes's analysis of the symbolic speech claim is too narrow. He is correct that a mask and a hood typically are sufficient to convey the fact that a person is associated with the KKK. That other aspects of the regalia communicate the same message does not render a mask useless in communicating a message. And more important, as Skinner-Thompson's scholarship has wisely demonstrated, the act of wearing a mask communicates an independent message of the wearer's interest in anonymity. Skinner-Thompson points to the use of Guy Fawkes masks by members of the hacking group Anonymous, which among other things criticizes government surveillance, and the use of masks by some Occupy Wall Street protesters in 2011, which led to some citations.[63]

Cabranes's rulings on the case's most important issue, the right to anonymous speech, is difficult to reconcile with Judge Miller's opinion in *Goshen*. In a thorough review of First Amendment anonymity challenges to antimask laws published in 2013, Margot Kaminski identified several cases in which courts both upheld and struck down such restrictions. Kaminski observed "how widely the splits between courts are developing."[64]

Of the courts that refused to strike down antimask laws, Kaminski wrote, they have done so for different reasons, including a failure to show a link between anonymity and expression and finding that the regulation of conduct is not a regulation of speech.[65] Judge Cabranes's opinion, Kaminski observed, "appears to be an outlier in its decision that the Supreme Court protection for anonymity is limited to compelled disclosures of names."[66]

Other courts, Kaminski noted, have taken a more nuanced approach to upholding the constitutionality of antimask laws.[67] In doing so, they have imposed some requirements that narrow their application. For instance, the Georgia Supreme Court upheld Georgia's antimask law, but held that it restricts only conduct "that is intended to conceal the wearer's identity and that the wearer knows, or reasonably should know, gives rise to a reasonable apprehension of intimidation, threats or impending violence."[68] Such a ruling would be somewhat easier to square with Judge Miller's ruling, as the Goshen ordinance applied more broadly to the use of masks to disguise or conceal the wearer's identity.

Even with the lack of harmony among courts about the constitutionality of antimask requirements, the opinions generally demonstrate the enduring legacy of *Talley*, *McIntyre*, and the other Supreme Court decisions protecting anonymous speech, and the willingness of courts to at least consider the application of these rights to new contexts. "Despite the breadth of the court split in anti-mask cases," Kaminski wrote, "there is a generally common understanding that anonymity is valuable and should in at least some circumstances be protected as a speech right or as an aspect of speech."[69]

An antimask law will impact groups other than the Ku Klux Klan. In 2012, three women wearing balaclavas while protesting outside the Russian Consulate in Manhattan, in support of the band Pussy Riot, were arrested and charged with violating the antimask statute. Balaclavas are brightly colored ski masks that were associated with Pussy Riot, a band that openly opposed Russian president Vladimir Putin's policies. The women challenged the constitutionality of the antimask law and prosecutors dropped the charges related to the masks.[70]

The Pussy Riot protesters focused mainly on the Speech Motivation for anonymity; the face coverings, they argued, were central to the message that they were conveying. "The balaclava is the trademark or defining symbol of Pussy Riot and integral to their substantive message advocating gender equality, political engagement, and protest against the repressive Russian government," the women's lawyers wrote in a brief to the court.[71]

The Pussy Riot protesters' goals were far different from those of Jeff Berry's Ku Klux Klan. The former wore masks to make a statement about Putin's authoritarian regime in Russia, while the latter relied on masks to spread their racial hatred. Yet they both faced restrictions under the same New York antimask law.

And therein lies a key challenge in developing anonymity rules. Shielding anonymous activities may protect the free speech of idealistic activists who are looking to improve democracy, but it also can foster the expression of ideas from some of the nation's most pernicious and hateful groups. For that reason, a balanced approach to anonymity is desirable. And courts eventually adopted such a nuanced legal framework as they determined how to apply anonymity rules to the Internet.

Part II

THE RIGHT TO ONLINE ANONYMITY

"On the Internet, nobody knows you're a dog," reads the caption beneath Peter Steiner's famous 1993 *New Yorker* cartoon depicting a dog behind a computer.

As homes and businesses rapidly acquired computers in the 1990s, anonymity moved from pamphlets and protests to the Internet. People often used pseudonyms—or sought to remain entirely anonymous—as they posted information to the masses.

The Internet-related legal disputes would look different from the litigation over antimask laws, pamphleteering restrictions, and canvassing rules. Often, the dispute was not between the government and a dissident, but two private parties. The plaintiff might be a company that was filing a defamation lawsuit against the person who anonymously criticized the business on a message board. Or the plaintiff had her life turned upside down by lies from an anonymous troll.

The challenge for courts is to determine when to require Internet service providers (ISPs) and websites to help the plaintiffs unmask the anonymous posters. Although these disputes look different from the anonymous pamphleteering cases, the courts have found a First Amendment right to online anonymity that traces back to those victories. This right to online anonymity is far from absolute; as in the early Supreme Court anonymity cases, courts balance competing factors, such as privacy and free expression, in determining whether to order the unmasking of anonymous Internet users.

Although online poster subpoenas differ from campaign literature regulations, the disputes share many of the same competing interests. In his 2007 book, *The Future of Reputation*, Daniel Solove aptly described these values as applied to the Internet. People may seek online anonymity, he wrote, "because they fear social ostracism or being fired from their jobs," and a lack of anonymity may discourage people from expressing "controversial ideas." On the flipside, Solove notes, anonymity makes it "easier to say harmful things about others when we don't have to take responsibility" and allows deception because people "can readily masquerade as other people in creating blogs and profiles."[1]

When courts confront requests to unmask anonymous Internet users, they balance these competing values. It often is difficult to predict the outcome of anonymity disputes, as both sides often have compelling arguments, and the result often turns on a judge's subjective judgments of the magnitude of the harms and benefits of anonymity.

The courts have recognized a First Amendment right to online anonymity that is not absolute and can be defeated in particularly strong cases. By subjecting unmasking requests to stringent review, courts generally have struck the appropriate balance between free speech and the need to combat online harms.

This part examines how courts have handled requests from civil litigants—often large companies—to unmask anonymous online posters, applying the same First Amendment principles reflected in the victories of Manuel Talley and Margaret McIntyre. It then investigates the relatively weaker protections in copyright infringement cases and criminal investigations, and compares US anonymity protections to those in other nations. Moreover, protections for online anonymity come not only from the First Amendment, but from technology that enables users to mask identifying information such as their Internet Protocol addresses. This part looks at these technological protections for anonymity, including Tor, which arose from a technology developed by US military researchers in the 1990s.

6

CYBERSMEAR

"BONUSES WILL HAPPEN—BUT WHAT ARE THEY REALLY?"[1]

That was the title of a November 1, 1998, thread on the Yahoo! Finance bulletin board dedicated to tracking the financial performance of Raytheon, the mammoth defense contractor. Like many publicly traded companies at the time, Raytheon was the subject of a Yahoo! Finance message board, where spectators commented and speculated on the company's financial status. Yahoo! allowed users to post messages under pseudonyms, so its Finance bulletin boards quickly became a virtual—and public—water cooler for rumors about companies nationwide.

The Yahoo! Finance boards largely operated on the "marketplace of ideas" approach to free speech theory,[2] which promotes an unregulated flow of speech, allowing the consumers of that speech to determine its veracity.[3] Although Yahoo! Finance may have aspired to represent the marketplace of ideas, the market did not always quickly sort the false from the true. During the dot-com boom of the late 1990s, Yahoo! Finance users' instant speculation about a company's financial performance and stock price took on new importance to investors and companies. But some of these popular bulletin boards contained comments that were not necessarily helpful to fostering productive financial discussion. "While many message boards perform their task well, others are full of rowdy remarks, juvenile insults and shameless stock boosterism," the *St. Petersburg Times* wrote in 2000. "Some boards are abused and fall prey to posters who try to manipulate a company's stock, typically by pushing up its price with misleading information, then selling the stock near its peak."[4]

Corporate executives and public relations departments routinely monitored the bulletin boards, keenly aware that one negative post could affect employee morale and, more importantly, stock prices. And they did not have faith in the marketplace of ideas sorting out the truth from the falsities. While companies were accustomed to handling negative press coverage, the pseudonymous criticism on Yahoo! Finance was an entirely different world. Executives knew to whom they could complain if a newspaper's business columnist wrote about inflated share prices or pending layoffs. Yahoo! Finance's commenters, on the other hand, typically were not easily identifiable. They could be disgruntled employees, shareholders, or even executives.

The reputation-obsessed companies and executives could not use the legal system to force Yahoo! to remove posts that they believed were defamatory or contained confidential information. In February 1996, Congress passed Section 230 of the Communications Decency Act, which generally prevents interactive computer services—such as Yahoo!—from being "treated as the publisher or speaker" of user content.[5] In November 1997, a federal appellate court construed this immunity broadly,[6] and other courts soon followed. Congress passed Section 230 in part to *encourage* online platforms to moderate objectionable content, and the statute creates a nearly absolute bar to lawsuits for defamation and other claims arising from third-party content, whether or not they moderate.[7] Section 230 has a few exceptions, including for intellectual property law and federal criminal law enforcement. Section 230 meant that an angry subject of a Yahoo! Finance post could not successfully sue Yahoo! for defamation, but could sue the poster. That person, however, often was difficult to identify by screen name.

Not surprisingly, the Yahoo! Finance bulletin boards would become the first major online battleground for the right to anonymous speech.

Companies' attempts in the late 1990s to unmask Yahoo! Finance posters would set the stage for decades of First Amendment battles over online anonymity.

A November 1, 1998, reply in the Raytheon bonuses thread came from a user named RSCDeepThroat. The four-paragraph post speculated on the size of bonuses. "Yes, there will be bonuses and possibly for only one year," RSCDeepThroat wrote. "If they were really bonuses, the goals for each segment would have been posted and we would have seen our progress against them. They weren't, and what we get is black magic. Even the segment execs aren't sure what their numbers are." RSCDeepThroat predicted bonuses would be less than 5 percent. "That's good as many sites are having rate problems largely due to the planned holdback of 5%. When it becomes 2%, morale will take a hit, but customers on cost-plus jobs will get money back and we will get bigger profits on fixed-price jobs."[8]

RSCDeepThroat posted again, on January 25, 1999, in a thread with the title "98 Earnings Concern." The poster speculated about business difficulties at Raytheon's Sensors and Electronics Systems unit. "Word running around here is that SES took a bath on some programs that was not discovered until late in the year," RSCDeepThroat posted. "I don't know if the magnitude of those problems will hurt the overall Raytheon bottom line. The late news cost at least one person under Christine his job. Maybe that is the apparent change in the third level."[9] The poster speculated that Chief Executive Dan Burnham "is dedicated to making Raytheon into a lean, nimble, quick competitor." Although RSCDeepThroat did not provide his or her real name, the posts' discussion of specifics—such as the termination of someone who worked for "Christine"—suggested that RSCDeepThroat worked for Raytheon or was receiving information from a Raytheon employee.

RSCDeepThroat and the many other people who posted about their employers on Yahoo! Finance had good reason to take advantage of the pseudonymity that the site provided. Perhaps the most important driver was the Economic Motivation; if their real names were linked to their posts, they likely would lose their jobs. Likewise, the Legal Motivation drove their need to protect their identities, as many employers had policies against disclosing confidential information, and some companies required their employees to sign confidentiality agreements. And the Power

Motivation also was a likely factor in the behavior of some Yahoo! Finance posters—suddenly, the words and feelings of everyday employees mattered to the company's top executives.

Raytheon sought to use its legal might to silence anonymous posters. The prospect of inside information being blasted across the Internet apparently rankled Raytheon's executives so much that the company sued RSCDeepThroat and twenty other Yahoo! Finance posters for breach of contract, breach of employee policy, and trade secret misappropriation in state court in Boston. In the complaint, the company wrote that all Raytheon employees are bound by an agreement that prohibits unauthorized disclosure of the company's proprietary information.[10] Raytheon claimed that RSCDeepThroat's November post constituted "disclosure of projected profits," and the January post was "disclosure of inside financial issues."[11]

Raytheon's complaint stated only that the company sought damages in excess of twenty-five thousand dollars. Litigating this case might cost more than any money the company would recover in settlements or jury verdicts. The lawsuit would, however, allow Raytheon to attempt to gather information to identify the authors of the critical posts.

Raytheon's February 1, 1999, complaint was among the earliest of what would become known as a "cybersmear lawsuit," in which a company filed a complaint against (usually pseudonymous) online critics.[12] Because of its high visibility and large number of pseudonymous critics, Yahoo! Finance was ground zero for cybersmear lawsuits.

Because Raytheon only had the posters' screen names, the defendants listed on the complaint included RSCDeepThroat, WinstonCar, DitchRaytheon, RayInsider, RaytheonVeteran, and other monikers that provided no information about the posters' identities. To appreciate the barriers that the plaintiffs faced, it first is necessary to understand the taxonomy that applies to the levels of online identity protection. This was best explained in a 1995 article by A. Michael Froomkin.[13] He summarized four levels of protection:

- Traceable anonymity: "A remailer that gives the recipient no clues as to the sender's identity but leaves this information in the hands of a single intermediary."[14]

- Untraceable anonymity: "Communication for which the author is simply not identifiable at all."[15]
- Untraceable pseudonymity: The message is signed with a pseud-onym that cannot be traced to the original author. The author might use a digital signature "which will uniquely and unforgeably distin-guish an authentic signed message from any counterfeit."[16]
- Traceable pseudonymity: "Communication with a *nom de plume* attached which can be traced back to the author (by someone), although not necessarily by the recipient."[17] Froomkin wrote that under this category, a speaker's identity is more easily identifiable, but it more easily allows communications between the speaker and other people.[18]

Although traceable anonymity and traceable pseudonymity are not substantially different from a technical standpoint—in both cases, the speakers can be identified, Margot Kaminski argues that a speaker's choice to communicate pseudonymously rather than anonymously might have an impact on their expression because pseudonymous communica-tion "allows for the adoption of a developing, ongoing identity that can itself develop an image and reputation."[19]

Yahoo! Finance largely fell into the category of traceable pseudonymity. Yahoo! did not require users to provide their real names before posting. But it did require them to use a screen name and asked for an email ad-dress (though there often was no guarantee that the email address alone would reveal their identifying information). It automatically logged their Internet Protocol (IP) addresses, unique numbers associated with a par-ticular Internet connection. Plaintiffs could use the legal system to obtain this information, which could lead to their identities, albeit with no guar-antee of success.

On the day that Raytheon filed its lawsuit, it asked the court for per-mission to conduct discovery on Yahoo! for a wide swath of informa-tion that the company maintains about the twenty-one posters, including their email addresses, IP addresses, and any communications between the posters and Yahoo! Two days later, the judge approved the motion.[20] At the time, Yahoo! often provided identifying information to litigants after receiving a subpoena without first notifying its users and providing them an opportunity to challenge the subpoenas in court. Because Yahoo! did not require real names—and subscribers might use throwaway email addresses to register with the site—Yahoo! might not necessarily have been able to deliver notice to subpoena targets. Yet it could have tried to notify the targets via their listed email addresses or via a post on Yahoo! Finance.

But Yahoo!'s compliance with Raytheon's requests did not necessarily lead to the identities of the posters. An IP address is only a series of numbers that is associated with the user's connection provided by an ISP. Email addresses also might not reveal the poster's actual name. That required Raytheon to issue a second set of discovery requests, this time to the companies that provided the email accounts or Internet connections.

A month after the judge approved its request to Yahoo!, Raytheon issued a new set of discovery requests from Internet service providers including America Online, EarthLink Network, and Hotmail for information about seven of the posters. "Without additional discovery," the company's lawyers wrote in a court filing, "Raytheon will be unable to serve process or otherwise prosecute this action against those defendants."[21]

One of Raytheon's requests to America Online related to RSCDeep-Throat. That is likely because RSCDeepThroat used his America Online email address to register with Yahoo! Finance. Unlike Yahoo!, America Online's practice at the time was to notify users if their identifying information was the subject of a civil discovery request, providing them with the opportunity to challenge the subpoena in court.

America Online's more privacy-friendly approach stemmed from careful internal deliberation. David Phillips, who was America Online's associate general counsel in the mid-1990s, said that beginning in about 1995 the company started to get subpoenas for its users' identifying information. The trickle of subpoenas grew into a flood, with plaintiffs claiming that America Online users defamed them and divorce lawyers seeking information about the infidelities of their clients' spouses. Phillips estimated that America Online eventually would receive between sixty and eighty civil subpoenas each week.

These requests sparked discussions that reached the company's highest executives, including chief executive Steve Case, Phillips recalled in an interview for this book. "Steve Case really cared about these policy issues and getting it right, and saying, 'Hey, we're the founders of a new Internet, a sort of new world, a sovereign unto itself,'" Phillips said. "We were just trying to figure this out and create some standards that were a middle ground between common carrier/AT&T and a newspaper or publisher."[22]

America Online's leadership eventually determined that this middle ground meant providing notice to users before revealing their identifying information, Phillips said. "We decided that we would give notice to the account holder we had received this and we'd comply by a certain date to give them an opportunity to object," he said.[23]

America Online's policy was particularly important for protecting users' anonymity because, unlike Yahoo!, America Online was far more likely to have accurate information about its subscribers' true identities. Although America Online allowed customers to use pseudonyms as their email addresses and login names, America Online needed the subscribers' real names to bill them for Internet access charges.

When America Online received the discovery request for information about the email address registered to RSCDeepThroat, it notified the email account's owner, Mark Neuhausen. Neuhausen was, in fact, RSCDeep-Throat. He also was a vice president in Raytheon's Arlington, Virginia, office, and joined Raytheon after it acquired the company that employed him. When Neuhausen received the notice from America Online, he chose not to attempt to challenge it in court. "I did nothing," he said. "I didn't really think I posted anything proprietary."

Even if he persuaded a court to quash Raytheon's request to America Online, he had already been unmasked. His America Online address included his first name, last initial, and birthdate. Once Yahoo! provided the email address to Raytheon, his employer likely could identify him fairly easily. "I got no notice from Yahoo!," Neuhausen recalled in an interview with me. "My view at the time was Yahoo! was sleazy by responding and not letting me know at all."

The ease with which Raytheon obtained his identifying information was disconcerting, Neuhausen said. "Someone does a subpoena with no burden of proof at all and says someone posted something that's trade secrets or proprietary, and we're subpoenaing the courts to get their identity," he said. "It was annoying to me."[24]

Soon after Raytheon sent the discovery request to America Online, Neuhausen received a visit from a human resources executive, he recalled. The executive said that the company did not believe that anything was wrong with his posts, but they did not like that he was posting,

Neuhausen recalled. Neuhausen said that if this were the case, he was willing to stop. The executive told Neuhausen that they needed to find some punishment for him, and Neuhausen replied that, as a father, he did not believe in punishing his children if they did nothing wrong.[25]

The next week, Raytheon fired Neuhausen, he recalled. Although the experience was unsettling, Neuhausen said he was not heartbroken because he had been unhappy at Raytheon. He found another job soon after the termination, though some defense contractors said they couldn't hire him. "They said, 'We heard about what happened at Raytheon, and we can't touch you right now,'" he recalled.[26]

If Raytheon intended to convey a message to employees by suing, it may have achieved its goal. The lawsuit—and Neuhausen's termination— were the subject of national media coverage. "We've tried to convey something to employees," Phyllis Piano, then Raytheon's vice president of corporate communications, told the *Wall Street Journal* at the time. "We encourage people to air their views. But they can't cross the line and divulge proprietary information."[27]

Raytheon's ability to unmask Internet posters with relative ease caught the attention of privacy advocates. "This kind of case is happening more and more as conversations which used to take place in private have migrated to the Net where private, even anonymous communication, becomes public," Barry Steinhardt, associate director of the American Civil Liberties Union, told the *San Jose Mercury News* in April 1999.[28]

Raytheon's lawsuit received significant media coverage. But many other cybersmear lawsuits proliferated around the turn of the century. An April 1999 article in the *New York Law Journal* reported that on average for each week since June 1998, companies had filed one or two cybersmear complaints in the court system of Santa Clara County, California, where Yahoo! was headquartered.[29] That figure did not include lawsuits filed in other jurisdictions—such as Raytheon's—where the plaintiff then sought to conduct out-of-state discovery on Yahoo!

"The word is clearly out among in-house corporate counsel that this is the way to deal with the problem of online criticism," David Sobel, general counsel for the Electronic Privacy Information Center, told *The Industry Standard* in November 1999.[30]

The early cybersmear lawsuits often claimed that the posters violated employee confidentiality agreements, disclosed trade secrets, breached fiduciary duties, or defamed the companies.[31] "At the beginning, the companies were more abusive than the posters," Jon Sobel, who served as Yahoo!'s general counsel from 1998 to 2003, recalled in an interview for this book. "The companies were very thin-skinned."[32]

Companies often filed the lawsuits merely to seek the identities of the posters. As the *Oregonian* newspaper described in an October 2000 article about cybersmears: "Companies file a lawsuit, then use the power of subpoena to learn the true identities of the John Does. Once they have the names, the companies drop the suits and fire the John Does who are employees."[33] Indeed, on May 20, 1999, less than five months after filing its lawsuit against the twenty-one John Does, Raytheon voluntarily dismissed the complaint.[34]

Because many companies did not intend to litigate the cybersmear cases past the initial discovery round, it often did not matter whether they stated a viable claim in their complaint. For instance, in the Raytheon lawsuit, one of the twenty other John Doe defendants was a poster named onerainone, who on September 17, 1998, posted: "Out west we have been ordered to accelerate personel [sic] reductions planned for 1999 and make the cuts in 1998 istead [sic]. I think another 4–7% will leave this year. Possibly before the Thanksgiving holiday."[35]

Raytheon included onerainone in its lawsuit, claiming that the post constituted "disclosure of internal manpower projections."[36] It is hard to imagine why such a post caused a multibillion-dollar company to sue an employee. Even if the seemingly innocuous prediction violated Raytheon's internal policies, onerainone could argue that there is a strong public interest in employees commenting on working conditions. If Margaret McIntyre had the right to distribute anonymous campaign literature, why did onerainone not have the right to anonymously complain about a corporate workplace? Why could a private company use the power of the judiciary to unmask onerainone?

But onerainone and the twenty other Raytheon message board posters did not have a chance to challenge the discovery of their information from Yahoo! because they were unaware of the lawsuit and subpoenas. In a 2000 article, David Sobel, the privacy advocate, wrote that Yahoo!'s failure to notify its users of subpoenas meant that the users "frequently have no opportunity to quash subpoenas and the courts have no role in evaluating the propriety of requests for identifying information."[37]

Yahoo! publicly acknowledged the torrent of subpoenas that it was receiving, but argued that it simply could not challenge each subpoena in court on behalf of its users. "That's not realistic," a senior producer of Yahoo! Finance told a reporter in 1999. "You'd be talking about potentially overwhelming legal costs."[38] But even if Yahoo! did not choose to defend its users' anonymity rights in court, it would cost very little to notify the users of the subpoena at the email address on record.

Although many anonymous posters could not challenge subpoenas for their identifying information because they were unaware of the litigation, that would soon change.

The Yahoo! Finance discussion board for Xircom was home to the heated, colorful, and sometimes offensive debate that could be expected in discussions of tech stocks in the late nineties. Xircom, a California-based modem manufacturer, sparked intense speculation over its financial performance. The posters on the board had names such as "marketwzrd" and "NeedleDickHump." The posts had titles such as "coms up 8 percent on takeover rumor!" and "Hans-ols Flunks Doggy School." One poster wrote, "I'm so sick of this piece of shit stock. Gimme 1 reason to hold on to this dog."[39]

Posts that caught Xircom management's attention, however, came from a poster named "A_VIEW_FROM_WITHIN." In April 1999, he wrote that he was a Xircom engineer, and he criticized the quality of the company's products and its inability to retain employees. "Xircom use [*sic*] to be a fun place to work but there is now a heavy dark cloud surrounding the environment at Xircom," the poster wrote on Yahoo! Finance.[40] He also wrote that "management seems disconnected from the work force" and that the company's sales director is "more concerned with finding his lost hair gel than he is about sales growth."[41]

Some posters questioned whether the poster worked for Xircom. "You are obviously one of the dead wood engineers that were dumped because of incompetence. . . . You are a FRAUD," one wrote.[42] Still, the prospect of an employee posting public criticism of Xircom caused the company to sue A_VIEW_FROM_WITHIN in Ventura County, California, state court on May 5, 1999, alleging breach of contract, defamation, interference with prospective commercial advantage, unfair competition, and breach of fiduciary duty.[43] On the day that it sued the poster, Xircom subpoenaed Yahoo! for his identifying information.[44]

In a typical cybersmear case in 1999, Xircom would have quietly obtained A_VIEW_FROM_WITHIN's identifying information from Yahoo! and the poster's ISP. Unfortunately for the company, three days after it filed the complaint—and before it could obtain identifying information from Yahoo!—the *Ventura County Star* ran a front-page story about the lawsuit, entitled "Xircom Files Suit for Web Postings."[45]

When reached for comment from the newspaper, Xircom attorney Randall Holliday said that the posts upset the company because they apparently were written by one of its employees. "What puts this action in an entirely different space is that the author claims to be an employee and if that is in fact true we have major problems," he told the newspaper. "There could be violation of company policies on proprietary information and trade secrets."[46]

Three days after the *Ventura County Star* article, the *Los Angeles Daily News* wrote a story about the lawsuit. The newspaper interviewed law professor Matthew Spitzer, who warned that posts on public message boards such as Yahoo! Finance could lead to defamation lawsuits. "Don't post messages on the Internet unless you're comfortable about them being published on the front pages of a newspaper," Spitzer warned.[47]

The poster behind the A_VIEW_FROM_WITHIN moniker happened to read one of the newspaper articles and began calling lawyers to see if they would represent him in fighting the subpoena before Yahoo! turned over his information.[48]

No lawyer specialized in defending subpoena targets in cybersmear cases, as there had not yet been any challenges to these lawsuits. So he called Los Angeles technology attorneys, with little success. He was seeking free legal advice, and lawyers at white shoe law firms had little incentive to provide pro bono services to a Yahoo! Finance message board poster.

One evening in May 1999, his luck changed when he called Megan Gray.[49] After a stint as a foreign newspaper correspondent, Gray attended the University of Texas School of Law. When she graduated in 1995, Gray moved west to practice intellectual property and media law. She first landed at the Los Angeles office of megafirm O'Melveny and Myers.

Unlike other new associates at big law firms, who ground out billable hours on tedious projects like document review, Gray was laser-focused on building her own client base. Soon after joining the firm, she landed her first paying client. The firm was not thrilled, as they preferred that she serve the firm's existing multibillion-dollar clients, she recalled.

A year after joining O'Melveny, Gray moved to the Los Angeles office of Baker & Hostetler, a global firm with a respected media and technology practice, well-suited for the former journalist. Her intellectual property work included helping entertainment industry clients seize counterfeit goods. This eventually led to work on Internet-based infringement cases. Soon enough, Gray was the firm's Internet law guru, at a time when the Internet was just emerging as a commercial enterprise.

By the time she was a fourth-year associate in 1999, Gray had a large book of business, eventually her own secretaries and paralegals, and even junior associates working for her. As she acknowledged in an interview for this book, it was "super weird" for a mid-level associate at a big firm to have her own staff.

Gray continued to build her expertise—and her reputation—in Internet law. That is likely how her name ended up on A_VIEW_FROM_WITHIN's radar. When Gray spoke with him on that May evening, she understood the sort of case that he was asking her to handle. "I quickly realized, 'Oh, this is Raytheon. OK, I've heard about this.'"

Because she was bringing in her own clients, she had enough clout to convince the firm to allow her to take on the case pro bono. But the firm had a policy that associates could not file pleadings in court without also having a partner's name on the document. So she asked one of her firm's established First Amendment partners if he would work on the case with her. "That's fine, but you're going to do the work,'" she recalled him telling her.

Gray immediately thought of *McIntyre* and the other Supreme Court anonymity cases, but it was unclear how a court would react to such a First Amendment argument. Gray knew that she had to move quickly, before Yahoo! provided Xircom with the information.

She could not simply call Xircom and try to convince the company to withdraw the subpoena. Notifying the company that her client was aware of the subpoena might cause the company to withdraw the complaint and refile, perhaps in another court. Her client might not learn of the new lawsuit. That would allow Xircom to quietly subpoena Yahoo! "Strategically, it was often best to get something on file with the court before you approached opposing counsel," Gray said.

So Gray worked late nights and weekends at her Wilshire Boulevard office to piece together a motion to quash a subpoena for an anonymous online poster's identifying information. On May 25, 1999—less than three weeks after Xircom sued her client—Gray filed a fifteen-page motion to quash, along with fifteen exhibits. "Xircom is a large, publicly traded company that has filed a meritless lawsuit in an attempt to squelch a person who dares to criticize its performance in the marketplace," Gray wrote in the opening paragraph of the brief. "Such criticism is rampant on one area of the internet devoted to discussing Xircom. Xircom has filed this lawsuit, and publicized it extensively, in a concerted effort to chill the speech of individuals discussing Xircom on the internet."[50]

The subpoena violates the First Amendment's protections of anonymous speech, Gray argued, pointing the California judge to the Supreme Court's ruling in *McIntyre*. "This Court should not permit the judicial branch to become a clearing house for lawsuits filed with only the most frivolous pretense—lawsuits with the true purpose of providing private detective agency services through the subpoena power to persons seeking to learn the identity of people using Yahoo! message boards," Gray wrote.[51]

Gray focused on the need to protect anonymity on new online technologies. She pointed to a 1997 Supreme Court decision that struck down a federal law that penalized the transmission of indecent online content to minors. "Because the internet is so easily used by anyone with a computer and modem, entitling anyone to speak his mind and be heard, it has become the focal point for much legislation in an attempt to control the outspoken masses," Gray wrote. "Such laws, however, have been uniformly struck down as unconstitutional impingements of the First Amendment."[52]

Gray stressed that she was not seeking an absolute bar on subpoenas for anonymous posters' identities. Rather, she argued that the court should quash Xircom's subpoena because it was "groundless."[53] She explained that Xircom could not succeed in its defamation claim, as the company is a public figure that must meet a high burden of proof to win a defamation claim, and because statements of pure opinion cannot be the basis for defamation lawsuits.[54] Gray argued that the trade secrets and fiduciary duty-related claims also could not succeed because her client was not a Xircom employee, and his posts did not include trade secrets.[55]

Xircom's lawsuit, Gray argued, also should be dismissed under a California statute known as an "anti-SLAPP law" (SLAPP stands for "strategic lawsuit against public participation.") California's legislature enacted the law to combat the "increase in lawsuits brought primarily to chill the valid exercise of the constitutional rights of freedom of speech and petition for the redress of grievances."[56] The law makes it harder for a plaintiff to bring a weak lawsuit arising from the exercise of free speech and allows the defendant to recover attorney's fees if the lawsuit is dismissed. Xircom's lawsuit should be dismissed under the California anti-SLAPP statute, Gray argued, because the company could not demonstrate that it suffered damage from her client's two posts, out of thousands on Xircom's Yahoo! Finance board. She noted that Xircom's stock price rose after her client's two postings.[57]

At a June 14, 1999, hearing, Judge John Hunter granted Gray's request to block Xircom's subpoena, but not because he concluded that it violated the First Amendment. Instead, Hunter agreed with Gray's alternative argument: that the subpoena violated California procedural rules, including a requirement that the plaintiff wait twenty days after serving a complaint before conducting discovery.[58] Hunter rejected the First Amendment argument, allowing Xircom to issue a new subpoena to Yahoo! that would conform to California's procedural rules.[59] "We will continue to seek (identifying) information," Xircom attorney Holliday told a reporter after the hearing. Gray at the time said her client would continue to challenge Xircom's attempts to unmask him.[60]

Because Judge Hunter would have allowed a new subpoena, Gray tried to persuade Xircom to back down. The company believed that A_VIEW_FROM_WITHIN was a Xircom employee. "I told them, 'You have this whole conspiracy theory that is not reality.'" She offered to review a list of names that Xircom suspected might be the poster, and then sign a declaration that her client was not among those listed.

Gray's tactics worked, and in July her client reached a settlement with Xircom. The company did not reveal the settlement terms, but its announcement stated that A_VIEW_FROM_WITHIN had never been employed by Xircom and was not an engineer.[61]

Despite the anticlimactic end to the dispute, Gray's efforts did not go to waste. The case's publicity quickly earned her a reputation as the go-to lawyer for John and Jane Does seeking to fight subpoenas for their identifying information. Demand for her services became especially high in 2000, when Yahoo! changed its policy and began notifying users by email of subpoenas for their identifying information, and providing them fifteen days to challenge the subpoena.[62]

Gray estimated that over the next two years, she represented about fifty John Does, seeking to block companies' attempts to unmask them. Representing John Does posed challenges that she wouldn't face with other clients. She never called John Does by their real names, nor did she speak with them in the presence of other attorneys or support staff at her firm. While some cases were pro bono, many clients could cover litigation costs through their home insurance policies. But she had to ensure that the law firm's billing department had no access to her clients' real names. These were far from the typical cases that big law firms handled.

As soon as Gray began representing a John Doe, she would contact Yahoo! to let the company know that she was objecting to the subpoena. ("It was always Yahoo!" she said.) She then would send the plaintiff a template letter, along with many news clippings about her defense of anonymous posters. "You didn't even know this was a thing," she said she conveyed in her letters. "So I'm telling you this is a thing. I am proud to represent this John Doe. And I can't wait for more publicity for my Texas heart."

Gray's tactics usually led to her clients remaining anonymous. Still, the subpoenas kept coming, from large and small companies alike, usually for innocuous—and often childish—insults about the companies' financial performance and stock prices.

Why were the companies so intent on unmasking Gray's clients?

When asked this question in 2020, Gray paused, and recalled an incident that occurred as she was receiving national notoriety for her First Amendment and privacy advocacy. She had built a million-dollar book of business—unheard of for a mid-level associate—and the managing partner of her office enthusiastically supported her new practice. But one of the firm's prominent partners in another office read an article about a case that Gray had handled. "And he was disgusted and offended that I would be helping somebody badmouth the CEO of any company," Gray said. In a memo to Gray and copied to the firm's policy committee, the partner noted that he was a director of many companies, and had been attacked by people on bulletin boards. Gray was prohibited from representing John Does.

Gray said that she resigned from the firm, but after the executive committee reversed the decision within twenty-four hours, she returned to the firm. Although she was once again allowed to represent John Doe defendants, the experience taught her a lesson about why the Yahoo! Finance boards rankled corporate executives—and their lawyers—to the point that they would sue to unmask posters. The Internet had completely upended the power structure that the companies had always relied on.

"I had not appreciated the white powerful privilege that an older generation felt," Gray said. "They really had never been talked back to in a manner that seemed in their face. They knew subconsciously, people would talk about them behind their back, but they never paid attention to that. This was now in their face and it was in print."

Corporate executives generally had not faced public criticism from their subordinates, or their wives, or their children. Suddenly, people with names like RSCDeepThroat and A_VIEW_FROM_WITHIN were not only questioning their judgment and character, but doing so in public. "It was unerasable," Gray said. "And it really got under their skin."

After three years of fending off John Doe subpoenas, Gray left Baker & Hostetler in 2002 to move to Washington, DC, where she worked for a privacy advocacy group, in private practice, and at the Federal Trade Commission. In 2018, Gray began working as General Counsel of DuckDuckGo, a search engine that touts its protections for user privacy.

The anonymous online poster lawsuits would continue for years. And courts would soon be forced to decide how much protection they should provide for John Does, and how to play referee in a new forum with a completely foreign power dynamic.

Among the first scholars to write substantively about the John Doe lawsuits was Lyrissa Barnett Lidsky, then a law professor at the University of Florida. In a landmark *Duke Law Journal* article published in February 2000—in the very early days of the John Doe lawsuits—Lidsky aptly described the role that these new lawsuits had in suppressing the free speech that made the Internet so unique. She wrote that "the Internet allows ordinary John Does to participate as never before in public discourse, and hence, to shape public policy."[63]

The lawsuits, she observed, threatened to "reestablish existing hierarchies of power, as powerful corporate Goliaths sue their critics for speaking their minds." Because the anonymous posters often did not have enough money to litigate against large corporations, Lidsky wrote, the lawsuits threatened "not only to deter the individual who is sued from speaking out, but also to encourage undue self-censorship among the other John Does who frequent Internet discussion fora."[64]

Lidsky did not find all complaints about Yahoo! Finance postings to be meritless. A single post on the Internet can have great reach and impact, so an unprincipled John Doe could easily cause great damage. "He can pollute the information stream with defamatory falsehoods, which may in turn influence other investors to question the corporation's credibility or financial health," Lidsky wrote. "Moreover, once the defamatory information enters the information stream, it may have a greater impact than if it had appeared in print."[65]

The postings that led to cybersmear cases were a significant concern not only to companies, but to securities regulators. In the late 1990s and early 2000s, the Securities and Exchange Commission monitored financial bulletin board postings and was concerned about stock price manipulation.[66] In a 1999 speech, Richard Walker, then the SEC's chief enforcement officer, warned of the threat that online speech posed for securities fraud. Fraudsters, Walker warned, used misinformation to manipulate companies' share prices. "Often perpetrated by short sellers, this fraud is intended to drive down a stock price on the basis of false information," Walker said. "These scams routinely involve 'microcap' stocks—which are low-priced thinly traded securities. In conducting these scams, the Internet has served as the modern day 'boiler room' replacing the traditional army of salespersons working the phones with scripts in hand." Enforcing securities laws on "the vast universe of the Internet," Walker said, is the commission's greatest challenge.[67]

Figuring out how to mitigate the chilling effects of John Doe subpoenas while still providing injured plaintiffs with some recourse and combatting stock price manipulation was challenging. Due to a lack of direct First Amendment protection for online anonymity, Lidsky advocated for protecting some John Doe posters via the First Amendment's "opinion privilege," which protects pure statements of opinion—rather than factual assertions—from defamation claims. Many of the Yahoo! Finance posts could be reasonably interpreted only as mere bloviation, and not statements of fact. The opinion privilege is particularly attractive for John Doe defendants, Lidsky wrote, because it can be asserted in the early stages of a lawsuit, often averting substantial legal fees.[68]

The opinion privilege would not be a panacea for anonymous poster cases. As Lidsky demonstrated in her review of opinion privilege cases, courts were not always clear and consistent in determining what types of statements were protected opinion. Another limitation of the opinion privilege is that it applies only to defamation lawsuits, and many anonymous poster lawsuits—including those filed by Raytheon and Xircom— also included other claims, such as trade secret disclosure and breach of contract, where the opinion privilege would not apply.

But as of early 2000, John Doe defendants did not have any certain legal defenses against these unmasking attempts. Although Gray had recently begun making this argument in court, no binding legal precedent applied *McIntyre*'s protections to subpoenas arising from online speech. "Existing First Amendment doctrine currently provides defendants no protection from having their anonymity stripped away once a libel action is filed, although one might argue that the First Amendment right to speak anonymously should be extended to provide such protection," Lidsky wrote.[69]

In a 2001 article, Shaun B. Spencer focused on the lack of process that existing laws provide to subpoena targets. "Under existing procedures, John Doe sometimes receives no notice, and when he does, he may lack the time or money to retain counsel to challenge the subpoena," Spencer wrote. "Although some message board hosts and ISPs provide one or two weeks' notice, they are not required to give any notice and not all do."[70] Spencer proposed an amendment to the Electronic Communications Privacy Act that would require ISPs to notify subpoena targets at least thirty days in advance, and allow them to contest the subpoena in court.[71]

Spencer's proposal—which Congress has not adopted twenty years later—made a good deal of sense; rather than relying on the off-chance that a poster might read about a lawsuit in the news, it would provide the poster with a meaningful chance to contest the subpoena's legality. Plaintiffs in the late 1990s had carte blanche to subpoena identifying information because they largely managed to obtain the information without alerting the targets. Likewise, in 2000, Bruce P. Smith wrote of the lack of clarity for protecting anonymity from John Doe subpoenas.[72] Unlike newspapers and television stations, which used their substantial resources and libel insurance policies to fight First Amendment battles for decades, John Doe defendants typically had a harder time financing their defense, Smith observed.[73]

Lawyers for anonymous posters and civil liberty groups faced years of heavy lifting to create a workable legal standard that protects online anonymity. The path would be long and uncertain. And it would begin in an unlikely place: a candy store.

7

SETTING THE RULES FOR
ONLINE ANONYMITY

The legal standards for anonymity on the Internet began not with an inflammatory Yahoo! Finance post, but in a quotidian intellectual property
dispute. Judge D. Lowell Jensen was not the most likely candidate to serve
as the trailblazer for online anonymity protections. Jensen served as the
Alameda County, California, district attorney from 1969 to 1981, where
he prosecuted high-profile defendants, including Patty Hearst's kidnap-
pers.[1] "Lowell is a gentleman of the old standard," James Jenner, Alameda County's chief public defender, told the *New York Times* in a 1986
profile of Jensen.[2] He moved east to work in Ronald Reagan's administration, where he rose to be the deputy attorney general, second in command
of the Justice Department. Reagan appointed him to the northern California federal court in 1986.[3]

More than a decade into his service as a federal judge, at age seventy-
one, Jensen presided over what at first appeared a rather unremarkable
case. On February 22, 1999, Columbia Insurance Company, which was
assigned the trademarks for the See's Candy Shops retail chain, sued the

owner of the seescandy.com domain name.[4] Seescandy.com allegedly sold candy via the website, using See's Candy's trademarks without the company's approval.[5]

Columbia alleged trademark infringement and related claims, arguing that the defendant harmed its business by operating under its trademarked name.[6] Columbia also sought a temporary restraining order to bar the defendant's use of seescandy.com and to order the defendant to pay damages for the infringement.

Columbia had a fairly straightforward case for trademark infringement, so granting the temporary restraining order seemed like a no-brainer. But Columbia had a problem: nobody knew for sure who operated the website. Throughout 1998 and 1999, the seescandy.com domain was registered to various names and addresses or post office boxes in California. The email addresses and phone numbers of the domain name operator also changed, at one point listing 408-555-1212, the number for directory information.[7] The host of the seescandy.com website also changed in 1999.[8] The complaint named as defendants Seescandy.com, four companies, and six people's names that had been somehow associated with seescandy.com's domain registration. But there was no way to verify who was behind seescandy.com based on those records.

In his March 8, 1999, opinion, Jensen wrote that he would not yet grant the temporary restraining order, as it would be "futile" because Columbia "has not been able to collect the information necessary to serve the complaint on defendants."[9] Federal civil procedure rules typically require plaintiffs to identify and serve defendants with complaints. In "rare" circumstances, Jensen wrote, courts can allow a plaintiff to sue, and then use the discovery process to identify the defendants.[10] Although many judges in 1999 and 2000 did not hesitate to allow this sort of discovery in cyber-smear cases such as the one filed by Raytheon, Judge Jensen determined that such discovery was reserved for extraordinary circumstances.

Jensen noted the increase in Internet-related litigation involving not only trademark infringement, but also defamation, and observed that plaintiffs often have "little or no hope" of identifying the defendants. He recognized that in these types of cases, courts may need to help the plaintiffs identify those who are causing harm. "However, this need must be balanced against the legitimate and valuable right to participate in online forums anonymously or pseudonymously," Jensen wrote. "People are permitted to interact pseudonymously and anonymously with each other so long as those acts are not in violation of the law. This ability to speak one's mind without the burden of the other party knowing all the facts about one's identity can foster open communication and robust debate."[11]

Online anonymity, Jensen wrote, also can prevent people from embarrassment when they seek sensitive information on the Internet. "People who have committed no wrong should be able to participate online without fear that someone who wishes to harass or embarrass them can file a frivolous lawsuit and thereby gain the power of the court's order to discover their identity," he wrote.[12]

To balance these concerns with the plaintiffs' need to fight online harms, Jensen developed four factors for a court to consider before allowing early discovery in Internet disputes. First, the plaintiff must "identify the missing party with sufficient specificity such that the Court can determine that defendant is a real person or entity who could be sued in federal court."[13] Second, the plaintiff "should identify all previous steps taken to locate the elusive defendant."[14] Third, the plaintiff must convince the court that the lawsuit would overcome a motion to dismiss (meaning that the plaintiff has a viable legal claim). To meet this bar, Jensen wrote, "plaintiff must make some showing that an act giving rise to civil liability actually occurred and that the discovery is aimed at revealing specific identifying features of the person or entity who committed" the act that triggers that liability.[15] This requires at least some evidence to support the claim. Jensen likened this to the requirement, in criminal investigations, that the government demonstrate probable cause.

Jensen appeared to conclude that Columbia had satisfied these three prongs, but he added a fourth prong to the test: he ordered the company to file a specific request to him, specifically outlining and justifying the discovery that it planned to conduct.[16] Eleven days after he issued his order, Columbia's counsel sent a letter to Jensen forgoing more discovery. They had identified a defendant, and the case settled (it is unclear from the case's record how Columbia identified him).

Although the *seescandy.com* case ended with a whimper, it was the first time that a federal court engaged in a substantive analysis of the concerns with unmasking people on the Internet. Jensen's opinion is particularly noteworthy because it was the judge—and not a civil liberties group or defense lawyer—who decided to make anonymity an issue in the case. The operator of seescandy.com had not hired a lawyer to make the case for anonymity protections. Rather than merely providing Columbia with sweeping discovery tools, Jensen carefully considered the anonymity implications.

Jensen did not explicitly rely on *NAACP v. Alabama, McIntyre v. Ohio Elections Commission*, or any of the other landmark Supreme Court anonymity opinions. Jensen did not even mention the First Amendment. But his pragmatic analysis about the impact of discovery reflects a deep concern about the First Amendment implications. And his analysis would shape how other judges would approach First Amendment challenges to John Doe subpoenas.

In the same month that Columbia sued the operator of seescandy.com, another company sued five anonymous America Online chatroom posters in an Indiana state court.[17] The company claimed that the defendants transmitted defamatory and confidential information, breaching fiduciary and contractual obligations.[18]

The company then went to state court in Virginia, where America Online was based, to issue subpoenas for the identities of subscribers to four America Online email addresses. America Online refused to produce the information, partly because the company had sued anonymously in the Indiana court.[19] Why should America Online help a company unmask its users when the company had the benefit of litigating the case anonymously? The company did not even fully quote the allegedly harmful chatroom posts in its public court filings.

America Online asked the Virginia court to quash the subpoena in October 1999. The anonymous company provided Judge Stanley P. Klein with a copy of the chatroom posts to review in his chambers, but the posts identifying the anonymous company were inaccessible to America Online or any members of the public.[20] America Online's motion was particularly remarkable because the challenge to the proposed unmasking was coming not from a John Doe defendant, but from the defendant's service provider. America Online was not legally required to advocate for its clients' anonymity, but it did so anyway.

Klein recalled to me that he spent a long time thinking about the issues in the case, and he recognized that there was little precedent to guide him. Klein realized that he needed to strike a delicate balance between the competing issues. "I don't think the First Amendment protections should be set aside very easily," Klein said. "On the other hand, it didn't mean the First Amendment protections are impenetrable."[21]

The plaintiff (which was identified in court filings as Anonymous Publicly Traded Company) argued to Judge Klein that only the John Doe defendants—and not America Online—had standing to challenge the subpoenas. In a January 31, 2000, opinion, Klein rejected this argument, pointing to the Supreme Court's 1958 ruling in *NAACP v. Alabama*, in which the Court allowed the NAACP to advocate for the anonymity of its members.[22] "It can not be seriously questioned that those who utilize the 'chat rooms' and 'message boards' of AOL do so with an expectation that the anonymity of their postings and communications generally will be protected," Klein wrote. "If AOL did not uphold the confidentiality of its subscribers, as it has contracted to do, absent extraordinary circumstances, one could reasonably predict that AOL subscribers would look to AOL's competitors for anonymity."[23]

AOL raised two objections to the subpoena: that it was unfair to allow the company to litigate anonymously, and that the subpoenas infringed AOL users' First Amendment rights. Klein declined to overturn the Indiana court's decision to allow the company to sue under a pseudonym.[24] But he concluded that the First Amendment applied to the subpoena dispute, pointing to *McIntyre, Talley*, and other landmark First Amendment cases. "Inherent in the panoply of protections afforded by the First Amendment is the right to speak anonymously in diverse contexts," Klein wrote. "This right arises from a long tradition of American advocates speaking anonymously through pseudonyms, such as James Madison, Alexander Hamilton, and John Jay, who authored the Federalist Papers but signed them only as 'Publius.'"[25]

Although state and federal courts had long recognized such anonymity rights in disputes surrounding antimask laws, pamphleteering, and so many other contexts, Klein's ruling marks the first published opinion on record in which a court explicitly applied the First Amendment's anonymity protections to a subpoena for online posters' identities.[26] "To fail to recognize that the First Amendment right to speak anonymously should be extended to communications on the Internet would require this Court to ignore either United States Supreme Court precedent or the realities of speech in the twenty-first century," Klein wrote.[27] Klein acknowledged

Jensen's ruling in *seescandy.com*, but noted that Jensen's ruling "focused solely on the procedural propriety of allowing discovery before service of process was effected."[28]

Even though Klein's analysis was rooted in the First Amendment, he declined to adopt America Online's proposed speech-protective approach, which would have required the plaintiff to make specific claims that, on their face, show that the company had a valid case, and that the identifying information was "centrally needed" to support that case.[29] Instead, Klein wrote, a court can require an Internet service provider to disclose identifying information: "(1) when the court is satisfied by the pleadings or evidence supplied to that court (2) that the party requesting the subpoena has a legitimate, good faith basis to contend that it may be the victim of conduct actionable in the jurisdiction where suit was filed and (3) the subpoenaed identity information is centrally needed to advance that claim."[30]

Klein's First Amendment test is perhaps less anonymity-protective than Jensen's *seescandy* framework. Jensen required the plaintiff to demonstrate that the case would survive a motion to dismiss. Although it is unclear exactly what (if any) evidentiary support Jensen would require, Klein's test merely requires the plaintiff to have a "legitimate, good faith basis" for a lawsuit and to ensure that the judge is "satisfied by the pleadings or evidence" that the plaintiff has supplied. Klein's framework also does not require the plaintiff to describe the steps taken to try to locate the anonymous poster.

"I felt under the circumstances of this case that this was the best way to protect First Amendment rights and to protect parties from being defamed or breaches of fiduciary duty," Klein said in 2020. "I didn't think that I was writing something everyone had to agree with." After reciting his test, Klein concluded that the plaintiffs had met the three prongs.[31]

America Online appealed Klein's ruling to the Virginia Supreme Court, focusing on the unfairness of allowing an anonymous plaintiff to use the courts to unmask defendants. The company, APTC, had argued that anonymity was necessary to prevent harm to its business. APTC's "conclusory" justification was insufficient for the Virginia Supreme Court, which noted that the company failed to present evidence to support its argument for anonymity. The Virginia Supreme Court reversed Judge Klein.

Although America Online did not have to provide the subscribers' identities, the Virginia Supreme Court did not overrule Klein's First Amendment analysis of the subpoena. His ruling was the first published opinion to consider the First Amendment implications of a John Doe subpoena. A Virginia trial court judge's opinion was not binding on any other courts. But with no higher court rulings on the issue, other judges might have no choice but to adopt Klein's framework.

Among the lawyers closely watching the earliest online poster decisions was Paul Levy. Levy is a lawyer at Public Citizen, a consumer advocacy group that Ralph Nader founded in 1971. Levy had worked for the group since 1977, focusing on union members' rights. Levy first became involved in online speech issues at the turn of the century, when he helped represent two union-member flight attendants who operated a flight attendant website that Northwest Airlines accused of advocating a sick-out on New Year's Eve of 1999. Northwest sued, and the federal magistrate judge allowed the company to seize the flight attendants' hard drives. Northwest also sought information to identify posters to the website's bulletin board (though that likely was unnecessary, as the website publicly listed posters' IP addresses.)[32]

The Northwest case fizzled out when the company dropped the lawsuit, but it helped Levy build a reputation as an advocate for online speech. He became involved in other anonymous poster cases, and worked on an ad hoc task force of free speech advocates to address John Doe subpoenas. Levy and the other free speech advocates knew that they needed to convince a higher court to create a strong First Amendment precedent that would protect anonymity. Logistically, this goal was difficult. Because many John Doe defendants were unaware that they were even the subject of subpoenas, they could not bring a challenge in court. And even if the civil liberties advocates identified a worthy case, they risked appearing before a judge who was not sympathetic to First Amendment anonymity arguments.

Levy needed the perfect case. And he found it in New Jersey.

TheStreet.com was the Bible for investors in the hot stock market of the late 1990s. A tidbit of gossip or criticism on the website could jolt a company's stock, particularly when it reverberated across Yahoo! Finance.

"Does Dendrite Do Right With The Way It Handles Software Expenses?" read the headline on Herb Greenberg's September 3, 1999, column on TheStreet.com.

"Dendrite" was Dendrite International, a New Jersey–based producer of sales software for pharmaceutical and consumer products companies.[33] Its stock was publicly traded on NASDAQ, and not surprisingly, the company was the subject of a lively Yahoo! Finance discussion board.

"Never heard of Dendrite International?" Greenberg asked. "I hadn't either until a numbers-crunching source pointed it out and steered me in the direction of its accounting (in conjunction with its zooming stock price)." Among his observations was that the company had recently stated that it might begin to recognize revenue at the moment it delivered its products, rather than as customers installed and used the products, which "could mean more revenue up front."[34] Also in September 1999, the Center for Financial Research and Analysis released a report that concluded that Dendrite's change in revenue recognition increased the company's reported earnings and might have "masked weaknesses in the company's core segments."[35]

Although Dendrite publicly rebutted the reports that it changed its revenue recognition, posters on the company's Yahoo! Finance bulletin board seized on the news. Throughout the first half of 2000, a poster going by the name of "xxplrr" posted nine comments on the board, three of which focused on the company's revenue recognition practices. In one, he wrote that John Bailye, Dendrite's chief executive, "got his contracts salted away to buy another year of earnings—and note how they're changing revenue recognition accounting to help it." In another post, xxplrr wrote that "Bailye has his established contracts structured to provide a nice escalation in revenue. And then he's been changing his revenue-recognition accounting to further boost his earnings (see about 100 posts back)." The poster also wrote that the company "signed multi-year deals with built in escalation in their revenue year-over-year (pharma cares most about total price of the contract, so they don't care; nor do they care if the price is in software or services). They also have been able to restructure their contracts with Pfizer and Lilly the same way."[36]

The pseudonymous poster also asserted that Dendrite was seeking another company to acquire it. "[Dendrite] simply does not appear to be competitively moving forward . . . John [Bailye, Dendrite's CEO] knows it and is shopping hard. But Siebel and SAP already have turned him down. Hope Oracle does want in bad (and that's what they'll get). But it doesn't help job prospects in Morristown any does it?"[37] This upset Dendrite, which said at the time it was not looking to sell the company.[38]

The posts did not offer any hints as to the identity of xxplrr, but one could infer that the poster was interested in promoting a decline in the company's share price. "If you got in at 15, today you're a happy camper and smart for having recognized the unnatural dip. . . . But at 22, do you feel lucky?" xxplrr asked. In another post, xxplrr argued that "the analysts have caught on to the lack of prospects here. That's why the stock has plunged and no short term tweaking is going to help, much." In yet another post, he wrote that analyst reports about Dendrite "are just trying to cover their positions from having backed the stock when it was in the 30's. That 'all those declines make this a great buy' line is one of the oldest games; it fails to generate much juice when the basics of the business have changed."[39]

Although it was unclear who xxplrr was, the poster at least suggested he worked for a company within Dendrite's sector, writing that he had two reasons to care about Dendrite's share prices: "first, one can make money at this stock, but information helps; [another poster's] response to my last posting helped fill in a missing gap for me—so i [sic] got something tangible out of it; second, the spin on the stock is so out of control when reality hits its [sic] going to taint the whole sector, my firm included."[40]

Or was he a Dendrite employee? In at least one post, he hinted that he had access to nonpublic information about the company that is "not the stuff you'll find in 10-K's, or even reports from analysts, who aren't close enough to the market. . . . Read the 10-K's and Q's all you'd like, its [sic] good homework. But they can't tell you what's going to happen—and this is such an esoteric segment the analysts can't track it well."[41]

Dendrite was paying attention to the Yahoo! Finance bulletin board, as it believed that some comments were at least correlated with stock price declines. For example, after xxplrr posted a message on March 28, 2000, Dendrite shares fell 3 percent.[42]

On May 24, 2000, Dendrite sued xxplrr in New Jersey state court, alleging defamation and misappropriation of trade secrets.[43] The suit also included claims against three other Yahoo! Finance pseudonymous posters: implementor_extrodinaire, ajcazz, and gacbar.[44] The claims against each of the four defendants varied; for instance, implementor_extro-dinaire and ajcazz had indicated in their postings that they were current or former Dendrite employees, causing Dendrite to sue them for breaching a contractual prohibition on disclosing confidential or proprietary informa-tion.[45] The complaint listed the defendants as John Doe Nos. 1–4; xxplrr was named John Doe No. 3.

Soon after suing, Dendrite asked Judge Kenneth C. MacKenzie to allow it to conduct discovery against Yahoo! to identify the four defen-dants. Rather than reflexively approving the discovery request—as so many judges had been doing for the past few years—MacKenzie ordered that a notice of the potential discovery be posted on Dendrite's Yahoo! bulletin board, allowing the defendants to object to Yahoo! disclosing their identities.[46]

Lawyers for two of the four defendants—xxplrr and gacbar—challenged the discovery, while the other two did not respond.[47] xxplrr retained a lawyer from a small New Jersey firm. But MacKenzie's required bulletin board posting caught the attention of someone else: Paul Levy of Public Citizen.

Levy recalls that he learned of the bulletin board posting from another member of the ad hoc working group on John Doe subpoenas. He im-mediately saw the Dendrite dispute as an ideal case for creating strong precedent for anonymous online speech. Most important, Levy noted that MacKenzie went out of his way to attempt to notify the defendants *before* deciding whether to unmask them. "When I saw the notice, my immedi-ate reaction was, 'This is a judge who gets it,'" Levy said. "'This is a case where we ought to focus our efforts.'"[48]

Levy filed an amicus brief in July 2000, asking MacKenzie to deny Dendrite's discovery request. Levy urged MacKenzie to consider whether Dendrite had viable legal claims against the poster. Many Yahoo! bulletin boards, Levy wrote, are understood as expressing opinions rather than factual assertions. "The notion that most members of the public would treat the average message board posting as a reliable statement of fact on which to base major investment decisions is almost laughable; that is certainly true of the repartee in which many of the posters on the Dendrite message boards tend to be engaged," Levy wrote.[49]

Later that month, MacKenzie held oral arguments and heard from the lawyers for Dendrite and the posters, as well as Levy.[50] Levy said he left the hearing with a positive feeling. "The judge was engaged," Levy recalled. "He saw an opportunity to do something interesting."[51]

Levy's instincts were right. Four months later, MacKenzie issued a twenty-two-page, single-spaced opinion, allowing Dendrite to uncover the identities of implementor_extrodinaire and ajcazz (who claimed to have worked for Dendrite and did not oppose discovery), but quashing the subpoenas for identifying information about xxplrr and gacbar.

MacKenzie followed the *seescandy* framework, and much of his analysis focused on whether Dendrite's claim could survive a motion to dismiss. Dendrite's defamation claim against xxplrr could not survive a motion to dismiss, MacKenzie ruled, because Dendrite did not adequately demonstrate that all of xxplrr's statements were false, nor did the company show that it suffered harm due to the postings.[52] MacKenzie wrote that he was "unwilling to acknowledge any nexus between the posting of allegedly defamatory messages on the internet and a drop in stock prices."[53]

Although MacKenzie applied the *seescandy* analysis, he also made some broader statements about the importance of applying the First Amendment to the Internet. The two posters, he wrote, "were utilizing the soapbox that the internet provides in order to express their personal opinion."[54] MacKenzie also concluded that the misappropriation claim against both posters was not strong enough to survive a motion to dismiss because the company did not provide evidence that the information they posted constituted trade secrets.[55]

Dendrite appealed the denial of xxplrr's identifying information to the Appellate Division, New Jersey's intermediate appellate court.[56] Another judge could have faithfully applied the *seescandy* test and concluded that Dendrite's defamation claim would have survived a motion to dismiss. As Dendrite noted in its appellate brief, New Jersey plaintiffs need not prove their claims when fending off motions to dismiss; the court's job at that early stage is to determine whether the facts alleged in the plaintiff's complaint could constitute a viable legal claim.[57] But the New Jersey appellate court was not bound by the *seescandy* test, which was decided by a district court judge in California. The New Jersey court could create a different test—one that required evidence supporting the plaintiff's claim.

Levy recognized this opportunity and, in a fifty-six-page amicus brief that he wrote with the American Civil Liberties Union of New Jersey, he proposed a new test for courts to apply when deciding whether to un-mask anonymous online posters. Levy derived the test from landmark Supreme Court cases such as *McIntyre* and *Talley*, cases in which media defendants in libel cases are asked to reveal their anonymous sources, and some of the early online poster cases, including *seescandy*.[58] Levy argued that there is a qualified—rather than absolute—privilege to post anonymously online that "requires courts to review a would-be plaintiff's claims, and the evidence supporting them, to ensure that the plaintiff has a valid reason for piercing each poster's anonymity."[59] Levy then articulated a five-part test for courts to apply when determining whether to unmask an anonymous poster.

First, the plaintiffs should attempt to notify anonymous posters of the subpoenas, as MacKenzie required Dendrite to do.[60] Second, the plaintiff's complaint should specifically identify the anonymous poster's statements that led to the lawsuit. Dendrite satisfied this requirement, Levy wrote, but many plaintiffs do not, and "instead, they may quote one or two messages by a few individuals, and then demand production of a larger number of identities."[61] Third, the judge should examine the statements to determine whether they give rise to a viable legal claim.[62] For instance, if a post is clearly an opinion rather than a factual assertion, it cannot be defamatory.

The fourth element of Levy's proposed test clarified some uncertainty in MacKenzie's opinion: Levy explicitly proposed requiring the plaintiff to produce some evidence to support the legal claim.[63] In a footnote, Levy acknowledged that MacKenzie's opinion was "somewhat inconsistent" as to whether evidence is required for an anonymous poster subpoena, but Levy wrote that requiring evidence is the right approach to protect First Amendment values.

So far, Levy's proposal was not drastically different from the framework that MacKenzie applied. But Levy and his colleagues proposed a fifth prong of the analysis, in which the court weighs the need for unmasking against the need for confidentiality, otherwise known as "balancing the equities."[64] This test, Levy wrote, could prevent lawsuits that are filed merely to identify and punish an employee.[65] The balancing test that he proposed was derived partly from "reporter's privilege" cases in which courts decided whether to require journalists to reveal their anonymous sources. At the federal level, the qualified reporter's privilege is grounded in the First Amendment or common law. At the state level, most state legislatures have passed statutes known as shield laws. Although the court rulings and statutes vary in terms of their strength of protection, they generally provide reporters with a limited—rather than absolute—ability to prevent the compelled disclosure of their anonymous sources. Courts use various balancing tests to determine whether the need for the reporter's testimony outweighs the harm to freedom of the press.

Some of the other free speech advocates, Levy acknowledged, were not as enthusiastic about the balancing approach, and hoped for a more absolute proposal. But Levy did not want to argue for an absolute bar against unmasking. Levy—whose group has long represented consumers who battle large corporations—recognized that there also may be cases in which plaintiffs were seriously harmed and had compelling reasons to identify defendants.

Levy thinks that the New Jersey court appreciated his position and viewed him as a neutral expert who could guide the judges in developing a framework. "They were plainly looking at me as somebody who wasn't representing an interest in the case who cared about the law, who cared about standards, who cared about the interests of both sides," Levy said.

Indeed they did. At the start of its unanimous opinion on July 11, 2001, the three-judge panel adopted a test that was remarkably similar to Levy's proposal, including an evidentiary evaluation.[66] (The court phrased this prong as requiring the plaintiff to "produce sufficient evidence supporting each element of its cause of action, on a prima facie basis, prior to a court ordering the disclosure of the identity of the unnamed defendant.")[67] Perhaps most notably, the court adopted Levy's suggestion for a balancing test, in which the court "must balance the defendant's First Amendment right of anonymous free speech against the strength of the prima facie case presented and the necessity for the disclosure of the anonymous defendant's identity to allow the plaintiff to properly proceed."[68]

The judges affirmed MacKenzie's decision to quash the subpoena, agreeing that Dendrite had not shown that it was harmed by the comments. "The record does not support the conclusion that John Doe's postings negatively affected the value of Dendrite's stock, nor does Dendrite offer evidence or information that these postings have actually inhibited its hiring practices, as it alleged they would," the judges wrote.[69]

Perhaps because the ruling came from an appellate court, the "*Dendrite* test" soon became a predominant framework for assessing John

Doe subpoenas, with many state and federal courts around the nation either directly following the test or using it to develop their own modified frameworks.[70] For instance, in 2009, the Court of Appeals of Maryland concluded that the *Dendrite* test "most appropriately balances a speaker's constitutional right to anonymous Internet speech with a plaintiff's right to seek judicial redress from defamatory remarks."[71]

Dendrite's equities balancing test—the final prong—is particularly attractive to judges, as Levy anticipated. As Nathaniel Gleicher observed in a 2008 *Yale Law Journal* note, this prong "provided flexibility to judges faced with a landscape of rapidly evolving technology and law, and gave them an avenue to consider concerns that were outside the scope of earlier standards, such as the potential for the defendant to be harmed if his identity were revealed."[72]

Michael Vogel, who represented Dendrite before the trial and appellate courts, said in an interview with me that he appreciated Levy's nuanced proposal, even though Vogel advocated for a less stringent standard. "I think he was successful because he took seriously what my clients were arguing in terms of the importance of their claims," Vogel said. "And I took seriously what his clients were arguing in terms of the importance of the anonymity and First Amendment interests."[73]

Still, Vogel believes that the court's balancing test creates tremendous uncertainty for plaintiffs, even if they have legitimate claims supported by evidence. "This is an exceedingly broad level of authority to grant to a single, trial-level judge, and is inconsistent with the spirit of such rights as due process and the right to trial by jury that generally animate judicial decision-making at the pre-trial stage," Vogel wrote in a 2004 *Oregon Law Review* article.[74]

Vogel's critique of *Dendrite* highlights a broader tension that has pervaded anonymity disputes for decades: the trade-offs between speakers' need for anonymity against the harms that the anonymity causes to others. In 1960, Los Angeles officials could not convince the Supreme Court that their need for the names of pamphleteers was so great that it outweighed the harms that Manuel Talley might have faced while organizing boycotts in the civil rights era. On the other hand, New York officials persuaded the Second Circuit that the city's interest in promoting safety outweighed the Ku Klux Klan's need for masking their own identities during rallies.

At bottom, much of First Amendment anonymity law balances the benefits against the harms of anonymity. The *Dendrite* framework—particularly the final factor—reflects this approach by giving judges flexibility to consider the social consequences of allowing or prohibiting anonymity. But some litigants—and judges—demand more certainty about whether a speaker can remain anonymous and whether a plaintiff can recover for harm. A few years after the New Jersey court's landmark ruling against Dendrite, a court to the south would chart another way to deal with John Doe subpoenas.

The town of Smyrna sits on Duck Creek in north-central Delaware. The town was founded in the early 1700s as the village of Salisbury, and its economy at first focused on shipbuilding and shipping food and fertilizer. In 1806, the state of Delaware renamed the town Smyrna, likely after the ancient Aegean port.[75] As its economy modernized, the population grew, reaching about six thousand people. As with so many small towns, its politics were heated and colorful.

Smyrna resident Patrick Cahill in 2003 received a municipal citation for abandoned property because a thirty-foot sailboat was in his yard; he said he was fixing it. After Cahill won an appeal of the citation, the town council unsuccessfully tried to pass an ordinance defining immovable boats as "solid waste." This caused Cahill to successfully run for the town council the next year.[76]

Cahill butted heads with Smyrna's mayor, Mark Schaeffer, who also was his next-door neighbor. In September 2004, when Cahill's wife, Julia, was changing in their upstairs bedroom, she said she looked out the window to see a camera pointed toward her. The Cahills called the police, which investigated and found no evidence that the camera was operational or pointed at the Cahills' bedroom.[77]

On September 17, 2004, the *News Journal* newspaper in Wilmington, Delaware, wrote about the dispute. Schaeffer's attorney told the newspaper that Cahill's claims were "ridiculous" and said that it was a motion-activated security camera that could not zoom into a neighbor's property. Patrick Cahill alleged to the newspaper that Schaeffer operated not a security camera, but a surveillance camera. "This camera is clearly pointed at my property, not at all at his property, and that makes it very obvious to me that he's simply recording everyone who comes in and out of my house," he said.[78]

Not surprisingly, this story had already been the subject of discussion on the "Smyrna/Clayton Issues Blog," a graphics-free website operated by the company that owns the *Delaware State News*. The blog allowed community members to post comments about local issues, either with their real names or with pseudonyms. The blog was a long string of comments, with the most recent comment at the top.[79]

On September 15, 2004, a poster by the name of "Stymied" wrote: "I hear schaeffer put up a surveillance camera to watch cahills [*sic*] house. It looks right into their bedroom, isn't that illegal? Is this just another stab at intimidating and harassing that poor man and his wife? HE HAS GOT TO GO. He runs out all his neighbors, and anyone who goes against him. I'm sure the police will do nothign [*sic*] about it again."

The next comment that day came from a poster identifying himself as Pat Cahill, noting that this was the first time he had posted on the blog. He wrote that Schaeffer had been surveilling his home. "He has installed a camera high up on his garage wall that as of yesterday was pointed directly at an [*sic*] second floor bedroom window."

Some pseudonymous posters supported Cahill. "That mayor has gone too far," a poster named "Angela" wrote on September 17, the day that the newspaper article was published. "Harassing and intimidating a council member, what does that mean he does to regular people?"

But not all the comments were positive. The day after the article, a poster named "Proud Citizen" wrote:

> If only Councilman Cahill was able to display the same leadership skills, energy and enthusiasm toward the revitalization and growth of the fine town of Smyrna as Mayor Schaeffer has demonstrated! While Mayor Schaeffer has made great strides toward improving the livelihood of Smyrna's citizens, Cahill has devoted all of his energy to being a divisive impediment to any kind of cooperative movement. Anyone who has spent any amount of time with Cahill would be keenly aware of such character flaws, not to mention an obvious mental deterioration. Cahill is a prime example of failed leadership— his eventual ousting is exactly what Smyrna needs in order to move forward and establish a community that is able to thrive on economic stability and a common pride in its town.

Those with disparaging remarks regarding the Mayor are either misinformed, uneducated on the truth, or simply cannot stand the fact that he has been successful in his role as a leader, humanitarian, and goal achiever.

"Resident" responded later that day: "Who are you trying to kid!" Resident wrote, in part,

The Town of Smyrna is growing to [*sic*] fast thanks to the Mayor and his yes people. Cahill is the only one on Council that has any since [*sic*]. He is doing what he was elected to do. But the Mayor cannot stand any one that is not his yes man. Cahill is his own person. That is why the Mayor has been harrassing [*sic*] the Cahills for the last 2 years. When you try to have someone fired from their job, peep in their windows, send a member of their family to walk through and about their yard just to harrass [*sic*] them.

Proud Citizen responded:

I'm not trying to kid anyone. "Resident Without Since" has a distorted perception of reality and ought to attend a few council meetings to get their facts straight.

Peeping in windows? Surely you jest. Per the paper, Cahill's wife was "getting dressed in the upstairs bedroom when she looked down to see a camera pointed at her." Well . . . this is exactly the point in time where one would not want to capture a moment on tape.

This prompted a reply from the poster who identified himself as Pat Cahill, implying he knew who "Proud Citizen" was: "Well, you give a rat enough time it will eventually come out of it's [*sic*] hole where you can see it in the light of day," he wrote. "You just gave yourself away with your vicious comment toward my wife. So why don't you turn your video camera around 180 deegrees [*sic*] and take a good look at yourself. Then maybe you'll see what the rest of Smyrna sees."

No response. The user calling himself "Pat Cahill" wrote another post, including his phone number. "Folks, I'll have to finish my comments about the video monitor at another time," he wrote.

Proud Citizen then responded that day: "Gahill [*sic*] is as paranoid as everyone in town thinks he is. The mayor needs support from his citizens and protection from unfounded attacks. A call to his constituents: make your voice heard on this blog!"

That was the last post by "Proud Citizen" on the Smyrna blog. But the invectives continued from other anti-Cahill accounts.[80] At the height of the personal attacks on October 1, a poster who apparently is the moderator of the forum (identified as "MODERATOR") reminded the posters that "most Blogs like this track posts by IP address, which is a unique network address that can be tracked down to the exact workstation where the comments are being made from. So think twice, before going off the deep-end again."

A month later, the Cahills sued four posters—including Proud Citizen—for defamation and invasion of privacy in Delaware state court.[81] Less than a month later, Judge Joseph R. Slights III approved the Cahills' request to use the discovery process to obtain the four posters' IP addresses from the newspaper's parent company, which operated the blog. The Cahills then issued subpoenas to Comcast, the Internet service provider for the four posters, seeking their identifying information. Federal law requires cable companies such as Comcast to notify its customers of such subpoenas before providing the information.[82]

Proud Citizen retained a lawyer, who asked Judge Slights to block Comcast from providing the Cahills with identifying information. In an emergency motion, Proud Citizen's lawyer urged the judge to apply the *Dendrite* test and prevent the unmasking. Cahill is a public figure and cannot prove actual malice, Proud Citizen's lawyer wrote. He also argued that his client's First Amendment rights outweigh the Cahills' need to obtain the identifying information.[83]

In an interview for this book, Slights recalled that this was new territory for him; he had never before dealt with a discovery dispute involving an online service. He also recognized that the lawsuit was in the very early stages, and discovery rulings at that point typically favored the plaintiffs. "In the discovery context we're just trying to determine whether the parties seeking the discovery have some reasonable grounds for it," said Slights, now a vice chancellor of the Delaware Court of Chancery. "There is some presumption to allow reasonable discovery. It's different from assessing whether someone has stated a viable claim."[84]

In a June 16, 2005, opinion, Slights wrote that the *Dendrite* test "goes further than is necessary to protect the anonymous speaker and, by doing so, unfairly limits access to the civil justice system as a means to redress the harm to reputation caused by defamatory speech."[85] The test, he wrote, delegates to the plaintiff the "nearly impossible task of demonstrating as a matter of law that a publication is defamatory before he serves his complaint or even knows the identity of the defendant(s)."[86]

Slights instead adopted the "less burdensome" framework from the *America Online* case in Virginia, requiring a "good faith" basis for the claim, and a demonstration that unmasking the defendant is "centrally needed" for the lawsuit. Applying this test, Slights approved the Cahills' subpoena to Comcast. "Given that Mr. Cahill is a married man, [Proud Citizen's] statement referring to Mr. Cahill as "Gahill" might reasonably be interpreted as indicating that Mr. Cahill has engaged in an extramarital same-sex affair," Slights wrote. "Such a statement may form the basis of an actionable defamation claim."[87]

Slights told me that the comments seemed egregious enough that the Cahills should be able to litigate the case. "I wasn't judging the merits of the claim," Slights said. "It just struck me that there was enough there to let the case go forward. The good faith standard lets you get to that place."

Proud Citizen appealed to the Delaware Supreme Court. No other state supreme court had articulated a standard for unmasking anonymous online posters, so this case was particularly important. Levy of Public Citizen filed an amicus brief, encouraging the court to adopt the *Dendrite* test. Levy argued that the test is fair and provides courts with flexibility needed to balance competing interests.[88]

In a unanimous decision, the Delaware Supreme Court reversed Slights' ruling. The justices relied heavily on the US Supreme Court's anonymity precedent, and concluded that it applies to the Internet. "Anonymous internet speech in blogs or chat rooms in some instances can become the modern equivalent of political pamphleteering," they wrote.[89] But the justices did not take Levy's advice and apply the complete *Dendrite* framework. Instead, they created a new test for anonymous poster subpoenas that included some—but not all—of *Dendrite*'s protections. The court agreed that "to the extent reasonably practicable under the circumstances," a plaintiff seeking identifying information "must undertake efforts to notify the anonymous poster that he is the subject of a subpoena or application for order of disclosure." The court also largely agreed with requiring the plaintiff to present evidence supporting the lawsuit, though the Delaware justices framed it as "facts sufficient to defeat a summary judgment motion."[90] Under this standard, the justices reasoned, "scrutiny is likely to reveal a silly or trivial claim, but a plaintiff with a legitimate claim should be able to obtain the identity of an anonymous defendant and proceed with his lawsuit."[91]

The Delaware justices did not adopt the *Dendrite* requirement to specify the defamatory statements, as they believe that already is required by their summary judgment standard. More notably, the justices believed that *Dendrite*'s balancing test "adds no protection above and beyond that of the summary judgment test and needlessly complicates the analysis."[92] Applying this new standard, the justices denied the subpoena because "no reasonable person could have interpreted these statements as being anything other than opinion."[93]

The Cahills' defamation lawsuit proceeded, and the next year Mayor Schaeffer said that his adult stepdaughter had written some of the posts at issue in the lawsuit (though it is unclear from the media coverage which of the posts she had written).[94] The Cahills said that a computer expert had traced some of the posts to the mayor's home. In 2006, the Cahills' attorneys confirmed that the case settled.[95]

Fifteen years after the Delaware Supreme Court reversed him, Slights believes that the court probably struck the right balance in setting a higher standard. But there are trade-offs, he said. "The practical reality of that is that it does make prosecuting a defamation case against an anonymous speaker extraordinarily difficult," he said.[96]

The dispute between the Cahills and their online antagonists produced an alternative framework judges can use to evaluate anonymous poster subpoenas. Since 2005, courts confronting these subpoenas often apply *Dendrite*, *Cahill*, or modifications of the two tests.

Which test is more protective of anonymity? Although the Delaware Supreme Court's opinion suggested that the *Dendrite* balancing test was unnecessary, Levy believes that *Dendrite* provides another level of protection for anonymous defendants. "The Doe defendants are more likely to prevail if they can throw in another argument for balancing," Levy said.

Yet Jane Kirtley in 2010 observed that judges nationwide have inconsistently interpreted *Cahill*. "Courts have variously interpreted the standard as more burdensome, or less burdensome, than *Dendrite*," she wrote.[97] Even under *Cahill*, the plaintiff must introduce enough evidence to overcome a summary judgment motion—a particularly difficult task for a plaintiff who has been unable to gather evidence through the discovery process.

Regardless of whether a court is applying *Dendrite* or *Cahill*, the plaintiff has a heavy lift. Just as the plaintiffs in both *Dendrite* and *Cahill* failed to convince the court to unmask anonymous posters, plaintiffs in more recent cases that applied versions of those tests have often seen their subpoenas quashed.[98]

The frequency of courts' denial of unmasking suggests that the *Dendrite* and *Cahill* precedents have generally been effective in protecting online anonymity. There are outliers in which the standards for anonymity have dipped below those applied in *Dendrite* and *Cahill*. In a business dispute between companies, a Nevada federal district court applied the *Cahill* test to the plaintiff's attempts to discover the identities of anonymous posters. In a 2011 opinion, the US Court of Appeals for the Ninth Circuit suggested that this test might have been too rigorous for a business dispute. Unlike *Cahill*, the court wrote, "this case does not involve expressly political speech."[99] The Ninth Circuit's opinion suggests that the type of speech should dictate the level of First Amendment anonymity protections.

Generally, though, when courts have applied First Amendment anonymity standards and ordered unmasking, the plaintiffs' cases often are compelling. For instance, in 2008, a federal district court judge allowed two Yale Law School students to subpoena the identifying information of a defendant in a case arising from a campaign of persistent harassment that they experienced on AutoAdmit, a law school–related discussion website. Among the posts, which included the plaintiffs' real names, were that a poster "hope[s] she gets raped and dies," and allegations that the plaintiff had abused heroin, had sexually transmitted diseases, and had rape fantasies.[100] One poster, identified as "AK47," posted a message about one of the plaintiffs, known as Jane Doe II, that falsely asserted: "Alex Atkind, Stephen Reynolds, [Doe II], and me: GAY LOVERS." Despite repeated complaints from both plaintiffs, AutoAdmit's administrator refused to delete any of the threads.

The behavior on AutoAdmit reveals some of the worst effects of online anonymity: writing horrific posts can upend someone's life. At least some of these posters were current or aspiring law students. It is hard to imagine that any of them would post rape threats and vile lies about these women if the posters' names were attached to the comments. If they were publicly associated with these comments, their own careers likely would never get off the ground. The anonymity that AutoAdmit purported to provide them was a catalyst for this behavior.

The two law students sued thirty-nine pseudonymous posters for libel, invasion of privacy, infliction of emotional distress, and copyright violations. Less than two weeks after the lawsuit was filed, AK47 posted on AutoAdmit "Women named Jill and [Doe II] should be raped," and a week after that AK47 began a thread with the subject "Inflicting emotional distress on cheerful girls named [Doe II]."[101]

AutoAdmit did not maintain logs of IP addresses, which made discovery more difficult than the standard anonymous poster case, though users needed to provide an email address for registration.[102] The plaintiffs managed to uncover an AT&T IP address associated with AK47, and subpoenaed AT&T for the IP address subscriber's identifying information. AT&T notified AK47 of the subpoena and told him that it would produce the information unless he moved to quash before February 25, 2008. He filed a motion to quash on February 25, and AT&T provided his identifying information to the plaintiffs the next day.

The subpoena apparently frightened AK47. On February 25, the plaintiffs' lawyer received a five-page single-spaced letter from AK47, expressing "deepest regret for being associated with Autoadmit.com," but then launching into a rambling attack on the lawsuit. "I cannot and will not be dragged into this huge mess simply because I made an inane, non-threatening and certainly non-actionable comment on the site," AK47 wrote. The poster then threatened to create a website devoted to the litigation. "The website will detail all the allegations and allegedly harmful comments in the case, and will feature the actual names of [Doe II] and [Doe I] as well as information pertaining to why they are suing me, and so on," AK47 wrote. The poster threatened to send links to the site to students at Yale and other universities.[103]

The Does' lawyers were not intimidated by the threat. They wisely filed the letter with Judge Christopher Droney. In his opinion deciding the motion to quash, Droney noted AK47's letter, writing that "the ostensible purpose of such a website was to formulate his defense to this action, although he also admitted it would likely be harmful to the plaintiffs."[104]

Droney applied a modified version of the *Dendrite* test, and denied the motion to quash because Doe II presented sufficient evidence for a libel claim. The "GAY LOVERS" statement, Droney wrote, "is defamatory, because any discussion of Doe II's sexual behavior on the Internet tends to lower her reputation in the community, particular [*sic*] in the case of any potential employers who might search for her name online."

She also presented sufficient evidence of harm to her reputation, Droney wrote. "In her interviews with potential employers in the Fall of 2007, Doe II felt she needed to disclose that existence of this and other such comments on AutoAdmit and explain that she had been targeted by pseudonymous online posters," Droney wrote. "In addition, this statement has contributed to difficulties in Doe II's relationships with her family, friends, and classmates at Yale Law School."[105] Although he did not apply the final step of *Dendrite*'s analysis in detail, Droney ruled that "the balancing test of the plaintiff's interest in pursuing discovery in this case outweighs the defendant's First Amendment right to speak anonymously."

Droney's analysis was legally mechanical and well reasoned. But it is hard to ignore the pragmatic realities of the tragic circumstances of the case. The AutoAdmit case was quite different from many of the high-profile cybersmear cases. The plaintiffs were not publicly traded companies like Raytheon or Dendrite, nor were they public officials like Patrick Cahill. The plaintiffs were law students whose online reputations were devastated by a crowd of vile sociopaths. As Lyrissa Lidsky observed about the AutoAdmit case in 2009, "It bears emphasizing that the plaintiffs apparently became targets of abuse not because they ran a business, held public office, or sought to influence public affairs, but simply because of gender, intelligence, and appearance. Although their suit was clearly brought to silence their critics, there was relatively little danger of silencing discussion on matters of public concern."[106]

The success of the AutoAdmit plaintiffs—and the failure of Dendrite and the Cahills—shows that the courts have developed robust yet reasonable protections for online anonymity, providing judges with sufficient discretion to allow unmasking in strong cases that often involve particularly egregious behavior by the defendants. As Levy envisioned when he sought to persuade the courts to create a balancing test for anonymity, judges generally have wisely used their discretion to balance First Amendment rights against the harms that plaintiffs have suffered.

The mere prospect of unmaskings in strong cases, such as the one that occurred in the AutoAdmit lawsuit, likely has a deterrent effect against future harmful online behavior. "Being unmasked, or even the fear of being unmasked, may prompt some defendants to express contrition and remorse," Lidsky wrote.[107]

The system, however, is far from perfect. In some respects, the legal framework discourages plaintiffs from bringing even meritorious lawsuits against anonymous posters, as they face a particularly high burden to unmask the defendants. Lidsky correctly notes that such deterrent effect comes from "strategic use of litigation" and not libel law, which does not require websites such as AutoAdmit to take down the defamatory content.[108]

The practical realities of litigation make it difficult to rely on the perseverance of plaintiffs to bring lawsuits against malicious anonymous posters. The AutoAdmit plaintiffs were represented pro bono by renowned law professors and litigators. And even with that exceptional legal representation—which most plaintiffs lack—the AutoAdmit plaintiffs suffered further harassment after they sued.

In my research for this book, I found that few of the John Doe subpoena cases with published opinions involved individual plaintiffs such as those in *AutoAdmit*; plaintiffs seeking to unmask anonymous posters were more likely to be companies that were upset about criticism or gossip about their business performance. Large companies have more resources to litigate, and they also stand to lose less from bringing lawsuits against anonymous posters.

In her book, *Hate Crimes in Cyberspace*, Danielle Citron documented the harassment that the AutoAdmit plaintiffs faced for years after their lawsuit. Anonymous trolls tried to ruin their job prospects and even falsely accused the husband of one of the plaintiffs of plagiarizing a law review article. One of the plaintiffs eventually worked at the US Justice Department, and AutoAdmit users posted her email address and that of her supervisor. "As the law student told me, some of the harassment was frightening; some damaged her professional reputation; some was simply bothersome," Citron wrote.[109]

As Citron demonstrates, plaintiffs in some of the most meritorious cybersmear cases—such as *AutoAdmit*—face substantial harm merely by suing. And what do they have to gain? Lidsky observes that defamation lawsuits against anonymous posters—even when successful—often cannot repair the damage done to the plaintiff. Even if a defamation lawsuit results in a settlement with or verdict against a once-anonymous poster, the plaintiff's reputation may be irreparably harmed. The AutoAdmit plaintiffs, Lidsky wrote, "did not want every person who Googled their names to discover they had been the targets of young men's verbal abuse and sexual objectification. They wanted the ability to manage their own self-representations in the online environment."[110]

It is hard to address this concern without examining the role of Section 230 of the Communications Decency Act. As I documented in a 2019 book, *The Twenty-Six Words That Created the Internet*, by preventing platforms from being on the hook for multimillion-dollar judgments arising from user posts, Section 230 is responsible for the business models of Facebook, Twitter, YouTube, and so many of the dominant US platforms.

In fact, Section 230 has allowed a website to continue hosting material even if it has been adjudicated defamatory. In a 2018 case, *Hassell v. Bird*,[111] the plaintiff obtained a default judgment in a defamation lawsuit against the poster of a Yelp review. As part of the default judgment, the trial court ordered Yelp to remove the post. Yelp challenged the order up to the California Supreme Court. In a split decision, the plurality held that Section 230 blocked the takedown order. The court reasoned that such a removal order "can impose substantial burdens on an Internet intermediary," and in such a case "a seemingly straightforward removal order can generate substantial litigation over matters such as its validity or scope, or the manner in which it is implemented."[112]

While the plurality is correct that takedown orders burden speech, Section 230 is not an absolute bar on any lawsuit that might reduce online speech. Section 230 prevents platforms from being *treated as the publisher or speaker* of third-party content. In *Hassell*, the lawsuit was filed not against Yelp, but against the person who posted the allegedly defamatory review. The takedown order was issued to Yelp only after the trial court's defamation judgment. "Yelp has not been sued, and its only responsibility in light of the judgment and injunction against [the defendant] is to avoid violating that court order," the dissent asserted. "Section 230 does not extend protection to a provider or user who violates an injunction by instead promoting third party speech that has been deemed unlawful by a California court."[113]

Although both sides presented reasonable arguments, the plurality's broad interpretation of Section 230 may have stretched the statute a bit beyond its text and legislative history. And the practical impact of the ruling is that even if a court rules that a post is defamatory—and not protected by the First Amendment—a website could refuse a takedown order.

The confusion over this aspect of Section 230—and the resulting inequity—might warrant consideration of a modest amendment to Section 230 to clarify that it does not block an order to take down material that has been adjudicated to be defamatory. As I wrote in *Twenty-Six Words*, any amendments to Section 230 must be precise and carefully crafted, as even modest tweaks to the law could have significant impacts on online speech. This clarification would allow plaintiffs the ability to bring lawsuits against the most egregious anonymous posters and get the relief that they are most likely to want—removal of the content.

We do not want to create a system in which a platform is liable for content once it receives a complaint from the plaintiff that it is defamatory (this is effectively the system that was in place under the common law, before Congress passed Section 230 in 1996). That would create a chilling effect that would suppress far too much speech, as risk-averse platforms would sooner delete a post than litigate its veracity in court. With this change to Section 230, the takedown could only occur after a court, in a lawsuit between the subject of the post and the poster, ruled the post to be defamatory or otherwise illegal. The First Amendment would prevent companies from abusing this mechanism to take down critical material, as plaintiffs still would need to meet the high bar for proving defamation. But this change would at least provide plaintiffs with hope that their efforts to rehabilitate their reputations are not for naught.

Moreover, any changes to Section 230 that guarantee the removal of material pursuant to a court order must contain sufficient safeguards to ensure that orders are not falsified or obtained by false pretenses. This is not merely a theoretical concern. Eugene Volokh and Paul Levy have documented cases when people have falsified court orders to persuade companies to remove material or employed techniques to obtain court orders by collusion or falsified consent.[114] (Although Section 230 might

prevent hosting companies or other platforms from being required to remove material, many have adopted policies to voluntarily remove third-
party content that is the subject of such an order.)

Critics of such a change to Section 230 also might fear that plaintiffs
could abuse the process and file lawsuits even if anonymous posts are not
defamatory. Because it is unlikely that many anonymous posters would
appear in court to defend against the claims, the plaintiffs might seek default judgments even if they do not have viable defamation claims. This
concern is valid, and might be addressed by allowing the platforms to appear in court to contest attempts to obtain a court order, even if the poster
does not. Moreover, even in the case of default judgments, courts should
apply some scrutiny as to whether the complaint states a viable claim. And
every state and the federal government should enact "anti-SLAPP" laws
that discourage plaintiffs from filing meritless defamation claims.[115]

Even allowing such takedowns would not remove all disincentives to
victims of anonymous harassment. Although courts allow plaintiffs to file
their lawsuits anonymously in an "unusual case" when anonymity "is
necessary . . . to protect a person from harassment, injury, ridicule or personal embarrassment,"[116] they still might be identified in news reports or
online postings, drawing even more attention to the initial harmful posts.
The AutoAdmit plaintiffs filed their suits as Jane Doe I and Jane Doe II,
but that did not prevent even more posts from appearing on AutoAdmit,
using their real names.

By suing, plaintiffs run the risk of drawing more attention to the harmful content than it otherwise would have received. This is a version of the
"Streisand effect," a term that *Techdirt* editor Mike Masnick coined in
2005. It was inspired by Barbra Streisand's unsuccessful lawsuit against
a photographer who published a photograph of her home, leading to far
more attention to the photograph than if she had not sued.[117]

The AutoAdmit case highlights a second obstacle that creates a disin-
centive for plaintiffs to sue bad actors: in some of the worst cases, they
cannot be tracked down. The plaintiffs and their skilled litigation counsel
managed to identify some of the thirty-nine defendants,[118] but AutoAdmit's failure to log IP addresses certainly created a significant barrier to
unmasking.

Under Michael Froomkin's anonymity taxonomy described in chapter 6, AutoAdmit at least tried to operate under a system of untraceable

pseudonymity, by requiring posters to use a screenname but failing to log their IP addresses. One could argue that by requiring an email address at registration, AutoAdmit used traceable pseudonymity, though there was no guarantee that the email address was associated with the poster.

In a 2009 article, "Cyber Civil Rights," Danielle Citron proposed conditioning Section 230 protections on a standard of care for the platforms to exercise. That standard includes a requirement of traceable anonymity, or retaining logs of IP addresses. "This would allow posters to comment anonymously to the outside world but permit their identity to be traced in the event they engage in unlawful behavior," Citron wrote.[119] The proposal attempts to strike a balance. By providing platforms with a strong incentive to retain IP addresses, the traceable anonymity condition might increase the likelihood that plaintiffs could obtain the IP addresses through litigation and hold the defendants accountable.

Traceable anonymity might avoid some difficulties arising from AutoAdmit's failure to log IP addresses, though a site like AutoAdmit, which trafficked in scurrilous content, might make the strategic choice to continue not logging IP addresses and forgo Section 230 protections. (That strategy might soon lead to AutoAdmit being sued into oblivion.)

Some critics of the proposal might argue that the mere prospect of the platforms turning over IP addresses would chill anonymous speech. Froomkin wrote that Citron's traceable anonymity proposal is unconstitutional under the line of First Amendment anonymity cases starting with *Talley* and *McIntyre*. "At the very least, when wholesale bans on anonymous speech such as proposed in *Cyber Civil Rights* reach core First Amendment speech they are not allowed," Froomkin wrote.[120]

The strength of such objections to traceable anonymity depends on whether you view IP logging as a wholesale anonymity ban. In *Talley* and *McIntyre*, the authors were required to include their identities on their writings. Those laws undoubtedly were wholesale anonymity prohibitions. Conditioning Section 230 protections on maintaining IP logs surely makes it easier to unmask some posters, but it is not analogous to the complete anonymity bans in *Talley* and *McIntyre*. First, many online services routinely log IP addresses already, though this voluntary action is different from a law that encourages them to do so. Second, platforms still would have the option of not logging IP addresses and therefore not receiving Section 230 protections (though this probably would be an unattractive choice, leading to substantial potential liability). Third, even when the platforms log IP addresses, the plaintiff or government would need to use some sort of legal process, such as a subpoena, to obtain the IP address information. Those requests likely would be subject to the robust First Amendment protections of *Dendrite* or *Cahill*. Fourth, even with the IP address, the plaintiff or government often needs to use a second round of subpoenas or other legal process to obtain identifying information that matches the IP address to a user, allowing another avenue for legal challenges.

Froomkin raised a compelling point about the potential misuse of identifying data. "Dissidents around the world rely on US servers to get out their message," he wrote. "It's probably not a good idea to engineer our communications in a way that might tempt our government to cozy up to foreign bad guys by slipping them information about the dissidents (think Nixon or Kissinger) who after all don't have First Amendment rights here when based abroad."[121] Such concerns should not be minimized, and the risks of such abuses undoubtedly increase if platforms are pressured to maintain identifying information. But those potential abuses—and many others—already exist given the vast amount of identifying information that companies already voluntarily collect. To mitigate some of this risk, Congress should pass legislation that protects identifying information from unauthorized disclosure, as I describe in chapter 16. And any traceable anonymity provision should only encourage companies to retain IP addresses for a limited time.

In a 2013 article, Bryan H. Choi made another case for the ability to pierce anonymity protections in some cases. Choi wrote that abuses of online anonymity threaten the Internet's generativity, which Jonathan Zittrain has defined as "a system's capacity to produce unanticipated change through unfiltered contributions from broad and varied audiences." Anonymity, Choi wrote, allows abuses of generativity "to be committed with impunity."[122] The future of a generative Internet requires some restrictions on anonymity, Choi wrote. Choi suggested technical improvements to increase the likelihood of being able to identify the users of particular devices.

On the flipside, anonymity may aid generativity by providing a safe environment for people to experiment online in manners that they would avoid if their identities were linked to their words and actions.

The challenge in determining policies for anonymity and generativity is to encourage the next prolific Wikipedia editor who contributes to communal knowledge while allowing some recourse against the next horrific AutoAdmit-like troll. Traceable anonymity attempts to strike this balance, provided that the identifying information is protected by a sufficiently high legal standard, such as that set in *Dendrite* and *Cahill.*

Of course, traceable anonymity is not a panacea for plaintiffs. Malicious posters might use technological means such as VPNs or Tor (described in chapter 11), in which case the platform where the defendant posted the harmful content might not have an accurate IP address for the defendant. Or the defendant might use a public Wi-Fi connection, such as that in a coffee shop. The plaintiff might be able to obtain the coffee shop's identity, but it could be hard to trace the post back to the particular poster, depending on whether the coffee shop required posters to register before accessing the connection. Still, traceable anonymity might decrease the likelihood that litigation against a John Doe will result in a dead end, and therefore increase the likelihood that a plaintiff would take the risk of suing a bad actor.

Although commentators differ on some important policy details such as traceable anonymity, the courts have generally settled on a rigorous level of anonymity protection for subpoenas in civil actions such as defamation. Plaintiffs have a heavy lift to unmask anonymous online posters, but it is possible to do so if they have a compelling case and sufficient evidence. This is the appropriate balance, and it reflects the strong value of anonymous speech that courts had articulated decades before the modern Internet.

But the anonymity protections of *Dendrite* and *Cahill* are strongest in certain types of civil actions, such as defamation, and are weaker in other types of litigation. As I argue in the next two chapters, some courts have provided insufficient protection for anonymity in copyright lawsuits and criminal investigations and cases.

8

ONLINE ANONYMITY AND COPYRIGHT

At the turn of the century, the phrase "P2P" sent fear—and anger—through record companies' corporate headquarters. P2P, or peer-to-peer, allows users to share media files—including songs—with one another at no cost. The rapid growth of personal computer usage—and the faster speed of broadband connections—made P2P an attractive option for people who wanted to listen to music on their computers rather than on compact discs.

There was a problem—P2P services did not compensate record labels or artists for their music, and iTunes, Spotify, and other commercial services that could legally distribute music in digital format did not yet exist. The recording industry argued that P2P systems and their users infringed their copyright. They sued Napster, then the hottest P2P service, and won a court case in the US Court of Appeals for the Ninth Circuit in April 2001, effectively shutting down Napster.[1]

But shutting down Napster did not solve the recording industry's P2P problem. Newer P2P services emerged. The most prominent new

P2P software was KaZaA, which was not as centralized as Napster. Napster used a "central directory" maintained by the company to index the files that were stored on users' computers and available for download, while KaZaA relied on a network of "super-peer" computers to perform the same task.[2] A single lawsuit against Napster could—and did— effectively end its file sharing. KaZaA's decentralization, however, made the service harder to battle through litigation.

Yet some viewed file sharing as a threat to the recording industry. A June 2003 article by Stan J. Liebowitz that examined record sales and file sharing concluded that "MP3 downloads are causing significant harm to the record industry," though it is unclear "whether such downloading in our current legal environment will cause a mortal blow to the industry."[3]

Although the record labels could not easily or effectively sue the P2P services, they still could sue the users who were downloading—and sharing—their music and infringing their copyright. The users typically did not use their real names on P2P services, but their IP addresses often were publicly available. That meant that the record labels typically needed only to send one subpoena to the Internet service provider associated with the IP address, and they would have the name of the subscriber to that account.

Unlike Raytheon and the other cybersmear plaintiffs of the early aughts, the recording industry could obtain some subscribers' identities without even suing. A 1998 law, the Digital Millennium Copyright Act (DMCA), allows copyright owners to obtain a subpoena to identify alleged infringers from the clerk of any federal district court with a sworn declaration that the subpoena seeks to identify an infringer and the information "will only be used for the purpose of protecting rights" under US copyright law.[4] The subpoena powers under Section 512(h) of the DMCA are more plaintiff-friendly than the tests developed by *Dendrite* and the other anonymous poster cases, as the DMCA lacks notification, First Amendment balancing, and other key anonymity protections.

The Recording Industry Association of America (RIAA) announced on June 25, 2003, that it would begin gathering identifying information of people who shared large amounts of music on P2P networks. In its announcement of its subpoenas, the RIAA included supportive quotes from dozens of high-profile musicians. "If you create something and then someone takes it without your permission, that is stealing," Mary J. Blige said in the RIAA announcement. "It may sound harsh, but it is true."[5]

But the RIAA's plans—and, in particular, its use of the DMCA procedures—quickly drew criticism from civil liberties groups. "It is an automatic process where there is no judge and no judicial oversight," Fred von Lohmann of the Electronic Frontier Foundation told the *Milwaukee Journal-Sentinel* at the time. "Anyone can get your information, and it is an incredible invasion of our privacy. It treats us as guilty until proven innocent."[6]

RIAA served subpoenas on Internet service providers and universities (which provide Internet access to students), and on September 8, 2003, sued 261 P2P users across the country. "Nobody likes playing the heavy and having to resort to litigation," RIAA president Cary Sherman said at the time. "But when your product is being regularly stolen, there comes a time when you have to take appropriate action." Also that day, RIAA announced an "amnesty" program, in which people who had not yet been sued could voluntarily come forward and provide RIAA with an affidavit in which they agree to respect copyrights.[7]

Among the 261 defendants was Patrick Little, a Daly City, California, musician. He told the *Los Angeles Times* that his twin teenage daughters had downloaded or distributed songs including "Another Brick in the Wall" by Pink Floyd and "I Can't Let U Go" by Usher.[8] "I'm just pretty upset," he told the *Los Angeles Times* on the day the suit was filed. "I told the girls they shouldn't be doing that. Now here I am. I can't afford to pay whatever they're charging. I don't know what I'm going to do."[9] In January 2004, Little settled with the RIAA, agreeing to pay $2,795.[10]

By September 2003, the RIAA had reportedly sent more than 1,500 DMCA subpoenas.[11] But not all Internet service providers were willing to turn over their customers' identifying information. In July 2002, RIAA subpoenaed Verizon for the information of a customer who allegedly offered for downloading more than six hundred copyrighted files on KaZaA in one day.[12] Verizon refused to fulfill the request, not on First Amendment grounds, but because Verizon believed that the DMCA's subpoena powers apply only if the copyrighted content is stored with the service provider, and not, as here, on the customer's hard drive.[13] The RIAA asked a federal judge in the District of Columbia to enforce the subpoena. The case went to Judge John D. Bates, a former prosecutor who was appointed to the DC court by President George W. Bush in 2001.[14]

Although Verizon focused its argument on how the judge should interpret the DMCA, a coalition of eleven consumer groups filed an amicus brief, arguing that the DMCA subpoenas violate the First Amendment right to anonymity. Their lawyer? Megan Gray, who by that time had moved from California to Washington, DC.

Gray used her knowledge of anonymity from dozens of cybersmear cases to make a similar First Amendment argument to the DC court. She pointed to the rulings in *seescandy.com*, *Dendrite*, and other John Doe cases as evidence of a qualified but strong right to anonymity. "Although the tests vary somewhat, all of them share a key critical characteristic that is absent from Section 512(h): the requirement that a court of law review the evidence and allegations and balance them with the constitutional right of anonymous speech before the anonymity of an Internet user is breached," Gray wrote.[15]

Although the files that someone stores on a hard drive might not be the same as a post on a bulletin board, Gray wrote that the files can reveal a good deal about a person. The files also might give a false impression, she wrote. "For example, if an individual has a bunch of gangsta rap files available through P2P on his computer, one might form a misleading opinion of him, if it was not also known that he had those files in order to teach his seminar class on the perceptions of African-American culture in modern society," she wrote.[16]

Gray's argument, however, did not persuade Bates. Because Verizon had not made a First Amendment argument, he gave it little weight. In a January 21, 2003, opinion, Bates focused on the arguments that Verizon made about the scope of the DMCA subpoena statute. But he wrote that the First Amendment does not apply to copyright infringement.[17]

Bates's analysis focused on what he viewed as the nonexpressive nature of music file sharing, distinguishing it from anonymity cases such as *McIntyre* and *Watchtower Bible & Tract Society*. "To be sure, this is not a case where Verizon's customer is anonymously using the Internet to distribute speeches of Lenin, Biblical passages, educational materials, or criticisms of the government—situations in which assertions of First Amendment rights more plausibly could be made," Bates wrote.[18]

After Bates's initial ruling, Verizon argued that another RIAA subpoena violated the First Amendment. In an April 24, 2003, opinion, Bates again minimized the First Amendment concerns, writing that "when the Supreme Court has held that the First Amendment protects anonymity, it has typically done so in cases involving core First Amendment expression."[19] Because the DMCA "does not directly impact core political speech," Bates reasoned, it does not warrant the same level of scrutiny as applied to Margaret McIntyre and others.[20] The DMCA's subpoena provisions, he wrote, satisfy the lower level of review by, for instance, requiring the plaintiff to provide a sworn declaration before obtaining a subpoena.[21]

Bates too quickly assumed that the acts of downloading music and making that music available for others to download are not sufficiently expressive to warrant First Amendment protection. Anyone who, as a teenager, made a mix tape (or mix CD, or mix playlist) knows that the selection of songs certainly carries expressive value.

In a footnote to his first opinion, Bates noted the RIAA's observation that "the alleged infringer is not truly anonymous—Verizon knows the identity."[22] Indeed, it is increasingly rare for commercial online communications to operate entirely in a world of untraceable anonymity or pseudonymity. The early cybersmear cases mostly involved Yahoo!, which operated under a system of traceable pseudonymity, but that did not stop courts from conducting First Amendment balancing tests to determine whether to allow the subpoenas. Even some posters on AutoAdmit—which consciously chose not to log IP addresses—left behind enough clues for the plaintiffs to identify them. But protections for anonymity do not simply vanish because identities are traceable. Verizon's knowledge of its customers' identities does not reduce the privacy and free speech concerns associated with disclosing their identities to a trade association that is suing them.

Unlike the cybersmear subpoena opinions such as *Dendrite* and *Cahill*, Bates's opinion does not require evidence of actual copyright infringement, merely an allegation that depends on the imperfect use of IP addresses in a sworn declaration. As Sonia Katyal correctly observed, this distinction between "core First Amendment expression" and copyright infringement leads to an inequity for copyright defendants seeking to protect their anonymity. "By drawing this unduly stark line between First Amendment rights of expression and copyright infringement, the court

mistakenly presumed that the individual in question—indeed, every individual potentially subject to a DMCA notice—was already guilty of infringement, and thus was not entitled to any First Amendment protections," she wrote.[23]

Verizon appealed to the US Court of Appeals for the DC Circuit, and Gray again led the public interest groups in arguing that the subpoena violated the First Amendment. Verizon persuaded the DC Circuit to reverse Bates, but on narrow grounds: the appellate court concluded that the DMCA subpoena provision applied only to service providers that host allegedly infringing content, not those that merely transmit it.[24] Because it agreed with Verizon's interpretation of the DMCA, the DC Circuit declined to address whether it agreed with Gray's First Amendment argument.[25]

The ruling was a mixed bag for anonymity advocates. By avoiding the First Amendment issue altogether, the DC Circuit allowed Bates's minimization of those concerns to stand. But the appellate court's narrow interpretation of the DMCA subpoena power dealt a blow to the RIAA's 2003 antipiracy campaign, which focused on issuing subpoenas to service providers, as the users typically stored the music files on their own computers rather than with the companies. Because the RIAA could issue DMCA subpoenas en masse, without even suing, the DC Circuit eliminated a useful tool.

Still, the DC Circuit opinion did not prevent the RIAA from filing lawsuits against anonymous alleged infringers and using discovery in those cases to subpoena the identifying information of the defendants. The RIAA could use the same procedures that corporations used in their cybersmear cases against anonymous critics on Yahoo! Finance.

A few months after the DC Circuit's opinion, Sony Music Entertainment and sixteen other record companies sued forty people who allegedly infringed their copyrights on peer-to-peer networks. The record companies named the defendants John Does 1–40, and identified them only by their IP addresses. "The true names and capacities of the Defendants are unknown to Plaintiffs at this time," they wrote in the complaint, filed in Manhattan federal court.[26]

Judge Denny Chin approved the record companies' request to subpoena the defendants' Internet service provider, Cablevision, for the defendants' identifying information. After receiving the subpoenas on February 3,

2004, Cablevision notified the targeted customers, as required by Judge Chin: "Unless we hear from you, or your attorney, in writing by February 20, 2004, that you have filed the appropriate papers with the US District Court for the Southern District of New York to have the subpoena set aside, we will disclose your subscriber information to the plaintiffs, as required by the enclosed subpoena," the company wrote.[27]

On February 19, an attorney representing one of the defendants notified Chin that he planned to move to quash. Yet Cablevision fulfilled the subpoenas four days later because it believed the lawyer had not filed a formal motion with the court. Although Cablevision had already turned over the identifying information, Chin could order the record labels to return the information or prevent them from using it in the case. Chin allowed defendants to move to quash the subpoenas, and four of the defendants did so.[28]

Recognizing the potential for the RIAA's new legal strategy to undercut online anonymity, Public Citizen, the ACLU, and the Electronic Frontier Foundation filed an amicus brief urging Chin to quash the subpoena. The groups urged Chin to apply the *Dendrite* balancing test in evaluating the evidence of copyright infringement.

The recording industry argued to Judge Chin that the subpoenas simply did not raise First Amendment concerns because online music distribution is not "constitutionally protected expression," pointing to Bates's opinion.[29] The privacy advocacy groups pushed back on the minimization of the First Amendment values of music sharing. "The First Amendment does not protect libel or revelation of trade secrets or any of the variety of other wrongs that are commonly alleged in the lawsuits for which the courts have developed John Doe proceedings, any more than it protects copyright infringement," they wrote. "However, at the initial stage of the lawsuit, no court has determined that anyone has committed any such wrongs."[30]

The record companies partly framed the dispute as a Fourth Amendment issue, and noted a 1979 opinion in which the Supreme Court concluded that a phone company can provide law enforcement with business records without violating the Fourth Amendment.[31] Their focus on the Fourth Amendment is somewhat off base because the main remedy in Fourth Amendment disputes is suppression of evidence in criminal trials, and this lawsuit was a civil copyright dispute. Their argument reveals a key shortcoming in their approach to First Amendment anonymity claims: they imply that courts may judge the value of the expression at issue. Under their reading, an anonymous critic of a city council member might receive more protection than a Metallica fan who is accused of sharing a music collection on a peer-to-peer network.

Judge Chin, too, hesitated to find a robust right to anonymity for file sharers. In a July 26, 2004, opinion, Chin denied the motions to quash. Downloading, distributing, and making available copyrighted music, Chin wrote, "qualifies as speech, but only to a degree." File sharing, he wrote, is not "true expression" because the "individual is not seeking to communicate a thought or convey an idea. Instead, the individual's real purpose is to obtain music for free." Given the nature of the expression involved in peer-to-peer sharing, he wrote, the defendants' distribution and downloading is entitled to "limited" First Amendment protection that "is subject to other considerations."[32]

Applying this lower level of anonymity protection, Chin determined that the record labels met their burden in justifying the subpoenas by listing the allegedly infringed songs and the times at which the defendants shared or downloaded the music via specific IP addresses.[33] The defendants had "minimal expectation of privacy," Chin wrote, because Cablevision's terms of service bar the use of its services for copyright infringement and reserve the right to disclose customer information to fulfill legal obligations.[34] Also weighing in favor of the subpoenas, Chin wrote, was that the subpoenas were "sufficiently specific," there were not other ways to identify the defendants, and the identities were "centrally needed" for the lawsuit.[35]

Judge Chin's test provides some protections for anonymity, but they are not as robustly articulated as some of the defamation opinions such as *Dendrite*. Because Chin was among the first judges to address copyright subpoenas, hundreds of court opinions would rely on his analysis. In a separate copyright dispute six years later, the US Court of Appeals for the Second Circuit wrote that Chin's test is the "appropriate general standard" for such subpoenas.[36]

Sony involved defendants who had allegedly distributed and downloaded copyrighted music. Even cases that purport to target only those who allegedly distributed copyrighted music sweep in many defendants who used P2P services to download music but had not disabled the function on the P2P program that allowed others to access their music catalogues. The opinion failed to adequately address the First Amendment values embodied in downloading and listening to music. In a 1965 opinion, *Lamont v. Postmaster General*, the Supreme Court invalidated a postal law that required the detention and screening of mail for "communist political propaganda." If the authorities determined that mail is communist political propaganda, they would destroy the mail unless the recipient completed and returned a reply card. The cards allowed recipients to ask the Post Office for delivery in the future of any "similar publication."[37]

The Supreme Court struck down this law as a First Amendment violation because "the addressee, in order to receive his mail, must request in writing that it be delivered."[38] Conditioning the receipt of mail on the completion of a reply card "is almost certain to have a deterrent effect, especially as respects those who have sensitive positions." Other recipients, as well, are "likely to feel some inhibition in sending for literature which federal officials have condemned as 'communist political propaganda,'" Justice Douglas wrote for the majority.[39] In a concurrence, Justice Brennan more directly addressed the right to receive information. "The dissemination of ideas can accomplish nothing if otherwise willing addressees are not free to receive and consider them," Brennan wrote. "It would be a barren marketplace of ideas that had only sellers and no buyers."[40]

Although *Lamont* does not directly address anonymity, it shows that an interference with someone's receipt of information raises First Amendment concerns. In a 1996 article, Julie Cohen persuasively argued that *Lamont*, as well as other opinions such as *McIntyre* and *NAACP v. Alabama*, "suggest the glimmerings of judicial recognition of a broad right of anonymity extending to *all* of the constitutive activities of communication." Receipt of information and speaking, Cohen wrote, are "symbiotic": "One cannot exist without the other, and any definition of 'speech' in the constitutional sense properly encompasses both."[41]

While Chin considered the accused file sharers' privacy interests in his analysis, he minimized the importance of those interests. I do not suggest that copyright plaintiffs should never be able to obtain defendants' identities. But just as defamation plaintiffs must make a particularly strong showing before obtaining defendants' identifying information, copyright plaintiffs should as well. Judges should fully consider the evidence and the chilling effect of such subpoenas on both anonymous expression and receipt of content.

The RIAA file-sharing lawsuits often involved popular music, so it might be difficult to understand how a lack of anonymity for file sharers would chill expression. Even with more rigorous First Amendment scrutiny, the RIAA cases still may have resulted in the unmasking of the file sharers. The need for anonymity would become more apparent over the next decade when a company representing the makers of pornographic films would eclipse the recording industry in lawsuits against anonymous online file sharers.

Matthew Sag and Jake Haskell took on the ambitious task of tallying the thousands of copyright lawsuits filed against John Doe defendants in 2015–2016. They found that the most frequent plaintiff was not Sony, Arista, or any other recording label. Rather, a company called Malibu Media filed 2,646 copyright cases against John Does—nearly 62 percent of all such cases.[42]

Malibu Media is a porn company. And it aggressively pursues people who it believes have shared its movies on peer-to-peer sites. Between 2012 and 2016, Sag and Haskell found, Malibu Media filed nearly six thousand copyright cases, paying more than $2 million in filing fees alone.[43]

Although Malibu Media's copyrighted material differs from those of the record labels, Malibu Media uses litigation procedures like those used in the record labels' 2004 case in Manhattan. After identifying the IP addresses of suspected file sharers, Malibu Media files John Doe lawsuits and asks the court for permission to subpoena the Internet service providers for the subscribers' IP addresses.

From a John Doe defendant's perspective, the stakes likely are far higher in a Malibu Media case than in a recording industry lawsuit. It's one thing to be publicly accused of sharing a Top 40 song. It's another to be accused, in a public court document, of sharing a movie called *Sex for Three by the Sea*. It is particularly disconcerting for defendants who did not engage in the alleged file sharing, as IP addresses are imperfect methods of identifying file sharers. For example, the alleged infringement may have been committed by a houseguest, or someone who accessed an unsecured Wi-Fi connection. Yet the subscriber to that Internet connection faces the prospect of being named.

Not surprisingly, after defendants learn that Malibu Media has filed a copyright lawsuit, defendants have a strong incentive to settle.

Although judges often allow defendants to temporarily litigate anonymously, the threat of public unmasking looms. A lawyer for Malibu Media told the *New Yorker* in 2014 that most defendants reach confidential settlements of between two thousand and thirty thousand dollars.[44]

Although the defendants might have a greater interest in anonymity, the lawsuits boil down to copyright infringement, and Chin already set a relatively low standard for subpoenas in copyright cases. For instance, in 2012, Malibu Media sued a John Doe in New York who allegedly shared a Malibu Media movie, *Leila Last Night*, on BitTorrent.[45] After receiving notice of a subpoena from his Internet service provider, the defendant moved to quash the subpoena. A Manhattan federal judge denied the motion. "Courts in this district have recognized that internet users have a limited First Amendment privacy interest in anonymous internet usage, including the use of peer-to-peer file-sharing networks, but this interest does not protect those who use their anonymity to infringe the copyrights of others," Judge Edgardo Ramos, pointing to Chin's *Sony* opinion, wrote.[46] About two weeks later, the case settled on undisclosed terms, and John Doe was never publicly unmasked.

Some judges, however, have pushed back against Malibu Media's litigation. Perhaps the most notable example resulted from an April 26, 2012, lawsuit that the company filed in Los Angeles federal court against ten John Does who allegedly used BitTorrent to upload or download a film called *Blonde Ambition*.[47] A few weeks later, Malibu Media filed an eight-page motion to serve subpoenas on the defendants' ISPs for identifying information, relying largely on the low standard that Chin set in the *Sony* case. "Obviously, without learning the Defendants' true identities, Plaintiff will not be able to serve the Defendants with process and proceed with this case," the company wrote.[48]

The case went to Judge Otis Wright, a former Los Angeles County sheriff's deputy whom George W. Bush had appointed to the federal bench five years earlier. Wright's June 27, 2012, order in the case made it clear that he held a dim view of Malibu Media's litigation tactics.

Wright first expressed skepticism that the information that Malibu Media sought from the ISPs would reveal the identities of the people who infringed the copyrights. "For instance, a person may be the subscriber, but his roommate is the actual infringer," Wright wrote. "And the subscriber may have his home network configured to allow visitors, including strangers, to access the Internet—and use BitTorrent. Further, the subscriber may be a business (e.g., a coffee shop), and Internet access may be open to all employees and customers."[49]

Wright also questioned the sufficiency of Malibu Media's evidence that a particular IP address was involved in copyright infringement. On BitTorrent, movie files are divided into thousands of pieces, and distributed to a downloader from a "swarm" of computers that already have the movie available for sharing.[50] Although Malibu identified particular IP addresses that shared parts of the movie, Wright wrote, they may have shared only one small piece, and "individual BitTorrent file pieces are worthless—by themselves they can never be reconstructed into the original file."[51] Because the litigation was in its early stages, Wright refrained from ruling whether transmitting only some pieces of a movie constitutes copyright infringement, but he noted that "Malibu's case is weak if all it can prove is that the Doe Defendants transmitted only part of all the BitTorrent pieces of the copyrighted work."[52]

Recognizing that the case involved pornography, Wright worried that Malibu might abuse the discovery process. "To save himself from embarrassment, even if he is not the infringer, the subscriber will very likely pay the settlement price," Wright wrote. "And if the subscriber is a business, it will likely pay the settlement to save itself from the hassle and cost of complying with discovery—even though one of its customers or employees is the actual infringer."[53]

Despite his concerns about the evidence and the potential for bullying the defendant into a settlement, Wright allowed Malibu Media to subpoena the information of one of the defendants, but he did not allow the other nine defendants to remain in the lawsuit because he saw no evidence that they worked together to infringe the company's copyright.

After partly allowing the subpoena, Wright emphasized his distaste for pornography companies' use of the judiciary to extract settlements. "These lawsuits run a common theme: plaintiff owns a copyright to a pornographic movie; plaintiff sues numerous John Does in a single action for using BitTorrent to pirate the movie; plaintiff subpoenas the ISPs to obtain the identities of these Does; if successful, plaintiff will send out demand letters to the Does; because of embarrassment, many Does will send back a nuisance-value check to the plaintiff," Wright wrote.[54]

The cases typically settle, and the parties rarely litigate whether the defendant infringed the copyright. "The federal courts are not cogs in a plaintiff's copyright-enforcement business model," Wright wrote. "The Court will not idly watch what is essentially an extortion scheme, for a case that plaintiff has no intention of bringing to trial." To address this problem, Wright said, he would require such companies to file individual lawsuits, "making this type of litigation less profitable."[55]

Wright set the tone for increased skepticism for copyright infringement lawsuits against anonymous file sharers, particularly those involving pornography. Dozens of judges would quote from his opinion in their own rulings involving copyright subpoenas, often from Malibu Media. For instance, in a 2017 order in which he threatened to block any further Malibu Media lawsuits unless the company demonstrated the accuracy of its geolocation technology, San Francisco federal judge William Alsup quoted extensively from Wright's opinion. "Although Malibu Media now files individual cases against each defendant in this district (rather than one mass lawsuit), its practices evidently remain the same as those Judge Wright described," Alsup wrote.[56]

Wright's opinion was particularly consequential because a federal judge called the lawsuit as he saw it: an "extortion scheme." Although he allowed at least some of the requested discovery, Wright recognized the high stakes of unmasking a defendant who would be publicly accused of viewing pornography. The harm is to the defendants' reputations, and not only because they are accused of stealing copyrighted material but because of the nature of that material. Although Malibu Media's pornography is legal, a defendant may face a social stigma in being publicly listed as a consumer—and thief—of porn.

Yet Malibu Media would have the courts believe there is no anonymity interest because its cases involve the illegal act of copyright infringement. Do the mere allegations that the defendants violated copyright law override their very real concerns about the impacts of being unmasked? In a different context, the Supreme Court has suggested that the answer is a complex one. In a 1969 opinion, *Stanley v. Georgia*, the Supreme Court considered the constitutionality of a defendant's conviction for possessing obscene films in a drawer in his bedroom. A Georgia law criminalized "knowingly hav[ing] possession of . . . obscene matter."[57]

The Supreme Court had ruled that obscenity is not constitutionally protected, but that case involved defendants who distributed or sold obscene material. *Stanley v. Georgia*, the Court ruled, was different because it dealt only with the defendant *possessing* the obscene material in private. "This right to receive information and ideas, regardless of their social worth, is fundamental to our free society," Justice Thurgood Marshall wrote for the majority.[58]

That right to receive information, Marshall wrote, can be traced to cases such as *Lamont* and others that protect against government invasions of privacy. "He is asserting the right to read or observe what he pleases—the right to satisfy his intellectual and emotional needs in the privacy of his own home," Marshall wrote. "He is asserting the right to be free from state inquiry into the contents of his library."[59] Julie Cohen correctly observed that Marshall's ruling is "privacy language, and has been recognized as such, but it is anonymity language as well."[60]

Marshall recognized that Georgia's law applied only to obscene materials, but he wrote that this classification does not justify the "drastic invasion" of First Amendment rights. "Whatever may be the justifications for other statutes regulating obscenity, we do not think they reach into the privacy of one's own home," Marshall wrote. "If the First Amendment means anything, it means that a State has no business telling a man, sitting alone in his own house, what books he may read or what films he may watch. Our whole constitutional heritage rebels at the thought of giving government the power to control men's minds."[61]

Malibu Media's copyright infringement cases, of course, differ from *Stanley v. Georgia*. *Stanley v. Georgia* involved a criminal conviction that deprived the defendant of his liberty, while a copyright infringement case seeks civil damages as well as the ability to unmask the defendant as someone who steals pornography online. The stakes are higher in a criminal obscenity case, and in that respect there is an even greater reason to provide some First Amendment protection than in a civil copyright case.

Yet there also is an argument that a defendant in a Malibu Media case is entitled to *more* First Amendment protection than a defendant in a criminal obscenity case. Although the defendant's alleged act—infringing copyright—is not protected by the First Amendment, constitutional protections should fully apply when the allegations are unproven. At the discovery stage, the plaintiff has not proven a case on the merits. The defendant's actions might not constitute infringement, or the identified subscriber may not have even been the person who downloaded. Yet the mere possibility of unmasking the anonymous people who are associated with these accounts threatens privacy interests recognized by the Supreme Court.

While the Malibu Media cases seek only to prevent infringement of copyright—rather than entirely ban the consumption of legal pornography—these cases also threaten the privacy interests in possessing and consuming information that the Supreme Court recognized in *Stanley v. Georgia*. As Wright aptly demonstrated in his opinion, there are both procedural and technical shortcomings with the methods that companies use to identify copyright infringers, yet unmasking and publicly accusing them in open court can harm their reputations and have broad chilling effects.

Cases such as *Lamont* and *Stanley v. Georgia* are rooted in the First Amendment, but they revolve around privacy interests as much as free expression. Likewise, the Malibu Media cases, while impacting the receipt and viewing of pornography, pose a direct threat to the privacy of people by publicly associating their identities with pornography. Privacy and anonymity are two different values; privacy protects personal information, and anonymity protects the identity associated with that information. But protecting anonymity often overlaps with protecting privacy, and protecting privacy often overlaps with protecting anonymity.

The use of subpoenas to unmask—and effectively extort—people who allegedly viewed or shared legal pornography raises its own privacy concerns.[62] A corporation uses the force of the government to compel another corporation to turn over its customers' private information, and then threatens to publicly unmask them unless they settle for thousands of dollars. The unmasking could lead to a public shaming that reveals intimate details of the customers' personal lives. The Privacy Motivation for anonymity understandably drives people to seek to remain anonymous in these file-sharing cases.

Yet many judges mechanically apply Chin's *Sony* test to subpoenas from Malibu Media and other pornography companies. These tests show little regard for privacy of viewing information. They often do not factor in the potential humiliation that a John Doe would face for being publicly accused of downloading *Triple Blonde Fantasy*. They do not consider the immense leverage that companies have in pressuring the defendant to settle rather than face public shame. Nor do they consider the role that the court system plays in helping companies use that shame to exact settlements.

The success of unmasking in pornography copyright cases suggests that privacy is simply not a significant concern in the framework under which courts analyze subpoenas. This framework is rooted in the First Amendment and focuses almost exclusively on the impacts that subpoenas have on people who create speech rather than those who receive the speech. This hyperfocus on speech creation ignores the very real First Amendment concerns about restricting information that the Supreme Court expressed in *Lamont* and *Stanley*. Although copyright infringement is not constitutionally protected, the First Amendment should impose adequate safeguards to ensure that the plaintiff has sufficient evidence of infringement before being able to unmask and publicly accuse a defendant.

While *Dendrite*, *Cahill*, and similar tests are a significant step toward a balanced framework for online anonymity, they protect some online activities far more than others. We cannot rely on this precedent to fully satisfy society's expectations for online anonymity. To provide broader protection for anonymity, courts should require a heightened evidentiary showing in *any* cases in which a subpoena would unmask an anonymous user. The standard would not provide absolute protection; rather, just as in *Dendrite*, the court would consider the strength of the evidence of copyright infringement. This requirement would, at the very least, address Wright's concern about inaccurately flagging a defendant as a file sharer.

Judges could retain the *Sony* test for copyright cases but more seriously consider the privacy implications of unmasking file sharers. They have a roadmap for this analysis from Royce Lamberth, a former federal prosecutor whom President Reagan appointed to the District of Columbia federal district court in 1987. In 2018, Lamberth denied a discovery request from Strike 3 Holdings, a pornography company that sought identifying information of a John Doe who allegedly infringed its copyright. Although he applied the *Sony* test, Lamberth placed a far greater emphasis on the defendant's privacy interests, particularly because Strike 3 failed to provide Lamberth with sufficient certainty that the defendant was the person who actually infringed the company's copyright. "Imagine having your name and reputation publicly—and permanently—connected to

websites like *Tushy* and *Blacked Raw*. Google them at your own risk,"
Lamberth wrote. "How would an improperly accused defendant's spouse
react? His (or her) boss? The head of the local neighborhood watch? The
risks of a false accusation are real; the consequences are hard to overstate
and even harder to undo."[63] Lamberth's opinion incorporates the substantial Privacy Motivation for anonymity in these cases. Unfortunately,
the US Court of Appeals for the DC Circuit reversed Lamberth in 2020.
"The mere fact that a defendant may be embarrassed to have his name
connected to pornographic websites is not a proper basis on which to diminish a copyright holder's otherwise enforceable property rights," Judge
Neomi Rao wrote for the three-judge panel.[64] The reversal of Lamberth's
privacy-protective opinion demonstrates the relatively lax standards for
anonymity that some courts apply in copyright cases.

Distribution and receipt of information is just as vital to online communications as creation of that information. So heightened anonymity
protection in copyright cases would better preserve the culture of anonymity empowerment. Yet even under the current US regime, with weaker
protection for distribution and receipt of information, the United States
provides among the strongest anonymity protections in the world.

Just as copyright cases tend to involve weaker protections for anonymity than other civil litigation such as defamation lawsuits, courts presiding
over criminal cases and grand jury investigations tend to place less emphasis on protecting anonymity.

9

WHEN THE GOVERNMENT WANTS TO UNMASK YOU

The cybersmear and copyright cases involved private parties trying to use the judicial system to unmask anonymous defendants. Yet the government also may seek to unmask anonymous Internet users for grand jury investigations, criminal prosecutions, and regulatory actions.

Americans have good reason to seek to protect their identities during government investigations. Of the six motivations for anonymity, the Legal Motivation is perhaps the most relevant. Being unmasked in a government investigation could lead to heavy legal fees, fines, and even prison time.

Government investigations are constrained by the Fourth Amendment, which protects against "unreasonable searches and seizures" and requires warrants to be supported by probable cause. Electronic surveillance also is governed by statutes such as the Stored Communications Act and Wiretap Act. Yet the restrictions on government searches do not guarantee anonymity protections. If a search violates the Fourth Amendment, courts will often (but not always) suppress any of the evidence from being used against the defendant in a criminal trial. This is a powerful incentive for law enforcement to respect the privacy of criminal suspects.

In 1967, the US Supreme Court ruled that the Fourth Amendment requires a warrant for a wiretap of a telephone call in a phone booth, as a person has a "reasonable expectation of privacy" in the contents of that conversation.[1] Courts have found that people have a reasonable expectation of privacy in the contents of their email.[2]

But warrants are not required for all information. In 1979, the Supreme Court allowed the warrantless installation of a pen register, which recorded the phone numbers that a criminal suspect dialed.[3] The Court reasoned that "a person has no legitimate expectation of privacy in information he voluntarily turns over to third parties."[4] The "third-party doctrine" also prevents the Fourth Amendment from applying to banking records.[5] Most relevant to anonymity concerns, courts have held that a criminal defendant does not have a reasonable expectation of privacy in IP address data and other subscriber information stored by Internet service providers.[6] The third-party doctrine reduces the likelihood that the Fourth Amendment will provide much protection for the anonymity of criminal defendants or suspects, or for potential witnesses in criminal cases.

The Fourth Amendment's conception of privacy does not always cover anonymity. Jeffrey M. Skopek highlighted the weaknesses in the Fourth Amendment doctrine's focus on the reasonable expectation of privacy and argued that it also should protect individuals' expectations of anonymity. "Although anonymity and privacy are similar in that both maintain the secrecy of personal information, they differ in a fundamental and legally relevant way: Privacy hides the information, whereas anonymity hides what makes it personal," he wrote. "Understanding this difference reveals the reasons why and ways in which the Fourth Amendment should be interpreted to protect not only reasonable expectations of privacy, but also 'reasonable expectations of anonymity.'"[7]

A key barrier to recognizing a Fourth Amendment reasonable expectation of anonymity is the third-party doctrine. The Supreme Court in recent years has limited the reach of the doctrine but has not entirely eliminated it. In a 2018 case, *Carpenter v. United States*, the Supreme Court indicated that it might limit the sweep of the third-party doctrine. In that case, the government had warrantlessly obtained 127 days of Timothy Carpenter's cell site location information—a list of the cell towers that a phone had pinged—allowing the government to place him near the scene of four robberies. The Supreme Court agreed with Carpenter that, even though the cell phone company had access to the records, he had a reasonable expectation of privacy (and the Fourth Amendment requires a warrant). "Given the unique nature of cell phone location information, the fact that the Government obtained the information from a third party does not overcome Carpenter's claim to Fourth Amendment protection," Chief Justice Roberts wrote for the majority.[8]

The case was a setback to governmental efforts to avoid the Fourth Amendment's warrant requirements for electronic surveillance. Yet Roberts emphasized that the decision is "narrow" and does not "call into question conventional surveillance techniques and tools, such as security cameras" or "other business records that might incidentally reveal location information."[9] This means that, post-*Carpenter*, courts must individually assess the privacy intrusion of a government search to determine whether the Fourth Amendment applies.

So far, it does not appear that *Carpenter* has markedly strengthened online anonymity protections for criminal defendants and suspects. In a 2019 child pornography transmission case, *United States v. Hood*, the government identified the defendant by warrantlessly obtaining his IP addresses from his messaging app, and then warrantlessly obtaining the location information for the IP addresses from the Internet service providers.[10]

The defendant argued that *Carpenter* requires a warrant for the IP address, which, like cell site location information, leads to his location at a particular time. The US Court of Appeals for the First Circuit rejected this argument, reasoning that unlike cell site location information, which tracks the defendant's location at all times, the defendant produces IP addresses for logs "only by making the affirmative decision to access a website or application."[11] What the decision failed to adequately address was the key role that IP addresses, combined with other data, play in unmasking anonymous Internet users. The decision suggests that, even after *Carpenter*, the Fourth Amendment provides only limited protection, at best, for anonymity.

Even if a reasonable expectation of privacy does exist and there is not an exception to the warrant requirement, the government can obtain a warrant upon a showing of probable cause. When law enforcement obtains warrants, they can be applied in a way that unmasks people even if they were not involved in the suspected crime. For instance, when investigating an arson case, Florida police served Google with a "keyword warrant" for information about "users who had searched the address of the residence close in time to the arson."[12] Similarly, law enforcement in recent years has used "geofence warrants," which require Google to provide identifying information of anyone whose mobile device's GPS system located them near the scene of a crime.[13] While both keyword warrants and geofence warrants are useful tools for law enforcement, they also run the risk of identifying innocent people and linking them with high-profile crimes merely because they had the bad fortune to search for the wrong term or be physically located near a crime.

Nor do electronic privacy statutes always prevent the government from unmasking people. For example, the federal Stored Communications Act sets a lower bar for the government to demand that an Internet service provider turn over any customer records other than the content of communications. To obtain customer records, the government can use a warrant, a subpoena, or a "(d) order," which requires the government to provide "reasonable grounds" to believe that the records are "relevant and material to an ongoing criminal investigation," a standard that is higher than the review of a subpoena, but lower than the probable cause required for a warrant.[14] Like the Fourth Amendment case law, the Stored Communications Act and other statutes differentiate between content and noncontent information, but do not place any additional protections on noncontent information just because it might identify someone who was anonymous online.

Although the Fourth Amendment and electronic communications privacy statutes provide only limited protection for anonymity, criminal suspects, defendants, and witnesses in criminal cases still are entitled to First Amendment protections of their identities. Yet it is hard to state with certainty whether the First Amendment anonymity rights are as robust in criminal cases as they are in civil cases like defamation claims, as very few criminal investigations or prosecutions have led to published court opinions that analyze the anonymity interests. That is at least partly because the unmasking often occurs during a criminal investigation, when the subject is often not aware of the inquiry and therefore cannot challenge it in court.

In the few criminal and regulatory published opinions that have addressed the issue, courts have recognized that defendants and suspects have a First Amendment right to anonymity. But as in the civil cases, this right is qualified, and the courts suggest that a criminal suspect or target of a grand jury investigation may be less likely to succeed in preventing a court from allowing the unmasking.

The Twitter user's pen name was Atticus Guevara, and his Twitter handle was @RUretarted.[15] As of February 2012, Atticus Guevara had fewer than 750 followers, but that did not stop him from providing vulgar and highly offensive commentary.[16] Below is a sampling of his tweets from the summer of 2011:

> Godamn I smacked my wife with my Dick . . . Now she has a cock shaped bruise on her face. . . . Take that take that take that
> Alternate use for semen Homemade (liquid skin) for when bandaids are just not an option.
> sheep keep doing what they do . . . Having already gotten used to being fucked they wander around oblivious to everything questioning nothing.[17]

His political leanings appeared to be liberal, and he expressed them through shock comments. Among his tweets that summer:

> @loograt you can only stab non-whites in Texas 4per week And you are allowed to drag at least one black person behind your truck per month.
> "@seanhannity: Unlike when Obama speaks @SpeakerBoehner is on time. We'll air it live." –does Boehner pay you every time you blow him?
> So I visited the westboro Baptist church . . . And took a massive shit on the pulpit . . . To my surprise no one was offended.[18]

Atticus Guevara was particularly fired up on August 2, 2011. He tweeted that "the Medias (fox networks) manipulation Of the politically ignorant Goes to prove the people really are as dumb as they look . . ." and

"There's a 50/50 shot you may have drunk piss! If you have ever refreshed yourself with a cold beverage from McDonalds #fuckMcdonalds."[19]

But the Atticus Guevara tweet that caught the attention of federal authorities that day was sent at 9:32 p.m. eastern time: "I want to fuck Michelle Bachman [sic] in the ass with a Vietnam era machete."[20]

Michele Bachmann at the time was a Republican congresswoman from Minnesota who had recently announced her campaign for the Republican presidential nomination. Bachmann was a high-profile leader in the conservative movement. In a June 2011 *Daily Beast* profile, titled "Bachmann's Unrivaled Extremism," Michelle Goldberg wrote that "no other candidate in the race is so completely a product of the evangelical right as Bachmann."[21] Bachmann's right-wing politics made her the frequent target of attacks from the left.

But Atticus Guevara's tweet was more than the standard rant about her politics or religion. Taken literally, the machete tweet might be read as a threat to rape, injure, and possibly murder Bachmann. Unlike merely controversial speech, true threats are not protected by the First Amendment.

At least some federal authorities appeared to believe that the tweet was a threat to a member of Congress. Three days later, a federal grand jury subpoenaed Twitter for "any and all records pertaining to the identity of user name @RUretarded Atticus Guevara." The subpoena requested the contact information for Atticus Guevara and the IP address associated with the Bachmann tweet.[22] Twitter notified the user that it received a subpoena. Atticus Guevara contacted the Washington, DC, chapter of the American Civil Liberties Union, which represented the poster and asked the federal court in Washington to quash the subpoena.

Pointing to *Talley, McIntyre,* and the other important First Amendment anonymity rulings, the ACLU argued that Atticus Guevara had a right to speak anonymously.[23] "The First Amendment's protection of anonymous speech emphatically extends to speech on the Internet, which has largely taken over the role of pamphlets, leaflets and soapboxes as the means by which ordinary people can communicate their views to the public," the ACLU wrote.[24]

Subpoenas that chill political speech, the ACLU wrote, deserve special scrutiny. "Federal law enforcement officers showing up at a person's workplace and neighborhood, asking unsettling questions about whether the person has made threatening statements, has criminal proclivities, has alcohol or drug problems, or is mentally unstable, could easily have drastic consequences including the loss of employment and social ostracism for the person and the person's family, even if no indictment ever issues," the ACLU wrote.[25] The tweet about Bachmann, the ACLU added, was not a true threat. The machete comment was "absurdist" and "an obviously outlandish and crude attempt at expressing contempt or disgust about a political figure, not a warning of any actual intent to do physical harm."[26]

The ACLU's motion went to Judge Royce Lamberth, the District of Columbia federal judge who in 2018 refused to unmask the defendant who allegedly infringed a pornography company's copyright.[27] Recognizing the First Amendment stakes in the ACLU's motion, Lamberth applied grand jury case law to conclude that the government could subpoena Twitter only if "the information sought is truly necessary to the grand jury's investigation."[28]

Despite the ACLU's insistence that the tweet did not constitute a true threat, Lamberth allowed the subpoena, reasoning that it could help the grand jury decide whether probable cause exists. "The grand jury ought to know if [Atticus Guevara] has a history of making threats to political candidates in other forums, or has stalked or engaged in other sinister behavior toward Ms. Bachmann, or happens to actually own a Vietnam-era machete," Lamberth wrote. "The government and the grand jury surely must know the identity of an individual making a threat in order to ascertain whether he intended the threat to be 'true.'"[29]

Lamberth, however, had "grave doubts" about whether the grand jury would indict Atticus Guevara. "There appears to be nothing serious whatsoever about [Atticus Guevara's] Twitter page, except perhaps the severity of mental depravity that would lead a person to produce such posts," Lamberth wrote.[30] Yet he was not deciding whether Atticus Guevara committed the crime, only whether the government should obtain his identity to further investigate. And the government, he wrote, "must take seriously all threats against a major presidential candidate such as Ms. Bachmann, unless and until it is satisfied that there is no likelihood that the threat was legitimate."[31]

Lamberth acknowledged the potentially "absurd results" to which his conclusion might lead. "Under this line of reasoning, the government could presumably subpoena any Web site any time any anonymous user made any post containing a mere scintilla of violence," Lamberth wrote. "The government could require Twitter to divulge the identity of a teenager who tweets, 'My parents are so mean! I want to toss them in a ditch.' Anonymity on the Internet would be sufficiently compromised to warrant this Court's concern."[32] But the Atticus Guevara tweet, he wrote, involves a threat to a political candidate and does not reach that "slippery slope."[33]

Lamberth's ruling shows the difference in standards applied for unmasking in criminal and civil proceedings. Had Lamberth been applying *Dendrite, Cahill,* or another standard for civil subpoenas, he may not have found sufficient evidence to support the subpoena, or a privacy interest that overrides the government's need for the identifying information. Yet because he was applying grand jury subpoena standards, Lamberth did not need to evaluate whether the prosecutors had enough evidence at that point; to the contrary, Lamberth seriously questioned whether the grand jury ever would indict.

Lamberth's predictions proved correct. Atticus Guevara agreed not to appeal Lamberth's ruling, provided that federal investigators interview him, with ACLU lawyers present, and not speak to his neighbors or employer unless the investigators still had concerns. After the interview, the government closed the investigation, and he never was indicted.[34]

Although some FBI agents and prosecutors learned Atticus Guevara's identity, he managed to prevent more widespread unmasking. Still, the publicity of the subpoena may have had a chilling effect, and not only for people who write similarly vulgar comments on Twitter. Anyone who has an interest in maintaining anonymity on social media is on notice that prosecutors might be able to unmask them, even with a flimsy claim of a potential criminal case.

And at least one court has applied an even lower standard of review to grand jury unmasking subpoenas, this time in a case involving Glassdoor, the site on which employees and job candidates post reviews of companies. In 2017, the US Court of Appeals for the Ninth Circuit affirmed the district court's denial of a motion to quash a grand jury subpoena for posters' identifying information as part of an investigation into a government contractor. Rather than apply more rigorous First Amendment anonymity precedent, the Ninth Circuit applied the lower standard that the Supreme Court used in *Branzburg v. Hayes,* which involved a grand jury subpoena seeking information about journalists' confidential sources. The court rejected Glassdoor's First Amendment challenge because the company "has neither alleged nor established bad faith on the part of the government in its investigation."[35] This "good faith" standard appears even less rigorous than Lamberth's requirement that the government demonstrate a true necessity for the information that the subpoena seeks.

Should the standard of proof be lower for a grand jury subpoena than it is for subpoenas in civil litigation? The government likely would argue that it should be, as a grand jury investigation into a potential crime is in the public interest and designed to prevent further danger to the public. Yet the nature of criminal proceedings also could weigh against the lower standard for grand jury subpoenas. The standard remedy in civil cases is the defendant paying money to the plaintiff. Criminal cases may end with the defendant going to prison. This potential consequence—the deprivation of liberty—is one of the most serious outcomes in the legal system.

The government, however, does not always seek to put wrongdoers in prison. Federal and state administrative agencies bring regulatory actions against companies and people, raising the potential for significant fines or settlements. Should the defendants in these administrative actions receive more anonymity protection—or less—than criminal defendants?

Using the trademarks of the late Bob Marley, Jammin' Java marketed coffee products such as "Marley Coffee." At the beginning of 2011, the stock price for the Beverly Hills–based company was well under $1. By May, the shares exceeded $6. By August, the shares were under $1 again.

The Securities and Exchange Commission noticed the volatility, and in May 2011 opened a formal investigation. The SEC learned of newsletters, posted to Yahoo! Finance and other websites in the spring of 2011, that the SEC believed contained misrepresentations about Jammin' Java's operations. Among the claims: the company farmed its coffee (the SEC says it did not); the company offered blue mountain coffee (the SEC says it rarely did); the company was doing a "rollout of Jammin' Java coffee across North America" (the SEC says it was not); and that the company's shares would reach $10 (the SEC says there were no grounds for that prediction).[36]

The SEC believed that the stock fluctuations were part of a "pump-and-dump" scheme, in which fraudsters buy stock at a low price, artificially inflate the share prices with false information, and sell at a high price.[37] As part of its investigation into this scheme, the SEC issued administrative subpoenas to Google for identifying information for the users of three Gmail addresses: jeffreyhooke@gmail.com, aurorapartners@gmail.com, and marketingacesinc@gmail.com. The user (or users) behind each of these email accounts asked the federal court in northern California to quash the subpoena.[38]

The anonymous emailers urged the court to apply a standard, similar to *Cahill*, that allowed subpoenas for identifying information only if the government provided enough evidence to defeat a summary judgment motion. "The SEC has not established *any* evidence supporting its legal claims," the lawyer for jeffreyhooke@gmail.com wrote. "It has not even revealed the *nature* of its legal claims, beyond conclusory assertions that the Securities Act may have been violated."[39]

At an October 2011 hearing on the motion, Keith Scully, who was representing two of the three John Does, emphasized to Magistrate Judge Nandor J. Vadas the lack of evidence behind the SEC's subpoena.

"Can you imagine a police officer coming into court, raising his hand and saying, 'My probable cause is I think there was a murder in this house. Please give me a search warrant to go in and get it?'" Scully asked.

Vadas retorted that police do not have to meet a high evidentiary standard to obtain telephone records, which he believed were much like what the SEC was seeking.

"The level of judicial scrutiny isn't just they have to stand up and wave the flag of fraud and say 'trust us,'" Scully said. "I mean, that—there might as well not be judicial review."[40]

At the heart of Scully's objection to the SEC's subpoena was the impact of unmasking the anonymous person or people behind the email accounts. Yet this case dealt with a government search, and therefore the focus was on the rules that apply to government surveillance. And those rules simply do not provide the same level of protection to identifying information as they do to the content of communications. Nor do they provide the same amount of safeguards to anonymity as defendants receive in civil suits between two private parties.

Not surprisingly, Vadas refused to quash the subpoenas. He rejected the higher *Cahill*-like standard that the John Does' lawyers proposed, writing that those come from discovery disputes between private parties, "not cases balancing the needs of a legitimate government investigation with the interest of a party wishing to remain anonymous."[41] Instead, Vadas applied a much lower standard for administrative subpoenas, requiring only procedural compliance and a demonstration that the information is "relevant and material to the investigation." Applying this standard, Vadas allowed the subpoena because the "identity of a potential touter of the Jammin Java stock 'touches' the SEC's Jammin Java investigation and thus is relevant."[42]

The subpoena targets asked District Judge Charles Breyer to review the magistrate judge's decision. Breyer affirmed Vadas, but thoroughly inquired into the government's interest and whether the subpoena was the least restrictive means to obtain the information. The higher summary judgment standard, Breyer wrote, "has never been applied in the context of an investigative subpoena issued by a government agency."[43] In 2015, the SEC filed a civil complaint against the company and nine people.[44]

The grand jury subpoena cases and the SEC investigation of Jammin' Java recognized that the subpoena targets have a First Amendment right to be anonymous. But in criminal and regulatory proceedings, that anonymity right is not always as strong as the rights of defendants in private civil lawsuits. The Fourth Amendment—which is the primary safeguard to protect against unreasonable government searches—simply does not provide many protections for anonymity interests.

This is not to suggest that criminal defendants should be entitled to more anonymity protections than civil litigants. The government should be able to uncover the identity of people suspected of distributing child pornography, making threats, and committing other illegal and harmful acts. But the courts should, at the very least, require more than just a statement that the identifying information is relevant to a government investigation. The First Amendment should require the government to present some evidence that the subpoena target has committed a crime or violated government regulations.

Like the copyright lawsuits, the government surveillance cases reveal the uneven application of the First Amendment protections. Defendants in defamation cases are more likely to be able to avail themselves of the First Amendment—and protect their identities—than criminal defendants.

Neither the First nor Fourth Amendments, as interpreted by courts nationwide, provide sufficient protection for anonymity in government investigations. Courts should reconsider the generally lax Fourth Amendment scrutiny that they apply to the government's attempts to unmask criminal suspects. Moreover, courts should apply more rigorous First Amendment standards to the government's requests for identifying information and use the same analytical frameworks that apply to civil subpoenas.

Yet even in areas such as copyright and criminal investigations, where US courts place less emphasis on anonymity protection, the United States is among the world's leaders in protecting anonymity.

10

ANONYMITY WORLDWIDE

The United States places a high value on anonymity, both offline and online. While the right to anonymity is far from absolute, it is stronger and better articulated than that of many other countries. As Jason A. Martin and Anthony L. Fargo wrote, "The legal right to anonymity is not defined anywhere else to the degree that it is in the United States."[1]

Perhaps the starkest contrast between the United States and some other countries can be seen in attempts to enact real-name laws, or legal requirements for people to use their real names when posting content on the Internet. China has an extensive history of imposing real-name mandates, including a 2003 requirement that Internet cafes gather their users' identifying information, in an effort to combat crime.[2] This was followed by local real-name registration requirements.[3]

In 2012, China enacted the Decision of the Standing Committee of the National People's Congress on Strengthening Online Information Protection, which provides that "network service providers should require their users to supply true identification information when signing [an] agreement to provide them with website access, fixed line telephone, mobile phone access, or allow them to post information via the network."[4] This decision was a significant step toward nationally requiring real names at registration for online services.

China continued down the path toward real names in 2017, when the government of President Xi Jinping enacted regulations to implement its Cybersecurity Law. These regulations require, among other things, message boards and other online forums to deny service to users who do not register under their real names. The regulations also require users to register their real names when posting social media comments.[5]

As Samm Sacks and Paul Triolo noted, the erosion of anonymity is part of China's construction of a "social credit system" that monitors its citizens' behavior and ranks their trustworthiness.[6] Sacks and Triolo observed that some companies worldwide, such as Facebook, have adopted real-name registration requirements, but few governments have been able to prohibit anonymity. "Beijing's effort, accelerated under Xi, to eliminate anonymity online in the name of cybersecurity appears to be one of the Communist Party's most well-organized activities, legally and bureaucratically," they wrote.[7]

Although China has received the most attention for its extensive real-name rules, other nations have cracked down on anonymity. Brazil's Federal Constitution bans anonymity, and a Brazilian regulation requires customers to provide personal information when they sign up for mobile phone service.[8] In 2014, Russia enacted a "bloggers law" that requires bloggers who have at least three thousand readers to sign up with the nation's media oversight agency.[9] And Iran requires Internet users to register their IP addresses.[10]

Authoritarian governments have an easier time cracking down on anonymity than other countries. As Martin and Fargo wrote, "Countries with authoritarian media regulation or developing economic systems tend to take a more conservative approach toward anonymous expression."[11]

In nonauthoritarian regimes, however, anonymity often receives greater protections. For instance, a South Korean law that went into effect in 2009 mandated websites with more than 100,000 visitors a day to require real-name registration. Rather than complying with the law, YouTube prevented comments and video uploads from South Korean servers.[12] But in 2012, South Korea's Constitutional Court struck down the requirement as a violation of free speech. "Expressions under anonymity or pseudonym allow (people) to voice criticism on majority opinion without giving into external pressure," the court wrote. "Even if there is a side effect to online anonymity, it should be strongly protected for its constitutional value."[13]

The positions of US courts on anonymity are closer to those of South Korea than China or Russia. In the United States, if a law even comes close to requiring an Internet user to provide real identifying information, it is unlikely to pass constitutional muster. In 1997, a federal judge struck down a Georgia criminal law that prohibited the use of computers "to falsely identify" a person.[14] The court rejected Georgia's argument that the statute helped prevent fraud, reasoning that the law "could apply to a wide range of transmissions which 'falsely identify' the sender, but are not 'fraudulent' within the specific meaning of the criminal code."[15]Likewise, the next year, a federal judge in New Mexico struck down a New Mexico law that prohibited the electronic transmission of material harmful to minors. The statute allowed website operators and others to avoid the criminal penalties by limiting access to indecent materials via age-gating technology such as requiring a verified credit card.[16] In striking down the law, the judge wrote that the verification requirement "would bar many adults who lack such identification from access to information appropriate for them."[17]

Even when the government establishes a strong and specific need for a law that requires the defendant to unmask himself, US courts are highly skeptical of the constitutionality of such laws. In 2014, the US Court of Appeals for the Ninth Circuit struck down a California law that required registered sex offenders to provide law enforcement with a list of all Internet identifiers that they use. The California law allowed law enforcement to publicly release the identifiers for public safety reasons. The Ninth Circuit ruled that the law "chills anonymous speech because it too freely allows law enforcement to disclose sex offenders' Internet identifying information to the public."[18] Sex offender online identification laws are a closer call, however. In 2010, the US Court of Appeals for the Tenth Circuit rejected a constitutional challenge to a Utah law that required registered sex offenders to disclose their Internet identifiers, but that law did not allow law enforcement to disclose those identifiers to the public.[19]

These cases show that US courts are very likely to strike down laws that require Internet users to identify themselves. Such laws diverge from

First Amendment anonymity precedent, and at the very least, the government has to provide a compelling reason for prohibiting anonymity.

Courts in many western democracies protect anonymous and pseudonymous speech. But those courts are more likely to focus on privacy concerns, while US courts are inclined to emphasize free speech interests. In some cases, the difference in the legal framework will make it less likely for a court to protect anonymity.

For instance, Finland's Protection of Privacy and Data Security in Telecommunications Act allowed the police to demand identifying information from telecommunications only for certain offenses. Malicious misrepresentation, however, was not among those offenses.[20] In 1999, a man emailed a twelve-year-old boy, asking to meet and "then to see what you want."[21] He was responding to a dating website advertisement for the boy. The ad stated that the boy wanted a relationship with a boy "to show him the way." The ad provided his personal information, and linked to a website that contained his picture and phone number. The boy had not placed the advertisement, but it was impossible to tell from reading it who the author was.[22]

The boy's father contacted the police, who unsuccessfully tried to obtain the account information from the ISP that provided the IP address from which the advertisement was posted. The police requested the Helsinki District Court to require the ISP to provide the identifying information, but the court denied the request, saying it was not authorized to do so by the Finland telecommunications privacy law.[23] The Court of Appeal affirmed the district court, and the Supreme Court denied review.[24] The boy then challenged the Finnish law in the European Court of Human Rights.

Many of the US anonymity cases focused on the free expression and privacy rights of the anonymous speaker who was the target of the unmasking attempt. Yet in this European case, the focus was on the privacy rights of the boy. He asserted that the advertisement violated his rights under the European Convention on Human Rights, which states that all people have "the right to respect for his private and family life, his home and his correspondence."[25] The boy's lawyers argued to the European Court that the Finnish law prevented him from holding the poster accountable for this privacy violation.[26]

The European Court concluded that the Convention not only prevented the government from invading a person's privacy, but it might impose "positive obligations inherent in an effective respect for private or family life," such as preventing others from invading privacy.[27] This is a significant difference from the negative obligations set forth in the US Bill of Rights, which focus on constraining the government.

The Finnish government argued that its laws allowed the child to sue the service provider, but the court ruled that this was insufficient to protect his privacy interests. "It is plain that both the public interest and the protection of the interests of victims of crimes committed against their physical or psychological well-being require the availability of a remedy enabling the actual offender to be identified and brought to justice," the court wrote.[28]

To allow for investigations into such privacy violations, the court wrote, the law cannot prevent the service provider from disclosing the poster's identity. The court gave little weight to anonymity protection. "Although freedom of expression and confidentiality of communications are primary considerations and users of telecommunications and Internet services must have a guarantee that their own privacy and freedom of expression will be respected, such guarantee cannot be absolute and must yield on occasion to other legitimate imperatives, such as the prevention of disorder or crime or the protection of the rights and freedoms of others," the court wrote.[29] The Finnish law, the court concluded, violated the boy's privacy rights under the European Convention, and the court ordered the government to pay him three thousand euros.

The case, *K.U. v. Finland*, represents the contrast between the United States and European approaches to privacy and free expression, and how those values shape the courts' approaches to anonymity. Europe values privacy as a fundamental human right, as seen not only in the European Charter on Human Rights, but also in its sweeping General Data Protection Regulation, which went into effect in 2018 and provides Europeans with the ability to access, delete, and correct the personal information that companies store about them.

The United States, in contrast, has a relatively weak system of privacy protections. Although the Fourth Amendment protects against certain government privacy invasions, and various provisions of the Constitution, taken together, have been found to provide "penumbral rights" of privacy,[30] the US Constitution does not explicitly provide a right of privacy. The United States also lacks a general, nationwide privacy law, with federal laws instead focusing only on particular sectors such as healthcare and financial institutions.

But the United States places far greater value on free speech than many other Western democracies. As Robert Sedler wrote in 2006, the US Supreme Court's strong First Amendment precedent means that the "constitutional protection afforded to freedom of speech in the United States is seemingly unparalleled anywhere else in the world."[31] Had *K.U. v. Finland* been a dispute in the United States, the US court likely would have assessed whether any statutes restrict the service provider's ability to disclose the information, and it also would have engaged in some form of First Amendment analysis of the police department's demand for the identifying information.

By framing anonymity as a value protected under free speech rights, it is unsurprising that, at least in some cases, the European courts would be less likely than US courts to recognize a strong right to anonymity. The court in *K.U. v. Finland* focused on providing the boy with a remedy for the egregious privacy violation that he suffered, so it naturally would conclude that the denial of the identifying information violated the Convention.

As Daniel Solove correctly observed in 2007, "Anonymity is a form of privacy protection, yet it can also facilitate privacy violations."[32] Piercing anonymity may protect the privacy rights of the person who was the subject of the initial harm, but it also may implicate the privacy rights of the poster. A shortcoming of both the US and European approaches to anonymity is that they view anonymity as mostly a free speech concern. But as seen in the Malibu Media cases and so many other attempts to unmask anonymous Internet users, anonymity is more than just about the ability to express oneself. It is a privacy concern.

Courts in both the United States and Europe should consider the privacy intrusion caused by unmasking an anonymous online poster. By weighing unmasking as both a free speech and a privacy issue, the European and US courts likely would be in better harmony in their analysis of unmasking. I am not suggesting that courts cease their assessments of the impact of unmasking on free speech. But the courts should also analyze the privacy impacts of unmasking.

The substantial role that US free speech doctrine plays in anonymous speech becomes particularly clear when foreign courts handle corporate cybersmear cases.

Totalise was a posterchild for the dot-com boom in the United Kingdom. Founded in 1999, the Internet service provider tried to lure new customers by offering them free shares of its stock.[33] Like many US companies during the early Internet heyday, Totalise was a frequent topic of discussions on online stock bulletin boards. In August 2000, Totalise noticed posts on The Motley Fool financial discussion website, from a user named "Z Dust," that it believed were defamatory.

Totalise requested that Motley Fool remove the posts, claiming they were defamatory. On the same day that it received the request, Motley Fool responded that it had deleted the posts and revoked Z Dust's access to the site. Yet Motley Fool eventually allowed Z Dust to post on the site again. After more complaints from Totalise, Motley Fool permanently banned Z Dust. Totalise then asked Motley Fool to disclose Z Dust's identifying information, but Motley Fool refused, citing a UK privacy law.[34]

This wasn't the end of Z Dust's commentary about Totalise. In early 2001, the company learned that the poster had moved to a second site, Interactive Investor, and posted nearly ninety messages about Totalise. Totalise demanded that Interactive Investor provide Z Dust's identifying information, and Interactive Investor refused, citing the same privacy law as Motley Fool.

Although both websites said they removed the posts, Totalise wanted to hold Z Dust personally accountable. Z Dust's posts are no longer online or part of the public record, but a judge would later describe the post as calling "into question both the competence and integrity of [Totalise's] management and the company's solvency, suggesting that it is on the point of collapse."[35]

Totalise asked Justice Robert Owen of the High Court of Justice, Queen's Bench Division, to order the websites to provide Z Dust's identifying information. Totalise sought what is known as a *Norwich Pharmacal* order, named after a 1974 House of Lords case that allows a plaintiff to conduct early discovery to identify defendants. Owen granted the request, recognizing the company's need to identify the poster and protect its reputation. Totalise, Owen wrote, "does not know, and has no means of discovering, the identity of Z Dust." Owen rejected the websites' argument that the British privacy law barred the disclosure, pointing to an exception that allows for disclosure of personal information in legal proceedings or as required by a court order.

Motley Fool also argued that the request violated a provision in the Contempt of Court Act, which bars courts from requiring parties to "disclose the source of information contained in a publication for which he is responsible" unless for the "interests of justice," national security, or crime prevention. Owen reasoned that this law is only intended to help journalists protect the confidentiality of their sources, and it does not apply to websites who are asked for identifying information about their posters. The websites "take no responsibility for what is posted on their discussion boards," Owen wrote. Even if the Contempt of Court Act applied to this request, unmasking the anonymous poster is "necessary in the interests of justice," Owen wrote. Totalise, he reasoned, presented a "strong prima facie case" of defamation that poses a "considerable threat" to Totalise. The comments are "very serious" because they question the company's ability to survive and the competence of the company's management, he wrote. "The potential audience is vast," Owen wrote. "It has no geographical limit." He also concluded that the poster was "hiding behind the anonymity" of both bulletin boards, and that Totalise had "no other practical means" of identifying the poster.[36]

Even though both websites have confidentiality policies, Owen wrote, he must compel them to provide the identifying information. "To find otherwise would be to give the clearest indication to those who wish to defame that they can do so with impunity behind the screen of anonymity made possible by the use of websites on the internet," Owen wrote. Owen also required the websites to cover Totalise's litigation costs.[37]

Interactive Investor successfully appealed Owen's decision to require it to cover Totalise's costs. Although the company did not appeal the order to disclose the identifying information, the Court of Appeal noted that it believed that Owen failed to consider "relevant matters," including "the effect upon Interactive of voluntarily disclosing confidential details."[38]

What is noteworthy about both rulings in the case is that they glossed over the impact of the order on anonymous speech. The rulings focused narrowly on the requirements of an easily circumvented privacy law and did not examine the broader free speech implications of forcing service providers to unmask their users and subject them to defamation lawsuits.

Now consider how a similar dispute would play out in a US court. Free speech interests would be front and center in any US court's decision on unmasking a cybersmear defendant. As seen in *Dendrite* and its progeny, the plaintiffs would face an uphill battle to persuade a court to allow the subpoenas.

Owen's analysis is a far cry from that of *Dendrite*. Although he summarily concluded that it was "perfectly plain" that the postings were "highly defamatory," he did not engage in the detailed evidentiary analysis that a US court likely would apply before ordering a defendant's unmasking. Even if he had conducted a thorough analysis, the bar for succeeding in a defamation lawsuit is much lower in the United Kingdom than it is in the United States. And a court applying the *Dendrite* test would not only evaluate the sufficiency of the evidence, but also would conduct a balancing test that weighs the strength of the case against the free speech interests. The United Kingdom further demonstrated its relative concerns about anonymous online speech when it enacted the Defamation Act of 2013.

The law explicitly immunizes website operators for statements on their sites that were not written by the website operators. But a plaintiff can overcome this defense if, among other things, "it was not possible for the claimant to identify the person who posted the statement."[39] The regulations issued under the law also require the websites to contact the poster upon receiving a complaint about a post and set a framework for the website to provide the complainant with the poster's contact details.[40]

The regulations do not absolutely require a website to attribute every statement to each poster, but if the site cannot reach the poster, it can only retain its immunity if it removes the post within forty-eight hours of receiving a complaint. Although the law does not prohibit entirely anonymous posts, it creates a strong incentive for a website to require posters to provide their identifying information. At the very least, it discourages the policies of some websites, such as AutoAdmit, which went out of its way to avoid logging IP addresses. And if the poster is truly anonymous and untraceable, the law strongly encourages the platform to remove the anonymous speech upon receiving a complaint.

Canada, like Europe and the United Kingdom, also emphasizes privacy over free speech in its anonymity analysis. A 2000 case from the Ontario Superior Court of Justice, *Irwin Toy v. Doe*, reveals the contrast with the United States.

An anonymous Internet user sent an email regarding Irwin Toy and its president, George Irwin, to about seventy-five people. The company claimed that the email defamed George Irwin and contained attachments with confidential corporate information.[41] Irwin Toy tracked the email to an IP address provided by iPrimus Canada, an ISP. iPrimus told Irwin Toy that it would provide the subscriber's identifying information only if the company obtained a court order, and that iPrimus would not oppose the order.[42]

Rather than merely grant the unopposed order for unmasking the defendant, Judge John C. Wilkins saw the need to issue a written opinion outlining his reasoning, as he anticipated "that the courts will be seeing motions of this nature on a more frequent basis, as members of the public become curious to determine the true identity of the originator of messages, and/or information passed through the internet, or posted on 'notice boards' or disclosed in 'chat rooms' therein."[43] If courts were to automatically unmask online posters, he wrote, "the fact of the anonymity of the internet could be shattered for the price of the issuance of a spurious Statement of Claim and the benefits obtained by the anonymity lost in inappropriate circumstances."[44]

Despite his apparent desire to set the rules of the road for online speech in Canada, Wilkins gave rather short shrift to any free speech concerns associated with unmasking the emailer. Wilkins allowed the disclosure of the identifying information, reasoning that Irwin Toy had laid out a "prima facie" case for defamation and conversion of private and confidential information.[45] Although that sounds like the analysis in *Dendrite* and *Cahill*, Wilkins did not describe exactly what portions of the email were defamatory or contained confidential information, nor did he state what amount of evidence (if any) suffices to meet his test for unmasking.

Other times, the focus on privacy results in strong anonymity protections. In 2004, the Federal Court of Canada, Trial Division, refused record companies' request to order Internet service providers to disclose the identities of twenty-nine customers who had allegedly distributed music online. The copyright lawsuit was similar to the recording industry's US claims in 2003 and 2004.

To evaluate the unmasking request, the trial judge developed a five-part test, including the strength of the claim, involvement in the dispute by the service provider, the lack of other sources for the information, and compensation to the ISP for the costs of discovery. But the fifth factor was the most noteworthy—and most distinct from US courts' approach—that "the public interests in favour of disclosure must outweigh the legitimate privacy concerns."[46]

While that balancing test might sound like the final factor in the New Jersey court's *Dendrite* analysis, it differs because the court must weigh the *privacy* interests rather than the free speech interests. Explicitly incorporating privacy into an anonymity balancing test allows a court to place a higher value on activities, such as downloading, that are not very expressive.

Judge Konrad von Finckenstein reasoned that this balancing test weighed against disclosure of the information. To grant an unmasking request, he wrote, he "must be satisfied that the information about to be disclosed is reliable." Because the record companies waited months before requesting the discovery, he reasoned, the information was less likely to be reliable, and there was an increased risk of "an innocent account holder being identified."[47] Soon after, Canadian technology law scholars Ian Kerr and Alex Cameron wrote that the ruling "must unquestionably be read as a victory for privacy and as an endorsement for preserving online anonymity unless there are strong reasons to justify compelling the disclosure of identity."[48] The Federal Court of Appeal affirmed von Finckenstein, writing that privacy is an "important consideration."[49] In this regard, Canada's anonymity protections are arguably stronger than those in the United States, at least for online activities such as file sharing that some US judges do not view to be sufficiently expressive to warrant rigorous First Amendment protections. By grounding its anonymity rights in privacy rather than expression, Canada could cover a wider range of online activities.

Canadian courts can more easily justify their privacy-focused anonymity analyses. In 2000, Canada enacted the Personal Information Protection and Electronic Documents Act, a nationwide privacy law. As Judge von Finckenstein noted in his opinion, one of the "primary purposes" of the law is "the protection of an individual's right to control the collection, use and disclosure of personal information by private organizations."[50] Because the Canadian privacy law has an exception that allows disclosure with a valid court order, von Finckenstein concluded that the law, combined with previous court rulings, requires the explicit weighing of privacy interests before allowing the unmasking.

Although many US states have passed their own privacy laws, and Congress regulates particular sectors, the United States does not have a similar generally applicable, nationwide privacy law. That may eventually change, as members of Congress introduce nationwide privacy and data protection bills that would give Americans control over their data, in the same manner as Europe's General Data Protection Regulation. As I explain in chapter 15, a European privacy model is a positive step toward preserving anonymity, as companies have unprecedented access to identifying information. Although the United States has long relied on the First Amendment to protect anonymity, those free speech protections may no longer be sufficient.

Whatever the shortcomings of the US legal protections for anonymity, they are only one mechanism by which people can separate their words from their identities. Widely available technology also allows people to control the dissemination of their identifying information.

11

TECHNOLOGICAL PROTECTIONS
FOR ANONYMITY

First Amendment precedent has been essential in creating an atmosphere for online anonymity empowerment in the United States. But precedent tells only part of the story.

To fully understand anonymity in the United States, you also must understand the technology that protects anonymity. To understand the technology that protects anonymity, you must understand a revolutionary anonymity protection, the Tor browser. To understand the Tor browser, you must understand the concept on which it is based, onion routing.

And to understand onion routing, you must understand pizza.

Pizza deliveries, that is. To be more specific, pizza deliveries to the Pentagon. Wolf Blitzer, who was CNN's Defense Department reporter in 1990, said that he noticed pizza deliveries to the Pentagon late at night, and suspected that they were dealing with Iraq's invasion of Kuwait, as Desert Shield would become Desert Storm.

"Later, by the way, when I was CNN's senior White House correspondent, I always knew there was some sort of crisis going on in the West

Wing after hours when I saw the arrival of pizzas," Blitzer told *Stars and Stripes* newspaper in a 2010 email. "Bottom line for journalists: Always monitor the pizzas."[1]

The Pentagon probably did not want Blitzer or any other reporter to know that the situation in the Middle East was escalating, and the pizza deliveries at least partly prevented officials from keeping that information secret. The compromise was not in the content of the message being sent to or from the pizza shop—it didn't matter to the reporters whether the pizzas had pepperoni or green peppers. The valuable information was that it was the *Pentagon* that was ordering the pizza late at night.

What the Pentagon needed was anonymity.

About five years later, three Defense Department scientists would confront anonymity in a different context, with lessons that could apply to the Pentagon's pizza problem. The Naval Research Laboratory in Southwest Washington, DC, is responsible for the US Navy's and Marine Corps' applied and basic research.[2]

David Goldschlag was a computer scientist in the lab's more theoretical formal methods section, which uses math to address problems in systems and software, and Michael Reed was a computer scientist in the lab's computer security section. In 1995, as the Internet was rapidly moving from an academic and military technology to home and business computers worldwide, researchers were increasingly concerned with how to secure the technology. At the Naval Research Laboratory, scientists were tasked with thinking about the big-picture issues that warranted further research.

One day in 1995, Goldschlag and Reed discussed whether it is possible to prevent outside observers from learning the identities of the parties that are communicating with each other on the Internet, Reed recalls. This was precisely the sort of challenge that the lab's scientists loved to tackle.

"NRL is a neat place," Reed said in an interview. "It's a lot like being in academia except you don't have the teaching responsibilities."

This academic question was a particular challenge. Some early computer science literature had addressed how to communicate anonymously, but none was directly applicable to real-time or near real-time communication on the Internet. As seen in the many unmasking disputes discussed earlier in this book, anonymity is hard to come by on the Internet. Even if users do not operate under their real names, they can be identified by their Internet Protocol (IP) address. Every computer—including servers and end-user terminals—is identified by an IP address, a unique sequence of numbers. If you visit www.google.com, the data are exchanged between your IP address and Google's IP address.

If you visit a website from home, that site's operator can identify your IP address and see that the traffic is coming from a Comcast account. If you visit a website from the Pentagon, the operator can see that the Pentagon is looking at the site. More concerning, third parties—such as Internet service providers and authoritarian foreign governments that conduct surveillance—could use IP addresses to identify two parties that are communicating, even if the content of the communication is encrypted.

The question also was important for the military. Just as the Pentagon did not want Wolf Blitzer to gain insight into its operations by monitoring its pizza deliveries, the Pentagon and federal intelligence agencies also did not want outside observers monitoring the sources of information that they were accessing on the Internet. Intelligence agencies rely partly on "open-source"—or publicly available—intelligence. If adversaries could see which areas of the Internet the intelligence agencies were exploring, their operations could be compromised. Goldschlag had worked at the National Security Agency before joining the lab, and he knew that the identity of the parties communicating was almost as important as the content of their communications.

Reed and Goldschlag went to Paul Syverson, a Naval Research Laboratory researcher with graduate degrees in math and philosophy who carpooled with Goldschlag. Syverson had joined the lab's formal methods section in 1989 and had worked on problems such as devising epistemic logics to reason about secure communication as might, for example, occur between an ATM and a bank when someone makes a withdrawal. They all were intrigued, and saw a comparison to the Pentagon's pizza problem. Imagine if, one day, people could order pizza over the Internet. "They wouldn't even need to camp outside of the Pentagon to see what was going on," Syverson said. "They could just watch the network, and that would be easier."

To Syverson, the need for anonymity reached far beyond the intelligence and defense community, into other areas of government. Suppose that an examiner at the US Patent and Trademark Office is searching the Internet to see if other companies have created technology that is like a patent application that the examiner is evaluating. That examiner would not want anyone knowing that the Patent and Trademark Office is researching the technology.

Reed, Goldschlag, and Syverson spent many days tossing around ideas and sketching diagrams of a structure that would allow connections while preventing anyone—including the person on the other end of the communication—from learning the IP address. The structure had to encompass a connection to handle the low latency and interactivity requirements of things like remote login or connecting to a webpage. The result was onion routing. They called it onion routing because the connection was created by a virtual onion, composed entirely of layers of encryption.

Here is a very high-level version of how it works. Let's say that computer A wants to connect to a website hosted on computer E. If A were to connect to E directly, then anyone who could observe the connection (including the organization that owns computer E, computer A's ISP, computer E's ISP, and possibly a government surveillance agency) could see A's IP address.

In onion routing, A uses a randomized series of intermediary computers—or "proxy nodes"—to act as middlemen between A and E. Let's say these proxy nodes are computers B, C, and D. Assume that each computer is located in a different country. If A's message simply routed from B to C to D to E without an onion, there would be little anonymity protection because someone in the middle could intercept the routing instructions and deduce the originator's IP address. This is where the onion comes in.

A makes a connection to B with an "onion" of encrypted layers of routing information. Only B can decrypt—or peel back—that first layer of the onion, which reveals the next destination, C, along with a shared key known only to A and B. B sends the remaining layers of the onion to C. Only C can peel back the next layer of the onion, revealing the next destination, D, along with a key known only to A and C. (C does not know who it is sharing this key with, only that it arrived in the onion.) C sends the remaining layer of the onion to D. Finally, D decrypts that final layer of the onion, revealing a key, and waits. The first data A sends down this "cryptographic circuit" are encrypted with the shared keys in the onion. What arrives unencrypted at D is an instruction to connect to the final destination, E. The next data are the beginning of a web connection between A and E. The connection goes over a circuit so that E can securely send messages back (such as the content of a webpage), and so A and E can communicate interactively as long as the connection is open. Communication from web server E going back to A gets a layer of encryption as it passes D, C, and B. B hands this to A, which strips all the encryption off and reads the web server's response.

Onion routing protects anonymity because of the multiple "hops" along the route. Someone conducting surveillance on A could see only that A made a connection to B, but would not know that the ultimate intended destination was E, as that routing information is buried far inside multiple layers of encryption.

What if the people operating computer B were secretly working with an adversarial nation? They could see that the connection came from A, and that they were forwarding it along to C. Yet anyone with access to computer B would have no idea that traffic from A moving along this connection was destined for E or that traffic coming back started at E.

Likewise, anyone with access to computer E would have no way of tracing the message back to A's IP address. They could see only that messages were being passed to and from D. Because onion routing is designed to work with ordinary web servers that know nothing about it, all E knows is that it received an ordinary web connection from D.[3]

To understand the genius of onion routing, it is useful to compare it with another anonymity technology, the Virtual Private Network, or VPN. VPNs are services that offer encrypted tunnels through which people connect to the Internet. Let's say that a user on computer A connects to website C via VPN B. Provided that the VPN is working perfectly (and that does not always happen), people with access to C's server logs would see only that a user of VPN B is connecting; they would not see A's IP address. Although VPNs provide security and some anonymity, there is a possibility that A's IP address could be revealed if VPN B was compromised (whether through an inside actor, an outside hacker, or government surveillance). VPNs also might not provide adequate protection against the websites that are visited, and identifying information might leak through an ISP connection. Under a system of onion routing, by contrast, a compromise of one of the three proxy routers would not reveal the user's identity, as the routing metadata are distributed across multiple "hops." Additionally, imagine that a Defense Department employee accesses a DOD VPN from an overseas hotel. Although the traffic may be encrypted, an employee of that hotel's ISP might be able to identify that the traffic involves the DOD—or at least the US government—because the Defense Department VPN may have a well-known address.

The three scientists published their first paper on onion routing, titled "Hiding Routing Information," at a May 1996 Workshop on Information Hiding in Cambridge, United Kingdom. The emphasis of their research was not necessarily anonymous communications, but rather anonymous traffic routing. Onion routing allows the parties that are communicating to set their own rules for identification.

"Our goal here is not to provide anonymous communication, but, to place identification where it belongs," they wrote. "The use of a public network should not automatically reveal the identities of communicating parties. If anonymous communication is undesirable, it is easy to imagine filters on the endpoint machines that restrict communication to signed messages."[4]

They had sketched out a rough concept for the technological framework of onion routing. The three researchers continued to refine onion routing. They faced logistical challenges. Imagine that the US government used a technology that blocked anyone else from observing its IP addresses via onion routing. If the government was the only organization using the technology, then it would do little to conceal the fact that government agencies were behind the Internet traffic.

"The critical thing is you can't have the government be the only customer of this," Goldschlag said in a 2019 interview. "Then you're not hiding what the government's doing. It depended on large amounts of use by lots of other people in order to provide the anonymity that the system required."

They also faced some technical challenges in the initial designs that they would overcome in further iterations of onion routing. Onion routing relies on "symmetric keys"—meaning that B uses the same encryption key that A used to encrypt the message. But how do A and B know the encryption key? In the initial version of onion routing, A's computer exchanged the encryption keys with each of the other computers via public key encryption—in other words, the sender encrypts the information with the recipient's public key, and the recipient decrypts it with a private key.

Goldschlag left the Naval Research Laboratory in 1997, and Reed left in 2000—both for the private sector. Syverson remained at the laboratory, and built partnerships to address both the technical and logistical challenges of onion routing. Most critically, beginning in 2002, Syverson worked with recent Massachusetts Institute of Technology graduates Roger Dingledine and Nick Mathewson to develop the next generation of onion routing, which they named Tor. They received research funding from the Office of Naval Research and the Defense Advanced Research Projects Agency.

Among the most critical developments in Tor was addressing the concern that a compromise in the public key encryption system could effectively break the system's security. Tor uses a key establishment protocol to create a symmetric key by combining public and private key information, avoiding the possibility of a compromise. "We can have a symmetric key we share without ever actually transmitting that key on the wire," Syverson said. "You don't see the key." Tor also introduced important improvements like directory servers for clients to learn which relay nodes were in the network and which were expected to be currently up and running.

Syverson, Dingledine, and Mathewson described Tor in a 2004 security symposium paper. "We are now at a point in design and development where we can start deploying a wider network," they wrote.[5] Also in 2004, Tor began receiving funding from the Electronic Frontier Foundation, and by the end of the year there were more than a hundred Tor nodes.[6]

A nonprofit organization, The Tor Project, was founded in 2006 to continue the work. The most consequential development in deploying Tor to the masses began in 2008, when the Tor Project began work on the Tor browser, which allows everyday users to more easily access onion routing.[7] By 2014, Tor had six thousand relay nodes in about eighty-nine countries and estimated that about 2.5 million people used the Tor browser each day.[8]

A particularly high-profile use of Tor came in 2010 and 2011, not in the United States but in the Middle East and Northern Africa during the Arab Spring uprisings. Authoritarian governments blocked access to social media, and many activists circumvented these restrictions via Tor. Daily Tor sessions in Egypt surged from 250 in December 2010 to 2,500 two months later.[9]

For instance, the Tor Project reported that dissidents in Egypt circumvented government-imposed blocks on social media sites such as Twitter by using the Tor browser. Tor is a key tool for circumventing such censorship and enabling the dissemination of dissenting viewpoints.[10]

Likewise, after Turkey's government in 2014 prohibited certain social media to prevent the discussion of government corruption allegations, its residents flocked to Tor. The number of new Turkish users per week increased 700 percent after the ban.[11] Other dictators noticed Tor's success in combatting oppressive regimes. In 2014, Russia's interior ministry offered a reward of $114,000 for assistance in unmasking Tor users.[12]

The use of Tor by dissidents worldwide shows the value of anonymity that dates to the days of Junius and Thomas Paine. Proponents of anonymity worldwide have a strong Legal Motivation and Safety Motivation for separating their identities from their words; had they been identified, they would have faced increased chances of prosecution and punishment. Tor has operationalized many of the greatest benefits of anonymity that societies have relied on for centuries.

Awareness of Tor gradually built throughout the 2010s, and not only in authoritarian regimes. For instance, in 2014, Lifehacker, a popular US website, wrote about the benefits—and limits—of Tor. "On a more general level, Tor is useful for anyone who wants to keep their internet activities out of the hands of advertisers, ISPs, and web sites," Thorin Klosowski wrote for the site. "That includes people getting around censorship restrictions in their country, police officers looking to hide their IP address, or anyone else who doesn't want their browsing habits linked to them."[13]

While the courts have been fostering the protection of anonymity for decades, the more recent technological developments such as Tor helped integrate anonymity into everyday online life. Tor—along with encrypted messaging apps such as Signal—"are designed with privacy and anonymity in mind and help inculcate those values as they spread and are adopted," Dr. Gabriella Coleman, an anthropologist at McGill University and one of the foremost experts on anonymity, wrote in 2019.[14]

Tor also has some inefficiencies. Its structure often makes it far slower than traditional web surfing. Rather than sending traffic directly to and from a web server, Tor directs it through three intermediaries, which may be located in different parts of the world.[15] And some commercial websites do not allow connections from Tor.[16] Despite the drawbacks, Tor use has continued to grow. As of mid-2020, the Tor Project reported well over

2.5 million users directly connecting to Tor relays. More than 22 percent of those users came from the United States, followed by Russia (16 percent), Germany (8 percent), and France (4 percent).[17]

Tor has helped protect at-risk populations in the United States. For years, the Tor Project has been working with domestic violence shelters to help victims prevent their abusers from monitoring their movements online. Dr. Kelley Misata, an information security expert, worked at the Tor Project from 2012 to 2014 after her own experience of being cyberstalked for years by a man who used Tor to evade legal responsibility. Misata said in a 2019 interview that she saw the possibility of Tor being used not as a weapon against women, but as a shield that allowed them to communicate without fear of being monitored by their abusers. "It perpetuates a confidence that can be built up over time that allows you to manage wherever your journey takes you," she told me.[18]

The vast majority of Tor browser traffic—more than 95 percent—goes to webpages accessible via normal web browsers.[19] The remaining traffic goes to "onion services," which are sites that are accessible only via a Tor browser. Rather than ending in ".com" or ".org," onion sites end in ".onion."

Some onion services are identical to or much like public-facing versions. Facebook in 2014 announced an onion service to ensure that Tor users could access the social media site.[20] In 2016, investigative journalism nonprofit ProPublica announced its onion service. "Our readers should never need to worry that somebody else is watching what they're doing on our site," Mike Tigas of ProPublica wrote. "So we made our site available as a Tor hidden service to give readers a way to browse our site while leaving behind less of a digital trail."[21]

Idealistic tech companies and journalism organizations are not the only organizations running onion services. In 2019, the Central Intelligence Agency announced that it was operating an onion service that provided all the features of its public website. "Our global mission demands that individuals can access us securely from anywhere," Brittany Bramell, CIA's director of public affairs, said when announcing the onion service. "Creating an onion site is just one of many ways we're going where people are."[22]

Some onion services that get substantial public attention, however, are not associated with public websites. They are also known as "hidden services," and a subset of them traffic in horrific and criminal content such as child sex abuse material, drug dealing, and murder-for-hire.[23] These sites, known colloquially as the "dark web," get significant media coverage, or at least media speculation. They also attract criticism from some in law enforcement.

"Tor obviously was created with good intention but it is a huge problem for law enforcement," Leslie Caldwell, then the assistant attorney general in charge of the Justice Department's Criminal Division, said at a 2015 conference. She pointed to the range of harmful hidden sites. "There are a lot of online supermarkets where you can do anything from purchase heroin to buy guns to hire somebody to kill somebody," she said. "There are murder-for-hire sites."[24]

The debate over these onion services is often conflated with the more general use of the Tor browser, but some critics make the crucial distinction. In a 2020 opinion piece, University of Massachusetts computer security experts Brian Levine and Brian Lynn wrote that while the Tor browser "provides an important anonymity service for individuals," they have concerns about hidden services that facilitate child sex abuse and other crimes: "Hidden services are creating resilient archives of child sexual abuse images that inflict pain long into the victims' adulthood. Because the internet has no physical boundaries, hidden services extend the reach of illicit content—including child pornography and illegal drugs—into all communities." Levine and Lynn encouraged Tor to "halt the failed hidden services project and start researching a different technology for enabling free speech."[25]

The users and operators of criminal onion services often are anonymous— and therefore out of reach of criminal prosecution. But they are not always able to remain anonymous. A prominent example of unmasking onion service users came in 2015, when the FBI successfully unmasked users of Playpen, an onion service that hosted child sex abuse material. Playpen was listed on a hidden service page devoted to child sex abuse material.[26] FBI agents in Maryland learned of the site and began connecting to it on September 16, 2014.[27]

Those who arrived at Playpen were greeted with pictures of partially clothed prepubescent girls with their legs spread, along with site registration instructions.[28] Users who clicked on the registration link would see a notice, informing them not to enter a real email address, as the site does not send confirmation emails. "This board has been intentionally configured so that it WILL NOT SEND EMAIL, EVER," the administrator wrote. "Do not forget your password, you won't be able to recover it."[29]

Users who registered for Playpen then had access to forums and subforums. Among the forum titles were "Jailbait—Boy," "Jailbait—Girl," "Preteen—Boy," and "Preteen—Girl," with more than six thousand posts between the four forums. Some of the other forum titles were "Toddlers," "Bondage," "Scat," and "Spanking."[30] The forum threads often contained images of children being raped by adults.[31] Playpen allowed private messages that appeared to foster child exploitation. For instance, in one post on a Playpen forum, a user wrote, "Yes i can help if you are a teen boy and want to fuck your little sister. write me a private message."[32] More than 11,000 users visited Playpen weekly. Some Playpen users were frequent posters—about 100 users had posted at least 100 times on the site, and 31 posted at least 300 times.[33] From August 2014 to February 2015, the website accumulated more than 95,000 posts and had more than 150,000 members.[34]

The FBI received a tip in December 2014 from a foreign law enforcement agency that Playpen might be operated on an IP address in the United States. The next month, the FBI obtained a search warrant to copy the Playpen server. The FBI suspected a Naples, Florida, resident, Steven W. Chase, as Playpen's administrator and tracked Playpen to a server in Lenoir, North Carolina.[35] The FBI arrested the suspected administrator in February 2015, and then took control of Playpen, operating it from a government server in Virginia.[36]

Although the FBI had obtained the server copy, any IP address logs that it might have contained would be of little use because all its visitors used Tor. The FBI received a warrant from a Virginia federal magistrate judge to deploy a "network investigative technique" to identify visitors to the site. Using this technique, the Playpen server caused visitors' computers to transmit their real IP addresses and other information to a government computer.[37] The FBI operated the Playpen server for two weeks beginning in February 2015.[38]

The investigative technique succeeded. By May 2017, the federal government had arrested at least 350 people in the United States associated with Playpen.[39] By circumventing the anonymity protections, the FBI peeled back the masks of hundreds of Americans and revealed that they had allegedly violated child sex abuse material laws.

Many defendants challenged the legality of the network investigative technique, arguing that federal criminal procedure rules did not allow a magistrate judge in Virginia to authorize a nationwide search warrant. Although many judges agreed that the warrant did not comply with the procedural rules, they generally rejected Fourth Amendment challenges, concluding that the FBI conducted its investigation in good faith.[40]

One of the people identified in the FBI's investigation operated under the username waytocool. This user accessed Playpen for 25.05 hours over two months. Among the posts that waytocool accessed was a link to a contact sheet that depicted the rape of a toddler by an adult male.[41] The FBI determined that Mediacom Communications Corporation was the ISP that provided waytocool's IP address and issued an administrative subpoena for the subscriber's identity. The FBI's investigation led to an apartment in Waseca, Minnesota, whose sole occupant was Terry Lee Carlson, Sr.[42]

The FBI used this information to obtain a warrant to search the apartment and found a hard drive with child pornography images and videos. The FBI also concluded that Carlson had produced and distributed child pornography.[43] The FBI found chats from years earlier in which Carlson bragged about molesting young boys.[44]

In November 2016, Carlson was indicted in Minnesota federal court, charged with five counts of production of child pornography, four counts of distribution of child pornography, one count of receipt of child pornography, and one count of possession of child pornography.[45] During an interview with law enforcement after his arrest, Carlson admitted that he had produced child pornography.[46] Despite a magistrate's recommendation to suppress much of the evidence, a federal judge denied Carlson's motion to suppress, and Carlson then pled guilty to one count of child pornography production.[47]

Carlson sought to persuade Judge John R. Tunheim to impose the minimum required sentence. In a six-page handwritten letter to Tunheim, Carlson told of the emotional toll he suffered after a divorce and the death of his father, whom Carlson had chosen not to connect to life support. "I blamed myself for my dad's passing," he wrote. "Asking myself for years to follow, what if I made the wrong choice?"

At that point, Carlson wrote, he became addicted to pornography. "I was alone and didn't have anyone I could confide in or spend time with," he wrote. He soon found groups online that trafficked in child pornography. "I felt I had made friends," he wrote. Some groups required members to contribute child pornography, and at that point he "betrayed the friendship" of a minor who had trusted him, he wrote.[48]

At Carlson's sentencing hearing on April 4, 2018, Assistant United States Attorney Carol Kayser recounted, in great detail, the evidence against Carlson, including the online chats in which Carlson bragged to others about molesting boys.[49]

"The record in this case shows that the defendant is a committed tenacious predator who thinks that children come on to him and want to be molested by him," Kayser said, seeking a prison sentence of twenty-five years.

Carlson's attorney requested the mandatory minimum sentence of fifteen years in prison.

"I made a mistake," Carlson told Tunheim at the hearing. "I did something wrong. It was terrible, and I feel bad about it."

Carlson's justification could not convince Tunheim to sentence him to the mandatory minimum. Instead, Tunheim issued a sentence of 262 months—nearly 22 years.

"It is obviously a serious crime that has a significant impact on victims, and that's something that the Court can't ignore," Tunheim said.

Were Tor, onion services, or the "dark web" the sole cause of Carlson's horrific acts? No. To be sure, the technology facilitated his (and others') use of Playpen. Without the anonymity that Tor provided, Carlson may have been caught sooner, or Playpen may have never existed in the first place. But he also very well may have found another way to view child sex abuse material. His court record suggests that the "dark web" was not the sole venue for his crimes, which began years before his documented access to Playpen. Among the FBI's evidence was a 2008 chat in which he bragged to another user that he had viewed child sex abuse material for six years. In the chat, he also discussed his use of GigaTribe, a peer-to-peer service, to distribute child sex abuse material. The chat took place on Yahoo, under the same username that he later would use on Playpen.[50] "In certain of his chats, you can tell that he was learning about GigaTribe in 2008, and by late July, early August of 2008, he was an enthusiastic user of GigaTribe, and he was encouraging his other chat partners to download the software to get on GigaTribe so that they could share and distribute child pornography," Kayser said at Carlson's sentencing hearing.[51]

While the public record does not indicate whether Carlson used anonymizing technology to access the chat or the peer-to-peer services, Yahoo and GigaTribe are a far cry from hidden services such as Playpen. The court record does not reveal whether Carlson's accessing of child sex abuse material was always anonymous, but it was not confined to hidden services such as Playpen.

Carlson's story illustrates some of the complexities of the battle against child sex abuse material. He accessed the illegal material on a hidden service, Playpen, but his online activities involving child sex abuse materials began years before Playpen was started in 2014, on more mainstream platforms. A subset of onion services enables anonymous dissemination of abusive images. That is an inescapable truth that must be considered when assessing the anonymity that onion services provide. But abusive online behavior is an inescapable use of the Internet as a whole, and it is not limited to onion services.

A tool such as Tor, which protects anonymity, is likely to have both legal and illegal uses. Fully quantifying how Tor is used is challenging, though some statistics about its use are publicly available.

Onion services are a small fraction of overall Tor use, and hidden services with criminal purposes are only a fraction of those onion services. And onion services constitute a small percentage of overall online child exploitation. A 2017 report from the Internet Watch Foundation found that of the tens of thousands of global webpages with child sexual abuse content, fewer than 1 percent were hidden onion services.[52]

"Yes, there's some horrible things, and I hope they get them and get rid of them," Syverson said, "but it's just not where a lot of it is."

A 2019 *New York Times* investigation into online child sex abuse material depicted the scope and complexity of the problem. The investigation highlighted some of the "dark web" forums in which people trafficked in the material, but noted that the "surge in criminal activity on the dark web accounted for only a fraction of the 18.4 million reports of abuse last year. That number originates almost entirely with tech companies based in the United States." The paper's investigation concluded that tech companies "have known for years that their platforms were being co-opted by predators, but many of them essentially looked the other way."[53]

The mere fact that a site like Playpen could exist—with thousands of users promoting horrific acts against children—is a tragedy that we must confront with the full force of the government's prosecutorial and investigative powers. I've heard the stories from Justice Department child exploitation investigators who are thwarted by the anonymity of hidden services. Has the technology been misused by some? Absolutely, and we must figure out how to stop this misuse, both by addressing the tools *and* the underlying causes of the misuse. The distinction that Lynn and Levine draw—focusing on hidden services rather than Tor as a whole—is worth further exploration, including an examination of both the costs and benefits of hidden services as a whole.

If even a tiny sliver of Tor use is harmful, it would be a disservice to ignore those harms when evaluating the technology. Similarly, it would be a disservice to ignore the tremendous benefits that Tor has fostered worldwide. Tor has done so much good for dissidents, whistleblowers, and other marginalized communities, not to mention the potential benefits it has had for the government intelligence operations that onion services initially were designed to serve. Tor has provided technological protections for anonymity just as the long line of First Amendment cases has provided legal protections. As with the legal protections for anonymity, the technological protections present a complex menu of costs and benefits.

As Syverson pointed out to me, Tor is far from the first communication innovation to be the scapegoat for society's ills. He notes that as far back as seventeenth-century England, the printing press was viewed as a national security threat. Syverson points to a classic and apt quote from psychologist Julian Jaynes: "Civilization is the art of living in towns of such size that everyone does not know everyone else. Not a very inspiring definition, perhaps, but a true one."[54]

While it would be easy to argue that Tor has harmed society—as cases such as Playpen reveal how it could be misused in devastating ways—I think that such a reaction would be shortsighted and a misreading of the complete body of evidence about Tor. As described throughout this book, harm occurs throughout the Internet, often without Tor or other anonymizing technologies. Some people remain anonymous merely by using unsecured Wi-Fi connections. Some steal the identities of others before committing crimes. Others simply take risks of being unmasked. And still others harass, stalk, and torment with their personal information in full public view. If we were to argue that cases such as Carlson's mean that Tor should not exist, then we also might conclude that the Internet as a whole should not exist, as so much documented abuse and crime occurs on non-onion services. But the root of the problem is not Tor—or the Internet more generally—rather it is the fundamental nature of some humans that *causes* them to use these online tools to harm others.

In my research for this book, perhaps nobody captured this complexity better than Kelley Misata, who suffered years of Tor-enabled cyberstalking before she took a job with the Tor Project and used the technology to empower abuse victims.

"I wasn't victimized by the technology," Misata said. "I was victimized by the person. The technology is just the vehicle."

Part III

LIVING IN AN ANONYMOUS WORLD

The culture of anonymity empowerment provided by the First Amendment and technology such as Tor has enabled users to communicate online with an unvarnished level of candor that very well may have been impossible if their names were linked to their expression and action. This has led to the good, the bad, and everything in between. Many people feel free to post about their intimate personal lives, and unpopular political views in ways that they never would in face-to-face interactions. Employees are empowered to expose the wrongdoings of their employers. But there also is a dark side to the culture of anonymity empowerment. Anonymous attackers launch harassment campaigns that ruin their targets' careers and personal lives. This part examines both the costs and benefits of the culture of anonymity empowerment. The stories in chapters 12 and 13 show just some of the ways that people have used the American culture of anonymity empowerment.

The legal and technological safeguards for anonymity enable much of the anonymous behavior—both good and bad—that we see on the

Internet. But it also becomes clear that anonymity is not the sole cause of this behavior. The crusading privacy journalist profiled in chapter 12 sought justice and equity long before the Internet emerged in everyday life. And while the cyberstalker portrayed in chapter 13 used technological anonymity protections to torment his victims, he had issues with interpersonal relations that went beyond the Internet.

While anonymity does not cause the good and bad acts that are carried out online, it amplifies and often enables them.

12

ANONYMITY AS A SHIELD

The qualified culture of anonymity empowerment has allowed people to conduct activities online that they might otherwise not have engaged in if they were forced to associate with their real names. Perhaps nowhere is that more true than in the blurry line between online activism and journalism, where anonymous and pseudonymous bloggers try to speak truth to power. The ability to hide part or all of their identities empowers them.

These bloggers and citizen journalists most often operate not under pure, untraceable anonymity, but in various forms of pseudonymity, enabling them to build credibility among readers. As David Post wrote in 1996, "By serving as storehouses of reputational capital, pseudonymous entities add value to social interaction in a way that anonymous speech does not."[1]

When the psychologist's seven-year-old son was upset about commercial whaling, she told him to start boycotts or write letters. "You have to do something," she told him.[2]

He wrote a letter to President Reagan, who did not respond. When George H. W. Bush took office, her son wrote to him. Still no response. "'OK,'" she recalls telling him, "now you've got to go over the President's head.' So he wrote a letter to Mrs. Bush."

The young child continued his letter-writing campaign and worked with Greenpeace, attaining some publicity. He wrote letters to the editor for their local newspaper in New York. This led to the family receiving threats at their home. But she was undeterred. "There's a lot of people out there with anger issues and self control problems who will threaten, who will come after you, who will stop you, who will show up at your doorstep, God only knows why," she said. "Are we going to live our lives in fear this way?"

This, in a nutshell, reveals the psychologist's fearless idealism. She proudly describes herself as a "child of the 60s." So it isn't surprising that as the Internet allowed people to voice their beliefs, she would take full advantage of the new platform. Nor is it a surprise that online anonymity would be crucial to her as she uncovered the truth and challenged the powerful.

The story of the psychologist—who uses the online pseudonym "Dissent Doe"—demonstrates the essential role that anonymity and pseudonymity have played for online activism and journalism. She wasn't always Dissent Doe. When she began posting in online psychology forums in the 1990s, she used her real name. One man whom she describes as a "want-to-be psychologist" did not believe that a psychology degree was necessary for the profession. She responded by critically analyzing the research that he cited.

"So he got upset and started harassing me, sent me vile email with sexual kinds of crap," she recalled.

She publicly responded to him, asking him to not contact her again. But the harassment escalated. He complained about her to her state's licensing board, and threatened to show up at conferences where she spoke. She knew his name—and that he had a gun—but she did not know what he looked like.

The Federal Bureau of Investigation suggested that she go offline for a while, and she did. She also befriended some white-hat hackers, and they gave her advice about how to protect herself online. She finally returned online—anonymously—in 2002 to launch a website about cyberstalking, with tips to stay safe online and protect anonymity. But she worried that because she described specific cases on the site, people might figure out her identity, and she pulled the plug on the website.

She still wanted to blog about privacy and anonymity, so in 2006, with a friend whom she met online, she founded a website dedicated to privacy news aggregation. They were inspired by a classic line—"We have met the enemy and he is us"—from the 1970 Pogo comic strip.

"I felt that that applied to privacy as well as to the environment," she said. "We were our own worst enemies. We were giving away information about ourselves to total strangers and to companies. And if you want to protect your privacy, you are your own worst enemy."

So they named the site PogoWasRight. The psychologist adopted the apt screen name of "Dissent Doe." Her collaborator, who would later part ways with the site, was "Ziplock." Because of her background as a psychologist, Dissent Doe was particularly interested in healthcare data breaches. She started a site, PHIprivacy.net. PHI is "protected health information," which are the data that are covered by US health privacy laws, and the site documented healthcare breaches.

"When you're a mental health professional, you really are keenly aware of the importance of privacy and confidentiality and keeping secrets, because most people feel safe to share information," she said.

She also received reports of breaches in other sectors, so she created a third site, DataBreaches.net, which eventually subsumed the health breaches site.

By 2020, Dissent Doe had accumulated more than twenty thousand posts on DataBreaches.net, still with a larger focus on healthcare than other sectors. Breaches of credit card data, for instance, do not concern her as much as a hospital that has leaked sensitive medical records. "Once people start getting your deep dark secrets, your really sensitive information, your medical information, that concerns me," she said.

Anonymity was crucial as Dissent Doe built an online following because she maintained her day job as a psychologist. She bluntly gives her opinions, particularly about medical privacy, and she digs deep to expose breaches of patient data, unafraid of upsetting her reporting subjects. "I didn't want my patients knowing what I was saying or thinking," she said. "I wanted to keep that clean."

Anonymity also is particularly important to Dissent Doe because she routinely writes about hackers and data breaches. Dissent Doe uses Tor when researching hackers' activities on the dark web. For more routine web browsing, she uses a VPN to anonymize herself. She also relies on throwaway email addresses and false names when necessary.

Hackers or security researchers will contact Dissent Doe to let her know about a breach, often of a hospital. Sometimes they will send the breached data to her as evidence. Her ultimate goal is to ensure that the hospital has disclosed the breach, as required by law. Dissent Doe views herself as not only a journalist, but also an advocate. She has filed complaints with regulators when she sees companies that refuse to remediate a data breach. Some of her complaints have led to enforcement actions by the Federal Trade Commission and other regulators.

"I want transparency," she said. "I want patients protected. I don't believe patients can protect themselves if information is withheld from them that they need."

Dissent Doe recounts an example of her journalism/activism. In April 2018, she was contacted by a hacker who told her that he had hacked a clinic two years earlier, and the organization failed to disclose the hack to its patients or the government, as required by law. The clinic also refused to pay the hacker the extortion fee that he had demanded, so he decided to let Dissent Doe know about it. "He says, 'I want you to have this information because they never told anybody,'" she recalls. The hacker provided her with the entire patient database, she said.

She says she spoke with the healthcare organization's external counsel in May 2018 to get a statement about the breach. But before she could publish a post about it, the clinic issued a press release two days later stating that it first learned of the breach in March 2018, when the clinic claimed that the hacker first notified the clinic of the alleged breach. Dissent Doe wrote a post about the clinic's press release, and her communications with the hacker.

The clinic's story would place the clinic within the sixty-day time frame in which federal law requires it to notify of data breaches. But this rendering of events conflicted with what the hacker told Dissent Doe: that the clinic had known about the breach since 2016. She filed Freedom of Information Act requests with both the federal and state health authorities, but both said they had received no reports in 2016. But she hit paydirt when she contacted the local police department, which provided her with a re-dacted report of a hacking that the clinic filed in July 2016. She wrote a second post about her discovery and also informed federal health privacy regulators.

In some cases, Dissent Doe must use her real name when communicat-ing with regulators. "I cannot let that issue stop me from doing some-thing, if it's really important and patient safety and patient privacy is on the line," she said. "That's my priority."

What if the United States were to pass a law that prohibited online anonymity and pseudonymity, such as the real-name requirements in countries such as China? She said that she is "an opinionated son of a bitch" who would continue to blog. "Will it chill some of the stuff I do? Probably," she said.

Anonymity, Dissent Doe said, was particularly important when she first launched her blogs. "If I had to start out under my real name, I would not have been able to start," she said. "Because then all my patients would have known and it would have chilled the way I spoke. It would have chilled the things I could do."

One aspect of her identity that Dissent Doe has not hidden is that she is female, and she thinks that has contributed to some of the harassment that she has experienced over the years. "If I were male, I don't think people would feel as comfortable coming after me and attacking me," she said.

Dissent Doe's anonymity has been compromised over the years, par-ticularly as she has upset the subjects of her reporting. She estimates that she receives legal threats at least monthly. On DataBreaches.net, Dissent Doe warns of the inefficacy of threats. "If you want to send me legal threats about my reporting or comments, knock yourself out, but don't be surprised to see me report on your threat, any confidentiality sig blocks you may attach notwithstanding," she writes. "I have been threat-ened with lawsuits many times, and to be blunt: there is NOTHING you can threaten me with that will scare me even 1/10th as much as the day both my kids got their driver's licenses within 15 minutes of each other."

Dissent Doe's blogging shows the benefits of the culture of anonym-ity empowerment that has shaped the United States. She uncovers truths about companies, and takes great personal risk by writing about the exploits of some of the world's most prolific hackers. She uses public records requests to get to the bottom of stories. She speaks her mind with little filter, and she produces excellent journalism. I have worked in cybersecurity law for more than a decade, and her blogs are consistently a must-read for me.

Dissent Doe is not a "journalist" in the traditional sense of a *New York Times* business reporter, who at least strives for objectivity. Dissent Doe proudly shares her goals of improving privacy and data security. She not only writes about data breaches, but she reports some companies to regulators. That simply is not the sort of journalism that you would see in a daily newspaper; indeed, a newspaper reporter might lose her job for reporting an article subject to regulators.

Dissent Doe's bias does not reduce her very real need for anonymity. Her speech produces a public good, and that speech depends on anonymity. The pamphleteers and newspaper scribes who lambasted the English colonization of America similarly lacked objectivity, yet their words served an important public interest. And anonymity was essential to their speech and advocacy.

With some online sleuthing, it is possible to discover Dissent Doe's true identity, as some people who have been unhappy with her journalism have managed to identify her at times. She does not fall into the "untraceable anonymity" category that A. Michael Froomkin described in 1995 as a "communication for which the author is simply not identifiable at all."[3] Instead, Dissent Doe would fall into Froomkin's category of "traceable pseudonymity," which is "communication with a *nom de plume* attached which can be traced back to the author (by someone), although not necessarily by the recipient."[4] (Dissent Doe refers to her status as "pseudo-anonymous.") On the spectrum of traceable pseudonymity, Dissent Doe is among the more traceable.

Speakers have long guarded their identities even if they did not have absolute anonymity. People had speculated about Hamilton, Madison, and Jay as the possible authors of the Federalist Papers, yet they carefully guarded their pseudonymity as "Publius." The Supreme Court protected the anonymity of the door-to-door canvassers, even though they may have been identifiable by their faces.

The culture of anonymity empowerment has not meant absolute protection from being identified, but that people can at least partly control the amount of information that others can obtain about them. And that is precisely what Dissent Doe does. By contacting regulators and other outside parties, she runs a real risk of being publicly unveiled, to her own professional detriment. Yet the culture of anonymity empowerment in the United States allows Dissent Doe to determine how much information about her is public.

Both law and technology contribute to this culture of anonymity empowerment. Dissent Doe can protect her anonymity due to the combination of the First Amendment legal protections and the technological safeguards such as Tor and VPNs.

As of 2020, Dissent Doe was winding up her psychology practice, but her blogs continued to operate at full-speed ahead. I asked her whether she has thought about retiring from the blogging world as well, rather than battle the constant torrent of threats.

She does not hesitate before telling me no. Absolutely not.

"I was part of the civil rights movement," she said. "I've been kicked. I've been beaten. I've been threatened. We went through hell in the sixties, and you don't back off. If you believe in something, you stand up for what you believe in."

Dissent Doe's story is a straightforward application of the culture of anonymity empowerment: a crusading speaker uses legal and technological tools to protect her identity, and engages in risky speech that she believes benefits society.

Sometimes, the culture of anonymity empowerment is harder to apply, even when the speech aims to advance the public good. Consider MakeThemScared.com. An anonymous group who say they are University of Washington students launched the site in 2018, in the midst of the MeToo movement that encouraged victims to speak out about alleged sexual assault and misconduct.[5] As the site describes itself, it is intended to "give survivors of sexual violence a voice and a place to expose the names of their sexual harassers/attackers."

As of mid-2020, MakeThemScared contained the names of about seventy-five men—both within and outside the University of Washington community—along with allegations of sexual assault or misconduct, with varying degrees of details. Although the men are named, the accusers are not.

Posters submit their reports via a submission form on the website. The submission form includes a question: "Is this really anonymous?" The response begins: "In the sense that any identifying information you do provide will not be disclosed to any party outside of the site moderators, who will make every possible effort to protect your anonymity. However, we do require some personal information in order to verify the claim." The moderators also state that they allow the submitters to request that certain portions of their answers not be displayed publicly.

The website provides readers with many caveats, including that its moderators cannot determine the guilt or innocence of the subjects of the posts. "This website is not a court of law. If someone's name is on the list, all it means is that we have received an accusation against them," the moderators wrote. "If the name of someone you know appears on this list, take note and proceed with caution, but it does not mean they have necessarily committed a crime."

I emailed the anonymous moderators of MakeThemScared to understand the motivations behind the site and the role that the culture of anonymity empowerment plays in its operations. I received a response from one of the moderators using a pseudonymous email address—the name of the site—and I do not know the identities of any of the moderators.

The moderator who responded said that MakeThemScared was inspired by what they saw as a shortcoming in the MeToo movement: that the stories focused only on alleged crimes and misconduct by celebrities. "Where was the justice for survivors outside of Hollywood and the film industry?" the moderator wrote.

The site's creators also felt that although MeToo exposed the extent of the problem, it did not have a "call to action" for the public. "If you looked at it and thought, 'Jeez, this is terrible, someone ought to do something about this,' there wasn't really anything else you could do. It magnified the sense of helplessness, and I struggled a lot with that feeling," the moderator wrote.

The moderator was talking with a friend, who mentioned that a coworker had been given only a "slap on the wrist" for harassment. "I realized how many people must know the name of their harasser or attacker and had either been let down by the institutions that were supposed to protect them or felt that because of the consequences they'd face if they reported to the police or school or sorority or fraternity, they had no other choice but to remain silent," the moderator wrote.

MakeThemScared was born from the moderators' attempts to address these shortcomings. Protecting the anonymity not only of themselves, but of the people submitting their stories, was key.

"We had the idea for a website where people could just post the name of their attacker or harasser anonymously, so they'd be shielded from the repercussions that survivors who speak out publicly face, and so that they could potentially warn others about a person who's probably out there trying to do the same thing to other people," the moderator wrote. "Once we had this idea, we looked up whether anyone had made anything like it before and it seemed like basically, they hadn't. It was such a simple idea that it felt wrong not to try to do it."

The moderators not only protect the anonymity of their posters, but they also protect their own identities. The moderator who responded to · my email pointed to times when women who had helped expose sexual misconduct had become the story, rather than the allegations that they were reporting.

"They—the person who was trying to stop sexual harassment—were the ones getting harassed, not the men on their lists accused of sexual harassment," the moderator wrote. "If our names had been made public, it would've drawn attention away from the issues we were trying to call attention to by creating the site and put the spotlight on us, and we didn't want that. We wanted the spotlight on the names on our list." Anonymity also was necessary to protect the moderators, as they "knew the list would probably make some people really angry."

Yet the site had to adjust some of its anonymity practices. When the site began operating in September 2018, the moderators did not require people to include their identifying information when sending a report to the site. Two days later, they changed that practice, and now require accusers to include a link to their social media profile and email address on the online reporting form. Although the site does not post this information— or any identifying information about accusers—the moderators use the information to resolve removal requests.

"The idea was that if we had the accuser's email address, and if the person they accused asked to have their name removed, we could ask the accuser for evidence, and if they provided it, we could leave the name up.

If they were unable to provide any evidence, then we could remove it," the moderator wrote.

The moderators also changed their anonymity policy to make it more difficult for people to create false submissions. Before the site required links to the social media profiles, they were bombarded with trollish submissions, including at least twenty that identified Bill Clinton as the perpetrator.

Although the site continues to warn that it has not verified the guilt or innocence of people who are listed on the site, it does at least some vetting before posting a submission. For example, the moderators look at the accuser's social media profile for any red flags, such as a newly created account, or a profile without a picture. If the accuser claims to have filed a police report, the moderators may check that claim.

The moderators also email the accuser at the given email address to confirm that they actually submitted the report. "It helps convince us the submission is real if the email address they give us to reach out to is an official school email with the accuser's name in it," the moderator wrote.

Even with these protocols, the moderator acknowledges it is not fail-proof. "We understand that our system isn't perfect, and ideally we would like to further investigate every report we get, but we're primarily concerned with creating a system that make[s] it as easy as possible for survivors to come forward with their stories," the moderator wrote. "That's the gap we were trying to fill, by creating a reporting system that was focused entirely on eliminating barriers for survivors. Right now, the reporting systems available to survivors are built more around concern for the safety, reputation, and wellbeing of the accused rapists than their victims. We were trying to create a system that worked the opposite way."

To some subjects of the posts, however, the list allows people to brand them with an accusation that might be among the first results that potential employers see when they search for their names online.

One University of Washington student, for instance, was a subject of one of the earliest MakeThemScared reports, before the site started requiring the accusers to provide their identities. As of mid-2020, the report was short, describing the incident only as "non-consensual sex/took advantage of drunkenness."

The University of Washington's student newspaper, *The Daily*, contacted the student for an October 2018 article. He told the newspaper that he did not recall the incident, but would not rule out the chance that something happened. He also provided the newspaper with an email he sent to MakeThemScared's moderators, in which he asked them to remove the post. The email included a message to the person who accused him of nonconsensual sex:

> Of course I want my name taken down of off this site. I AM scared. But I want to say sorry. I have always made sure to make my sexual encounters . . . consensual, but this advance was not. I want to say I am sorry I made you feel this way, but that sounds a bit like gaslighting. Your feelings are right.
>
> I am sorry I did something that I thought was okay, but wasn't. I am sorry that I put you in a position where you did not feel like you can say no. I know this won't rectify things, and make the trauma or experience magically go away. But I just want to communicate (semi-directly through this proxy) my shame and regret for doing this to you.[6]

The site has received criticism for its publication of the names of alleged harassers and assaulters. "It completely circumvents due process and trivializes the seriousness with which accusations ought to be received," *The Daily* wrote in an editorial. "It ends up lending more credit to the argument that even truthful accusations should be viewed with suspicion and as part of a vengeful agenda, not one that seeks justice. However, it isn't hard to imagine the feelings of helplessness that went into the creation of and contribution to this list. Despite #MeToo, it seems things haven't really changed."[7]

The site's moderators would not tell me whether they have received litigation threats or subpoenas for the identifying information of the posters. If any of the report subjects sued the website or its moderators for defamation, they might attempt to get the case dismissed under Section 230 of the Communications Decency Act, which prevents the operators of online platforms from being held liable for content provided by third parties. Courts have held that this protection applies if the website encourages users to post the allegedly defamatory content, and chooses which submissions to post.[8] Courts have also held that this protection applies if the site edits the post, as long as those edits do not materially contribute to the alleged defamation.[9] Some judges have pushed back on broad claims of Section 230 protections,[10] so it is hard to predict with certainty how a court would rule on a lawsuit against a site like MakeThemScared.

Even when Section 230 applies, the subjects could sue the accuser. As part of the lawsuit, the subject could subpoena MakeThemScared for identifying information. Presumably, the site would have the social media links and email addresses for most of the accusers. A court would then need to engage in a balancing test, such as *Dendrite* or *Cahill,* to determine whether the subject of the post had presented strong enough evidence of defamation, and consider other factors, such as the chilling effect on speech.

It is hard to predict the strength of the evidence for any potential case against a poster, in part because the posts vary in length and detail. Some are only a few words long, while others provide more specific allegations. Perhaps the toughest task for a court in such a case would be the final *Dendrite* requirement, to "balance the defendant's First Amendment right of anonymous free speech against the strength of the prima facie case presented and the necessity for the disclosure of the anonymous defendant's identity to allow the plaintiff to properly proceed." The considerations in a case involving MakeThemScared likely differ vastly from those involving a Yahoo! Finance posting about a company's stock price.

Alleging a sexual assault is among the most difficult things for a person to do, out of fear of retaliation, threats to personal safety, and individual privacy. The poster's right to anonymous speech in this type of case likely would be at its apex. How would a court weigh this vital interest against the strength of a defamation case brought by the subject of a post who was accused of sexual assault?

There is at least a chance that a person who is submitting a post to MakeThemScared could be unmasked, and subjected to unimaginable harassment and harms from armies of online trolls. Yet the culture of anonymity empowerment provides at least some safeguards that are not absolute, but they are sufficient to provide people with enough assurance to tell their stories.

And that is the world that the culture of anonymity empowerment has created. The culture broadly provides and encourages people to speak freely online, and control whether the outside world will receive any information that might identify them. Yet even if they choose to restrict that information, a court—or a technological failure—may still result in their unmasking.

Anonymity rules come down to balancing equities. For the first two days of its operations, MakeThemScared provided even greater anonymity protections by not requiring accusers to submit their email addresses and social media accounts, though their IP addresses still might have been traceable. But the administrators determined that a reduction in their overall anonymity protections was necessary for the site to at least try to verify the accusations.

Even its revised policies generated controversy, due to the impact on people who were named on the site. Yet MakeThemScared's publicly stated motives are laudable, and its moderators recognize the power that their commenters' anonymous speech carries. Their commenters use their anonymity as a shield to protect them from harmful consequences of speaking out. Others, however, have used anonymity as a sword to spread harassment and misinformation.

13

ANONYMITY AS A SWORD

A portrait of the culture of anonymity empowerment would be incomplete if it did not examine how malicious actors use their ability to control access to their identifying information when they inflict harm on other people. Cyberstalking, harassment, threats, misinformation, and other harms are easier to perpetrate under the cloak of anonymity. As Victoria Smith Ekstrand wrote, "The opportunity for anonymously fostering rumor, innuendo, and falsehoods online is greater than ever."[1]

Saul Levmore articulated the concerns over the harmful uses of Internet anonymity in a 2012 essay. Levmore describes the Internet as a far more effective medium for disseminating the sort of harmful speech that one might find on a bathroom wall.[2] Bathroom graffiti artists, Levmore wrote, "must work quickly to avoid detection and prosecution." In contrast, he observed, "the juvenilist on the Internet is empowered by the ability to communicate in leisurely fashion and to do so from afar."[3]

Levmore's analogy captures the relative ease with which the culture of anonymity empowerment allows bad actors to operate online. In some extreme cases, anonymous online speech reaches far beyond merely "juvenile," ruining lives and tearing communities apart.

The story of Ryan S. Lin and the cyberstalking campaign that he unleashed on his former roommate and others reveals some of the harmful ways that people can operate within the culture of anonymity empowerment. Although Lin's story received some media attention in 2018 when he was sentenced to 17.5 years in federal prison, none of the coverage that I read documented the full extent of the harms, and how his ability to shield some of his identifying information contributed to his persistent campaign of harassment.

The First Amendment's free speech protections did not directly hinder law enforcement's investigation into his campaign against his former roommate, as no First Amendment challenges to subpoenas or warrants provided roadblocks (had there been any such challenges, they likely would have been defeated due to the compelling need to identify the perpetrator). Rather, Lin relied on VPNs, Tor, and other anonymity technology to at least temporarily evade law enforcement. His persistent harassment of the roommate was fostered by the culture of anonymity empowerment, which allowed him to hide enough of his identifying information to cause harm. Anonymity-protecting technology is widely available, and the United States lacks real-name laws or other regulations that would reduce the likelihood of Lin operating anonymously. But because anonymity protections are not absolute, the government eventually was able to investigate, identify, and prosecute him.

This story comes from the extensive court record of his prosecution. As a warning, some details are graphic and shocking; I include them because it is important to avoid minimizing the damages of the cyberstalking campaign.

Ryan S. Lin was born in China in 1992, and moved to the United States a few years later.[4] As a young child in Connecticut, his mother said, he had exhibited antisocial behavior, though he received good grades.[5] His behavior appeared to deteriorate in middle school, when he was suspended for, among other reasons, an inappropriate message that he sent to a girl in his school. In seventh grade, he taught himself how to code. Lin was suspended six times in middle school. Lin was seen by a mental health provider, who concluded, "Ryan has his own rules and doesn't follow social rules." Due to his father's health problems, Lin's family did not continue Ryan Lin's therapy.[6] As a high school student, he hacked his classmates' Facebook profiles and harassed them.[7] He was admitted to Carnegie Mellon University, where he studied for three semesters. He studied at a community college, and then Rensselaer Polytechnic Institute, where he graduated magna cum laude with a computer science degree in 2015.[8] He served as webmaster of RPI's International Chinese Study Association, but as a result of a dispute he deleted the group's website.[9] Two classmates of Lin from Rensselaer would later tell federal law enforcement that Lin had harassed them, including by creating false social media accounts in one of the student's names. The students said that they reported Lin to school administration and received cease and desist orders against him.[10]

Lin moved to the Boston area after graduating, though he had problems at work due to conflicts with superiors, difficulties socializing with others, and troubles with focusing.[11]

He responded to an advertisement for a room rental in a Watertown, Massachusetts, house, and moved in in late April or early May 2016. Three other people were living in the house, including Jennifer Smith, a woman in her twenties who worked at a restaurant and in pet care.[12] (Jennifer Smith is not her real name; it is the pseudonym provided to her in an FBI affidavit, and I will use that pseudonym in this book.)

Within a few weeks of moving into the house, Lin purchased marijuana from Smith, according to the FBI. She awoke to him banging on her bedroom door in the middle of the night, alleging that she did not provide the agreed-upon amount of marijuana.[13] Lin sent text messages to Smith, at times referring to her recent abortion. "I understand abortions can be painful and the one you had in March probably has its lingering effects too. I agree Michael should not have treated you that way."[14]

Smith had not discussed her abortion with Lin or the other people in the house, but she had written about the abortion—and her former romantic partner, Michael—in an electronic journal that could be accessed from her MacBook.[15] Smith's laptop was not password protected, and contained a document with all her online account passwords. She stored the laptop in her bedroom, which did not lock.[16]

Toward the end of May, when Smith was alone in the house with Lin, their shared toilet overflowed. The plumber found in the toilet the bottles from Smith's anxiety and depression medications, which had been missing. Lin denied flushing the bottles. Smith moved out of the house within days.[17] About a month later, Smith returned to pack her belongings, and saw printouts of her journal in her bedroom, the FBI wrote. When she confronted Lin, he told her that he had not printed the journal.[18]

Lin had conflicts with the two remaining roommates. In a text message to one of the roommates, he identified her employer and exact earnings. He allegedly told one of the roommates that he had placed hidden cameras in the home.[19] The roommates complained to the landlord, and by around August 1, 2016, Lin was no longer living in the home.[20]

A few days before Lin was evicted from the house, an email was sent from an account that appeared to belong to Smith (but did not) to Lin, Smith, the two other housemates, and two other people, according to the FBI. The email included excerpts from Smith's online journal, along with explicit body images and pictures of Smith's face. Lin responded to the email chain. "It is fascinating how someone can be so incredibly depressed, paranoid, and slutty at the same time," he wrote. "I am quite sure I will never read such an intense story again that involves so much sluttiness and crazy thoughts."[21] Smith also began receiving offensive messages on social media. For example, an Instagram account named "jsnmma" in December 2016 posted, "It would be so nice if you could go back in time further and undo your abortion."[22]

Lin's unauthorized access to her computer and accounts provided him with not only the diary, but also private images and a sexually suggestive video of Smith, the government detailed in court filings. He created a collage that included pictures of Smith's face, Smith's buttocks in underwear, a female's naked breasts, and a vagina.[23] He distributed the diary, the video, and the images widely. For instance, in April 2017, an email account purporting to belong to Smith sent an email to local university staff, police department employees, staff at Smith's former schools, and others, that promised to teach the recipients how they could "spice up their sex life." The email included intimate portions of Smith's diary, the video, the collage, and her medical records.[24]

Lin also used text messaging services, often one based in Canada, to anonymously send messages to Smith. Among the messages that he sent her: "why get abortion?" "why dont [*sic*] u kill yourself," and "SUCH A DISGUSTING GIRL. KEEP YOUR LEGS CLOSED AND KILL

YOURSELF!!!!!!"[25] Pretending to be Smith, Lin posted ads on various dating websites, seeking people to fulfill fantasies of rape and violent sex.[26] One ad was titled "Would anyone like to tie me up tonight?"[27]

Lin took advantage of local police departments' anonymous tip submission system. On July 24, 2017, Lin caused the Waltham, Massachusetts, police to visit Smith's home by submitting tips that there was a bomb at the house, and that drug activity was occurring at the home.[28] The next month, he sent anonymous tips to four other local police departments about a bomb at Smith's home address. "The residents are not going to wake up to see the morning, or they will wake up disfigured. BOOM!"[29] Prosecutors also identified more than 100 anonymous bomb threats that Lin had fabricated, claiming that bombs had been planted at Bentley University, Waltham High School, and other nearby locations.[30]

Lin used information from Smith's online accounts to apply for unemployment benefits in Smith's name, cancel her driver's license registration, and apply for financial services from Bank of America.[31]

Smith was not the only target of Lin's harassment campaign. He repeatedly sent vulgar emails and text messages to Smith's mother, including threats to rape both Smith and her mother.[32] He emailed the collage and diary excerpts to Smith's mother and her mother's coworkers.[33] He emailed child pornography to Smith's mother, thanking her for the purchase and including the last four digits of her credit card number.[34]

Smith's father, a surgeon, also was among Lin's targets, prosecutors detailed. Pretending to be Smith, Lin sent an email to Smith's father and his coworkers. The email contained the collage, with a message: "I am very proud of my daddy who is a doctor here! He is such a great doctor and part of that is because I let him 'operate' on me when I was little! I still am and always will be daddy's little girl, so enjoy all."[35] The harassment caused her father to install an alarm system and security cameras at home and purchase two firearms to protect himself.[36]

Lin also focused his campaign on Smith's boss at the restaurant, the government wrote. Posing as both Smith and her boss, he posted rape fantasies on sex websites, including an invitation for a "gang bang" that included their work address and the boss's cell phone number.[37] He created a fake Facebook profile in the boss's name, with a threat to carry out a school shooting. This caused the police to visit her home.[38]

His harassment extended even outside of Smith's social circle, including two women who lived in the apartment next door to his new apartment, prosecutors wrote. Pretending to be the women's landlord, he emailed them: "Wow you look so nice, maybe one day I will break into your room when you are sleeping and rape you!"[39]

Anonymity and pseudonymity fostered Lin's continued campaign against Smith, her family, and others. When people saw Lin's messages, at least some may not have had any way of determining with certainty whether they came from the person he was pretending to be or from an impersonator. As federal prosecutors would write in court filings, many of his traumatized victims "suspected Lin but were not certain who their stalker was, why he had targeted them, how he had found them, or how he knew so much detailed personal information about them."[40] Even though law enforcement investigators suspected Lin, they would need evidence that he was the one sending these messages, and he at least tried to mask his identity while carrying out the cyberstalking and harassment. Investigators determined that Lin used Tor, VPNs, and other anonymity technology, as well as encrypted email and false names for social media accounts.[41] "The cyberstalking campaign against Smith and those connected to her has continued for months, despite significant efforts by local law enforcement, because the perpetuator of the harassment has used technology to conceal his identity," an FBI agent wrote in an affidavit in support of the criminal complaint against Lin.[42]

In a brief filed in federal court, prosecutors described the great care that Lin took to guard his identity when carrying out his crimes. "He used TOR to connect to VPNs and overseas providers, he encrypted his hard drives, he used over 1,000 different IP addresses in connection with his criminal conduct, he used hundreds of separate accounts with well-known overseas encrypted e-mail providers, he used dozens of spoofed text providers, and multiple VPN services," they wrote. "For the bomb threats in particular, when placing the threats, Lin used TOR and VPNs to then connect to the anonymous online tip lines, knowing that they were not logging his IP addresses. He alternatively used well-known overseas email providers that do not log and do not respond to law enforcement."[43]

These anonymity tools made it hard for law enforcement to gather sufficient evidence to tie Lin to the harassment campaign. Yet Lin left enough of a trail to allow dogged investigators to eventually link him to the acts. His actions reveal the sliding scale of anonymity; even when a speaker has left a trail of some information, that may not be enough to definitively identify the speaker.

It became clear to law enforcement that Lin sought to protect his anonymity online. The FBI eventually obtained access to records from his Gmail account, including screenshots of an iPhone that show anonymous texting and encrypted email apps. Lin also responded on Twitter to a VPN provider's tweet that it did not log its customers' traffic: "There is no such thing as VPN that doesn't keep logs. If they can limit your connections or track bandwidth usage, they keep logs."[44] This tweet would prove prophetic, as the lack of complete anonymity protections on VPNs would be essential to the FBI's ability to tie him to the cyberstalking.

A key piece of evidence came from Lin's activities on Rover, a pet service app that Smith used. The app matches pet care providers, such as Smith, with potential clients and allows clients to pay their pet care providers. In April 2017, "Ashley Plano" asked Smith via Rover to walk her dogs. Ashley Plano's Rover account had recently been created using teleportxf@gmail.com. Smith called Ashley's phone number, but nobody answered. Later that day, Ashley messaged to say she did not want Smith to walk her dog, but the communications caused Smith to disclose her phone number by calling "Ashley."[45]

A user of an anonymous text messaging service began text messaging Smith at that phone number two days later, with messages such as "IT WANTED TO LIVE AND YOU KILLED IT."[46] Also on that day, Ashley Plano requested the deletion of her Rover account.[47]

The FBI associated Lin with the "Ashley Plano" Rover account because the Gmail account that "Ashley Plano" used to create the Rover account was accessed on the same day as a Gmail address known to belong to Lin, from the same IP address. The IP address belonged to WANSecurity, a VPN provider. On three more days in April, the Rover account and Lin's Gmail account were accessed via the same IP addresses provided by another VPN provider, Secure Internet LLC.[48]

Records from another VPN provider, PureVPN, found that a user had accessed both Gmail accounts from the same IP address provided by WANSecurity. "Significantly, Pure VPN was able to determine that their service was accessed by the same customer from two originating

IP addresses: the RCN IP address from the home Lin was living in at the time, and the software company where Lin was employed at the time," an FBI agent wrote.[49]

Lin's former employer allowed the FBI to examine his old computer, but the former employer had already reinstalled the operating system on the computer when the FBI requested access. FBI employees recovered some artifacts, including visits to news articles about area bomb threats, visits to an anonymous text message site, and proof that PureVPN had been installed on the computer.[50]

When law enforcement arrested Lin on October 6, 2017, they conducted a search of his home and recovered parts of an electronic diary that Lin had kept. The diary entries document the methodological way in which Lin carried out his campaign against Smith and the role that anonymity played in his crimes. Among the excerpts:

Saturday—12/17/2016

Got to level 48 in World of Warcraft. Also continued to send [Smith] harassing emails about her abortion via email-to-SMS. It's funny how she can't block those messages because each message comes from a different phone number (lol).

Monday—3/20/2017

. . . Made a TorMail account and sent [Smith's] journals and abortion photos to her family (parents), friends, roommates, and coworkers over email and MMS. I also CCd both of her Gmail accounts (including the deleted one) and her iCloud account which I currently have access to. Shortly after that, she re-activated her Facebook profile after weeks of downtime. . . . either way, whatever I did I probably did have a profound impact on her this time, and I'm curious as to what the outcome and consequences will be. We shall see in the upcoming weeks:) **

Friday—5/5/2017

During the morning, sent text messages to [Smith's mother] from an anonymous phone number. I texted her all sorts of details about her personal life (like her gas problems and special diet) and she asked what it would take to stop, and how much money I wanted. I also sent some more mass emails of [Smith's] diary, suicide note, therapy notes, lingerie video, and naked photos to Waltham high school, JFK middle school, Brandeis, and Bentley university, literally hundreds of people at this point have seen all of her personal shit (LOL). It was raining heavily today, lunch by myself, went home at the usual time and did nothing but sleep for the entire day. For some reason I'm really tired today and I slept today. I didn't bother [Smith] at all during the evening like I have been consistently almost every single day for the past few days.

Thursday—4/20/2017

*** THE BIG DAY *** During the morning, I sent out [Smith's] diary to a TON of people on her contact list. I only got one reply though, from . . . (after checking during the evening after getting back home from work around 5:30pm). No contact from the police at all, I think at this point they have already given up trying to contact me via phone because they know that I won't bother picking up. No comments or anything posted to the Tumblr, however I did see that she tried to log into her old iCloud account. I think she realizes now (after seeing all the pictures posted on the Tumblr that I probably got them from the iCloud account) . . . she tried to unsuccessfully log in multiple times which resulted in the account getting locked. It doesn't matter though because she cannot reset it. *** Later in the evening, I made another Zoho account to continue sending her diary to everyone, this time from even larger email groups. I also started sending her those harassing abortion text messages again to her new phone number, this time from Zoho and 100% through TOR which makes things super safe and anonymous for me. Think I sent about 35 or so text messages, and it does not seem to be bound by a sending limit like Mail.com does. Although I cannot be completely certain. ***[51]

In May 2018, Lin pleaded guilty to cyberstalking, distribution of child pornography, hoax bomb threats, computer fraud and abuse, and aggravated identity theft.[52] But Judge William G. Young would not sentence him for another five months. Under the plea agreement, Lin faced a sentence of between seven and 17.5 years.[53]

While he was jailed in the Wyatt Detention Center, inmates said that he had tried to hack the Law Library's computers, and an officer found in Lin's cell papers that explained how to use anonymity technology such as Tor to access "CP" (presumably "child pornography"). A detainee informed the US Attorney's Office in August 2018 that Lin had told him that Lin planned to bomb two courthouses and kill two female prosecutors on his case.[54]

Victims, including Smith and her mother, spoke at Lin's October 3, 2018, sentencing hearing. They told Judge Young about the chaos that Lin caused in their lives and the community. "My life devolved into waiting for Ryan's next attack," Smith said at the hearing. "I couldn't work. I couldn't hide. I couldn't use my computer. I was afraid to leave the house. I also was afraid to be at home. The phone in my pocket was a weapon being used against me."[55]

Smith recounted the seemingly endless torrent of horror that Lin unleashed on her and others and the tremendous emotional and financial toll that it took on her for more than a year. "I hope that in the future the legal system will be more capable of quickly dealing with internet crimes to protect people from heinous abuse amplified by anonymity and the ubiquity of the current technologies in daily life," she said.[56]

Lin acted "untouchable" as he systematically harassed her and others, she told him at the hearing. "You're stupid to think you can remain anonymous forever on the dozens of platforms you used to attack me," she said. "You're a pervert and a coward and until recently you were never held accountable for your actions."[57] After Smith, her mother, and other targets of Lin's harassment campaign presented their stories, Waltham city officials told Young about the impact of Lin's repeated bomb threats to schools, day care centers, houses of worship, and other community institutions. "I've been in law enforcement for 38 years and I can't recall a single instance where one person caused so much fear and anxiety to so many people," Waltham police chief Keith MacPherson said.[58] Jack Flynn, superintendent of Waltham Public Schools, told Young that Lin was responsible for seventy-one bomb threats to the schools.[59] "Parents understandably made choices to keep their children home from school during parts of this terror that was caused by Mr. Lin," Flynn said.[60]

Despite the government's overwhelming presentation of individualized and communitywide harm, Lin's attorney requested that Young sentence Lin to seven years in prison—about ten years less than what the government sought. Central to Lin's request was his autism diagnosis. Lin relied on a psychologist's report, which stated that "an odd, illogical, inflexible, obsessive, compulsive, and self-destructive pattern of thought behavior appears to have motivated Mr. Lin to engage in using technology for socially inappropriate and disruptive purposes."[61]

At the sentencing hearing, Lin's lawyer, J. W. Carney Jr., stressed that Lin's "undiagnosed profound autism" had shaped his behavior, but Judge Young appeared to struggle with that excuse. "The criminal acts are not the pattern of someone who suffers with autism," Young told Carney. "Even if I grant those things, these criminal acts seem wholly at variance with what I know about autism."[62]

Lin's autism, Carney said, prevented him from fully appreciating the harms that he was causing. Still, Young said, Lin appeared to intend to cause harms. "It's not like he's mentally defective in any way and can't form the intent to commit the crime, he intentionally committed these crimes," Young said.[63]

Lin briefly addressed Young before receiving his sentence. He apologized to his victims. "I'm very sorry for turning your lives into a nightmare and I deeply regret my actions," Lin said. "And I really wish I could just turn back that clock and undo all those foolish decisions, but unfortunately that's clearly not possible."[64] Lin said he planned to continue receiving treatment while in prison, and that he hopes to use his "computer skills to, um—to do good things when I get out, to innovate and improve society rather than waste my life and my time just bothering people on the internet."[65]

His statement about using "computer skills" to help society was particularly jarring after witnesses testified that he upended lives and a community with those skills. The fact that he offered that possibility at his sentencing hearing might lend some support to his lawyer's argument that Lin did not fully appreciate the harms that he had caused.

Lin's apology did not appear to sway Young, who sentenced Lin to 17.5 years, which the government requested. "I'll grant you that you may not have fully appreciated the harm you did to your specific victims and to the community as a whole," Young said. "In the eyes of this Court, that does not diminish from the sentence which ought be imposed." Young said that Lin's conduct was "monstrous," and the fact that they were committed from a computer does not diminish the crimes. "In fact it ought to bring home to all of us how interconnected we are and what havoc can be wreaked by the improper evil criminal conduct in which you so gleefully engaged," Young said.[66]

Although I could not understand Lin's motives, I wanted to get a better understanding of what the impact was, beyond the black-and-white words of the court record. So I arranged to speak with Smith through her attorney, Carrie Goldberg, who specializes in representing victims of cyber harassment, stalking, and revenge pornography. (I count Goldberg as a good friend, and I deeply admire the crucial work that she performs.)

With remarkable candor, Smith discussed what it was like "watching this person who has no control or social aptitude to use every platform I have ever used to steal my identity, harass me."

Lin was someone who Smith lived with for a month and barely knew, making it hard to explain the barrage of emails and text messages to her coworkers, friends, and family. "That was one of the more confusing things to people who didn't know what was going on," Smith said.

From the start, Smith said, she knew Lin was behind the stalking and harassment. But the police were of little help because he disguised himself so well. One local police detective was determined to help her—a warrior, she called him. He even attended cybersecurity classes to learn more about the technology that Lin was using, and he issued subpoenas to many platforms. But he could not unmask Lin. "It really was all dead ends based on VPNs, Tor browser, extremely hidden user actions," Smith said. "The police weren't really able to do anything other than watch my house and try to make sure that nobody showed up."

Smith sought help from two different law firms, but they were of little use. One firm thought that the perpetrator was another former roommate of Smith and tried to convince her to hire a private investigator, but Smith was certain that it was Lin.

In the early summer of 2017, a coworker told Smith about her former classmate, Goldberg, and the work that she did representing people in similar situations. Smith called Goldberg, and approached her with suspicion, because by that point she was worried that anyone she spoke with might be part of Lin's harassment. She asked questions about her background to ensure that she was speaking with Carrie Goldberg, and not an impersonator. Goldberg had her secretary call Smith back from her main office line, helping to ease Smith's concerns. At that point, Smith knew that she found who she needed. "I realized it wasn't really just a lawyer I needed, but the combination of lawyers who are victims' advocates," Smith said. Goldberg worked with her contacts at the US Justice Department, including Mona Sedky, a veteran lawyer in the Justice Department's

Computer Crime and Intellectual Property Section who has prosecuted a number of high-profile and shocking crimes involving cyberstalking, sextortion, and other computer crimes. Within a few months, the Justice Department identified and charged Lin.

Smith recognizes that many other victims do not receive the same assistance from law enforcement. Documenting the constant barrage of evidence was like a second full-time job for Smith. "I was lucky because I was a sympathetic enough victim with the economic means to afford help and the fortitude to get justice," she said. She also questions whether federal authorities would have been interested if his harassment of her had not included bomb threats and child pornography. "It could have easily not been an FBI case," she said.

The child pornography and bomb threats contributed to the length of his sentence. Without those factors, the sentence might have been shorter. But to Smith, 17.5 years is like a ticking time bomb. I spoke to her about two years into the sentence, and she was convinced that when he is released, he will continue to target her. "I feel like I have a deadline," she said. She is taking computer classes to learn how to protect herself online. As of July 2020, she was not working. She had to withdraw from public interaction.

As Smith recounted Lin's persistent campaign against her and the way that it has effectively silenced her, I could not help thinking of feminist legal scholarship, beginning in the 1970s and 1980s with Andrea Dworkin and Catharine MacKinnon and extending to today's work by scholars such as Mary Anne Franks. They establish that advocacy for "free speech" often focuses on protecting the speech of men, even when it has a chilling effect on the speech of women. "Much contemporary free speech advocacy focuses on affirmatively providing outlets for violent expression as well as blocking attempts to mitigate the harms of myriad forms of abuse, including cyber stalking, harassment, misogynist propaganda, and 'revenge porn,'" Franks wrote.[67]

Ryan Lin's use of anonymity facilitated not only his horrific speech, but also an effective silencing of Jennifer Smith, extending long after Lin went to prison. The Jennifer Smith before Ryan Lin no longer exists, she told me.

"Now I'm a person who is waiting for his next attack."

I spent days immersed in Ryan Lin's case file, struggling to figure out how to prevent future devastation caused by similar online crimes. There are no easy law-based solutions, in part because Lin's use of anonymity is not straightforward. The harms arose not because Lin's identity was a complete mystery, but because he used anonymity protection to temporarily prevent his prosecution. Many of his victims suspected he was behind the harassment campaigns, but the anonymity technology such as Tor and VPNs made it harder for law enforcement to identify him with sufficient certainty for prosecution and likely enabled him to carry out the malicious acts for longer than he could have under his real name.

The First Amendment did not shield Lin's identity from disclosure. Had one of his targets sued "John Doe" for defamation and subpoenaed his identifying information, it is likely that a court applying *Dendrite* or *Cahill* would have required disclosure. Even the most stringent First Amendment anonymity safeguards allow for unmasking in particularly compelling circumstances, and a plaintiff could have a very strong case against Lin. The likelihood that a court would allow Lin's unmasking suggests that the First Amendment anonymity framework provides a reasonable balance between free speech and the need to redress harms. A shortcoming of the subpoena-based unmasking system is that by the time the perpetrator is identified, much harm already has occurred. And filing a civil lawsuit against Lin probably would not have helped Smith stop the barrage of harassment, as Lin still would have been free to keep posting, and a lawsuit may have angered Lin and prompted even more persistent online harassment. So reining in the First Amendment protections for anonymity would not necessarily prevent harassment campaigns such as the one carried out by Ryan Lin. The legal system eventually worked to unmask Lin and bring him to justice, but the harassment went on for far too long and had indelible effects on Smith and others.

It would have been harder, if not impossible, for Lin to carry out his campaign for so long had he been unable to use anonymizing technology such as VPNs and Tor and required to operate online under his real name. Yet it is difficult to conceive of how such a requirement could be effective, short of a law that requires all online platforms to register and display people's real names, while also banning anonymizing technology. Such a law would almost certainly run afoul of the First Amendment, as it would effectively silence not only harassers, but also citizen journalists such as Dissent Doe, political dissidents, and other speakers who have legitimate reasons to seek anonymity. And even if such a prohibition on any online anonymity could somehow pass constitutional muster, a dedicated harasser likely could circumvent the requirement, perhaps by falsifying identifying information or using contraband technology. While a real-name requirement and a legal prohibition on anonymizing technology might prevent some potential harassers from being anonymous online, I question whether such a ban would be effective for computer experts such as Lin. As with offline crimes, criminals will try to prevent their identities from being linked to their online crimes.

In her excellent memoir, *Nobody's Victim*, in which she recounts representing Smith and many other targets of cybercrime, Carrie Goldberg describes two schools of thought that drive abhorrent anonymous online behavior. The first, known as the "online disinhibition effect," holds that "people who engage in bad behavior online under masked identities have slipped into a sort of alternate reality," and that due to their online anonymity, they "feel free to engage in unbridled assholery with zero repercussions." Another line of thinking, Goldberg writes, is that online trolls are "more than merely a product of their environments," and are instead "evil, tending toward cruelty even when not online."[68] The second explanation suggests substantial challenges in combatting online harms, and that we must do more than just address whether people can remain anonymous. How do we combat that underlying cruelty?

Improvements to the criminal justice system might help to prevent some similar crimes, but that also is far from certain. As evidenced by Lin's 17.5-year sentence, many laws already presented the specter of substantial punishment. Judge Young sentenced him to the maximum number of years in prison allowed under the plea agreement. I agree with Young that the fact that the crimes were committed via computer does not diminish the harms. Lin's sentence is remarkably long compared to many other computer crime cases. Still, the existence of the federal criminal laws did not deter Lin from committing these persistent crimes. Perhaps Lin truly believed that his computer skills would prevent him from ever being identified. Perhaps Lin was unaware of the possible punishments. Or perhaps something else caused him to disregard the risk of substantial prison time. I can only hope that the media coverage of Lin's heavy prison sentence deters at least some potential cybercriminals. But Lin's case is unique in that skilled federal government cyber experts took on the investigation. The FBI's capacity and jurisdiction are limited, and we cannot expect that federal agents and prosecutors will be able to investigate every cybercrime. At the very least, local and state police need more dedicated cybercrime expertise, along with effective and punitive laws against cyberstalking and other computer crimes.

Ryan Lin's story reveals a broad societal failure. For years, a young person had harassed others without the necessary intervention from healthcare providers, schools, and law enforcement, despite repeated indications of problematic behavior. The many people who Lin victimized were harmed by the system's failure to address so many warning signs. Anonymity technology was a tool that allowed his harassment to last longer than it otherwise would have, but the underlying problems were rooted far deeper. Thanks to legal, technological, and social norms that have developed over decades, we live in a culture of anonymity empowerment. While this culture creates many opportunities for society, it also means that some people may misuse their anonymity to harm others. Our institutions must adapt to this culture of anonymity empowerment to better identify potential problems at the outset.

Any examination of modern online anonymity would be incomplete without a discussion of QAnon. But despite its name, the harmful disinformation movement has a complicated relationship with anonymity. QAnon did, in fact, begin with a series of pseudonymous posts on the 4Chan message board in 2017. Signed by someone identified as "Q"—which is an Energy Department security clearance level—the messages claimed to have insider knowledge of a massive deep state pedophilia ring that Donald Trump was combatting. Q gained a rapidly growing following of conspiracy theorists, waiting for "Q drops" of information on 4chan and then other message boards.[69]

The Q followers quickly spread conspiracy theories, largely focused on deep state plots against Trump. QAnon followers believe that a "Storm" will lead to widespread arrests of powerful people, and a "Great Awakening" when the public will realize that Q was correct.[70]

QAnon moved from the corners of the Internet to larger platforms such as Reddit, Facebook, and Instagram. The movement's popularity surged in the next few years, particularly leading up to the 2020 presidential election. An analysis conducted by research firm Storyful found that between March 2020 and July 2020, membership in ten large public Facebook groups related to QAnon grew by almost 600 percent.[71]

Family members of people who have become QAnon followers report that it has caused massive disruptions in their relationships and lives. A Minnesota woman, for instance, told Buzzfeed in 2021 of her mother's descent into QAnon conspiracy theories. In one text message, her mother warned of a blackout that would precede the Storm. "Something might be going down," her mother wrote. "Make sure your cars are gassed up, have plenty of food and drinking water. You can always fill up the bathtub for flushing the toilet. Also have cash on hand. We may not be able to communicate if there is a blackout." The woman tried to reason with her mother and point out that her information sources were not credible. "Believe it or don't," her mother replied. QAnon not only disrupted lives, but also strained family relationships. "We've kind of pushed away from each other because I don't believe her and she knows I don't believe her," another woman with a QAnon-following mother told Buzzfeed.[72]

QAnon has had even more dire impacts. In 2018, an armed QAnon follower used his truck to block the Mike O'Callaghan–Pat Tillman Bridge by the Hoover Dam in Arizona. The man held a sign indicating he was a QAnon follower and blocked traffic for almost an hour before trying to flee. After he was apprehended, he eventually pleaded guilty to a few crimes related to the incident.[73] The man wrote a letter to Trump from jail, in which he included a modification of a QAnon catchphrase, "For Where We Go One, We Go All."[74]

The Federal Bureau of Investigation designated QAnon as a "dangerous extremist group" in 2019, and many people indicted for participation in the January 6, 2021, storming of the Capitol had links to QAnon. For example, one leader of a group of rioters wore a "Q" shirt, and told investigators that he had "intentionally positioned himself" at the front so that people could see the shirt and Q would "get the credit."[75]

Precisely what role did anonymity play in the metastasis of QAnon? Pseudonymity was central to Q's posts. Just as the mystery associated with anonymous and pseudonymous speech has long added to the impact of speech, the debate over Q's identity has added to the profile and impact of

Q's speech. Speculation about Q's identity abounds on the Internet.[76] And many QAnon followers communicate on anonymous and pseudonymous forums.

But even some of QAnon's prominent advocates either used their real names or provided enough information to be identified. Two people who moderated the 4chan board on which Q posted, who used the screennames Pamphlet Anon and BaruchtheScribe, brought the posts to the attention of Tracy Diaz, who is popular on YouTube and had hosted a talk show. In 2018, NBC News reported that BaruchtheScribe is a web programmer named Paul Furber, and Furber confirmed the Q backstory to NBC. "A bunch of us decided that the message needed to go wider so we contacted Youtubers who had been commenting on the Q drops," Furber told NBC in an email. NBC managed to use property records and social media photos to also identify Pamphlet Anon. Diaz has blogged about how she and the two moderators of the 4chan board had promoted Q's posts in 2017.[77]

As QAnon supporters began posting on more mainstream platforms such as Facebook, they often identified themselves publicly.[78] In 2020, fourteen people who had expressed some support for QAnon ran for Congress, and two of those candidates won seats in the House.[79] In a QAnon-supporting chat room on Telegram, many of the fifteen-thousand-plus members post under their real names and include photos of their families in their profiles.[80] And as seen at the January 6, 2021, Capitol riot and other public gatherings, many QAnon supporters were not shy about wearing Q-themed apparel or waving QAnon signs. Despite the movement's name, anonymity is not terribly important to at least some followers of QAnon.

Anonymity is, however, important to many people who are concerned about loved ones who have fallen under the spell of QAnon. As of early 2021, more than 133,000 people had joined a Reddit forum called QAnonCasualties, where friends and family members of QAnon followers flocked to support one another and strategize. "It's exhausting loving someone and watching them get sucked into this cycle you can't break," a woman wrote about her husband. The woman did not use her real name on the forum or in an interview with *Politico*, which wrote that she "shared her story under the condition of anonymity because she fears [her husband's] retaliation and feels disloyal for speaking up."[81]

Anonymity has been key to the benefits that the forum provides to its posters. A review of the top posts on QAnonCasualties in February 2021 did not immediately find anyone who posted under an apparent real name or even a pseudonym that could be used to identify them. And the posters had good reason to hide their identities when posting on the forum. If their QAnon-following loved ones learned of the posts, the alienation likely would only be exacerbated. Their loved ones also might face ostracism or other retaliation.

While anonymous speech may have been part of the origins of QAnon, anonymity also is integral to a method that many people have developed to cope with the problems that QAnon has caused. And therein lies the complexity of anonymous speech. It would be disingenuous to deny that some anonymous speech—such as the original Q posts—has been evil and serves no redeeming social value. But it would be just as disingenuous to deny that other forms of anonymous and pseudonymous speech have been essential to open, honest, and valuable communications that could not have occurred with real names.

Some bad actors can use anonymity and pseudonymity to cause great harm. But a closer look at the stories shows why restrictions on anonymity would not necessarily solve all the problems. Rather, we need to have a better understanding of the underlying issues that cause people to commit atrocious acts—both anonymously and with their real names.

Part IV

THE FUTURE OF ANONYMITY

The First Amendment anonymity safeguards generally only protect against the use of subpoenas or governmental powers to unmask a speaker. The First Amendment anonymity protections prevent certain uses of government power to unmask people. Cases like *McIntyre* and *Talley* severely limit the government's ability to force the authors of publications to disclose their real names. And cases such as *Dendrite* and *Cahill* protect online anonymity only when a private party seeks to use a court-issued subpoena to compel the disclosure of identifying information. These cases do not restrict purely private activities that could compromise a person's anonymity. That is because they are rooted in the First Amendment, which only limits the government's abridgement of free speech. This principle, known as the state action doctrine, means that we cannot always rely on the First Amendment to fully safeguard anonymity.

Likewise, Tor, VPNs, and other technology only protect those who use it regularly and correctly. In my career as a cybersecurity lawyer, I worked with many people whose job is to protect the security and privacy of personal information, and they are among the most aware of the threats to personal privacy. Yet even many of them do not use Tor due to the latency of the network, and they often do not even use VPNs. And technology is not always available to prevent a person's identity from being revealed.

Thus, legal and technological safeguards do not fully protect anonymity. We disclose information to companies, the government, and other people that, when pieced together, can provide a straightforward roadmap to our identities. This occurs even when we assume that we are anonymous. As Helen Nissenbaum wrote in 1999, while anonymity in the computer age is not impossible, "achieving it is a more demanding business than merely allowing people to withhold their names."[1]

A. Michael Froomkin, one of the first legal scholars to write about online anonymity in the 1990s, wrote in 2015 of the "fairly grim" prognosis for online anonymity: "Several forces combine against it: ideologies that hold that anonymity is dangerous, or that identifying evil-doers is more important than ensuring a safe mechanism for unpopular speech; the profitability of identification in commerce; government surveillance; the influence of intellectual property interests and in requiring hardware and other tools that enforce identification; and the law at both national and supranational levels."[2]

Froomkin's outlook for anonymity is warranted. The vast amount of information that people provide—both knowingly and unknowingly—combines into a potent force that undercuts the anonymity that many expect.

This part outlines three challenges to maintaining anonymity in an increasingly connected society. First, many online platforms have adopted "real-name" policies, prohibiting their users from using their services anonymously or pseudonymously. Second, the vast amount of public information that is available about people enables them to be unmasked, even when they try to speak anonymously online. Third, companies maintain large databases of unregulated personal information that can make it more difficult to operate anonymously.

REAL-NAME POLICIES

Many ground rules for Internet anonymity are set not by courts or legislators, but by the private platforms that are the gateways to the Internet. Social media sites, online discussion forums, and other platforms are private companies that are not restricted by the First Amendment. They are free to decide the level of anonymity or pseudonymity that their users receive. And some platforms have decided to require all or most of their users to identify themselves by their real names.

Although the First Amendment does not prohibit platforms from deciding whether to limit anonymity or pseudonymity, these choices impact the culture of anonymity empowerment. Regardless of the protections that the First Amendment might provide for anonymity, a private company's decision to ban anonymity could make it more difficult for users to separate their identities from their speech.

The nation's largest social media provider, Facebook, has long had a fairly stringent real-name policy. In an interview in 2009, founder and chief executive Mark Zuckerberg told David Kirkpatrick that he always differed with those who said that Facebook should allow people to open separate profiles for their professional and social lives. "The days of you having a different image for your work friends or co-workers and for the other people you know are probably coming to an end pretty quickly," Zuckerberg said.[1]

Zuckerberg told Kirkpatrick that maintaining dual identities "is an example of a lack of integrity," and "the level of transparency the world has now won't support having two identities for a person."[2] He said that transparency enables people to be more accountable for their behavior. "To get people to this point where there's more openness—that's a big challenge," Zuckerberg said. "But I think we'll do it. I just think it will take time. The concept that the world will be better if you share more is something that's pretty foreign to a lot of people and it runs into all these privacy concerns."[3] Although Zuckerberg's comments did not explicitly criticize anonymity, a single-identity policy makes it difficult to engage in the anonymous and pseudonymous speech that has defined so much online discourse.

Soon after Zuckerberg's remarks were published, Michael Zimmer aptly noted that people routinely control what information they communicate depending on whether they are at work or socializing. "It is not that you pretend to be someone that you are not; rather, you turn the volume up on some aspects of your identity, and tone down others, all based on the particular context you find yourself," Zimmer wrote.[4]

Facebook's focus on a single identity stemmed from its commitment to "radical transparency." As Kirkpatrick described it, the philosophy goes like this: "Since the world is likely to become more and more open anyway, people might as well get used to it. . . . Everything is going to be seen."[5]

But as danah boyd pointed out in an essay responding to Zuckerberg's comments, Facebook had failed to be radically transparent in its own operations. Users, boyd noted, were often unaware of how their data were collected, used, and shared. "Users have no sense of how their data is being used and Facebook is not radically transparent about what that data is used for," boyd wrote in 2010. "Quite the opposite. Convolution works. It keeps the press out."[6]

Over the years, Facebook has enforced its real-name policy by locking accounts of some users who allegedly violated its rules. In 2011, the company reportedly closed the account of Chinese commentator Michael Anti, who was born with the name Zhao Jing. Although he had presented Facebook with a Harvard University certificate identifying him as Michael Anti, Facebook told him that he needed to present a government ID card containing the name. A Facebook spokesperson told the *Guardian* newspaper that its policy was designed to promote trust and safety: "We fundamentally believe this leads to greater accountability and a safer and more trusted environment for people who use the service. This view point has been developed by our own research and in consultation with a number of safety and child protection experts."[7]

While real-name requirements may be intended to promote safety, they also could threaten safety. In 2015, British journalist Laurie Penny's Facebook account was locked because she had been using a pseudonym. "Thanks to @facebook forcing me to use my real name, I am now at more risk of rape and death threats," Penny wrote on Twitter at the time. "But enjoy flogging that data, guys."[8]

Facebook has changed its real-name practices a bit over the years to accommodate some concerns. In 2014, San Francisco drag queens, including Sister Roma and Lil Miss Hot Mess, were suspended from Facebook due to its real-name policy. They met with Facebook representatives and argued that the real-name policy could hurt not only them, but many other groups, such as undocumented immigrants.[9] Facebook executive Chris Cox later released a statement explaining the company's reasoning for its real-name policy, but agreed there is "lots of room for improvement" in its procedures. "With this input, we're already underway building better tools for authenticating the Sister Romas of the world while not opening up Facebook to bad actors," Cox said. "And we're taking measures to provide much more deliberate customer service to those accounts that get flagged so that we can manage these in a less abrupt and more thoughtful way."[10]

In an online Q&A in June 2015, Zuckerberg clarified that Facebook's real-name policy did not necessarily require users to provide legal names. "Your real name is whatever you go by and what your friends call you," Zuckerberg said. "If your friends all call you by a nickname and you want to use that name on Facebook, you should be able to do that. In this way, we should be able to support everyone using their own real names, including everyone in the transgender community."[11]

The company changed its real-name procedures later that year, after criticism from advocates for the lesbian, gay, bisexual, and transgender community as well as domestic violence victims' advocates.[12] It began requiring people who flag false names to provide "additional context" for the review, seeking to reduce the amount of verification requests that it sends to users. Second, it developed a tool that it said would allow the users of flagged accounts to "let us know they have a special circumstance, and then give us more information about their unique situation."[13]

Facebook did not eliminate its real-name policy; it only promised two more procedural changes. And even those proved to be controversial. The Electronic Frontier Foundation (EFF), which has criticized real-name policies, said that the new tool that allows users to justify a "special circumstance" would effectively force "those who are most vulnerable to reveal even more information about their intimate, personal lives." Pressuring them to disclose more personal information results "in a remedy that is useless and risks putting them in a more dangerous situation should Facebook share those personal details," Eva Galperin and Wafa Ben Hassine of EFF wrote.[14]

Safety is a primary justification for Facebook's real-name policy. The company said it concluded that anonymity and pseudonymity can allow people to more easily harass, abuse, and intimidate others. In response to concerns that its real-name policies endangered some of its more vulnerable users, Facebook tried to mitigate these risks by offering the new tool to allow people to explain their unique situations that prevent them from complying with the policy. Yet even that solution raised safety concerns.

Facebook and other platforms have valid reasons for attempting to better identify the sources of user content. For instance, Brian Friedberg and Joan Donovan documented many cases of "pseudonymous influence operations," in which "politically motivated actors impersonate marginalized, underrepresented, and vulnerable groups to either malign, disrupt, or exaggerate their causes." Among the case studies that they document is Facebook's 2018 removal of fake accounts created by Russia's Internet Research Agency that purported to be run by Black and LGBT activists. Such pseudonymous operations, Friedberg and Donovan wrote, "intentionally or unintentionally reproduce social harm by degrading trust in the authenticity of marginalized people."[15] Pseudonymous speech is not the same as deceptive or false speech, and even platforms that allow pseudonymous accounts generally prohibit impersonation. But a policy that allows pseudonymity also may be more likely to pave the way for misleading accounts. The debate over real-name policies shows how the Safety Motivation for anonymity cuts both ways: while anonymity or pseudonymity would protect Facebook users from many types of threats, the company is just as concerned about the harmful potential uses of anonymity. Facebook is concerned about anonymity's use as a sword, while its critics argue that anonymity is a vital shield.

Despite the pushback that Facebook received and its procedural changes, as of early 2021, Facebook continued to have a real-name policy. "Facebook is a community where everyone uses the name they go by in everyday life," the company wrote in its online Help Center.[16] The company requires profile names to appear on an ID document such as, among other things, a government ID, bank statement, library card, utility bill, or car insurance card.[17] Although this policy is a bit less restrictive than one that permits only legal names, it curtails the full range of pseudonymous and anonymous speech. Merely having a real-name policy does not prevent every user from having fake names. During the first quarter of 2021, Facebook estimates, about 5 percent of its worldwide monthly active users were fake accounts, and the company took action on 1.3 billion fake accounts.[18]

The survival of Facebook's real-name policy despite persistent criticism reveals the power that companies wield in determining the level of anonymity that people may employ online. The First Amendment provides a baseline level of anonymity that the government may not restrict, but people may be unable to fully exercise those anonymity rights if the companies that serve as gateways to much of the Internet prohibit them from doing so.

Facebook is not the only platform to require real names. Websites of all sizes have experimented with various levels of anonymity and pseudonymity, and many concluded that the costs of anonymous comments outweigh the benefits. In 2013, the *Patriot-Ledger* newspaper in Quincy, Massachusetts, began requiring commenters to comment via their Facebook or LinkedIn profiles. "For some time, we've received complaints that the anonymous commenting system we've hosted on our online stories does little to enhance the conversation within our community," the newspaper wrote in an editorial announcing the change. "The criticism has been that some of the comments are hateful and sometimes, downright objectionable. We heard you and we agree."[19] Also that year, the *Huffington Post* began requiring commenters to post under their real names. "Freedom of expression is given to people who stand up for what they're saying and who are not hiding behind anonymity," Ariana Huffington, then the site's editor-in-chief, said. "Maintaining a civil environment for real conversation and community has always been key to the *Huffington Post*."[20]

Other platforms have taken a more anonymity-friendly approach. Reddit, a massive collection of online bulletin boards run by volunteer moderators, requires users to create usernames, but those need not be connected to their real names. As Reddit states in its content policy: "You don't have to use your real name to use Reddit, but don't impersonate an individual or an entity in a misleading or deceptive manner."[21] And many Reddit moderators have gone a step further, removing posts that "dox," or reveal the true identities of other posters.[22] "When people detach from their real-world identities, they can be more authentic, more true to themselves," Reddit chief executive Steve Huffman said in 2018.[23]

True selves are not always socially desirable. Some user-created boards, or "subreddits," have enabled some users to anonymously traffic in racist content, celebrity nude photos, and violence.[24] A 2019 study of six million Reddit posts created between 2011 and 2018 found "increasing patterns on misogynistic content and users as well as violent attitudes."[25] Yet Reddit's relative anonymity has fostered some of the communities that believed they were disenfranchised by Facebook's real-name policy. Emily VanDerWerff wrote of the welcoming communities for trans people that were created by anonymity on Reddit and Twitter. "The big reason to use an anonymous Twitter or Reddit account is to protect one's identity in the hope of exploring a new one," VanDerWerff wrote. "This is perhaps why anonymous social media accounts that people gradually start to use more than their 'real' accounts so frequently belong to trans women."[26]

Like Reddit, Twitter has taken a different approach from Facebook to anonymity and pseudonymity, reflecting the very real impact that corporate choices can have on identity disclosures. Twitter has had a longstanding policy against requiring users to publicly disclose their real names, though it does prohibit "accounts that pose as another person, brand, or organization in a confusing or deceptive manner."[27] At a 2011 town hall, Chief Executive Dick Costolo said that the lack of a real-name policy stemmed not from idealism, but from a desire to better serve consumer demand. "We're not wedded to pseudonyms," he said. "We're wedded to people being able to use the service as they see fit."[28] As Mathew Ingram wrote about Costolo's remarks, "Twitter realizes it can provide plenty of value for users (and thus for advertisers) without having to know your real name."[29]

Many Twitter users have long relied on the lack of a real-name policy. In an analysis of 2010 data from Twitter, New York University researchers found that 26 percent of Twitter accounts were either fully or partly anonymous (i.e., only providing part of a name). The researchers found that more than 20 percent of the followers of accounts in "sensitive" categories such as Islamophobia, gay/lesbian, and marijuana were anonymous, while fewer than 10 percent of the followers of "nonsensitive" categories were anonymous.[30]

The anonymity-permissive nature of Twitter has not been free of problems and criticism. In 2018, Twitter told the Senate Judiciary Committee that fifty thousand automated Russian accounts—or bots—were behind more than 4 percent of the retweets of Donald Trump's account from September 1 to November 15, 2016.[31] Fake Twitter accounts also enabled people to boost their numbers of followers. A 2018 *New York Times* article documented an underground industry of fake Twitter accounts, and estimated that up to 15 percent of Twitter's active users "are automated accounts designed to simulate real people, though the company claims that number is far lower."[32]

Billionaire Mark Cuban tweeted then that if the company "were to eliminate bots and accounts individuals won't put their real names behind, your revenues and user base and usage would skyrocket as a result of users and advertisers feeling safer on the platform."[33] But such a change would lead to some of the problems that Facebook has confronted with its real-name policy. "Think about closeted LGBT individuals who may not be in a position to be open about their identities," Matthew Hughes observed. "The anonymity Twitter offers means they have an avenue for personal expression, while remaining anonymous."[34]

Moreover, even companies that impose aggressive real-name policies may be susceptible to abuse by bad actors. For example, despite

Facebook's real-name policy for individual users, Russian propagandists managed to reach 126 million Facebook users during the 2016 presidential campaign.[35] As Special Counsel Robert Mueller's 2018 indictment of thirteen Russian propagandists outlined, Russians distributed the Facebook propaganda using fictitious groups such as "United Muslims of America" and "Being Patriotic," and they even managed to create a fictitious individual, "Matt Skiber," to organize an event for Trump.[36] It is impossible to quantify how much more Russian misinformation would have spread on Facebook had it not had a real-name policy, but the Mueller indictment shows that its policies were not a bulletproof method of preventing impersonation on its services.

The question that online services must address is whether the benefits of real-name policies outweigh the benefits of anonymity and pseudonymity. At least part of the answer comes from the free market. Consumer demand will ultimately determine whether a platform should have a real-name policy and any exceptions to that rule. If a platform's stringent real-name policy prevents its users from engaging in candid conversations, the platform may lose customers. But if a platform is overrun by anonymous trolls, it is unlikely to attract a broad user base, although there is a history of niche anonymous and pseudonymous sites such as AutoAdmit that can cause substantial damage despite having relatively small numbers of users.

But it is questionable whether requiring real names improves the level of discourse on social media. A 2016 analysis of a German online petition website reviewed more than half a million comments on more than 1,600 petitions. The researchers hypothesized that the commenters who used their real names would be more aggressive. "Aggressive commentors have nothing to hide: they stand up for higher-order moral ideals and principles," they wrote. And the research confirmed that hypothesis; they found that "more online aggression is obtained by non-anonymous commenters and not by anonymous commenters."[37]

Likewise, some research has found that pseudonymous online discussions tend to be of higher quality. Disqus, which provides online comment platforms for websites, reported in 2012 that commenters using pseudonyms commented nearly five times as often as those who were required to use their real names via Facebook logins and concluded that "pseudonyms are the most valuable contributors to communities because they contribute the highest quantity and quality of comments."[38]

A platform's determination that real-name policies are in its business interests does not necessarily mean that they are in the best interests of society. While companies such as Facebook have presented reasonable explanations for their real-name requirements, many harms that the policies seek to prevent will still occur, as the worst actors will be able to circumvent the real-name policies. Yet real-name policies can harm the transgender community, domestic violence victims, and others who might face serious consequences from the use of their real names. Because of the serious consequences for some of the most vulnerable groups, real-name policies often are not in the best interests of society.

15

OUT IN THE OPEN

Despite the legal and technical anonymity protections described in this book, anonymous and pseudonymous Internet users have been unmasked, often in very public ways. These unmaskings have taken place not because a court found an extraordinary circumstance that warranted disclosure. The disputes never made it to court. Nor did the unmasking occur due to a flaw in Tor or a VPN. The anonymous speakers' identities were disclosed because there were enough clues to enable others to put together these puzzle pieces to learn their identities.

Some of the most valuable personal information is "open source," often only a Google search away for the public. And people often disclose this information voluntarily on social media or in public places. Other identifying information is not open source, but is collected by companies or governments with few restrictions on its use in piercing anonymity both online and offline.

Academic research has long established that only a few data points are necessary to identify people. In a 2000 research paper, Latanya Sweeney used Census data to establish that 87 percent of Americans had a unique combination of five-digit ZIP code, gender, and birth date.[1] As Paul Ohm has correctly observed, the ease of reidentification of presumably anonymous data poses great threats to individual safety. "Our enemies will find it easier to connect us to facts that they can use to blackmail, harass, defame, frame, or discriminate against us," Ohm wrote. "Powerful reidentification will draw every one of us closer to what I call our personal 'databases of ruin.'"[2]

Famously, in 2006, America Online publicly released 20 million search queries as part of a public research initiative. Although the data were stripped of usernames, login names, IP addresses, and other traditionally identifying data, newspaper reporters managed to identify some users based on their search queries. The reporters identified a sixty-two-year-old widow, Thelma Arnold, based on her queries for landscapers in her small Georgia town, people who shared her last name, and "homes sold in shadow lake subdivision gwinnett county Georgia."[3]

In the years since Sweeney's groundbreaking research, the amount of open source information has surged, along with the popularity of social media. This phenomenon became particularly clear to me in the fall of 2015, shortly after I joined the faculty of the Naval Academy. I traveled to Clemson University to deliver a presentation about cybersecurity law. Also presenting was one of the Naval Academy's top students, Zac Dannelly. A senior (midshipman first class in Naval Academy parlance), Dannelly was a member of the Naval Academy's first graduating class of cyber operations majors.

My presentation about cybersecurity regulations went smoothly, though unremarkably. Dannelly's presentation, however, captivated the crowd. He demonstrated software used by a company where he had interned. The software compiles and analyzes publicly available data from social media to build geolocation-based profiles, allowing the user to track an individual's posts and check-ins across time and locations.

Dannelly chose a West Point cadet who had visited Annapolis to play a baseball game against the Naval Academy. With a few clicks, Dannelly managed to trace his movements, pinpointing details such as the cadet's hometown (and, in fact, home address thanks to geolocation tags on his social media posts) and where he visits for vacation. With the oratorial skills of a Top 40 radio DJ, Dannelly spoke of this baseball player's life in great detail. All of this came not from highly sensitive databases of confidential information, but social media posts and check-ins that the cadet voluntarily provided to the world.

Although there is nothing particularly shocking about a college student posting personal information on social media, it was striking to see how seamlessly Dannelly could gather and showcase a virtual dossier on a future military officer, based entirely on public data.

The vast amount of publicly available information allows anyone with a modicum of curiosity to use basic tools to identify people who would otherwise remain anonymous. My friend, Kate Klonick, a law professor at St. John's University, gave her students an assignment: pick a stranger in a public setting, and based on what you observe, use Google to identify them. Klonick based this project on Irwin Altman's 1975 theory that people may reveal private information in public if they assume they are anonymous.

The students succeeded in their surreptitious unmasking. One student overheard a man in her airplane as he arranged his ride from the airport. "He revealed enough in that conversation and she was able to find his name," Klonick wrote in a *New York Times* op-ed. Another student listened to a man talk on a train. "He overheard the man's first name and typed it in combined with the name of the college on his shirt," she wrote. "The student explained in his email to me that even without a last name, he was able to find the stranger's college major, minor and year of graduation. It helped that in one photo he was wearing the same outfit he wore that day on the train."[4]

The subjects of her students' experiments—much like Dannelly's West Point cadet—did not suffer irreparable harm. Yet the ease with which people can be unmasked can have serious consequences, particularly for people who believe they are anonymous.

Unmasking based on pieces of public information can be seen as one form of doxxing, particularly if the unmasking is made public. The term *doxxing* derives from the practice of publicly disclosing "private documents" about an adversary.[5] Doxxing can stem from the publication of private information, such as email. But as the US Department of Homeland Security notes, doxxers also may compile "information from multiple public-facing sources to reveal sensitive information about the victim, such as the victim's home address, family members, photos, workplace, and information about the individual's habits, hobbies, or interests."[6]

In some cases, doxxing also may stem from an anonymous speaker's overconfidence in the culture of anonymity empowerment, causing them to let down their guard. And when viewed broadly, doxxing is not something that is done only by someone with malicious intent. I take a broad interpretation of doxxing, and look at all the ways that an anonymous speaker might be unmasked based on identifying information that is available to others.

In his 2015 article, A. Michael Froomkin attributed some of the anonymity threats to "self surveillance" by people on social media. "Twitter, Instagram, Facebook, all offer opportunities to sabotage one's own privacy," he wrote. "Using a decent camera and increasingly accurate . . . facial recognition software, we have now gotten to a point where if you have a Facebook account, there is a 75% chance that a computer can match a picture taken of you to your Facebook account in less than 2 seconds. Not having a Facebook account is little protection. If somebody else on Facebook took a picture of you and tagged it, it is the same as doing it yourself."[7]

To see how easily someone can be unmasked based on a public data trail, we once again look at AutoAdmit. The self-described "law school discussion board" has remained online for well over a decade after the 2007 lawsuit filed against its pseudonymous users by the two female law students who were harassed online. A review of the website in 2020 found few posts related to law school admissions; rather, it is filled with sophomoric, hateful, racist, and misogynistic posts.

CharlesXII was a popular AutoAdmit poster who exemplified the character of the site. In June 2020, CharlesXII wrote, "Black doods staying inside playing Call of Duty is probably one of the biggest factors keeping crime down." Later that month, he wrote, "Honestly given how tired black people always claim to be, maybe the real crisis is their lack of sleep." In response to an August 2019 thread titled "We should just buy Canada and kick the Canadians out," CharlesXII wrote, "Okay but what do we do with the millions of Chinese people."[8]

CNN reporter Oliver Darcy received an anonymous email tip about the poster and, based on what CharlesXII disclosed on AutoAdmit and public information, published an article in 2020 identifying CharlesXII as Blake Neff, Fox News talk show host Tucker Carlson's lead writer.[9] "Among the details which make clear that CharlesXII and Neff are the same person: CharlesXII indicated on the board that he had gone to Dartmouth; Neff is an alumnus," Darcy wrote of his investigative process. "CharlesXII said he had been working for nearly four years in his current journalism job in Washington DC; Neff has been working for Carlson at Fox in Washington since February 2017, according to his LinkedIn profile, which appears to have been removed after his resignation from Fox News. CharlesXII said on the board that he got his start in journalism after he turned down law school and instead took a fellowship; Neff told the Dartmouth Alumni Magazine that he took a fellowship with the Collegiate Network."[10]

Neff also was the subject of a dating profile in a 2017 *Washington Post* article in which he referred to topics that CharlesXII had posted about on AutoAdmit, and CharlesXII posted pictures on AutoAdmit of a trip to Egypt, and Neff was seen in reflections in some of the pictures.[11]

CNN contacted Neff about its findings in July 2020, and the next day, Fox News said that Neff resigned. "Neff's abhorrent conduct on this forum was never divulged to the show or the network until Friday, at which point we swiftly accepted his resignation," Fox News executives wrote in a memo to employees. "Make no mistake, actions such as his cannot and will not be tolerated at any time in any part of our work force."[12]

Due to the abhorrent nature of his AutoAdmit posts, Neff's unmasking was understandably celebrated by many commentators. "As you might suspect, Neff himself is not exactly an argument for the notion that his is the Master Race," Jack Holmes wrote in *Esquire*. "He also showed off some toxic views of women and trafficked in homophobia. This apparently went on for five years, four of which he spent as Tucker Carlson's writer."[13]

Yet some other doxxing is more morally ambiguous. Consider NatSec-Wonk. This pseudonymous Twitter commentator gained a small but devoted following from 2011 to 2013 for tweets that were critical of the Obama administration's foreign policy. Among the tweets, he wrote of senior White House adviser Valerie Jarrett, "Someone at #aspenideas should ask Valerie Jarrett what it is she actually does at the White House #ihavenoideadoyou?"[14] He wrote of a Council on Foreign Relations event: "Is the Guiness [*sic*] World Record for largest density of tools in one room about to be broken?"[15]

A former Obama National Security Council official told the *Washington Post* that the tweets received attention in the administration. "We talked about it from time to time in the hallways, 'Did you see what @natsecwonk posted?'" the former official told the newspaper (anonymously, of course). "He probably heard people walking around saying things about the account."[16]

The tweeter also criticized members of the Beltway press. NatSecWonk wrote in July 2013 of *Daily Beast* reporters Eli Lake and Josh Rogin, "When was the last time you read a tough piece on GOP Members of Congress and their policies from @EliLake and @joshrogin? Yeah, me neither."[17]

A few months later, Rogin posted a story entitled "Exclusive: White House Official Fired for Tweeting Under Fake Name." On October 22, 2013, Rogin reported that a White House national security employee, Jofi Joseph, "has been surreptitiously tweeting under the moniker @natsecwonk, a Twitter feed famous inside Washington Policy circles since it began in February, 2011 until it was shut down last week."[18]

The *Washington Post* reported that Joseph worked on the White House team that negotiated with Iran. And the Obama administration went out of its way to identify him as the poster. According to the *Washington Post*, relying on an anonymous US official, Obama advisers tried to unmask Joseph by planting "inaccurate, but harmless information with him to see if it would pop up as a 140-character tweet." The *Post* could not confirm whether that operation led to the identification of Joseph as NatSecWonk. But the impact of the unmasking was swift; after Joseph was identified, he was booted from his office. "You've heard that phrase, 'You'll never work in this town again,'" a former NSC official told the *Post*. "Well, he's just thrown his career away."[19] Joseph issued an apology after the unmasking, writing to *Politico:* "What started out as an intended parody account of DC culture developed over time into a series of inappropriate and mean-spirited comments. I bear complete responsibility for this affair and I sincerely apologize to everyone I insulted."[20]

I failed to reach Joseph to interview him for this book, so I do not know whether he anticipated the risks when he tweeted pseudonymously. Joseph likely understood that his foreign policy career could implode if his name were linked to tweets that criticized his superiors and the media. Yet he made a risk-based decision that may have been based on his perception of the chances that he would be unmasked. Joseph's resume suggests that he is a smart person who would not make intentionally reckless decisions. There might have been a gap between his perception of the chances of being unmasked and the actual risk.

Nothing in the public reporting of Joseph's unmasking suggests that the White House used a subpoena or other legal process to unmask him, so the First Amendment protections of *Dendrite* and similar cases probably would not have helped him. Nor does the media coverage suggest that the White House used a particularly sophisticated technology to identify Joseph. If the *Washington Post's* article is correct, the White House may have used a simple operational technique—planting false information—to associate Joseph with the tweets that ended his foreign policy career.

Even absent an operation designed to pierce anonymity—as Joseph may have experienced—we may have forfeited our anonymity merely due to the vast amount of data that companies and governments collect about people, and what we have voluntarily placed in public view.

Whether Joseph's unmasking served the public interest is debatable. The White House may have had its justifications for imposing costs on employees who speak out of turn, particularly those who work in national security. Yet his speech was not comparable with the hatred that Neff spewed online, and Joseph may have had valid reasons for critiquing the media and powerful officials.

The ease with which people can be unmasked and tracked based on public information suggests that the anonymity empowerment provided by the First Amendment and technology also requires people to carefully assess the information that they are providing to the world. Even if this public information does not directly reveal their names or personally identifiable information, it could be pieced together to unmask them. Not all information that is available on the Internet was voluntarily posted by the data subjects. If a newspaper publishes an online article, the subjects of the article cannot restrict the online dissemination of that article due to well-established First Amendment protections. Although people cannot control the flow of this sort of potentially identifying information, they should be aware of the potential for such data to be linked to data that they voluntarily provide on public platforms like social media. The culture of anonymity empowerment requires not only laws and anonymity-protective technology, but self-empowerment.

EMPOWERING ANONYMITY THROUGH PRIVACY LAW

Even if people believe that they have hidden their identifying information from the public, it may not remain private online or offline. Sensitive, identifying data may exist in private corporate databases. That information can be used or bought by other companies and also is vulnerable to hackers. While anonymity and privacy are distinct, privacy laws may help to empower anonymity.

An entire industry has been built around personal data. The phenomenon was well described by Shoshana Zuboff in the 2019 book, *The Age of Surveillance Capitalism.* Surveillance capitalism, Zuboff writes, "unilaterally claims human experience as free raw material for translation into behavioral data" and "feeds on every aspect of every human's experience."[1]

Surveillance capitalism—coupled with weak privacy laws in the United States—has allowed companies to maintain vast amounts of information about people, and at least some of that information can be used to unmask people who had attempted to be anonymous. If a person uses an email address that does not indicate their name, there still is a chance that a data broker or other company has made the connection and maintains that linkage in their voluminous files about individuals.

And companies, the government, or bad actors could unmask people by combining their anonymous social media posts with data that companies maintain about people. For instance, many companies track web browsing histories to deliver advertising. Even if this web browsing history is not provided with the person's name, it is possible to predict the identity of the person based on other public information, such as social media posts. A 2017 study, based on browsing histories that subjects provided to the researchers, successfully predicted the identities of more than 70 percent of the subjects relying solely on their public Twitter posts. "Since users are more likely to click on links posted by accounts that they follow, these distinctive patterns persist in their browsing history," the authors wrote. "An adversary can thus de-anonymize a given browsing history by finding the social media profile whose 'feed' shares the history's idiosyncratic characteristics."[2]

And in some cases, companies have hoarded particularly sensitive personal data. A 2019 *New York Times* investigative report studied the troves of precise geolocation data that a company collected from individuals' mobile phones. The newspaper obtained a file containing more than fifty billion precise location points of more than 12 million Americans. "The companies that collect all this information on your movements justify their business on the basis of three claims: People consent to be tracked, the data is anonymous and the data is secure," Stuart A. Thompson and Charlie Warzel wrote. "None of those claims holds up, based on the file we've obtained and our review of company practices. Yes, the location data contains billions of data points with no identifiable information like names or email addresses. But it's child's play to connect real names to the dots that appear on the maps."[3]

A single geolocation point, such as a home or office, can easily lead to a person's unmasking. Only three people live in my house, and only one of us works at the Naval Academy in Annapolis. A company that has access to my geolocation movements can easily associate me with my phone. And that is precisely what the *New York Times* found.

"We followed military officials with security clearances as they drove home at night," the *Times* wrote. "We tracked law enforcement officers as they took their kids to school. We watched high-powered lawyers (and their guests) as they traveled from private jets to vacation properties." The *Times* noted that when advertising firms and data brokers purchase this data, it is accompanied by a mobile advertising ID, which is "used to combine location trails with other information like your name, home address, email, phone number or even an identifier tied to your Wi-Fi network."[4]

A French study in 2014 confirmed the utility of geolocation points as identifiers, even when they are not directly linked to a real name. The researchers described a method in which "the mobility of an individual can act as a signature, thus playing the role of a quasi-identifier." The use of pseudonyms, they wrote, "is usually not sufficient to preserve the anonymity of their identities because the mobility traces themselves contain information that can be uniquely linked back to an individual."[5]

Companies of all sizes—from mammoths such as Google to start-ups—collect geolocation data from users' smartphones. Even if the companies agree to limit their use and sharing of this information, like any data they are susceptible to breaches. For example, Animoto, which offers a cloud-based video production service, announced in 2018 that a hacker accessed its users' personal information, including names and geolocation information.[6] Likewise, in 2020, genealogy website ancestry.com announced that its users' data, including geolocation information, was left exposed online.[7]

One might expect that the sensitivity of geolocation information—and the ease with which it could unmask people who otherwise would be anonymous—warrants heightened legal requirements for companies that collect and use it. Many state and federal laws already impose greater protection for medical records, student data, and bank account information.

Yet in the United States, geolocation information often does not receive special privacy or data security protection. Every state, plus the District of Columbia, has a law that requires companies to notify their residents of the breach of certain types of personal information, such as bank account data and Social Security numbers. States define "personal information" differently, with some including email login credentials, and others including passport numbers. But no state requires companies to notify residents of the breach of their precise geolocation information. It is understandable that state data breach notice laws, many of which were passed in the mid-aughts, would seek to combat identity theft by giving special protection to bank account information. At the time, identity theft and credit card fraud were top concerns among cybersecurity professionals. But these laws fail to reflect more modern privacy concerns with technology such as geolocation, which threaten the ability of people to remain anonymous.

Still, we have some hope to preserve anonymity amid invasive new technologies. Some of the biggest success stories, at least in a few cities, involve the pushback against facial recognition technology. A January 2020 article in the *New York Times* received widespread attention for its reporting on Clearview AI, a company that developed an app widely used by law enforcement. "You take a picture of a person, upload it and get to see public photos of that person, along with links to where those photos appeared," Kashmir Hill wrote in the *Times*. "The system—whose backbone is a database of more than three billion images that Clearview claims to have scraped from Facebook, YouTube, Venmo and millions of other websites—goes far beyond anything ever constructed by the United States government or Silicon Valley giants." As Hill summarized, the app "could end your ability to walk down the street anonymously."[8]

Imagine the implications for the sliding scale of anonymity that has been a hallmark of American speech and dissent. The First Amendment allows canvassers to refuse to wear name badges, even though their faces are exposed. With technology such as the Clearview AI app, canvassers might be easily identified merely by exposing their faces in public. Such identification poses a great threat to speech, particularly if the person using the app is a police officer.

Hundreds of law enforcement agencies nationwide used Clearview AI's app. But one police department that did not was San Francisco's. In May 2019, the San Francisco Board of Supervisors voted 8–1 to ban its police and other city agencies from using facial recognition technology. Matt Cagle, an American Civil Liberties Union of Northern California lawyer who supported the ordinance, told the *New York Times* that facial recognition "provides government with unprecedented power to track people going about their daily lives."[9]

Some other municipalities, such as Boston, have followed San Francisco's lead and prohibited their agencies from using facial recognition.[10] And a few states have passed laws that restrict the use of biometrics, including face geometry and iris scans. These state laws are not absolute bans, and companies still can use facial recognition if they inform people of the technology and receive their consent.[11] Outside of this handful of cities and states, Americans have little control over companies' collection and use of information that could easily identify them.

Law enforcement's use of facial recognition is not the only threat that the technology poses to anonymity. Companies and individuals, too, could use facial recognition to pierce the veil of anonymity that exists in our online and offline lives. Consider a hypothetical that the writer Jessica Mason presented in 2020: a woman rebuffs a compliment from a man she met on the street. "What's to stop him from snapping a picture and finding her on social media and harassing her, or doxing her, or stalking and killing her?" she wrote.[12] Technology that enables people to pierce the veil of anonymity also defeats the substantial safety benefits that anonymity empowerment provides.

Despite the troubling ways in which the emerging technology can pierce anonymity and privacy, we also must keep in mind the substantial everyday benefits that the technology provides. While the *New York Times* article, for instance, reveals the potentially concerning uses of geolocation data, so many of us also rely on geolocation data every time we get in the car. The solution to concerns about anonymity compromises is not to ban the technology. Even if it were possible to prohibit all use of geolocation, facial recognition, and other technology, Americans might very well push back on such a sweeping change. Rather, we should use our legal and regulatory system to provide people with control over the use and disclosure of their identifying data, prohibit particularly nefarious uses, and encourage companies to better protect the data.

This is easier said than done. For years, members of Congress and consumer groups have advocated for a strong national privacy law, which would give Americans control over how companies collect, use, and share their personal information. Yet efforts to pass such a law have stalled, often due to debates over whether the federal law should override stronger state laws and whether it should provide people with a right to sue. Anonymity is not a common subject during the public debates, but a national privacy law can and should enable Americans to control the amount of identifying information that companies use and share.

The European Union provides an example of one attempt to address a sliding scale of anonymity in a privacy law. In 2018, the European Union's General Data Protection Regulation, or GDPR, went into effect. The law restricts the ability of companies to process Europeans' personal information and provides Europeans with broad rights to request access to and deletion of the personal information that companies hold.

The GDPR states that it does not regulate "anonymous information," but it defines that narrowly as "information which does not relate to an identified or identifiable person" or personal information that is "rendered anonymous in such a manner that the data subject is not or no longer identifiable." The GDPR clarifies that data are not anonymous— but pseudonymous, and still subject to the regulations—if it "could be attributed to a natural person by the use of additional information." In determining whether data are anonymous or pseudonymous, the GDPR accounts for means that are "reasonably likely" to use the data to identify a person, accounting for "all objective factors, such as the costs of and the amount of time required for identification, taking into consideration the available technology at the time of the processing and technological developments."[13]

The GDPR is an example of anonymity empowerment through privacy law. It encourages companies to fully anonymize data when possible and prevent it from being traced to a person. As the United Kingdom's data protection regulator wrote, for data to be considered anonymous under the GDPR, the company "must strip personal data of sufficient elements that mean the individual can no longer be identified."[14]

But if the data can be linked back to a person with reasonable effort, the company must abide by the GDPR and provide people with control over their data. And the GDPR also encourages pseudonymization. Although pseudonymous data are subject to the GDPR's requirements, the regulation requires companies to adopt a program to minimize privacy risks and explicitly cites pseudonymization as an example of an element of such a program.[15]

The United States is unlikely to adopt a privacy law that is quite the same as GDPR, as Europe has long valued privacy as a fundamental human right, and the US legal system is more likely to emphasize other rights, such as free expression. Privacy and free expression may conflict; for example, a 2014 Court of Justice for the European Union ruling created a "Right to Be Forgotten," which enables people to request that search engines deindex embarrassing search results from searches of their name. While there is some value in the Right to Be Forgotten, it is unlikely that such a legal requirement would pass muster in the United States, because of strong First Amendment free speech protections.

But US privacy law can—and should—adopt the features of the GDPR that provide people with control over certain identifying data that companies maintain about them. People can decide whether to exercise these rights, and they very well may do so if they would like to preserve their anonymity. Providing Americans with control over their personal information would allow them to reduce the likelihood that their behavior is being tracked online or that a company is maintaining a database of their geolocation information. Privacy law in the United States also should contain incentives for companies, when possible, to maintain data in an anonymous format so that it cannot be linked to a person.

Although Congress had not passed a generally applicable data protection law as of mid-2021, a few states, including California, Virginia, and Colorado, had done so. The laws generally are not as strong as the GDPR, but some provide incentives for companies to protect anonymity and pseudonymity. In 2021, Virginia enacted the Consumer Data Protection Act, which provides Virginia residents with the rights to access, delete, and correct their personal information. Many of the law's requirements do not apply to pseudonymous data, which it defines as personal information "that cannot be attributed to a specific natural person without the use of additional information, provided that such additional information is kept separately and is subject to appropriate technical and organizational measures to ensure that the personal data is not attributed to an identified or identifiable natural person." The law also does not apply to "de-identified data," which it defines as "data that cannot reasonably be linked to an identified or identifiable natural person, or a device linked to such person."[16] Like the GDPR, the Virginia law both empowers consumers to control their personal information and provides companies with an incentive to disassociate identifying information with other data that the companies store about consumers. The Virginia law perhaps does not go far enough to protect identifying information; for example, stating that de-identified data is that which "cannot be reasonably linked" to a person provides a good deal of flexibility for companies.

The California Privacy Rights Act, which voters approved in 2020, demonstrates another approach to empowering anonymity. The law creates a category of personal data known as "sensitive personal information," which includes geolocation and biometric information. It requires businesses to notify consumers about the collection and use of such sensitive personal information and allows consumers to ask that their sensitive personal information not be shared.[17]

But we cannot rely only on state legislatures to empower anonymity. Even if all fifty states were to pass data protection laws, it makes little sense to subject companies to a patchwork of laws that are based on the states where their consumers live. Congress should pass a stronger national data protection law that provides a national standard. As Congress develops a national data protection strategy, I hope that it will consider how the new law could help to continue the long history of anonymity and pseudonymity in the United States. Like the GDPR and the Virginia law, the US data protection law should empower anonymity by giving incentives to businesses to de-identify or pseudonymize the data. Key to the success of such statutory incentives will be stringent definitions of "anonymization" and "pseudonymization" that recognize the vast research (such as Sweeney's) that has found that it is possible to identify people based on purportedly anonymized data.[18] This research suggests that pseudonymization and anonymization incentives are not a panacea for concerns about anonymity. But these incentives might modestly reduce the likelihood of intrusions on anonymity.

Because anonymization and pseudonymization incentives probably are not enough to empower anonymity, Congress should ban particularly egregious anonymity threats, as San Francisco did with facial recognition. The law also should allow people, when possible, to request the deletion of their information and that it not be shared with other companies. But even when people have these rights, their identifying information could be compromised in a data breach or other sort of cybersecurity incident. Although some federal laws mandate data security safeguards in particular sectors such as finance and healthcare and the Federal Trade Commission enforces data security through its consumer protection law, the only generally applicable data security laws are imposed at the state level. And those laws are rather weak, mostly requiring "reasonable" data security without providing much guidance, and the laws generally are not terribly punitive.[19] To complement a national data protection law, Congress also should pass a strong cybersecurity law that requires companies to enact industry-standard technical, administrative, and physical safeguards to reduce the likelihood of unauthorized parties accessing personal information. While it is impossible to guarantee that personal information will be safe from data breaches, Congress and regulators should require companies to take responsible steps such as mandating employees use multifactor authentication and restricting access to personal information to employees who have a business need. Such steps could reduce the likelihood of a successful breach of identifying information.

Even strong data protection and cybersecurity laws will not fully address many threats to anonymity described in this chapter. The growing body of open source information, such as social media posts and online news articles, jeopardizes the ability of many people to remain anonymous or pseudonymous. Privacy laws should not restrict the use of such publicly available information, and such attempts would face First Amendment challenges. But a great deal of sensitive information, such as precise geolocation data, is not publicly available by default, and should receive rigorous privacy and security protections. By embedding anonymity values in national data protection and security laws, Congress would increase the control that Americans have over their identifying information. Privacy laws are not a panacea; rather, they could supplement First Amendment protections to further build a culture of anonymity empowerment.

Too often, anonymity is viewed as only a free speech issue, or only a privacy issue. It is both. The First Amendment protections are essential to preserving the history of anonymous speech that dates to colonial times. Yet protections from government intrusions on speech are insufficient to continue this tradition of anonymity empowerment. We need to not only preserve the First Amendment speech-based protections for anonymity, but develop a robust privacy legal framework that empowers anonymity in the age of surveillance capitalism.

CONCLUSION

As with so many free speech issues, it is challenging to quantify the costs and benefits of America's robust anonymity protections. If I only were to look at the Farmer in Pennsylvania or Dissent Doe, I would conclude that anonymity is an unalloyed societal good. And if I were to only look at AutoAdmit or Ryan Lin's harassment campaign, I would conclude that anonymity is the source of much that is wrong with society.

On balance, I conclude that the benefits of America's strong anonymity protections far outweigh the harms. From Thomas Paine to Manuel Talley to the anonymous employees on the late-nineties Yahoo! Finance boards, anonymous speakers have often been those who sought to challenge existing power structures. Limiting either the laws or technology that protect anonymity would too often also restrict the ability to speak freely about those in power.

When I consider the value of anonymity, I cannot help but think about Megan Gray's experience representing anonymous Yahoo! Finance posters at the dawn of the commercial Internet. I think about the powerful partner at a big law firm who was so threatened by the work of a young female associate. He was threatened because she helped employees and other anonymous critics of large companies avoid being unmasked. Gray's defense of their anonymity was ultimately a defense of their *ability* to speak out against powerful institutions. That this rainmaking partner was threatened by anonymity proves its value.

I also think about Al Sharpton's 1999 support of the Ku Klux Klan's challenge to New York's antimask laws. The Ku Klux Klan espouses views that Sharpton has worked tirelessly to combat through his activism. Still, Sharpton urged the court to allow the Klan to rally in masks and hoods. Sharpton's willingness to support the Klan's challenge reveals the enduring value of anonymity for marginalized communities.

I think about the dissidents in authoritarian countries who are voiceless because their governments have imposed online real-name requirements, enabling dictators to squelch even the slightest rumbling of opposition.

And I think about Junius, Publius, and so many others whose anonymous and pseudonymous writing laid the foundation for our democracy.

The anonymity debate is not always clearcut. The culture of anonymity empowerment has produced effects that are good, bad, and somewhere in between. Each American has had a different experience with anonymity—both from using anonymity as a tool online, and from experiencing the effects of other people's anonymous activities. Thus, each American also has a different—and equally legitimate—perspective about the merits of anonymity. And those mixed experiences with anonymity are reflected in the First Amendment protections, which are strong but far from absolute.

My personal experiences reflect the complex set of costs and benefits of living in a society that allows people, at least partly, to control whether their identities are linked to their actions. Based on these experiences—and my years of research for this book—I believe that America is better off due to the culture of anonymity empowerment.

My interactions with anonymous speakers have not been entirely pleasant. As the author of a book about Section 230 of the Communications Decency Act, I was on the receiving end of quite a bit of email, text messages, and phone calls as the statute became a heated subject of debate in Congress and the media in 2019 and 2020. Many messages were anonymous. Some people thoughtfully articulated their opinions about

Section 230. Some sought information about the law. But others hurled invectives, lies, anti-Semitic hate, and in some cases, threats. I often wondered whether they would use the same tone and inflammatory language if they were face to face with me at a conference, or even via the Internet if their names were linked to their hateful rhetoric.

The Section 230 debate wasn't the first time that I was on the receiving end of anonymous animosity. I was a journalist for nearly a decade before becoming a lawyer, and my newspaper printed reporters' email addresses at the end of each story. If I wrote an article about a politician, I could expect pseudonymous emails from all sides of the aisle, with some furious that I was in the tank for the politician, and others who thought I had a score to settle with that same leader. I responded to some of them, offering to talk with them on the phone. Not one person took me up on the offer, no matter how infuriated they sounded in their email. Anonymity empowered them to toss insults at me with a level of ferocity they probably would not have used if I knew their names or saw their faces.

But the angry emails only tell part of the story of my experience with anonymity. Perhaps my most extensive recent experiences with online anonymity have involved a website called D.C. Urban Moms and Dads, which I discovered in 2012 when my wife and I were looking to buy a house in the Washington, DC, area and start a family. This barebones site, almost entirely text based, contains dozens of forums on topics such as "General Parenting," "Trying to Conceive," "Real Estate," "Health and Medicine," and "Money and Finances." Although the site is based in DC, about half of its nearly 1 million monthly unique users come from outside the Washington, DC, area, to seek advice about, discuss, and debate so many topics that touch adult lives.

D.C. Urban Moms and Dads largely operates on the "traceable anonymity" prong of A. Michael Froomkin's framework: nearly all users are identified merely as "Anonymous," but the site's administrators maintain IP address logs. This anonymity has been crucial to my feeling comfortable over the years asking questions or voicing opinions about medical issues (I'm constantly anxious about my health), finances (I'm constantly anxious about going broke), and parenting (I'm constantly anxious about making the wrong choices as a parent). What benefits me is not only the ability to engage in these conversations without having my name associated with my questions, fears, or comments, but that other people are comfortable enough to respond to me with unvarnished honesty. Outside of a small group of friends, it is rare that I would discuss with the same level of candor as on the website.

Still, anonymity has not always made D.C. Urban Moms and Dads an online utopia. Posters also engage in polemics and ad hominem attacks, even though they don't know the name of the person on the receiving end of that attack. For example, in October 2020, a poster created a post entitled "Trump Just Lost My Vote," stating that while they had been "on the fence," about the upcoming presidential election, Donald Trump's response to Covid was the final straw. Dozens of people responded, mostly affirming the poster. Yet not everyone was supportive. "You took THIS long to see the light? You have to be the dumbest moron in the country," one person responded. "And frankly, we don't need your vote. It soils the rest of us. Just stay home. Let the smart people deal with this. Maybe in another ten years or so you can be trusted to vote, but for now, you should just STFU and do nothing."

I was so curious about the role that anonymity has played on the site that I reached out to its operators, Maria Sokurashvili and her husband, Jeff Steele. The two had worked in technology jobs in the DC area, and launched a parenting listserv in 2002. The listserv evolved into a website in 2005, and it eventually grew to be so popular that they managed to make the site their full-time jobs.

At first, the site's visitors registered with pseudonyms. But when the couple moved the site to new software in 2007, Steele said, they specifically looked for technology that allowed anonymous posting, and the site has been anonymous ever since. Steele believes that the site's success is due partly to a combination of anonymity and his willingness to step in and moderate discussions that go too far off the rails. "Websites that have some moderation and anonymity are few and far between," he said. A few times a year, Steele receives subpoenas for poster information. He generally complies with them, but at times first negotiates. But Steele usually can only provide IP addresses, as he generally does not collect email addresses or other identifying information.

Sure, there are some downsides of anonymity, Steele acknowledges. He points to "sock puppeting," which occurs when a poster responds to his own post, pretending to be a new poster. And some posters are sensitive to responses that criticize their posts, even though their names are not associated with the criticized posts. "Being anonymous doesn't completely mean you don't feel ownership," Steele said.

The candor that sometimes may make people feel uncomfortable also is the greatest strength of D.C. Urban Moms and Dads. Steele said he sought anonymity for the site because people feel welcome to share their life experiences, no matter how intimate. "People are free to be honest," Steele said. "On our site, if people think it's a bad idea, they'll say it's a bad idea. They will tell you. You get a lot of tough love."

One post, from December 2010, stands out to Steele as an example of the significant benefits of anonymity. A thirty-eight-year-old woman posted that she had just learned she was five weeks pregnant, and the father was a man she met three months earlier. She liked her new boyfriend, and was worried about how to break this shocking news to him. "So, I am quite eager to be a mother, but feel now I've started the whole thing ass-backward," she wrote.

People immediately responded, not with judgment or criticism, but with medical and legal advice, as well as their personal stories of having been in similar situations. "I was in the exact same position," one woman wrote. "We had already become very serious but this was something we were not expecting. To be honest my boyfriend became a raging asshole when I told him. So unsupportive and made the whole ordeal about him and what his needs and wants were. The only thing he wanted to happen was an abortion and quick. But I knew I was having that baby and I did . . . and he came around."

About a week later, the Original Poster (or "OP," a common term on the website to distinguish among the anonymous commenters) returned to say that her doctor told her she had a very high chance of miscarrying the early pregnancy. But the good news was that she told her boyfriend, and he was happy about the prospect of being a father. "A million thanks to all you wonderful moms and moms to be on this site," she wrote. "You totally saved me these last couple of days."

For Steele, this sort of conversation demonstrates the value of the site's anonymity. "I was just impressed in that whole thread that she would come and discuss this personal situation on our website and people would be so supportive," Steele said.

Anonymity has another benefit for D.C. Urban Moms and Dads post-ers, most of whom are women. If these posters were using their real names—or even pseudonyms—they very well might face the persistent harassment that is such a problem on the Internet. But purely anonymous posters do not face that problem, even if their comments might trigger the sort of person who would engage in pernicious harassment. "The fact that they don't have to worry about guys chasing them around and call-ing them ugly is a huge benefit," Steele said. "They can't get harassed or chased from thread to thread."

Some have used a lack of online anonymity as a sword against people—often women and minorities. danah boyd, for instance, tells a compelling story of an admissions officer from an Ivy League college who thought twice about accepting a Black student from south central Los Angeles after seeing gang insignia on his MySpace page. "Not everyone is safer by giving out their real name," boyd wrote. "Quite the opposite; many people are far LESS safe when they are identifiable. And those who are least safe are often those who are most vulnerable."[1]

As D.C. Urban Moms and Dads shows, the six motivations that justi-fied the anonymity of Junius and other newspaper and pamphlet authors are just as persuasive on the Internet. People have a strong Legal Motiva-tion for speaking anonymously; even if a defamation claim against an on-line poster would not ultimately succeed, defending against such a claim could be financially ruinous. The persistent harassment and stalking that people face online points to a Safety Motivation. Anonymous posters may communicate unpopular views that could cost them their jobs or damage their businesses, so a strong Economic Motivation remains for online ano-nymity. With the vast amount of personal information available online, the Privacy Motivation for anonymity remains stronger than ever; post-ers such as the thirty-eight-year-old woman who told her story on D.C. Urban Moms and Dads may not have done so with their real names, as it would communicate their most intimate details to the world. The Speech Motivation for anonymity is just as compelling online as it was in colonial pamphlets and newspaper articles. Dissent Doe has built an entire persona tied to her unique perspectives and compelling reporting about privacy and security issues. And the Power Motivation allows anonymous observ-ers and critics to speak out against politicians, businesses, and even their own employers.

My reasons for supporting a strong right to anonymity are similar to those of law professor David Kaye, who as United Nations Special Rapporteur on the promotion and protection of the right to freedom of opinion and expression issued a 2015 report urging states to strictly limit any restrictions on encryption and anonymity. Kaye recognized the criticism that encryption and anonymity could be used for crime, harassment, discrimination, and other social ills. "At the same time, however, law enforcement often uses the same tools to ensure their own operational security in undercover operations, while members of vulnerable groups may use the tools to ensure their privacy in the face of harassment," Kaye wrote.[2]

The discussion about the value of anonymity is not merely theoretical. As I was completing this book in early 2021, Andy Kessler wrote an op-ed in the *Wall Street Journal*, arguing that the solution to toxic online behavior was not amending Section 230 to hold platforms responsible, but to "end anonymity" online, perhaps by requiring a credit card or driver's license to use social media. "Sure, there's value to spontaneous users speaking freely about everything, but no one really knows how many fake accounts spewing fake news exist," Kessler wrote. "Truth is elusive. So why not impose know-your-customer on social-media companies."[3] The next day, Senator Ron Johnson of Wisconsin shared Kessler's op-ed on Twitter, and wrote, "I'm concerned that Congress's involvement in Section 230 reform may lead to more harm than good. One solution may be to end user anonymity on social media platforms. Social media companies need to know who their customers are so bad actors can be held accountable."[4]

While Kessler and Johnson raise reasonable doubts about whether changing Section 230 would prevent modern online harms, I worry that they do not fully account for the serious chilling effects of requiring real-name registration on social media. Even if such a change were to prevent some trolling and harassment—and it is not clear that it would—the requirement also would prevent gay teens from seeking support, women from speaking freely about their abusive relationships, and concerned citizens from criticizing their local governments.

To be clear, not all anonymous speech is valuable, desirable, or even safe for society. (Nor is a good deal of online speech that people post under their real names.) I do not and cannot defend all anonymous and pseudonymous speech on the Internet. Some anonymous speech is so destructive that we should not tolerate it, nor should we protect it with a cloak of anonymity. How do we foster the D.C. Urban Moms and Dads of the world while also protecting people from serial harassment and online stalking?

In large part, we already do, albeit imperfectly. The right to anonymity in the United States is strong, but not absolute. The First Amendment protections provide a good balance for anonymous speech, creating an atmosphere that prevents the government from mandating the real-name requirements and other anonymity killers seen in other countries. Yet the First Amendment protections allow courts to unmask bad actors in extraordinary circumstances.

This balance—reflected in the *Dendrite* and *Cahill* tests—puts a finger firmly on the scale in favor of anonymity, but also leaves room for courts to compel the unmasking of defendants in particularly egregious circumstances. This largely strikes me as an ideal level of anonymity protection. The First Amendment should prevent corporations from unmasking employees just because executives are upset about online criticism. Yet plaintiffs who have suffered extraordinary defamation or other wrongs, such as the AutoAdmit plaintiffs, should be able to try to identify their tormenters. The framework that courts have developed over the past two decades adequately captures these values. Judges should avoid less rigorous standards, and instead retain the final prong of the *Dendrite* test, which balances the poster's First Amendment anonymity right against the strength of the plaintiff's case.

One limitation of the *Dendrite* and *Cahill* tests, however, is that they often only apply in civil defamation claims and similar cases. And the need for anonymity extends beyond those disputes. Courts should provide equally strong anonymity protections for *distributing* and *receiving* information as they do for *expressing* information, such as copyright cases. Just as unmasking anonymous expression threatens to chill speech, unmasking the distributors and recipients of that speech also can have a chilling effect. If people fear that all of their online habits are easily accessible by a litigant who wants to commit extortion or merely embarrass them, those people may be less likely to freely seek out information online. Thus, judges in some of the copyright infringement cases have erred in minimizing the First Amendment anonymity protections for defendants. Although some might not view their acts of downloading or uploading music as being as "expressive" as posting on social media, threats to unmask them would similarly chill the flow of information online.

Likewise, courts should more thoroughly apply the First Amendment to the government's attempts to unmask people in criminal cases and investigations. The strong *Dendrite* and *Cahill* protections often only constrain civil litigants from using subpoenas to unmask defendants. Courts should apply equally strong First Amendment scrutiny to government requests to identify online posters, in addition to any Fourth Amendment or statutory search limits, such as the Electronic Communications Privacy Act. To be sure, the government might be able to satisfy the First Amendment requirements more easily than a civil litigant, as there may be strong public safety interests in unmasking someone. Still, the courts should consider the free speech implications of unmasking the government compels.

But we must ensure that our legal system sufficiently protects victims of anonymous harassment and stalking. Although anonymity has many beneficial uses, we cannot and should not ignore the bad actors who abuse anonymity protections to harm others. Rather than restricting anonymity protections for all Americans, the legal system should do far more to directly address and deter nefarious online behavior. A starting point would be ensuring that our criminal laws impose sufficient consequences for online harms. Harassment and stalking via computer can devastate a person's life, and our legal system must treat these crimes with the same seriousness as offline crimes. Law enforcement at the state, local, and federal level must have sufficient resources to investigate and prosecute cybercrime. This requires substantial training and hiring of experts who have a variety of technical and operational skills.

Also worth considering to assist victims of anonymous trolls is a change to Section 230 that would allow courts to enforce injunctions against platforms to take down material that has been adjudicated to be illegal or defamatory in a lawsuit between the subject of the material and the poster. This provides victims with the remedy that they most often want: removing illegal material from the Internet that has been ruining their reputations and lives.

Private platforms such as social media providers also must consider their social duties in maintaining a culture of anonymity empowerment.

Although the companies may have valid reasons for requiring users to disclose their real or legal names, the companies should carefully evaluate the harms that such policies cause for vulnerable communities who may be most in need of separating their online activities from their identities. In many cases, real-name policies are not in society's best interests.

Finally, we must conceive of anonymity not only as a free speech issue, but also as a privacy issue. This is particularly important as companies continue to develop biometrics, geolocation, and other technology that can easily identify someone who had wanted to remain anonymous. First Amendment protections only constrain the actions of the government (such as a court enforcing a subpoena), and they are of little use to people who want to restrict the private sector's use of deidentifying technology.

Privacy law can help to constrain companies' ability to unmask the anonymous. Unfortunately, the United States lacks a comprehensive privacy law, with the federal government only regulating particular industries such as healthcare and banking, and leaving the rest to the states, which have done an inadequate job in protecting privacy. The United States needs a strong national privacy law that gives people control over their personal information. While this national law would address many issues, one key value that it should maintain is anonymity empowerment. The national law should encourage companies to fully anonymize personal information when practical, and in other cases provide people with control over their identifying information, including the right to require a company to delete the data. Like some local governments that have restricted facial recognition, a national law should ban particularly egregious anonymity intrusions.

I agree with Michael Froomkin that there is reason to be skeptical about the future of anonymity in the United States, particularly because of the vast amount of information available about people due to technological developments. Moreover, we must address the very real harms that anonymous people have caused online, particularly harassment and stalking.

But I'm also not ready to give up on anonymity. Since our nation's founding, Americans have grappled with the right level of protections to provide to people who wanted to separate their names from their actions.

The culture of anonymity empowerment has been critical to the spirited dissent and debate that undergirds our democracy. The Supreme Court had good reason to protect the anonymity of the NAACP members in the 1950s, and the many court opinions that flowed from that ruling have all recognized the vital role of anonymity in American society. Courts, legislatures, the private sector, and every American should find the proper balance that leaves the door open for a Junius, Publius, Manuel Talley, Margaret McIntyre, or xxplrr of the future.

NOTES

Introduction

1. Glassdoor, About Us, https://www.glassdoor.com/about-us/.

2. Appendix of Exhibits in Support of Petition for Writ of Mandate or Other Appropriate Relief, Glassdoor v. Superior Court (Cal. Ct. App.) at 88; Glassdoor, Inc. v. Superior Court, 9 Cal. App. 5th 623, 626–27 (Cal. Ct. App. 2017).

3. Glassdoor, Inc. v. Superior Court, 9 Cal. App. 5th 623, 626 (Cal. Ct. App. 2017).

4. *Id.* at 627.

5. *Id* at 626–27.

6. *Id.* at 628.

7. Petition for Writ of Mandate or Other Appropriate Relief and Request for Stay; Memorandum of Points and Authorities, Glassdoor v. Superior Court, No. H042824 (Cal. Ct. App. Oct. 1, 2015).

8. Glassdoor, Inc. v. Superior Court, 9 Cal. App. 5th 623, 647–48 (Cal. Ct. App. 2017).

9. David Kaye, Report of the Special Rapporteur on the promotion and protection of the right to freedom of opinion and expression at 4 (2015).

10. See chapter 10 for a discussion of other countries' real-name requirements.

11. *See, e.g.,* Andy Kessler, *Online Speech Wars Are Here to Stay,* WALL ST. J. (Jan. 24, 2021). ("Sure, there's value to spontaneous users speaking freely about everything, but no one really knows how many fake accounts spewing fake news exist. Truth is elusive. So why not impose know-your-customer on social-media companies.")

12. Jillian York, *A Case for Pseudonyms,* ELECTRONIC FRONTIER FOUNDATION (July 29, 2011).

Part I. Developing the Right to Anonymity

1. In limited circumstances, the Supreme Court has held that the First Amendment restricts the actions of privately owned "public forums," such as company towns. But this exception is narrow, and only applies if the government "traditionally and exclusively performed the function." Manhattan Community Access Corp. v. Halleck, 139 S.Ct. 1921, 1929 (2019).

Chapter 1. America, the Anonymous

1. THE LETTERS OF JUNIUS, WOODFALL'S EDITION (Routledge 1890) at 128.
2. Robert Rea, THE ENGLISH PRESS IN POLITICS, 1760–1774 (1963) at 174–75.
3. LETTERS OF JUNIUS, WOODFALL'S EDITION at 57.
4. *Id.* at 15.
5. *Id.* at 103.
6. *Id.* at 76.
7. *Id.; see also Woodfall's Junius,* in CONTRIBUTIONS, BIOGRAPHICAL, LITERARY, AND PHILOSOPHICAL TO THE ECLECTIC REVIEW (John Foster, ed., 1844) at 316.
8. LETTERS OF JUNIUS, WOODFALL'S EDITION at 168.
9. *Id.* at 162.
10. Fred H. Peterson, *The Mystery of Junius,* 41 CAN. L. TIMES 527, 531 (1921).
11. LETTERS OF JUNIUS, WOODFALL'S EDITION at 240–41.
12. Peterson, *The Mystery of Junius,* 527, 528.
13. LETTERS OF JUNIUS, WOODFALL'S EDITION at 213–14.
14. Lance Bertelsen, *The Education of Henry Sampson Woodfall, Newspaperman,* in MENTORING IN EIGHTEENTH-CENTURY BRITISH LITERATURE AND CULTURE (Anthony W. Lee, ed. 2011) at 163.
15. Robert Rea, THE ENGLISH PRESS IN POLITICS, 1760–1774 (1963) at 177.
16. *Account of the Trial of Mr. Woodfall, the Original Printer of Junius's Letter to the King,* 46 THE UNIVERSAL MAGAZINE OF KNOWLEDGE AND PLEASURE 324, 324 (June 1770).
17. *Id.* at 325.
18. *Id.*
19. *Id.*
20. *Id.* at 326.
21. RICHMOND DISPATCH (Nov. 29, 1860).
22. LETTERS OF JUNIUS, WOODFALL'S EDITION at 245.
23. Edward J. White, LEGAL TRADITIONS AND OTHER PAPERS: A COLLECTION OF PAPERS AND ADDRESSES DELIVERED BEFORE BAR ASSOCIATIONS AND OTHER ORGANIZATIONS (1927).
24. Herman Merivale, *The Last Phase in the Junius Controversy,* 41 THE CORNHILL MAGAZINE 669 (1871).
25. Lord David Edmond Neuberger, *What's in a Name? Privacy and Anonymous Speech on the Internet Conference,* Keynote Speech (Sept. 30, 2014).
26. Victoria Smith Ekstrand, *The Many Masks of Anon: Anonymity as Cultural Practice and Reflections in Case Law,* 18 J. TECH. L. & POL'Y 1, 10 (2013).
27. Robert G. Natelson, *Does the Freedom of the Press Include a Right to Anonymity—The Original Meaning,* 9 N.Y.U. J.L. & LIBERTY 160, 184 (2015).
28. *See* Jeffrey M. Skopek, *Reasonable Expectations of Anonymity,* 101 VA. L. REV. 691, 720 (2015): "In sum, when 'personal information' is understood as an aggregation of two core components—a subject and a predicate—it becomes clear that there are two relevant ways in which it can be inaccessible to others. Under the first, we know the person's identity,

but not the information. This type of secrecy is what we generally call privacy. Under the second, we know the information, but not the personal identity. This is what we generally call anonymity."

29. Helen Nissenbaum, *The Meaning of Anonymity in an Information Age*, 15 THE INFORMATION SOCIETY, 141–44 (1999).

30. Victoria Smith Ekstrand, *The Many Masks of Anon: Anonymity as Cultural Practice and Reflections in Case Law*, 18 J. TECH. L. & POL'Y 1, 16 (2013).

31. Thanks to Tori Ekstrand for helping me develop this motivation in her thorough review of this manuscript.

32. Joseph Addison, Spectator No. 451 (Aug. 7, 1712), available at Project Gutenberg, https://www.gutenberg.org/files/12030/12030-h/SV3/Spectator3.html#section451.

33. *Id.*

34. Jason A. Martin and Anthony L. Fargo, *Anonymity as a Legal Right: Where and Why It Matters*, 16 N.C. J.L. & TECH. 311, 326 (2015): "In the realm of political speech, anonymous and pseudonymous publishing was common in the colonial period in the United States through the Revolutionary War and beyond. Opponents of British rule during the pre-war period often wrote anonymously or under pseudonyms to avoid arrest or, depending upon the pseudonym used, to rouse like-minded citizens."

35. Thomas R. Adams, *The British Pamphlet Press and the American Controversy, 1764–1783*, in 89 THE PROCEEDINGS OF THE AMERICAN ANTIQUARIAN SOCIETY Part 1, 41 (April 1979).

36. *Id.* "Some of the authors held positions in the government, and the appearance of their names might have impaired the appearance of impartiality that pamphlet publishers like to foster. Other tracts were written by comparatively obscure men, whose names would add nothing to a pamphlet's salability."

37. Stanley Nider Katz, *Introduction,* in A BRIEF NARRATIVE OF THE CASE AND TRIAL OF JOHN PETER ZENGER, PRINTER OF THE NEW YORK WEEKLY JOURNAL (1963) at 9.

38. *Id.* at 2–8.

39. Walker Lewis, *The Right to Complain: The Trial of John Peter Zenger*, 46 A.B.A. J. 27, 29 (1960).

40. *See* McIntyre v. Ohio Elections Commission, 514 U.S. 334, 361 (1995) (Thomas, J., concurring in the judgment).

41. Stanley Nider Katz, *Introduction,* in A BRIEF NARRATIVE OF THE CASE AND TRIAL OF JOHN PETER ZENGER, PRINTER OF THE NEW YORK WEEKLY JOURNAL (1963) at 9.

42. Lewis, *The Right to Complain.*

43. *Id.*

44. *Id.* at 30.

45. *Id.* at 111.

46. McIntyre v. Ohio Elections Commission, 514 U.S. 334, 361 (1995) (Thomas, J., concurring).

47. Jeffrey L. Pasley, TYRANNY OF PRINTERS (2001) at 35: "Anonymity also shielded from reprisal those gentleman Revolutionaries who had social or professional position to lose if they appeared too active against the British or performed badly on the public stage. A gentleman had a carefully built 'character' that could be damaged by a poor performance, while an artisan was a much humbler man with no such standing to lose."

48. Thomas R. Adams, AMERICAN INDEPENDENCE: THE GROWTH OF AN IDEA (1965) at xvii.

49. John Howe, LANGUAGE AND POLITICAL MEANING IN REVOLUTIONARY AMERICA (2004) at 130.

50. *Id.* at 131.

51. *Id.* at 131–32.

52. Massachusetts Historical Society, *The Townshend Acts*, available at https://www.masshist.org/revolution/townshend.php.

53. John Dickinson, Letters from a Farmer in Pennsylvania to the Inhabitants of the British Colonies, Letter 1.

54. *Id.* at Letter 2.

55. *Id.* at Letter 1.

56. William Murchison, The Cost of Liberty: The Life of John Dickinson (2013) at 61.

57. Carl F. Kaestle, *The Public Reaction to John Dickinson's Farmer's Letters*, American Antiquarian Society at 325–26: "The response to the Farmer's Letters was even more remarkable than the extent of the initial circulation. Immediately after the publication of the first letter, editors, politicians, and irate governors recognized a special significance in the pieces by the 'Pennsylvania Farmer.' He became a constant authority for writers exhorting their countrymen to action, warning of new dangers, and expounding more supporting arguments."

58. *Id.* at 334.

59. *Id.* at 335.

60. Arthur M. Schlesinger, Prelude to Independence (1958) at 88.

61. Murchison, The Cost of Liberty at 61.

62. *Id.* at 61–62.

63. Carl F. Kaestle, *The Public Reaction to John Dickinson's Farmer's Letters*, American Antiquarian Society at 333.

64. *Id.* at 333–34.

65. Philip Davidson, Propaganda and the American Revolution 1763–1783 (1941) at 15.

66. *Common Sense*, in The Writings of Thomas Paine (Moncure Daniel Conway, ed. 1894) at 85–86.

67. Howe, Language and Political Meaning at 129.

68. Alfred Owen Aldridge, Man of Reason: The Life of Thomas Paine (1959) at 35.

69. Letter from George Washington to Lieutenant Colonel Joseph Reed (April 1, 1776), available at https://founders.archives.gov/documents/Washington/03-04-02-0009#GEWN-03-04-02-0009-fn-0006.

70. Aldridge, Man of Reason at 43.

71. *Common Sense*, in Writings of Thomas Paine at 68.

72. Victoria Smith Ekstrand and Cassandra Imfeld Jeyaram, *Our Founding Anonymity: Anonymous Speech during the Constitutional Debate*, American Journalism (2011): "Freeing authors from direct attack to their reputations and their safety, anonymity provided a cloak of security and confidence to debate the merits of the proposed Constitution."

73. *Id.* "It encouraged readers to focus their attentions on the words, not the personalities, and rationally debate issues surrounding the Constitution rather than be persuaded by external influences."

74. Michael I. Meyerson, Liberty's Blueprint (2008) at 78.

75. McIntyre v. Ohio Elections Commission, 514 U.S. 334, 365 (1995) (Thomas, J., concurring) (quoting *Letters From the Federal Farmer No. 5*, Oct. 13, 1787, in 2 The Complete Anti-Federalist 254 (H. Storing ed. 1981)).

76. Liberty's Blueprint at 79.

77. Alexander Hamilton, Federalist Paper No. 1.

78. Gregory E. Maggs, *A Concise Guide to the Federalist Papers as a Source of the Original Meaning of the United States Constitution*, 87 B.U. L. Rev. 801, 812 (2007).

79. The Documentary History of the Ratification of the Constitution Digital Edition (ed. John P. Kaminski, Gaspare J. Saladino, Richard Leffler, Charles H. Schoenleber and Margaret A. Hogan) (2009).

80. *Id.*
81. *Id.*
82. *Id.*
83. Maggs, *A Concise Guide to the Federalist Papers,* 801, 811.
84. Eran Shalev, Rome Reborn on Western Shores (2009) at 177.
85. *Id.* "The mere name of Publius enriched the arguments presented in the essays with supplementary contexts, illuminated meanings and goals, and entrenched the notion of republican virtue within the many classical allusions deployed throughout the essays."
86. Natelson, *Does the Freedom of the Press Include a Right to Anonymity* 160, 198–99.

Chapter 2. Empowering Anonymous Association

1. Brown v. Board of Education, 347 US 483, 495 (1954).
2. *See* Thurgood Marshall, Legal Defense Fund, available at https://www.naacpldf.org/about-us/history/thurgood-marshall.
3. *See* David Martin, *The Birth of Jim Crow in Alabama 1865–1896,* Nat'l Black Law Journal 13(1) (1993): "One act prohibited enticement of a laborer away from his contract, another increased punishment for receipt and concealment of stolen property, and a third defined the duties between master and apprentice."
4. Brief for Petitioner, NAACP v. Alabama, Case No. 91 (Sept. 21, 1957) at 7.
5. *Id.* at 8.
6. *Id.*
7. *See* Dana Beyerle, *Legacy of Former Gov. John Patterson "Mixed,"* Gasden Times (June 13, 2004): "Patterson was an avowed segregationist who, although he didn't invite Klan support when he ran for governor, didn't refuse it either."
8. Appendix C to Petition for Writ of Certiorari to the Supreme Court of Alabama, NAACP v. Alabama (Mar. 20, 1957).
9. Brief for Petitioner, NAACP v. Alabama, Case No. 91 (Sept. 21, 1957) at 8.
10. *Id.* at 9.
11. Associated Press, *Organization Given 30 Days to File Answer,* The Troy Messenger (June 1, 1956).
12. Brief for Petitioner, NAACP v. Alabama, Case No. 91 (Sept. 21, 1957) at 9–10.
13. Robert L. Carter, A Matter of Law (2005) at 150.
14. *Id.* at 151–52.
15. Brief for Petitioner, NAACP v. Alabama, Case No. 91 (Sept. 21, 1957) at 10.
16. Appendix B to Petition for Writ of Certiorari to the Supreme Court of Alabama, NAACP v. Alabama (Mar. 20, 1957) at 15a–16a.
17. Brief for Petitioner, NAACP v. Alabama, Case No. 91 (Sept. 21, 1957) at 11.
18. Appendix A to Petition for Writ of Certiorari to the Supreme Court of Alabama, NAACP v. Alabama (Mar. 20, 1957) at 2a.
19. Petition for Writ of Certiorari to the Supreme Court of Alabama, NAACP v. Alabama (Mar. 20, 1957) at 22.
20. *Id.* at 23.
21. *Id.* at 27.
22. Brief and Argument in Opposition to Petition for Writ of Certiorari, NAACP v. Alabama (May 13, 1957) at 20.
23. Motion and Brief of Amici Curiae, NAACP v. Alabama (Oct. 7, 1957) at 33.
24. *Id.* at 37.
25. New York ex rel. Bryant v. Zimmerman, 278 U.S. 63 (1928).

26. Brief and Argument for Respondent, NAACP v. Alabama (Oct. 21, 1957) at 30.

27. Oyez Project, Transcript of Oral Argument, NAACP v. Alabama (Jan. 15, 1958) (NAACP Oyez Transcript).

28. *Id.*

29. *Id.*

30. *Id.*

31. *Id.*

32. Erin Miller, Glossary of Supreme Court Terms, SCOTUSblog (Dec. 31, 2009), https://www.scotusblog.com/reference/educational-resources/glossary-of-legal-terms/.

33. Letter of John Marshall Harlan, April 22, 1958, in the papers of Chief Justice Earl Warren (Library of Congress Manuscript Division).

34. NAACP v. Alabama ex rel. Patterson, 357 US 449, 460 (1958).

35. *Id.* at 462.

36. *Id.*

37. *Id.* at 463.

38. *Id.* at 464.

39. *Id.* at 465.

40. Justice Tom Clark, Memorandum to the Conference (June 30, 1958), in the papers of Chief Justice Earl Warren (Library of Congress Manuscript Division).

41. Anita L. Allen, *Associational Privacy and the First Amendment: NAACP v. Alabama, Privacy and Data Protection*, 1 ALA. C.R. & C.L. L. REV. 1, 13 (2011): "Thanks to *NAACP v. Alabama*, the government may not force even a controversial group to identify its members, absent establishing a compelling state interest in disclosure. The right of private free association belongs to all who respect the rights of others. It belongs to those who are for racial equality or against it. It belongs to Muslims, Jews, Christians, Hindus, and Buddhists. It belongs to communist, socialist, or liberal ideologues. And it belongs to the native born and the immigrant American."

42. Petition for a Writ of Certiorari to the Supreme Court of Arkansas, Bates v. Little Rock (Mar. 13, 1959) at 3–4.

43. *Id.* at 6.

44. *Id.* at 5–7.

45. *Id.* at 15.

46. *Id.* at 6–7.

47. Transcript of Record, Bates v. Little Rock (Supreme Court October Term 1959) at 9.

48. *Id.* at 11–12.

49. *Id.* at 12.

50. *Id.* at 25.

51. *Id.* at 60.

52. *Id.* at 65.

53. Bates v. City of Little Rock, 319 S.W. 2d 37, 43 (Ark. 1958).

54. Petition for a Writ of Certiorari to the Supreme Court of Arkansas, Bates v. City of Little Rock (Mar. 13, 1959) at 8–9.

55. *Id.* at 10.

56. Oyez Project, Transcript of Oral Argument, Bates v. Little Rock (Nov. 18, 1959).

57. *Id.*

58. Draft of Opinion, Bates v. Little Rock (Jan. 6, 1960) at 8, in the papers of Chief Justice Earl Warren (Library of Congress Manuscript Division).

59. *Id.* at 8–9.

60. Letter from William Brennan to Hugo Black, Bates v. Little Rock (Jan. 5, 1960) (in the papers of Justice Hugo Black, Library of Congress Manuscript Division).

61. Letter from William Brennan to Potter Stewart, Bates v. Little Rock (Jan. 7, 1960) (in the papers of Justice William Brennan, Library of Congress Manuscript Division).

62. Letter from Potter Stewart, Bates v. Little Rock (Jan. 19, 1960) (in the papers of Justice Hugo Black, Library of Congress Manuscript Division).

63. Letter from William Brennan to Potter Stewart, Bates v. Little Rock (Feb. 1, 1960) (in the papers of Justice William Brennan, Library of Congress Manuscript Division).

64. Bates v. Little Rock, 361 U.S. 516, 524 (1960).

65. *Id.* at 524–25.

66. *Id.* at 527.

67. *Id.* at 528 (Black, J., and Douglas, J., concurring).

68. Dale E. Ho, *NAACP v. Alabama and the False Symmetry in the Disclosure Debate*, 15 N.Y.U. J. LEGIS. & PUB. POL'Y 405, 407 (2012).

69. *Id.*

70. *Id.* at 441: "If *NAACP v. Alabama* continues to have enduring force, it is through the anti-suppression principle that anonymity may be an essential tool for protecting vulnerable minorities from repression at the hands of a hostile majority. These protections benefit not only minority speakers themselves but society as a whole by ensuring that the polity has access to disfavored views."

Chapter 3. Empowering Anonymous Speech

1. Letter from Martin Luther King, Jr. to Manuel D. Talley (Sept. 19, 1956), Stanford University, Martin Luther King Jr. Research and Education Institute.

2. *L.A. CORE Founder Manuel Talley Dies*, L.A. TIMES (Dec. 17, 1986).

3. *Four Charged in Café Disturbance*, ALBUQUERQUE JOURNAL (April 16, 1950).

4. *Negro Asks Judge to Dismiss Complaint*, CLOVIS NEWS-JOURNAL (April 18, 1950).

5. Transcript of Record, Talley v. California at 3–4.

6. *Id.* at 17.

7. *Id.* at 18.

8. *Id.* at 19.

9. *Id.* at 4.

10. Talley v. California, 362 U.S. 60, 60–61 (1960).

11. Transcript of Record, Talley v. California at 3.

12. *Id.* at 9.

13. *Id.* at 10, 20B.

14. *Id.* at 6.

15. *Id.* at 13–14.

16. *Id.* at 14.

17. *Id.* at 15.

18. *Id.*

19. People v. Talley, 172 Cal. App. Supp. 2d 797, 800 (1958).

20. *Id.* at 803.

21. *Id.* at 805 (Swain, J., concurring).

22. *Id.* at 807 (Bishop, P.J., dissenting).

23. Petitioner's Opening Brief, Talley v. California (Dec. 2, 1959) at 17; *Id.* at 20–21.

24. *Id.* at 21.

25. 229 U.S. 288 (1913).

26. *Id.* at 296.

27. Respondent's Brief, Talley v. California (Jan. 2, 1960) at 11.

28. The transcript of this oral argument comes from the Oyez Project, Transcript of Argument, Talley v. California (Jan. 13–14, 1960).

29. *Id.*

30. *Id.*

31. *Id.*

32. Talley v. California, 362 U.S. 60, 62–63 (1960).

33. *Id.* at 64.

34. *Id.* at 64–65.

35. *Id.* at 65.

36. Feb. 10, 1960 Letter from John Marshall Harlan II to Hugo Black, in the papers of Justice Hugo Black (Library of Congress Manuscript Division).

37. Talley v. California, 362 U.S. 60, 66 (1960). (Harlan, J., concurring).

38. *Id.* at 66–67.

39. *Municipal Ordinance Prohibiting Anonymous Handbills Declared Unconstitutional,* 22 OHIO ST. L.J. 220, 223 (1961).

40. David Lawrence, *Court Ruling on Handbills Inconsistent,* ITHACA JOURNAL (March 11, 1960).

41. Feb. 11, 1960 Memorandum for the Conference, Felix Frankfurter, in the papers of Justice Hugo Black (Library of Congress Manuscript Division).

42. Talley v. California, 362 U.S. 60, 67–68 (Clark, J., dissenting).

43. *Id.* at 70.

44. *Id.* at 71.

45. Jan Crawford Greenburg, *Free Speech Furor Began with a Leaflet,* CHICAGO TRIBUNE (Nov. 28, 1994).

46. Joint Appendix, McIntyre v. Ohio Elections Commission (Apr. 18, 1994) at 6.

47. *Id.* at 3; McIntyre v. Ohio Elections Commission, 514 U.S. 334, 338n3 (1995).

48. Joint Appendix, McIntyre v. Ohio Elections Commission (Apr. 18, 1994) at 15.

49. McIntyre v. Ohio Elections Commission, 514 U.S. 334, 338 (1995).

50. Joint Appendix, McIntyre v. Ohio Elections Commission (Apr. 18, 1994) at 3, 4.

51. *Id.* at 12.

52. *Id.* at 37.

53. *Id.* at 38–39.

54. *Id.* at 39.

55. *Id.* at 41–42.

56. *Id.* at 43.

57. Petition for a Writ of Certiorari, McIntyre v. Ohio Elections Commission (Dec. 16, 1993) at A-34.

58. *Id.* at A-34 to A-35.

59. *Id.* at A-21.

60. McIntyre v. Ohio Elections Comm., 67 Ohio St. 3d 391, 396 (1993).

61. *Id.* at 397 (Wright, J., dissenting).

62. *Id.* at 399.

63. Jan Crawford Greenburg, *Free Speech Furor Began with a Leaflet,* CHICAGO TRIBUNE (Nov. 28, 1994).

64. Motion to Substitute Executor Joseph McIntyre as the Proper Party in this Case, McIntyre v. Ohio Elections Commission (June 2, 1994).

65. The transcript of this oral argument comes from the Oyez Project, Transcript of Oral Argument, McIntyre v. Ohio Elections Commission (Oct. 12, 1994).

66. McIntyre v. Ohio Elections Commission, 514 U.S. 334, 357 (1995).

67. *Id.* at 343.

68. *Id.* at 344.

69. *Id.* at 347.

70. *Id.* at 348–49.

71. *Id.* at 351.

72. *Id.* at 353.

73. Abrams v. United States, 250 U.S. 616, 630 (1919) (Holmes, J., dissenting).

74. McIntyre v. Ohio Elections Commission, 514 U.S. 334, 348 (1995).

75. *Id.* at 353 (quoting First National Bank of Boston v. Bellotti, 435 U.S. 765, 777 [1978]).

76. Lyrissa Barnett Lidsky and Thomas F. Cotter, *Authorship, Audiences, and Anonymous Speech*, 82 NOTRE DAME L. REV. 1537, 1547 (2007).

77. McIntyre v. Ohio Elections Commission, 514 U.S 334, 358 (1995) (Ginsburg, J., concurring).

78. *Id.* at 371 (Scalia, J., dissenting).

79. *Id.* at 373.

80. *Id.* at 381.

81. *Id.* at 383.

82. *Id.* at 367 (Thomas, J., concurring in judgment).

83. *Id.* at 370.

84. *Id.* at 371.

85. Jonathan Turley, *Registering Publius: The Supreme Court and the Right to Anonymity*, 2001 CATO SUP. CT. REV. 57, 67 (2001–2).

86. David G. Post, *Pooling Intellectual Capital: Thoughts on Anonymity, Pseudonymity, and Limited Liability in Cyberspace*, 1996 U. CHI. LEGAL F. 139, 154 (1996).

87. Margot Kaminski, *Real Masks and Real Name Policies: Applying Anti-Mask Case Law to Anonymous Online Speech*, 23 FORDHAM INTEL. PROP. MEDIA & ENT. L.J. 813, 834 (2013).

88. *Id.* at 834–35: "The *McIntyre* Court based its protection for anonymous speech on a literary rather than political understanding of the First Amendment. The *McIntyre* Court conceived of anonymity as an editorial choice. Anonymity is a means of expressing oneself, and an author has the freedom to decide whether or not to disclose his or her true identity. An author may choose to be anonymous because of fear of retaliation, concern about social ostracism, or a desire to protect his or her privacy; the Court implied that the precise reason does not in fact matter."

89. Frederick Schauer, *Anonymity and Authority*, 27 J.L. & POL. 597, 602 (2012).

90. *Id.* at 605–6.

Chapter 4. The Scope of Anonymity Empowerment

1. David Kaye, Report of the Special Rapporteur on the promotion and protection of the right to freedom of opinion and expression (2015).

2. Jeffrey M. Skopek, *Reasonable Expectations of Anonymity*, 101 VA. L. REV. 691, 721 (2015).

3. A renowned and very kind Stanford environmental engineering professor is named "Jeff Koseff," causing me to occasionally receive invitations to conferences about wave dynamics and other topics about which I have absolutely no knowledge. I'd rather not know whether he receives correspondence intended for me.

4. David G. Post, *Pooling Intellectual Capital: Thoughts on Anonymity, Pseudonymity, and Limited Liability in Cyberspace*, 1996 U. CHI. LEGAL F. 139, 149 n. 26 (1996).

5. Bryan H. Choi, *The Anonymous Internet*, 72 MD. L. REV. 501, 542 (2013).

6. *Reasonable Expectations of Anonymity* at 725.

7. *See* John Hazlehurst, *How Can We Get Rid of Ballot Craziness?* COLORADO SPRINGS BUSINESS JOURNAL (updated Mar. 4, 2021).

8. *Id.*; Initiative & Referendum Institute, Colorado, available at http://www.iandrinstitute.org/states/state.cfm?id=5.

9. American Constitutional Law Foundation v. Meyer, 120 F. 3d 1092, 1096 (10th Cir. 1997).

10. Buckley v. American Constitutional Law Foundation, 525 U.S. 182, 188 n.5 (1999).

11. *Id.* at 189–90, n.8.

12. *Id.*

13. This book will focus only on the aspects of the lawsuit related to anonymity.

14. Brief of Respondents David Aitken, Jon Baraga, and Bill Orr, Buckley v. American Constitutional Law Foundation, No. 97–930 (June 19, 1998) at 3–4.

15. *Id.* at 3; American Constitutional Law Foundation, Inc. v. Meyer, 870 F. Supp. 995, 1001 (D. Colo. 1994).

16. *Id.* at 1002.

17. *Id.* at 1003.

18. American Constitutional Law Foundation v. Meyer, 120 F. 3d 1092, 1102 (10th Cir. 1997).

19. *Id.*

20. *Id.* at 1105.

21. Petition for Writ of Certiorari, Buckley v. American Constitutional Law Foundation at 11.

22. The transcript of this oral argument comes from the Oyez Project, *available at* https://www.oyez.org/cases/1998/97-930.

23. Buckley v. American Constitutional Law Foundation, 525 U.S. 182, 199 (1999).

24. *Id.* at 200.

25. *Id.* at 203.

26. Elizabeth Garrett, *Money, Agenda Setting, and Direct Democracy*, 77 TEX. L. REV. 1845, 1882 (1999) ("Because humans have limited abilities to gather, analyze, and use information, and because most voters pay little attention to politics, citizens enter the voting booth with incomplete information about their electoral choices. Such citizens vote *competently* when they vote on the basis of their limited information as they would if they had complete and accurate information at the time of the election. The content and quality of political information is particularly important to voter competence in initiative contexts because voters have far fewer informational cues than they do in other political contexts.").

27. Buckley v. American Constitutional Law Foundation, 525 U.S. 182, 210 (1999). (Thomas, J., concurring in judgment).

28. *Id.* at 233 (Rehnquist, C.J., dissenting).

29. *Id.* at 224 (O'Connor, J., concurring in the judgment in part and dissenting in part).

30. *Id.* at 221.

31. Andrew J. Tobias, *Workers at Embattled Jefferson County Coal Plant Look to Donald Trump to Help Their Cause*, THE HERALD (March 23, 2017).

32. Joint Appendix, Watchtower Bible and Tract Society of New York v. Village of Stratton, No. 00-1737 (Nov. 28, 2001) at 15a.

33. *Id.* at 14a, 16a.

34. *Id.* at 16a.

35. Petition for a Writ of Certiorari, Watchtower Bible and Tract Society of New York v. Village of Stratton, No. 00-1737 (May 18, 2001) at 3.

36. Joint Appendix, Watchtower Bible and Tract Society of New York v. Village of Stratton, No. 00-1737 (Nov. 28, 2001) at 16a.

37. *Id.* at 17a–18a.

38. *Id.* at 19a.

39. *Id.* at 19a–20a.

40. *Id.* at 11a–12a.

41. Watchtower Bible and Tract Society of New York v. Village of Stratton, 61 F. Supp.2d 734, 736 (S.D. Ohio 1999).

42. *Id.* at 737–39.

43. Watchtower Bible and Tract Society of New York v. Village of Stratton, 240 F. 3d 553, 563 (6th Cir. 2001).

44. *Id.*

45. Brief for Petitioners, Watchtower Bible and Tract Society of New York v. Village of Stratton, No. 00-1737 at 20.

46. *Id.* at 19 (internal quotation marks and citations omitted).

47. Brief for Respondents, Watchtower Bible and Tract Society of New York v. Village of Stratton, No. 00-1737 at 27.

48. Watchtower Bible and Tract Society of New York v. Village of Stratton, 536 U.S. 150, 167 (2002).

49. Margot Kaminski, *Real Masks and Real Name Policies: Applying Anti-Mask Case Law to Anonymous Online Speech*, 23 FORDHAM INTEL. PROP. MEDIA & ENT. L.J. 813, 838 (2013).

50. Watchtower Bible and Tract Society of New York v. Village of Stratton, 536 U.S. 150, 167 (2002).

51. *Id.*

52. *Id.*

53. *Id.* at 169.

54. *Id.* at 173 (Rehnquist, J., dissenting).

55. *Id.* at 169 (majority opinion).

56. James A. Gardner, *Anonymity and Democratic Citizenship*, 19 WM. & MARY BILL RTS. J. 927, 928 (2011) ("Because Americans so often reductively equate democratic politics with voting, when we think of anonymity in democratic politics we typically think mainly of the secret ballot. But political participation in modern democratic life can take many forms: financial contributions to candidates, political parties, and advocacy groups; petition signing; political speech and debate; communication with and lobbying of officials; attending public meetings; holding office; and any of a host of other obligations of citizenship such as paying taxes, obeying the law, or performing public service or charitable work in one's community.").

57. Buckley v. Valeo, 424 U.S. 1 (1976).

58. *Id.* at 63.

59. *Id.* at 63–64.

60. *Id.* at 66 (internal quotation marks and citation omitted).

61. *Id.* at 66–68.

62. *Id.* at 69.

63. McConnell v. Federal Election Commission, 540 U.S. 93 (2003).

64. *Id.* at 196.

65. *Id.* at 276 (Thomas, J., concurring in part and dissenting in part).

66. Lyrissa Barnett Lidsky and Thomas F. Cotter, *Authorship, Audiences, and Anonymous Speech*, 82 NOTRE DAME L. REV. 1537, 1555 (2007) (internal quotation marks and citations omitted).

67. Citizens United v. Federal Election Commission, 558 U.S. 310 (2010).

68. *Id.* at 366.

69. *Id.* at 370.

70. *Id.* at 369.

71. *Id.* at 370.

72. *Id.* at 371.

73. *Id.* at 480–81 (Thomas, J., concurring in part and dissenting in part).

74. *Id.* at 481–82.

75. *Id.* at 483.

76. Doe v. Reed, 561 U.S. 186 (2010).

77. *Id.* at 192.

78. *Id.* at 197.

79. *Id.* at 201.

80. *Id.* at 221(Scalia, J., concurring in the judgment).

81. *Id.* at 228.

82. *Id.* at 233–34 (Thomas, J., dissenting).

83. *Id.* at 238–39.

84. Branzburg v. Hayes, 408 U.S. 665 (1972).

85. *Id.* at 690–91.

86. *Id.* at 707–8.

87. *Id.* at 710 (Powell, J., concurring).

88. *See, e.g.,* Shoen v. Shoen, 48 F.3d 412, 416 (9th Cir. 1995); Miller v. Transamerican Press, 621 F.2d 721 (5th Cir. 1980); Riley v. City of Chester, 612 F. 2d 708 (3d Cir. 1979).

89. *See* Jonathan Peters, *Shield Laws and Journalist's Privilege: The Basics Every Reporter Should Know,* COLUMBIA JOURNALISM REVIEW (Aug. 22, 2016), https://www.cjr.org/united_states_project/journalists_privilege_shield_law_primer.php.

Chapter 5. Antimask

1. Ann Jacobson, *KKK Plans to Attend School Board Meeting,* SOUTH BEND TRIBUNE (May 17, 1998).

2. Plaintiff's Brief in Support of Motion for Summary Judgment, American Knights of the Ku Klux Klan, No: 3:98CV0403 (N.D. Ill. Jan. 1998) at 3.

3. *Id.* at 4.

4. Bill Moor, *Sowing Seeds of Racism,* SOUTH BEND TRIBUNE (Aug. 10, 1998).

5. Southern Poverty Law Center, Jeff Berry, available at https://www.splcenter.org/fighting-hate/extremist-files/individual/jeff-berry.

6. Randy Fabi, *Klan Rally Creates Uproar in Elkhart,* INDIANA DAILY STUDENT (April 14, 1998).

7. J. R. Ross, *KKK: Cities Try to Unmask Klan to Keep Out Message of Hate,* ASSOCIATED PRESS (Aug. 1, 1998).

8. *Id.*

9. Plaintiff's Brief in Support of Motion for Summary Judgment, American Knights of the Ku Klux Klan, No: 3:98CV0403 (N.D. Ill. Jan. 1998) at 8 (quoting deposition of Allan Kauffman).

10. Ross, *KKK.*

11. American Knights of the Ku Klux Klan v. Goshen, 50 F. Supp. 2d 835, 836 (N.D. Ind. 1999).

12. Interview with Alan Kauffman (March 16, 2020).

13. Beth Neff, *Anti-Mask Ordinance Wins Nod,* SOUTH BEND TRIBUNE (June 17, 1998).

14. *Id.*

15. American Knights of the Ku Klux Klan v. Goshen, 50 F. Supp. 2d 835, 837 (N.D. Ind. 1999).

16. Plaintiff's Brief in Support of Motion for Summary Judgment, American Knights of the Ku Klux Klan, No: 3:98CV0403 (N.D. Ill. Jan. 1998) at 8–9 (quoting deposition of Allan Kauffman).

17. *Id.* at 9 (quoting deposition of Allan Kauffman).

18. *Id.* at 18.

19. Southern Poverty Law Center, Ku Klux Klan, available at https://www.splcenter.org/fighting-hate/extremist-files/ideology/ku-klux-klan.

20. American Knights of the Ku Klux Klan v. Goshen, 50 F. Supp. 2d 835, 845 (N.D. Ind. 1999).

21. *Id.* at 839.

22. *Id.* at 840.

23. *Id.* at 841.

24. *Id.* at 842.

25. *Id.* at 841.

26. *Id.* at 842–43.

27. *Id.* at 843–44.

28. *Id.* at 844.

29. *Id.*

30. *Id.* at 845.

31. Interview with Alan Kauffman (March 16, 2020).

32. *Id.*

33. Dan Berry, *Shrunken and Splintered Klan Is Still a Potent Lure for the Disaffected*, N.Y. Times (Oct. 23, 1999).

34. Declaration in Opposition to Plaintiff's Motion for a Preliminary Injunction, Church of the American Knights of the Ku Klux Klan v. Safir, No. 99 Civ. 10635, Dkt. 5 (S.D.N.Y. Oct. 20, 1999) [hereafter "Declaration in Opposition"] at ¶ 2.

35. *Id.* ¶ 3.

36. Church of the Ku Klux Klan v. Kerik, 356 F. 3d 197, 204 (2d Cir. 2004).

37. Declaration in Opposition ¶ 5.

38. *Id.* at Ex. 2.

39. Larry Celona, *NYPD Says No to KKK's Hooded Hatefest*, N.Y. Post (Oct. 14, 1999).

40. Brief of the National Action Network, Inc., as Amicus Curiae in Support of Plaintiff's Motion, Church of the American Knights of the Ku Klux Klan v. Safir, 99 Civ. 10635 (Oct. 20, 1999) at 13.

41. Declaration in Opposition at Ex. 3, ¶ 20.

42. Transcript of preliminary injunction hearing, Church of the American Knights of the Ku Klux Klan v. Safir, No. 99 Civ. 10635, Dkt. 14 (S.D.N.Y. Oct. 21, 1999) at 5.

43. *Id.* at 43.

44. *Id.* at 43–44.

45. *Id.* at 44.

46. *Id.* at 57–58.

47. *Id.* at 59–60.

48. *Id.* at 101–2.

49. Church of the Ku Klux Klan v. Kerik, 356 F. 3d 197, 201n3 (2d Cir. 2004); Benjamin Weiser, *Appeals Court Bars Klan Masks; Group Still Plans to Stage Rally*, N.Y. Times (Oct. 23, 1999).

50. *Id.*

51. Church of the American Knights of the Ku Klux Klan v. Kerik, 232 F. Supp. 2d 205, 208 (S.D.N.Y. 2002).

52. *Id.* at 210.

53. *Id.* at 213.

54. *Id.* at 214.

55. *Id.* at 215.

56. *Id.* at 217–19.

57. Scott Skinner-Thompson, *Performative Privacy*, 50 U.C. Davis L. Rev. 1673, 1676 (2017).

58. Church of the Ku Klux Klan v. Kerik, 356 F. 3d 197, 209 (2d Cir. 2004).

59. *Id.* (internal citation and quotation marks omitted).

60. *Id.*

61. *Id.* at 206.

62. *Id.*

63. Skinner-Thompson, *Performative Privacy*, 1673, 1703: "The government's own response to the masks highlights their inherent expressive content—the government finds the concealment expressive and intimidating and uses its own reaction to the expressive masks to justify stripping individuals of privacy."

64. Margot Kaminski, *Real Masks and Real Name Policies: Applying Anti-Mask Case Law to Anonymous Online Speech*, 23 Fordham Intel. Prop. Media & Ent. L.J. 813, 876 (2013).

65. *Id.* at 872–73.

66. *Id.* at 873.

67. *Id.*

68. State v. Miller, 260 Ga. 669, 398 S.E.2d 547, 676 (1990).

69. Kaminski, *Real Masks and Real Name Policies*, 887–88.

70. Christopher Robbins, *City Dodges Legal Challenge to 1845 Anti-Mask Law*, Gothamist (Dec. 12, 2012).

71. Defendant's Memorandum of Law in Support of Their Motion to Dismiss, People v. Weldon, Docket No. 2012NY073843 (Crim. Ct. of City of N.Y. Nov. 21, 2012) at 2.

Part II. The Right to Online Anonymity

1. Daniel Solove, The Future of Reputation (2007).

Chapter 6. Cybersmear

1. Complaint, Raytheon v. John Does 1–21, Civil Action NO. 99–816 (Mass. Super. Ct. Feb. 1, 1999) at Ex. 22.

2. *See* Abrams v. United States, 250 U.S. 616, 630 (1919) (Holmes, J., dissenting): "But when men have realized that time has upset many fighting faiths, they may come to believe even more than they believe the very foundations of their own conduct that the ultimate good desired is better reached by free trade in ideas—that the best test of truth is the power of the thought to get itself accepted in the competition of the market, and that truth is the only ground upon which their wishes safely can be carried out."

3. Lyrissa Barnett Lidsky, *Silencing John Doe: Defamation & Discourse in Cyberspace*, 49 Duke L.J. 855, 900 (2000): "From a First Amendment perspective, the financial message boards contribute to the marketplace of ideas by encouraging citizens to participate in public decisionmaking. The financial message boards exercise a powerful democratizing effect on public discourse about the publicly held corporations that shape citizens' daily lives." As Frederick Schauer wrote in 1978, "Under this theory, trust in the operation of the marketplace implies a trust that the truth eventually will prevail. False ideas need not be suppressed, for the operation of the market ultimately will reject ideas that are in fact false." Frederick F.

Schauer, *Language, Truth, and the First Amendment: An Essay in Memory of Harry Canter*, 64 VA. L. REV. 263, 271–72 (1978).

4. Robert Trigaux, *The Fight to Speak Their Mind, Anonymously*, ST. PETERSBURG TIMES (May 28, 2000).

5. 47 U.S.C. 230.

6. Zeran v. America Online, Inc., 129 F. 3d 327 (4th Cir. 1997).

7. For a history of Section 230, *see* Jeff Kosseff, THE TWENTY-SIX WORDS THAT CREATED THE INTERNET (2019).

8. Complaint, Raytheon v. John Does 1–21, Civil Action No. 99-816 (Mass. Super. Ct. Feb. 1, 1999) at Ex. 22.

9. *Id.* at Ex. 23.

10. *Id.* at ¶ 8.

11. *Id.* at ¶ 15.

12. *See* Joshua R. Furman, *Cybersmear or Cyber-SLAPP: Analyzing Defamation Suits against Online John Does as Strategic Lawsuits against Public Participation*, 52 SEATTLE U. L. REV. 213, 214 (2001): "Threats to individual privacy and speech online have recently been stressed in so-called cybersmear lawsuits. These are defamation suits brought by companies against individuals who make disparaging remarks about a company on Internet discussion fora. The processes, results, and consequences of cybersmear litigation serve as a touchstone for the issues presented by abuse of civil discovery against online John Does."

13. A. Michael Froomkin, *Anonymity and Its Enmities*, 1 J. ONLINE L. art. 4 (1995).

14. *Id.* ¶ 14.

15. *Id.* ¶ 19.

16. *Id.* ¶ 33

17. *Id.* ¶ 36.

18. *Id.*

19. Margot E. Kaminski, *Real Masks and Real Name Policies: Applying Anti-Mask Case Law to Anonymous Online Speech*, 23 FORDHAM INTELL. PROP. MEDIA & ENT. L.J. 815, 822 (2013): "Pseudonymous individuals presumably abstain from abusing others more than anonymous individuals, because of the importance of ongoing reputation in pseudonymous communicative contexts. Or, perversely, pseudonymous individuals may be encouraged to abuse others, depending on the type of social reputation that matters most to them."

20. Plaintiff Raytheon Company's Motion for Commission to Take Out-of-State Discovery and Affidavit of Jeffrey C. Morgan, Raytheon v. John Does, Civil Action No. 99-816 (Mass. Super. Ct. Feb. 1, 1999).

21. Plaintiff Raytheon Company's Motion for Commission to Take Additional Out-of-State Discovery and Affidavit of Jeffrey C. Morgan, Raytheon v. John Does, Civil Action No. 99-816 (Mass. Super. Ct. March 5, 1999).

22. Interview with David Phillips (March 3, 2020).

23. *Id.*

24. Interview with Mark Neuhausen (Feb. 24, 2020).

25. *Id.*

26. *Id.*

27. William M. Bulkeley, *Raytheon Employees Resign in Wake of Lawsuit Protesting Internet Postings*, WALL ST. J. (Apr. 5, 1999).

28. Deborah Claymon, *Online Aliases No Shield from Law: Court Order Unmasks Dubious Commentary*, SAN JOSE MERCURY NEWS (Apr. 6, 1999).

29. Blake A. Bell, *Dealing with the Cybersmear: False Internet Rumors Target Companies, Stocks*, 221 N.Y. L. J. (Apr. 19, 1999).

30. Elinor Abreu, *EPIC Blasts Yahoo for Identifying Posters*, THE INDUSTRY STANDARD (Nov. 10, 1999).

31. *Id.*; David L. Sobel, *The Process that John Doe Is Due: Addressing the Legal Challenge to Internet Anonymity*, 5 VA. J.L. & TECH. 3 ¶ 13 (2000).

32. Interview with Jon Sobel (March 3, 2020).

33. *See* John Snell, *Prying into Posts*, THE OREGONIAN (Oct. 30, 2000).

34. Notice of Dismissal, Raytheon v. John Does 1–21, Civil Action No. 99-816 (Mass. Super. Ct. May 20, 1999).

35. Complaint, Raytheon v. John Does 1–21, Civil Action No. 99-816 (Mass. Super. Ct. Feb. 1, 1999) at Ex. 17.

36. *Id.* at ¶ 15.

37. Sobel, *The Process that John Doe Is Due* 1, ¶ 14.

38. Michael Hedges, *1st Amendment vs. Internet*, ARIZ. REPUBLIC (July 15, 1999).

39. Memorandum of Points and Authorities in Support of Motion to Quash and Request for Protective Order, Xircom v. Doe, Case No. Civ. 188724 (May 24, 1999) at 2.

40. Rebecca Fairley Raney, *Judge Rejects Online Critic's Efforts to Remain Anonymous*, N.Y. TIMES (June 15, 1999).

41. Deborah Adamson, *Xircom Sues over Online Comments; Firm Says Unknown User Hurt Company*, L.A. DAILY NEWS (May 11, 1999).

42. Memorandum of Points and Authorities in Support of Motion to Quash and Request for Protective Order, Xircom v. Doe, Case No. Civ. 188724 (May 24, 1999) at 3.

43. *Id.* at 10; Roger Harris, *Xircom Files Suit for Web Postings*, VENTURA COUNTY STAR (May 8, 1999).

44. Memorandum of Points and Authorities in Support of Motion to Quash and Request for Protective Order, Xircom v. Doe, Case No. Civ. 188724 (May 24, 1999) at 1.

45. Roger Harris, *Xircom Files Suit for Web Postings*, VENTURA COUNTY STAR (May 8, 1999).

46. *Id.*

47. Deborah Adamson, *Xircom Sues over Online Comments; Firm Says Unknown User Hurt Company*, L.A. DAILY NEWS (May 11, 1999).

48. Michael D. Goldhaber, *Cybersmear Pioneer*, NAT'L L. J. (July 17, 2000).

49. Unless otherwise noted, quotes from Megan Gray come from an interview with the author on April 15, 2020.

50. Memorandum of Points and Authorities in Support of Motion to Quash and Request for Protective Order, Xircom v. Doe, Case No. Civ. 188724 (May 24, 1999) at 1.

51. *Id.* at 6–7.

52. *Id.* at 9.

53. *Id.*

54. *Id.* at 11–12.

55. *Id.* at 12–13.

56. Cal. Code Civ. Proc. 425.16.

57. Memorandum of Points and Authorities in Support of Motion to Quash and Request for Protective Order, Xircom v. Doe, Case No. Civ. 188724 (May 24, 1999) at 14.

58. *Id.* at 4.

59. Laura Randall, *Judge Blocks Xircom's Subpoena of Yahoo*, NEWSBYTES (June 15, 1999).

60. Roger Harris, *'John Doe' Victorious in Latest Battle with Xircom*, VENTURA COUNTY STAR (June 15, 1999).

61. Deborah Adamson, *Xircom Settles 'John Doe' Suit*, L.A. DAILY NEWS (July 10, 1999).

62. Greg Saitz, *N.J. Firm's Lawsuit Tests Privacy Rights of Online Detractors*, STAR LED-GER (July 18, 2000).

63. Lyrissa Barnett Lidsky, *Silencing John Doe: Defamation & Discourse in Cyberspace*, 49 DUKE L.J. 855, 861 (2000).

64. *Id.*

65. *Id.* at 884–85.

66. Anne Colden, *Corporations Increasingly Suing Their Online Critics, Legal Experts Say*, DENVER POST (Jan. 15, 2001).

67. Securities and Exchange Commission, Remarks of Richard Walker at the National Press Club (April 5, 1999).

68. Lyrissa Barnett Lidsky, *Silencing John Doe: Defamation & Discourse in Cyberspace*, 49 DUKE L.J. 855, 946 (2000).

69. *Id.* at 904, n.256.

70. Shaun B. Spencer, *Cyberslapp Suits and John Doe Subpoenas: Balancing Anonymity and Accountability in Cyberspace*, 19 J. MARSHALL J. COMPUTER & INFO. L. 493, 499 (2001).

71. *Id.* at 520.

72. Bruce P. Smith, *Cybersmearing and the Problem of Anonymous Online Speech*, 18 COMM. LAW. 3 (2000): "For the moment, the immunity afforded Internet service providers strongly suggests that the burden of litigating cases of alleged cybersmearing will fall on individual John Does."

73. *Id.*

Chapter 7. Setting the Rules for Online Anonymity

1. U.S. JUSTICE DEPARTMENT, D. Lowell Jensen, https://www.justice.gov/criminal/history/assistant-attorneys-general/d-lowell-jensen.

2. Philip Shenon, *Working Profile: D. Lowell Jensen: "A Gentleman" in Line of Fire at Justice Dept.*, N.Y. TIMES (Jan. 13, 1986).

3. U.S. JUSTICE DEPARTMENT, D. Lowell Jensen.

4. Verified Complaint, Columbia Insurance Co. v. Seescandy.com, Civ. Action No. 99-0745 (N.D. Cal. Feb. 22, 1999).

5. *Id.* at ¶ 27.

6. *Id.* at ¶¶ 62–63.

7. Columbia Insurance Co. v. Seescandy.com, 185 F.R.D. 573, 576 (N.D. Cal. 1999).

8. *Id.*

9. *Id.* at 577.

10. *Id.*

11. *Id.* at 578.

12. *Id.*

13. *Id.*

14. *Id.* at 579.

15. *Id.* at 579–80.

16. *Id.* at 580–81.

17. Opening Brief of Appellant at 7, America Online v. Anonymous Publicly Traded Company, Record No. 000974 (Va. Sept. 28, 2000).

18. *In re* Subpoena Duces Tecum to America Online at *1, 52 Va. Cir. 26 (Va. Cir. Ct. Jan. 31, 2000).

19. *Id.*

20. Opening Brief, America Online v. Anonymous Publicly Traded Company, Record No. 000974 at 5 (Va. Sept. 28, 2000).

21. Interview with Stanley Klein (May 24, 2020).

22. *In re* Subpoena Duces Tecum to America Online, 52 Va. Cir. 26 (Va. Cir. Ct. Jan. 31, 2000) at *4.

23. *Id.* at *5.

24. *Id.* at *4.

25. *Id.* at *6.

26. To be sure, there may have been unpublished orders or opinions, or oral rulings, before Klein's opinion.

27. *In re* Subpoena Duces Tecum to America Online, 52 Va. Cir. 26 (Va. Cir. Ct. Jan. 31, 2000) at *6.

28. *Id.* at *8, n11.

29. *Id.* at *7.

30. *Id.* at *8.

31. *Id.*

32. Michael McCarthy, *Privacy: Can Your PC Be Subpoenaed?* ZDNet (May 24, 2000); Interview with Paul Alan Levy (May 18, 2020).

33. Brief on Behalf of Plaintiff-Appellant, Dendrite International v. Does, Docket No. MRS-C-129-00 (NJ. App. Div. March 7, 2001) at 11.

34. Herb Greenberg, *Does Dendrite Do Right with the Way It Handles Software Expenses?* TheStreet (Sept. 3, 1999).

35. Dendrite Intern. v. Doe No. 3, 775 A.2d 756, 762 (N.J. App. Div. 2001) (quoting the report).

36. *Id.* at 763.

37. *Id.*

38. Brief on Behalf of Plaintiff-Appellant, Dendrite International v. Does, Docket No. MRS-C-129-00 (NJ. App. Div. Mar. 7, 2001) at 12.

39. *Id.* at 14.

40. *Id.*

41. *Id.* at 16.

42. *Id.*

43. *Id.* at 3.

44. Unpublished Letter Opinion, Dendrite v. Does, Docket No. MRS-C-129-00 (NJ Super. Ct.—Chancery Div. Nov. 23, 2000) at 1.

45. *Id.* at 2.

46. Brief on Behalf of Plaintiff-Appellant, Dendrite International v. Does, Docket No. MRS-C-129-00 (NJ. App. Div. March 7, 2001) at 4.

47. *Id.* at 4.

48. Unless otherwise noted, quotations from Paul Levy come from an interview conducted on May 18, 2020.

49. Memorandum of Public Citizen as Amicus Curiae in Opposition to the Requested Discovery, Dendrite v. Does, Docket No. MRS-C-129-00 (NJ Super. Ct.—Chancery Div. July 11, 2000) at 14.

50. Brief on Behalf of Plaintiff-Appellant, Dendrite International v. Does, Docket No. MRS-C-129-00 (N.J. App. Div. March 7, 2001) at 4–5.

51. Unless otherwise noted, quotations from Paul Levy come from an interview conducted on May 18, 2020.

52. Unpublished Letter Opinion, Dendrite v. Does, Docket No. MRS-C-129-00 (NJ Super. Ct.—Chancery Div. Nov. 23, 2000) at 11–12.

53. *Id.* at 13.

54. *Id.* at 19.

55. *Id.* at 17.

56. Dendrite did not appeal the denial of the motion to discover information about gacbar, and its appeal regarding xxplrr's information focused only on the defamation claim, not the misappropriation claim.

57. Brief on Behalf of Plaintiff-Appellant, Dendrite International v. Does, Docket No. MRS-C-129-00 (NJ App. Div. March 7, 2001) at 21.

58. Brief of Amici Curiae Public Citizen and the American Civil Liberties Union of New Jersey, Dendrite v. Does, Docket No. A-2774-00 (NJ App. Div. March 29, 2001) at 22–29.

59. *Id.* at 29.

60. *Id.* at 32–33.

61. *Id.* at 34–36.

62. *Id.* at 36–37.

63. *Id.* at 37–41.

64. *Id.* at 44–46.

65. *Id.* at 45.

66. Dendrite Intern. v. Doe No. 3, 775 A.2d 756, 760–61 (N.J. App. Div. 2001). The judges framed it as a four-part test, by collapsing Levy's third and fourth elements into a single prong, but the substance of their guidelines was similar to Levy's.

67. *Id.* at 760.

68. *Id.*

69. *Id.* at 772.

70. *See* Nathaniel Gleicher, *John Doe Subpoenas: Toward a Consistent Legal Standard,* 118 YALE L. J. 320, 340 (2008): "*Dendrite* was a significant early development in John Doe subpoena standards, and it has been extensively cited by courts developing subsequent standards."

71. Independent Newspapers v. Brodie, 966 A.2d 432, 456 (Md. Ct. App. 2009).

72. Gleicher, *John Doe Subpoenas* at 340.

73. Interview with Michael Vogel (May 27, 2020).

74. Michael S. Vogel, *Unmasking 'John Doe' Defendants: The Case against Excessive Hand-Wringing over Legal Standards,* 83 OR. L. REV. 795, 808 (2004).

75. Town of Smyrna Delaware, History, https://smyrna.delaware.gov/history.

76. J. L. Miller, *Security Camera Inflames Smyrna Feud,* THE NEWS JOURNAL (Sept. 17, 2004).

77. *Id.*

78. *Id.*

79. The comments cited from the Smyrna/Clayton Issues Blog come from court filings and the Internet Archive capture of the site, http://newsblog.info/0405.

80. Cahill v. Doe, 879 A.2d 943, 946–47 (Del. Super. Ct. June 14, 2005).

81. *Id.*

82. *Id.* at 948.

83. Emergency Motion of Defendant John Doe No. 1 for a Protective Order, C.A. No. 04C-11-022 JJS, Cahill v. Does (Del. Super. Ct. Jan. 4, 2005).

84. Interview with Joseph Slights (June 10, 2020).

85. Cahill v. Doe, 879 A.2d 943, 952 (Del. Super. Ct. June 14, 2005).

86. *Id.* at 952–53.

87. *Id.* at 954–55.

88. Brief for Public Citizen, American Civil Liberties Union, Electronic Frontier Foundation, and American Civil Liberties Union of Delaware as Amici Curiae Urging Reversal, Doe v. Cahill, No. 266, 2005 (Del. Aug. 1, 2005).

89. Doe v. Cahill, 884 A.2d 451, 456 (Del. 2005).

90. *Id.* at 460.

91. *Id.* at 464.

92. *Id.* at 461.

93. *Id.* at 467.

94. ASSOCIATED PRESS, *Blogger at Center of Lawsuit Is Identified* (Feb. 3, 2006).

95. ASSOCIATED PRESS, *Settlement Reached in Smyrna Blogger Case* (June 23, 2006).

96. Interview with Joseph Slights (June 10, 2020).

97. Jane E. Kirtley, *Mask, Shield, and Sword: Should the Journalist's Privilege Protect the Identity of Anonymous Posters to News Media Websites*, 94 MINN. L. REV. 1478, 1487 (2010).

98. *See, e.g.*, Letter decision, Ciabattoni v. Teamsters Local 326, Case No. N15C-04-059 VLM (Del. Super. Ct. May 29, 2018); Order Vacating the Order of Magistrate Judge Dated December 18, 2015 and Denying Plaintiffs' Discovery Motion, East Coast Test Prep v. AllNurses.com, 167 F.Supp.3d 1018 (D. Minn. 2016); Doe v. Coleman, 497 S.W.3d 740 (Ky. 2016); Mortgage Specialists v. Implode-Explode Heavy Industries, 999 A.2d 184 (N.H. 2010); Independent Newspapers v. Brodie, 966 A.2d 432 (Md. Ct. App. 2009); Krinsky v. Doe 6, 72 Cal. Rptr. 3d 231 (Cal. Ct. App. 2008).

99. *In re* Anonymous Online Speakers, 661 F. 3d 1168, 1177 (9th Cir. 2011).

100. Doe v. Individuals, 561 F. Supp. 2d 249, 251 (D. Conn. 2008).

101. *Id.* at 252.

102. Kevin Fayle, *Defamation Lawsuit Seeks to Unmask Anonymous Cowards*, THE REGISTER (June 24, 2007): "Autoadmit.com allows users to post anonymously, and does not retain IP addresses for its users."

103. Declaration of Steve Mitra in Support of Motion for Limited Expedited Discovery supp. 4, Doe v. Individuals, Docket No. 3:07-cv-909, Dkt. No. 30-5 (D. Conn. Mar. 18, 2008).

104. Doe v. Individuals, 561 F. Supp. 2d 249, 252 n.4 (D. Conn. 2008).

105. *Id.* at 257.

106. Lyrissa Barnett Lidsky, *Anonymity in Cyberspace: What Can We Learn from John Doe*, 50 B.C. L. REV. 1373, 1389 (2009).

107. *Id.* at 1390.

108. *Id.*

109. Danielle Citron, HATE CRIMES IN CYBERSPACE 44 (2014).

110. Lyrissa Barnett Lidsky, *Anonymity in Cyberspace: What Can We Learn from John Doe*, 50 B.C. L. REV. 1373, 1389 (2009).

111. Hassell v. Bird, 5 Cal.5th 522, 545 (2018).

112. *Id.* at 545.

113. *Id* at 574 (Cuellar, J., dissenting).

114. *See* Eugene Volokh, *Two Past Prosecutions for Forged Court Orders in Libel Takedown Cases*, WASH. POST (April 21, 2017); Eugene Volokh & Paul Alan Levy, *Dozens of Suspicious Court Cases, with Missing Defendants, Aim at Getting Web Pages Taken Down or Deindexed*, WASH. POST (Oct. 10, 2016).

115. According to the Reporters Committee for Freedom of the Press, thirty-one states and the District of Columbia had anti-SLAPP laws as of June 2021, but their scope varies widely. Moreover, there is not a federal anti-SLAPP law. *See* Austin Vining and Sarah

Matthews, Reporters Committee for Freedom of the Press, *Overview of Anti-SLAPP Laws*, available at https://www.rcfp.org/introduction-anti-slapp-guide.

116. Does v. Advanced Textile, 214 F.3d 1058 (9th Cir. 2000) (internal quotation marks and citation removed).

117. Mike Masnick, *Since When Is It Illegal to Just Mention A Trademark Online?* TECHDIRT (Jan. 5, 2005).

118. David Margolick, *Slimed Online*, PORTFOLIO (March 2009).

119. Danielle Keats Citron, *Cyber Civil Rights*, 89 B.U. L. REV. 61, 123 (2009).

120. A. Michael Froomkin, *CCR Symposium: The Right to Remain Anonymous Matters*, CONCURRING OPINIONS (Apr. 14, 2009).

121. *Id.*

122. Bryan H. Choi, *The Anonymous Internet*, 72 MD. L. REV. 501, 506 (2013).

Chapter 8. Online Anonymity and Copyright

1. A&M Records v. Napster, 239 F.3d 1004 (9th Cir. 2001).

2. Jack Goldsmith and Tim Wu, WHO CONTROLS THE INTERNET 109 (2006).

3. Stan Liebowitz, *Will MP3 Downloads Annihilate the Record Industry? The Evidence so Far* in ADVANCES IN THE STUDY OF ENTREPRENEURSHIP, INNOVATION, AND ECONOMIC GROWTH, ed. Gary Libecap (2003) at 30.

4. 17 U.S.C. 512(h).

5. Press Release, RECORDING INDUSTRY ASSOCIATION OF AMERICA, *Recording Industry to Begin Collecting Evidence and Preparing Lawsuits against File "Sharers" Who Illegally Offer Music Online* (June 25, 2003).

6. Stanley A. Miller II, *Music Industry's Next Piracy Targets: Ordinary Folks*, MILWAUKEE JOURNAL-SENTINEL (June 26, 2003).

7. Press Release, RECORDING INDUSTRY ASSOCIATION OF AMERICA, *Recording Industry Begins Suing P2P File Sharers Who Illegally Offer Copyrighted Music Online* (Sept. 8, 2003).

8. Complaint, Capitol Records v. Little, C 03-4068 (N.D. Cal. Sept. 8, 2003) at Ex. A.

9. Alex Pham et al., *Surprise Is a Common Reaction of Those Sued*, L.A. TIMES (Sept. 9, 2003).

10. Stipulation to Judgment and Permanent Injunction, Capitol Records v. Little, C 03-4068 (N.D. Cal. Jan. 8, 2004) at ¶ 1.

11. Katie Dean, *Senator Takes a Swing at RIAA*, WIRED (Sept. 17, 2003).

12. Recording Indus. Ass'n of Am. v. Verizon Internet Servs. (*In re* Verizon Internet Servs., Inc., Subpoena Enf't Matter), 240 F. Supp. 2d 24, 28 (D.D.C. 2003).

13. *Id.* at 29.

14. Senior Judge John D. Bates, available at https://www.dcd.uscourts.gov/content/senior-judge-john-d-bates.

15. Brief of Amici in Support of Verizon's Opposition to RIAA's Motion to Enforce, Recording Indus. Ass'n of Am. v. Verizon Internet Servs. (*In re* Verizon Internet Servs., Inc., Subpoena Enf't Matter), Civ. No. 1:02MS00323 (D.D.C. Aug. 2002).

16. *Id.*

17. Recording Indus. Ass'n of Am. v. Verizon Internet Servs. (*In re* Verizon Internet Servs., Inc., Subpoena Enf't Matter), 240 F. Supp. 2d 24, 42 (D.D.C. 2003).

18. *Id.* at 43.

19. Recording Indus. Ass'n of Am. v. Verizon Internet Servs. (*In re* Verizon Internet Servs., Inc., Subpoena Enf't Matter), 257 F. Supp. 2d 244, 259 (D.D.C. 2003).

20. *Id.* at 260.

21. *Id.* at 262.

22. Recording Indus. Ass'n of Am. v. Verizon Internet Servs. (*In re* Verizon Internet Servs., Inc., Subpoena Enf't Matter), 240 F. Supp. 2d 24, 43, n.19 (D.D.C. 2003).

23. Sonia K. Katyal, *Privacy vs. Piracy*, 9 INT'L J. COMM'CNS L. & POL'Y 7 (2004–5).

24. Recording Industry of America v. Verizon, 351 F.3d 1229, 1236 (D.C. Cir. 2003).

25. *Id.* at 1231.

26. Complaint, Sony Music Entertainment v. Does 1–40, Civil Action No. 04 CV 00473 (S.D.N.Y. Jan. 24, 2004) at ¶ 21.

27. Sony Music Entertainment v. Does 1–40, 326 F. Supp. 2d 556, 560 (S.D.N.Y. 2004).

28. *Id.*

29. Plaintiffs' Opposition to Jane Doe's Motion to Quash and Response to the Memorandum of Amici Curiae Public Citizen, et al., Sony Music Entertainment v. Does 1–40, Case No. 04-cv-00473 (S.D.N.Y. April 7, 2004) at 4–5, 10.

30. Memorandum of Amici Curiae Public Citizen, American Civil Liberties Union and Electronic Frontier Foundation in Support of Motions to Quash, Sony Music Entertainment v. Does 1–40, Case No. 04-cv-00473 (S.D.N.Y. April 22, 2004) at 5 n.2.

31. Plaintiffs' Opposition to Jane Doe's Motion to Quash and Response to the Memorandum of Amici Curiae Public Citizen, et al., Sony Music Entertainment v. Does 1–40, Case No. 04-cv-00473 (S.D.N.Y. April 7, 2004) at 10–11.

32. Sony Music Entertainment v. Does 1–40, 326 F. Supp. 2d 556, 564 (S.D.N.Y. 2004).

33. *Id.* at 565.

34. *Id.* at 566.

35. *Id.*

36. Arista Records v. Doe 3, 604 F.3d 110, 119 (2d. Cir. 2010).

37. Lamont v. Postmaster Gen., 381 U.S. 301, 303 (1965).

38. *Id.* at 307.

39. *Id.*

40. *Id.* at 308 (Brennan, J., concurring).

41. Julie E. Cohen, *A Right to Read Anonymously: A Closer Look at Copyright Management in Cyberspace*, 28 CONN. L. REV. 981, 1014 (1996).

42. Matthew Sag and Jake Haskell, *Defense against the Dark Arts of Copyright Trolling*, 103 IOWA L. REV. 571, 578 (2018).

43. *Id.* at 580.

44. Gabe Friedman, *The Biggest Filer of Copyright Lawsuits? This Erotica Web Site*, NEW YORKER (May 14, 2014).

45. Complaint, Malibu Media v. Doe, 12 CV 3810 (S.D.N.Y. May 14, 2012).

46. Malibu Media v. Doe, 2013 U.S. Dist. LEXIS 99332, 12 CV 3810 (S.D.N.Y. July 16, 2013).

47. Complaint ¶¶ 11, 36–42, Malibu Media v. John Does 1–10, 2:12-cv-03623 (C.D. Cal. April 26, 2012) at 5.

48. Plaintiff's Notice of Motion and Motion for Leave to Serve Third Party Subpoenas Prior to a Rule 26(f) Conference; Memorandum of Points and Authorities in Support Thereof ¶ 5, Malibu Media v. John Does 1–10, 2:12-cv-03623 (C.D. Cal. May 4, 2012).

49. Order, Malibu Media v. John Does 1–10, No. 2:12-cv-03623 (C.D. Cal. June 27, 2012) at 4.

50. *20 Essential Tricks and Skills Every BitTorrent User Should Know*, PC GAMER (Nov. 11, 2009).

51. Order, Malibu Media v. John Does 1–10, 2:12-cv-03623 (C.D. Cal. June 27, 2012) at 5.

52. *Id.*

53. *Id.* at 4.

54. *Id.* at 6.

55. *Id.*

56. Order to Show Cause, Malibu Media v. Doe, No. C 16-05975 (N.D. Cal. May 10, 2017).

57. Stanley v. Georgia, 394 U.S. 557, 558–59 (1969).

58. *Id.* at 564 (citation omitted).

59. *Id.* at 565.

60. Julie E. Cohen, *A Right to Read Anonymously: A Closer Look at Copyright Management in Cyberspace*, 28 CONN. L. REV. 981, 1009 (1996).

61. Stanley v. Georgia, 394 U.S. 557, 565 (1969).

62. For an excellent discussion of the more general issue of sexual privacy, *see* Danielle Keats Citron, *Sexual Privacy*, 128 YALE L. J. 1870 (2019).

63. Strike 3 Holdings, LLC v. Doe, 351 F. Supp. 3d 160, 164 (D.D.C. 2018).

64. Strike 3 Holdings, LLC v. Doe, 964 F. 3d 1203, 1212 (D.C. Cir. 2020).

Chapter 9. When the Government Wants to Unmask You

1. Katz v. United States, 389 U.S. 347, 360 (1967) (Harlan, J., concurring).

2. *See* United States v. Warshak, 631 F.3d 266 (6th Cir. 2010).

3. Smith v. Maryland, 442 U.S. 735 (1979).

4. *Id.* at 743–44.

5. United States v. Miller, 425 U.S. 435 (1976).

6. *See* United States v. Ulbricht, 858 F.3d 71, 97 (2d Cir. 2017); United States v. Suing, 712 F.3d 1209, 1213 (8th Cir. 2013); United States v. Stults, 575 F.3d 834, 843 (8th Cir. 2009).

7. Jeffrey M. Skopek, *Reasonable Expectations of Anonymity*, 101 VA. L. REV. 691, 761 (2015).

8. Carpenter v. United States, 138 S. Ct. 2206, 2220 (2018).

9. *Id.*

10. United States v. Hood, 920 F.3d 87, 89 (1st Cir. 2019).

11. *Id.* at 92.

12. Alfred Ng, *Google Is Giving Data to Police Based on Search Keywords, Court Docs Show*, CNET (Oct. 8, 2020).

13. *Id.*

14. 18 U.S.C. 2703(d).

15. Motion to Intervene and to Quash Grand Jury Subpoena No. 11116275, *In re* Grand Jury Subpoena No. 11116275, No. 1:11-mc-00527 (D.D.C. Sept. 20, 2011) at 1.

16. *In re* Grand Jury Subpoena No. 11116275, 846 F. Supp. 2d 1 (D.D.C. 2012); because the poster used a male screenname, this book refers to the poster as "he" and "him," but the court documents do not reveal the poster's sex.

17. Motion to Intervene and to Quash Grand Jury Subpoena No. 11116275, *In re* Grand Jury Subpoena No. 11116275, No. 1:11-mc-00527 (D.D.C. Sept. 20, 2011) at 22–23.

18. *Id.*

19. *Id.* at 3.

20. *Id.* at 20. There was a slight dispute as to the wording of the tweet. The government claimed that it stated: "I want to fuck Michelle Bachmann in her ass with a Vietnam era Machete." *In re* Grand Jury Subpoena No. 11116275, 846 F. Supp. 2d 1, 3 n.2 (D.D.C. 2012).

21. Michelle Goldberg, *Bachmann's Unrivaled Extremism*, DAILY BEAST (June 14, 2011).

22. Motion to Intervene and to Quash Grand Jury Subpoena No. 11116275, *In re* Grand Jury Subpoena No. 11116275, No. 1:11-mc-00527 (D.D.C. Sept. 20, 2011) at 1.

23. *Id.* at 9–12.

24. *Id.* at 11–12.

25. *Id.* at 27.

26. *Id.* at 20–21.

27. Senior Judge Royce C. Lamberth, available at https://www.dcd.uscourts.gov/content/senior-judge-royce-c-lamberth.

28. *In re* Grand Jury Subpoena No. 11116275, 846 F. Supp. 2d 1, 5 (D.D.C. 2012).

29. *Id.* at 6.

30. *Id.*

31. *Id.* at 7.

32. *Id.* at 8.

33. *Id.*

34. American Civil Liberties Union of the District of Columbia, *In re* Grand Jury Subpoena No. 11116275, available at https://www.acludc.org/en/cases/re-grand-jury-subpoena-no-11116275.

35. *In re* Grand Jury Subpoena, No. 16-03-217, 875 F.3d 1179, 1191 (9th Cir. 2017). The court's "good faith" standard came from the reporter's privilege case, *Branzburg v. Hayes*, 408 U.S. 665 (1972), described in Chapter 4.

36. Complaint, Securities and Exchange Commission v. Jammin' Java, Case 2:15-cv-08921 (C.D. Cal. Nov. 17, 2015) at ¶¶ 83–90.

37. U.S. Securities and Exchange Commission's Opposition to John Doe's Motion to Quash Administrative Subpoena and Memorandum in Support Thereof, Doe v. Securities and Exchange Commission, Case No. 3:11-mc-80209 (N.D. Cal. Sept. 2, 2011) at 2.

38. Three separate motions to quash were filed, each with its own case number, and they resulted in very similar results. This book will focus on the filings in the case involving the jeffreyhooke@gmail.com subpoena, Case 3:11-mc-80209.

39. Memorandum in Support of Motion to Quash Administrative Subpoena, Doe v. Securities and Exchange Commission, Case No. 3:11-mc-80209 at 5 (N.D. Cal. Aug. 18, 2011).

40. Transcript of Proceedings of the Official Electronic Sound Record, Doe v. Securities and Exchange Commission, Case No. 3:11-mc-80209 at 17–18 (N.D. Cal. Oct. 4, 2011).

41. Order Denying Motion to Quash Subpoena, Doe v. Securities and Exchange Commission, Case No. 3:11-mc-80209 at 4 (N.D. Cal. Oct. 4, 2011).

42. *Id.* at 8.

43. Doe v. Securities and Exchange Commission, Case No. 11-cv-80209, 2011 WL 5600513, at *4 (N.D. Cal. Nov. 17, 2011).

44. Press Release, SECURITIES AND EXCHANGE COMMISSION, *SEC Obtains $58 Million Judgment against Perpetrator of International Pump-and-Dump Scheme Involving Marley Coffee* (Oct. 3, 2017).

Chapter 10. Anonymity Worldwide

1. Jason A. Martin and Anthony L. Fargo, *Anonymity as a Legal Right: Where and Why It Matters*, 16 N.C. J.L. & TECH. 311, 347 (2015).

2. Jyh-An Lee and Ching-Yi Liu, *Real-Name Registration Rules and the Fading Digital Anonymity in China*, 25 PAC. RIM L. & POL'Y J. 1, 11 (2016).

3. *Id.* at 11–12.

4. *Id.* at 13.

5. Samm Sacks and Paul Triolo, *Shrinking Anonymity in Chinese Cyberspace*, LAWFARE (Sept. 25, 2017).

6. *Id.* "The Social Credit System requires real-name information attached to the data it captures so that an individual's creditworthiness, from social/political and economic vectors, can be aggregated in the system's vast databases."

7. *Id.*

8. CODING RIGHTS, PRIVACY LATAM, & PRIVACY INTERNATIONAL, *The Right to Privacy in Brazil* at ¶ 28 (Sept. 2016).

9. David Kaye, REPORT OF THE SPECIAL RAPPORTEUR ON THE PROMOTION AND PROTECTION OF THE RIGHT TO FREEDOM OF OPINION AND EXPRESSION at 17 (May 22, 2015); Adi Robertson, *Putin Signs Law Forcing Bloggers to Register with Russian Media Office*, THE VERGE (May 7, 2014).

10. REPORT OF THE SPECIAL RAPPORTEUR ON THE PROMOTION AND PROTECTION OF THE RIGHT TO FREEDOM OF OPINION AND EXPRESSION at 17.

11. Jason A. Martin and Anthony L. Fargo, *Anonymity as a Legal Right: Where and Why It Matters*, 16 N.C. J.L. & TECH. 311, 367 (2015).

12. Eric Fish, *Is Internet Censorship Compatible with Democracy: Legal Restrictions of Online Speech in South Korea*, 10 ASIA-PAC. J. ON HUM. RTS. & L. 43, 85 (2009).

13. *South Korea's Real-Name Net Law Is Rejected by Court*, BBC NEWS (Aug. 23, 2012).

14. American Civil Liberties Union of Georgia v. Miller, 977 F. Supp. 1228, 1230 (N.D. Ga. 1997).

15. *Id.* at 1232.

16. American Civil Liberties Union v. Johnson, 194 F.3d 1149, 1152 (10th Cir. 1999).

17. American Civil Liberties Union v. Johnson, 4 F. Supp.2d 1029 (D.N.M. 1998), *aff'd* American Civil Liberties Union v. Johnson, 194 F.3d 1149 (10th Cir. 1999).

18. Doe v. Harris, 772 F.3d 563, 580 (9th Cir. 2014).

19. Doe v. Shurtleff, 628 F.3d 1217 (10th Cir. 2010).

20. Judgment, Case of K.U. v. Finland, Application no. 2872/02 (European Court of Human Rights 2008) at ¶ 11.

21. *Id.* ¶ 8.

22. *Id.* ¶ 7.

23. *Id.* ¶¶ 9–11.

24. *Id.* ¶ 12.

25. *Id.* ¶ 35.

26. *Id.* ¶ 36.

27. *Id.* ¶¶ 42–43.

28. *Id.* ¶ 47.

29. *Id.* ¶ 49.

30. *See* Griswold v. Connecticut, 381 U.S. 479, 485 (1965).

31. Robert A. Sedler, *An Essay on Freedom of Speech: The United States Versus the Rest of the World*, 2006 MICH. ST. L. REV. 377, 380 (2006).

32. Daniel Solove, THE FUTURE OF REPUTATION 140 (2007).

33. Tim Richardson, *Totalise Ends Free Share Offer*, THE REGISTER (Dec. 11, 2001).

34. Totalise Plc v The Motley Fool Ltd & Anor [2001] EWHC 706 (QB) (February 19, 2001).

35. *Id.*

36. *Id.*

37. *Id.*

38. Totalise v. Motley Fool, [2001] EWCA Civ 1897 at 7.

39. UK Public General Acts, 2013 c.26, Sec. 3.

40. United Kingdom Ministry of Justice, Complaints about Defamatory Material Posted on Websites: Guidance on Section 5 of the Defamation Act 2013 and Regulations.

41. Irwin Toy v. Doe, [2000] O.J. No. 3318 at ¶¶ 2–3.

42. *Id.* ¶¶ 4–6.

43. *Id.* ¶ 8.

44. *Id.* ¶ 17.

45. *Id.* ¶ 12.

46. BMG Canada Inc. v. John Doe (F.C.), [2004] 3 F.C.R. 241 at ¶13.

47. *Id.* ¶42.

48. Ian Kerr and Alex Cameron, *Nymity, P2P & ISPs*, in PRIVACY AND TECHNOLOGIES OF IDENTITY (Katherine Strandburg and Daniela Stan Raicu, eds.) (2006) at 287.

49. BMG Canada Inc. v. John Doe, [2005] F.C.J. No. 858, ¶37.

50. BMG Canada Inc. v. John Doe (F.C.), [2004] 3 F.C.R. 241, ¶38.

Chapter 11. Technological Protections for Anonymity

1. Jeff Schogol, *Does Pizza Signal a Crisis at the White House?* STARS AND STRIPES (July 27, 2010).

2. Much of the material in this chapter comes from interviews that the author conducted in 2019 with David Goldschlag, Michael Reed, and Paul Syverson.

3. Special thanks to Paul Syverson for taking a tremendous amount of time to walk me through the technical models of onion routing.

4. David M. Goldschlag, Michael G. Reed, and Paul F. Syverson, *Hiding Routing Information* (May 1996) at 1.

5. Roger Dingledine, Nick Mathewson, and Paul Syverson, *Tor: The Second-Generation Onion Router*, in PROCEEDINGS OF THE 13TH USENIX SECURITY SYMPOSIUM, Aug. 2004.

6. ONION ROUTING: HISTORY, available at https://www.onion-router.net/History.html.

7. *See* TOR PROJECT, HISTORY, available at https://torproject.org/about/history/.

8. *Tor Project's Struggle to Keep the "Dark Net" in the Shadows*, BBC (Aug. 22, 2014).

9. Amy E. Cattle, *Digital Tahrir Square: An Analysis of Human Rights and the Internet Examined through the Lens of the Egyptian Arab Spring*, 26 DUKE J. COMP. & INT'L L. 417, 446, n.162 (2016).

10. Ingmar Zahorsky, *Tor, Anonymity, and the Arab Spring: An Interview with Jacob Appelbaum*, UNIVERSITY FOR PEACE & CONFLICT MONITOR (Aug. 1, 2011).

11. Roshni Chakraborty, *The Deep Web: For the Nefarious or the Democratic?* HARV. INT'L REV., Fall 2018, at 18, 20.

12. Leonid Bershidsky, *Putin Sets Sights on Exposing Tor*, BLOOMBERG NEWS (July 28, 2014).

13. Thorin Klosowski, *What Is Tor and Should I Use It?* LIFEHACKER (Feb. 21, 2014).

14. Gabriella Coleman, *How Has the Fight for Anonymity and Privacy Advanced since Snowden's Whistle-Blowing?* 41(4) MEDIA, CULTURE, AND SOCIETY 565 (2019).

15. *See* Steve Alexander, *Tor Browser Is Secretive, Slow, and Can be Risky*, STAR TRIBUNE (Dec. 9, 2019).

16. Sophos, *Tor Users Being Actively Blocked on Some Websites*, available at https://nakedsecurity.sophos.com/2016/02/29/tor-users-being-actively-blocked-on-some-websites/ (Feb. 29, 2016).

17. *See* metrics.torproject.org.

18. Interview with Kelley Misata (Oct. 28, 2019).

19. TOR PROJECT, *Some Statistics about Onions*, available at https://blog.torproject.org/some-statistics-about-onions (Feb. 26, 2015).

20. FACEBOOK, *Making Connections to Facebook More Secure*, available at https://www.facebook.com/notes/protect-the-graph/making-connections-to-facebook-more-secure/1526085754298237/ (Oct. 31, 2014).

21. Mike Tigas, *A More Secure and Anonymous ProPublica Using Tor Hidden Services*, PROPUBLICA (Jan. 13, 2016).

22. Press Release, CENTRAL INTELLIGENCE AGENCY, *CIA's Latest Layer: An Onion Site* (May 7, 2019).

23. *See* Conor Pope, *Inside the Dark Web: 'The Truth Is There Is a Lot of Evil out There,'* IRISH TIMES (Oct. 13, 2018).

24. https://www.c-span.org/video/?324019-1/2015-state-net-conference&event=324019&playEvent.

25. Brian Levine and Brian Lynn, *Tor Hidden Services Are a Failed Technology, Harming Children, Dissidents and Journalists*, LAWFARE (Jan. 17, 2020).

26. Government's Response to Defendant's Memorandum in Support of His Motion to Suppress the NIT Warrant, United States v. Carlson, Criminal No. 16-CR-00317, at Ex 1., ¶ 10 (D. Minn. Jan. 31, 2017).

27. *Id.* at Ex. 1, ¶ 11.

28. *Id.* at Ex. 1, ¶ 10.

29. *Id.* at Ex. 1, ¶ 13.

30. *Id.* at Ex. 1, ¶ 14.

31. *Id.* at Ex. 1. ¶ 18.

32. *Id.* at Ex. 1. ¶ 21.

33. *Id.* at Ex. 1. ¶ 19.

34. *Id.* at 2.

35. *Id.* at Ex 1., ¶ 28; FEDERAL BUREAU OF INVESTIGATION, *Playpen Creator Sentenced to 30 Years* (May 5, 2017).

36. Government's Response to Defendant's Memorandum in Support of His Motion to Suppress the NIT Warrant, United States v. Carlson, Criminal No. 16-CR-00317, at Ex 1., ¶ 30 (D. Minn. Jan. 31, 2017).

37. *Id.* at Ex. 1., ¶¶ 33–34.

38. *Id.* at 3.

39. FEDERAL BUREAU OF INVESTIGATION, *Playpen Creator Sentenced to 30 Years* (May 5, 2017).

40. *See, e.g.*, United States v. Levin, 874 F.3d 316 (1st Cir. 2017).

41. Government's Response to Defendant's Memorandum in Support of His Motion to Suppress the NIT Warrant, United States v. Carlson, Criminal No. 16-CR-00317, at 6 (D. Minn. Jan. 31, 2017).

42. *Id.* at 7.

43. *Id.*

44. *Id.* at 8.

45. Memorandum Opinion and Order on Report and Recommendation of Magistrate Judge, United States v. Carlson, Criminal No. 16-CR-00317, at 7 (D. Minn. Aug. 7, 2017).

46. *Id.* at 7.

47. Carlson's plea was conditional on an appeal of the suppression motion, which the Eighth Circuit denied in 2019; *see* United States v. Carlson, No. 18-1829 (8th Cir. May 3, 2019).

48. Defendant's Exhibit A to Defendant Terry Carlson's Position on Sentencing Factors and Motion for Downward Variance, United States v. Carlson, Criminal No. 16-CR-00317 (D. Minn. March 21, 2017).

49. Sentencing Hearing Transcript, United States v. Carlson, Criminal No. 16-CR-00317 (D. Minn. April 4, 2018).

50. Sentencing Hearing Transcript at 11, United States v. Carlson, Criminal No. 16-CR-00317 (D. Minn. April 4, 2018).

51. *Id.*

52. Annual Report, 2017, Internet Watch Foundation at 19, available at https://annualreport.iwf.org.uk/pdf/IWF_2017_Annual_Report.pdf.

53. Michael H. Keller and Gabriel J.X. Dance, *The Internet Is Overrun with Images of Child Sexual Abuse. What Went Wrong?*, N.Y. TIMES (Sept. 29, 2019).

54. Julian Jaynes, THE ORIGIN OF CONSCIOUSNESS IN THE BREAKDOWN OF THE BICAMERAL MIND (1976) at 149.

Chapter 12. Anonymity as a Shield

1. David Post, *Pooling Intellectual Capital: Thoughts on Anonymity, Pseudonymity, and Limited Liability*, 1 UNIVERSITY OF CHICAGO LEGAL FORUM art. 5 (1996).

2. Much of this chapter is derived from phone interviews conducted with Dissent Doe in 2019 and 2020.

3. A. Michael Froomkin, *Anonymity and Its Enmities*, J. ONLINE L. art. 4 (1995).

4. *Id.* at ¶ 36.

5. Daniel Payne, *Make Them Scared Website Posts Uncorroborated Sexual Assault Claims against Male Students*, COLLEGE FIX (Oct. 5, 2018).

6. Manisha Jha, *In a Perfect System, Makethemscared Wouldn't Exist, Say Site Moderators*, THE DAILY (Oct. 8, 2018).

7. Editorial: *"Make Them Scared" Is a Symptom, Not a Solution*, THE DAILY (Oct. 5, 2018).

8. *See, e.g.*, Jones v. Dirty World Entertainment Recordings, 755 F.3d 398 (6th Cir. 2014).

9. *See, e.g.*, Batzel v. Smith, 333 F. 3d 1018 (9th Cir. 2003).

10. *See* Jeff Kosseff, *The Gradual Erosion of the Law that Shaped the Internet*, 18 COLUM. SCI. & TECH. L. REV. 1 (2017)

Chapter 13. Anonymity as a Sword

1. Victoria Smith Ekstrand, *The Many Masks of Anon: Anonymity as Cultural Practice and Reflections in Case Law*, 18 J. TECH. L. & POL'Y 1, 10, 23 (2013).

2. Saul Levmore, *The Internet's Anonymity Problem*, in THE OFFENSIVE INTERNET: SPEECH, PRIVACY, AND REPUTATION (Saul Levmore and Martha Nussbaum, eds.) at 53 (2012): "Whether the goal is to injure with offensive speech or spread socially useful information about another, the Internet is more appealing than the table or the wall; anonymity is more assured, it has the potential to reach a larger audience, it keeps the message alive, and it is searchable by interested parties who can then reproduce what they like for further publication."

3. *Id.*

4. Defendant's Sentencing Memo, United States v. Lin, Crim. No. 18-10092-WGY (D. Mass. Sept. 26, 2018) [hereinafter "Defendant's Sentencing Memo"] at 1.

5. *Id.* at 2.

6. *Id.* at 3.

7. *Id.*

8. *Id.* at 4.

9. *Id.*

10. Affidavit of Special Agent Jeffrey Williams in Support of a Criminal Complaint, United States v. Lin, Crim. No. 18-10092-WGY (D. Mass. Oct. 3, 2017) [hereinafter "Affidavit"] ¶ 63.

11. Defendant's Sentencing Memo at 3–5.

12. Affidavit ¶ 11.

13. *Id.* ¶ 14.

14. *Id.* ¶ 15.

15. *Id.* ¶ 15.

16. *Id.* ¶ 11.

17. *Id.* ¶ 16.

18. *Id.* ¶ 17.

19. *Id.* ¶ 18.

20. *Id.* ¶ 19.

21. *Id.* ¶ 20.

22. *Id.* ¶ 29.

23. Information ¶ 17., United States v. Lin, Crim. No. 18-10092-WGY (D. Mass. April 9, 2018) [hereinafter "Information"].

24. *Id.* ¶ 22.

25. *Id.* ¶ 26.

26. *Id.* ¶¶ 28–35.

27. *Id.* ¶ 32.

28. *Id.* ¶ 36.

29. *Id.* ¶ 38.

30. *Id.* ¶¶ 86–88.

31. *Id.* ¶¶ 40–45.

32. *Id.* ¶ 47.

33. *Id.* ¶ 48.

34. *Id.* ¶ 54.

35. *Id.* ¶ 61.

36. Government's Sentencing Memorandum at 9, United States v. Lin, Case No. 1:18-cr-10092-WGY (D. Mass. Sept. 28, 2018) [hereinafter Government's Sentencing Memorandum].

37. Information ¶ 63.

38. *Id.* ¶ 66.

39. *Id.* ¶¶ 82–84.

40. Government's Sentencing Memorandum at 8.

41. Affidavit ¶ 41; Information ¶ 14.

42. Affidavit ¶ 41.

43. Government's Sentencing Memorandum at 17.

44. Affidavit ¶ 42.

45. *Id.* ¶ 48.

46. *Id.* ¶ 49.

47. *Id.* ¶ 50.

48. *Id.* ¶ 51.

49. *Id.* ¶ 52.

50. *Id.* ¶¶ 36–37.

51. Government's Sentencing Memorandum at 4–5.

52. Plea Agreement, United States v. Lin, Case No. 1:18-cr-10092-WGY (D. Mass. May 9, 2018).

53. Sentencing Hearing Transcript, United States v. Lin, Case No. 1:18-cr-10092-WGY (D. Mass. Oct. 3, 2018) [hereinafter "Sentencing Hearing Transcript"] at 5.

54. Government's Sentencing Memorandum at 7.

55. Sentencing Hearing Transcript at 36.

56. *Id.* at 39–40.

57. *Id.* at 40.

58. *Id.* at 55.

59. *Id.* at 59.

60. *Id.* at 61.

61. Defendant's Sentencing Memo at 7.

62. Sentencing Hearing Transcript at 82–83.

63. *Id.* at 86.

64. *Id.* at 90.

65. *Id.* at 91.

66. *Id.* at 93.

67. Mary Anne Franks, *Beyond "Free Speech for the White Man": Feminism and the First Amendment,* in RESEARCH HANDBOOK ON FEMINIST JURISPRUDENCE (Cynthia Bowman and Robin West eds.) (2018).

68. Carrie Goldberg, NOBODY'S VICTIM: FIGHTING PSYCHOS, STALKERS, PERVS, AND TROLLS 144–47 (2019).

69. Mike Wendling, *QAnon: What Is It and Where Did It Come From?* BBC NEWS (Jan. 6, 2021).

70. Brett Forrest, *What Is QAnon? What We Know about the Conspiracy-Theory Group,* WALL ST. J. (Feb. 4, 2021).

71. Deepa Seetharaman, *QAnon Booms on Facebook as Conspiracy Group Gains Mainstream Traction,* WALL ST. J. (Aug. 13, 2020).

72. Stephanie K. Baer, *People Are Finding Comfort in Tweeting Their Family's Frantic Texts Pushing QAnon Lies,* BUZZFEED (Jan. 20, 2021).

73. William Mansell, *Man Pleads Guilty to Terrorism Charge after Blocking Hoover Dam Bridge with Armored Truck,* ABC NEWS (Feb. 13, 2020).

74. Richard Ruelas, *QAnon Follower Sentenced to Nearly 8 Years in Prison for Standoff near Hoover Dam,* ARIZONA REPUBLIC (Jan. 4, 2021).

75. Olivia Rubin, Lucien Bruggeman, and Will Steakin, *QAnon Emerges as Recurring Theme of Criminal Cases Tied to US Capitol Siege,* ABC NEWS (Jan. 19, 2021).

76. *See, e.g.,* Aaron Mak, *Was the Identity of Q Really Just Revealed?* SLATE (Sept. 25, 2020).

77. Brandy Zadrozny and Ben Collins, *How Three Conspiracy Theorists Took 'Q' and Sparked Qanon,* NBC NEWS (Aug. 14, 2018).

78. John Buckley, *"Stop the Cabal": What Is the Conspiracy Movement QAnon?* SYDNEY MORNING HERALD (Sept. 3, 2020): "As Q kept posting, followers made the transition from being anonymous 'anons' to posting under their real names on mainstream social media platforms."

79. Jason McGahan, *Inside QAnon, the Conspiracy Cult that's Devouring America,* LOS ANGELES MAGAZINE (Aug. 17, 2020).

80. Stephanie McNeal, *Gen Z Moms Are Building Their Brands Around QAnon,* BUZZFEED (Jan. 22, 2021).

81. Anastasiia Carrier, *"This Crap Means More to Him Than My Life": When QAnon Invades American Homes,* POLITICO (Feb. 19, 2021).

Part IV. The Future of Anonymity

1. Helen Nissenbaum, *The Meaning of Anonymity in an Information Age*, 15 THE INFORMATION SOCIETY 141 (1999).
2. A. Michael Froomkin, *From Anonymity to Identification*, 1 JOURNAL OF SELF-REGULATION AND REGULATION 120 (2015).

Chapter 14. Real-Name Policies

1. David Kirkpatrick, THE FACEBOOK EFFECT: THE INSIDE STORY OF THE COMPANY THAT IS CONNECTING THE WORLD (2010) at 199.
2. *Id.*
3. *Id.* at 200.
4. Michael Zimmer, *Facebook's Zuckerberg: "Having Two Identities for Yourself Is an Example of a Lack of Integrity"* (May 14, 2010), available at https://michaelzimmer.org/2010/05/14/facebooks-zuckerberg-having-two-identities-for-yourself-is-an-example-of-a-lack-of-integrity/.
5. Kirkpatrick, THE FACEBOOK EFFECT at 209.
6. danah boyd, *Facebook and 'Radical Transparency' (A Rant)* (May 14, 2010), available at https://www.zephoria.org/thoughts/archives/2010/05/14/facebook-and-radical-transparency-a-rant.html.
7. Tania Branigan, *Facebook's 'Real Name' Policy Attacked by Chinese Blogger*, THE GUARDIAN (March 9, 2011).
8. Nadia Khomami, *Journalist Laurie Penny Banned from Facebook for Using Pseudonym*, THE GUARDIAN (June 24, 2015).
9. Vauhini Vara, *Who's Real Enough for Facebook?* NEW YORKER (Oct. 2, 2014).
10. Chris Cox, Facebook post dated Oct. 1, 2014, available at https://www.facebook.com/chris.cox/posts/10101301777354543.
11. Facebook Q&A with Mark Zuckerberg (June 30, 2015), available at https://www.facebook.com/zuck/posts/10102213601037571?comment_id=10102213698751751&reply_comment_id=10102213934943421&total_comments=45&comment_tracking=%7B%22tn%22%3A%22R9%22%7D.
12. Melissa Chan, *Facebook Relaxes Controversial "Real-Name Policy" After Criticism*, TIME (Dec. 15, 2015).
13. Facebook, *Community Support FYI: Improving the Names Process on Facebook* (Dec. 15, 2015), available at https://about.fb.com/news/2015/12/community-support-fyi-improving-the-names-process-on-facebook/.
14. Eva Galperin and Wafa Ben Hassine, *Changes to Facebook's 'Real Names' Policy Still Don't Fix the Problem*, ELECTRONIC FRONTIER FOUNDATION (Dec. 18, 2015).
15. Brian Friedberg and Joan Donovan, *On the Internet, Nobody Knows You're a Bot: Pseudoanonymous Influence Operations and Networked Social Movements*, JOURNAL OF DESIGN AND SCIENCE (2019).
16. Facebook, *Managing Your Account, What Names Are Allowed on Facebook*, available at https://www.facebook.com/help/112146705538576.
17. Facebook, *Managing Your Account, What Types of ID Does Facebook Accept?*, available at *https://www.facebook.com/help/159096464162185?helpref=faq_content*.
18. Facebook, Community Standards Enforcement Report, Fake Accounts, *available at* https://transparency.fb.com/data/community-standards-enforcement/fake-accounts/facebook.
19. *We Heard You, No More Anonymous Comments*, PATRIOT-LEDGER (June 13, 2013).
20. Elizabeth Landers, *Huffington Post to Ban Anonymous Comments*, CNN (Aug. 22, 2013).

21. Reddit, Content Policy, available at https://www.redditinc.com/policies/content-policy.

22. Timothy B. Lee, *Why Reddit Just Banned a Community Devoted to Sharing Celebrity Nudes*, Vox (Sept. 8, 2014).

23. Rachel Gutman, *Reddit's Case for Anonymity on the Internet*, THE ATLANTIC (June 28, 2018).

24. Lee, *Why Reddit Just Banned a Community Devoted to Sharing Celebrity Nudes*.

25. Tracie Farrell, Miriam Fernandez, Jakub Novotny, and Harith Alani (2019). *Exploring Misogyny across the Manosphere in Reddit*, WEBSCI '19 PROCEEDINGS OF THE 10TH ACM CONFERENCE ON WEB SCIENCE 87.

26. Emily VanDerWerff, *Trans Twitter and the Beauty of Online Anonymity*, Vox (Sept. 23, 2020).

27. Twitter Help Center, *Impersonation Policy*, available at https://help.twitter.com/en/rules-and-policies/twitter-impersonation-policy#:~:text=Impersonation%20is%20a%20violation%20of,suspended%20under%20Twitter's%20impersonation%20policy.

28. Mat Honan, *Twitter Doesn't Give a Damn Who You Are*, GIZMODO (Sept. 9, 2011).

29. Mathew Ingram, *Why Twitter Doesn't Care What Your Real Name Is*, GIGAOM (Sept. 16, 2011).

30. Sai Teja Peddinti, Keith W. Ross, and Justin Cappos, *User Anonymity on Twitter*, IEEE SECURITY & PRIVACY (2017).

31. Donie O'Sullivan, *Russian Bots Retweeted Trump Nearly 500,000 Times in Final Weeks of 2016 Campaign*, CNN (Jan. 27, 2018).

32. Nicholas Confessore, Gabriel J.X. Dance, Richard Harris, and Mark Hansen, *The Follower Factory*, N.Y. TIMES (Jan. 27, 2018).

33. Tweet of Mark Cuban (Jan. 28, 2018), available at https://twitter.com/mcuban/status/957690629785440256.

34. Matthew Hughes, *Mark Cuban Has a Really Bad Idea for Fixing Twitter*, THE NEXT WEB (Jan. 29, 2018).

35. Mike Isaac and Daisuke Wakabayashi, *Russian Influence Reached 126 Million through Facebook Alone*, N.Y. TIMES (Oct. 30, 2017).

36. Indictment, at 34, 54, 62, United States v. Internet Research Agency, 1:18-cr-00032-DLF (D.D.C. Feb. 16, 2018).

37. Katja Rost, Lea Stahel, and Bruno S. Frey, *Digital Social Norm Enforcement: Online Firestorms in Social Media*, 11(6) PLoS ONE (2016).

38. Disqus, Pseudonyms Drive Communities (2012), *available at* https://mediacdn.disqus.com/1325732276/img/marketing/research/infographic_lg.jpg.

Chapter 15. Out in the Open

1. Latanya Sweeney, *Simple Demographics Often Identify People Uniquely*. Carnegie Mellon University, Data Privacy Working Paper 3. Pittsburgh 2000.

2. Paul Ohm, *Broken Promises of Privacy: Responding to the Surprising Failure of Anonymization*, 57 UCLA L. REV. 1701, 1705 (2010).

3. *Id.* at 1717–18.

4. Kate Klonick, *A 'Creepy' Assignment: Pay Attention to What Strangers Reveal in Public*, N.Y. TIMES (Mar. 8, 2019).

5. Nellie Bowles, *How 'Doxxing' Became a Mainstream Tool in the Culture Wars*, N.Y. TIMES (Aug. 30, 2017): "Online vigilantism has been around since the early days of the internet. So has 'doxxing'—originally a slang term among hackers for obtaining and posting private documents about an individual, usually a rival or enemy. To hackers, who prized their anonymity, it was considered a cruel attack."

6. Department of Homeland Security, *How to Prevent Online Harassment from "Doxxing"* (2017).

7. A. Michael Froomkin, *From Anonymity to Identification*, 1 JOURNAL OF SELF-REGULATION AND REGULATION 120, 129 (2015).

8. Oliver Darcy, *Tucker Carlson's Top Writer Resigns after Secretly Posting Racist and Sexist Remarks in Online Forum*, CNN (July 11, 2020).

9. *Id.*

10. *Id.*

11. *Id.*

12. Michael M. Grynbaum, *Writer for Tucker Carlson Resigns after 'Abhorrent' Online Posts Are Revealed*, N.Y. TIMES (July 11, 2020).

13. Jack Holmes, *Tucker Carlson Is on Another 'Vacation' after His Top Writer Was Fired for Doing Freelance Racism*, ESQUIRE (July 14, 2020).

14. Caitlin Dewey, *A Sampling of Controversial Tweets from @NatSecWonk*, WASH. POST (Oct. 23, 2013).

15. Michael Crowley, *The NatSecWonk I Know*, TIME (Oct. 23, 2013).

16. David Nakamura, Anne Gearan, and Scott Wilson, *Stung by a Twitter Renegade, Group in Obama Administration Launched Sting of Its Own*, WASH. POST (Oct. 23, 2013).

17. Caitlin Dewey, *A Sampling of Controversial Tweets from @NatSecWonk*, WASH. POST (Oct. 23, 2013).

18. Josh Rogin, *Exclusive: White House Official Fired for Tweeting under Fake Name*, DAILY BEAST (Oct. 22, 2013).

19. Nakamura, Gearan, and Wilson, *Stung by a Twitter Renegade*, WASH. POST (Oct. 23, 2013).

20. Glenn Thrush, *NSC Aide Admits Twitter Attack on White House*, POLITICO (Oct. 22, 2013).

Chapter 16. Empowering Anonymity through Privacy Law

1. Shoshana Zuboff, THE AGE OF SURVEILLANCE CAPITALISM 7, 9 (2019).

2. Jessica Su, Ansh Shukla, Sharad Goel, and Arvind Narayan, *De-anonymizing Web Browsing Data with Social Networks*, WWW '17: PROCEEDINGS OF THE 26TH INTERNATIONAL CONFERENCE ON WORLD WIDE WEB 1261 (April 2017).

3. Stuart A. Thompson and Charlie Warzel, *Twelve Million Phones, One Dataset, Zero Privacy*, N.Y. TIMES (Dec. 19, 2019).

4. *Id.*

5. Sebastien Gambs, Marc-Olivier Killijian, and Miguel Nunez del Prado Cortez, *De-Anonymization Attack on Geolocated Data*, 80 JOURNAL OF COMPUTER AND SYSTEM SCIENCES 1597 (2014).

6. Animoto, Important Security Announcement, available at https://help.animoto.com/hc/en-us/articles/360008114514-Important-Security-Announcement.

7. Phil Muncaster, *Genealogy Software Maker Exposes Data on 60,000 Users*, INFOSECURITY MAGAZINE (July 21, 2020).

8. Kashmir Hill, *The Secretive Company That Might End Privacy as We Know It*, N.Y. TIMES (Jan. 18, 2020).

9. Kate Conger, Richard Fausset, and Serge F. Kovaleski, *San Francisco Bans Facial Recognition Technology*, N.Y. TIMES (May 14, 2019).

10. Aaron Holmes, *Boston Just Became the Latest City to Ban Use of Facial Recognition Technology*, BUSINESS INSIDER (June 24, 2020).

11. *See, e.g.*, Illinois Biometric Privacy Act, 740 I.L.C.S. 14.

12. Jessica Mason, *The App That Lets People Search You via Your Face Is Real and TER-RIFYING*, The Mary Sue (Jan. 21, 2020)

13. GDPR, Recital 26.

14. United Kingdom Information Commissioner's Office, What is Personal Data, available at https://ico.org.uk/for-organisations/guide-to-data-protection/guide-to-the-general-data-protection-regulation-gdpr/what-is-personal-data/what-is-personal-data/.

15. GDPR, Article 25.

16. Va. Code 59.1-571 through 59.1-581.

17. Cal. Civ. Code 1798.135.

18. *See* Karl Bode, *Harvard Students Again Show 'Anonymized' Data Isn't Really Anonymous*, Techdirt (Feb. 10, 2020): "As companies and governments increasingly hoover up our personal data, a common refrain to keep people from worrying is the claim that nothing can go wrong because the data itself is 'anonymized'—or stripped of personal identifiers like social security numbers. But time and time again, studies have shown how this really is cold comfort, given it takes only a little effort to pretty quickly identify a person based on access to other data sets."

19. *See* Jeff Kosseff, *Hacking Cybersecurity Law*, 2020 U. Ill. L. Rev. 811 (2020); Jeff Kosseff, *Defining Cybersecurity Law*, 103 Iowa L. Rev. 985 (2018).

Conclusion

1. danah boyd, *'Real Names' Policies Are an Abuse of Power*, Zephoria (Aug. 4, 2011).

2. David Kaye, Report of the Special Rapporteur on the promotion and protection of the right to freedom of opinion and expression at 6 (2015).

3. Andy Kessler, *Online Speech Wars Are Here to Stay*, Wall St. J. (Jan. 24, 2021).

4. Mike Masnick, *No, Getting Rid Of Anonymity Will Not Fix Social Media; It Will Cause More Problems*, Techdirt (Feb. 1, 2021).

INDEX